Detention Empire

Justice, Power, and Politics

COEDITORS

Heather Ann Thompson
Rhonda Y. Williams

EDITORIAL ADVISORY BOARD

Peniel E. Joseph
Daryl Maeda
Barbara Ransby
Vicki L. Ruiz
Marc Stein

The Justice, Power, and Politics series publishes new works in history that explore the myriad struggles for justice, battles for power, and shifts in politics that have shaped the United States over time. Through the lenses of justice, power, and politics, the series seeks to broaden scholarly debates about America's past as well as to inform public discussions about its future.

More information on the series, including a complete list of books published, is available at http://justicepowerandpolitics.com/.

Detention Empire

**Reagan's War on Immigrants
and the Seeds of Resistance**

Kristina Shull

THE UNIVERSITY OF NORTH CAROLINA PRESS

Chapel Hill

*Published with the assistance of the Anniversary Fund
of the University of North Carolina Press.*

Designed by Jamison Cockerham
Set in Arno, Scala Sans, and Helvetica Now
by Jamie McKee, MacKey Composition

Cover illustrations: "Growth" by Michelle Angela Ortiz,
2020. Barbed wire, © Maravic/istockphoto.com

Manufactured in the United States of America

The University of North Carolina Press has been a member
of the Green Press Initiative since 2003.

LIBRARY OF CONGRESS CATALOGING-IN-PUBLICATION DATA
Names: Shull, Kristina, author.
Title: Detention empire : Reagan's war on immigrants
and the seeds of resistance / Kristina Shull.
Other titles: Justice, power, and politics.
Description: Chapel Hill : The University of North Carolina Press, [2022] | Series:
Justice, power, and politics | Includes bibliographical references and index.
Identifiers: LCCN 2022017135 | ISBN 9781469669854 (cloth ; alk. paper) |
ISBN 9781469669861 (paperback ; alk. paper) | ISBN 9781469669878 (ebook)
Subjects: LCSH: Noncitizen detention centers—United States—History. |
Immigrants—United States—History—20th century. | Immigrants—United
States—Social conditions—20th century. | United States—Emigration and
immigration—Government policy. | United States—History—1969–
Classification: LCC JV6483 .S57 2022
LC record available at https://lccn.loc.gov/2022017135

for Andis,

and for everyone sowing seeds of resistance

inside and outside the walls

I believe that seeds grow into sprouts

And sprouts grow into trees.

And, if I know anything at all,

It's that a wall is just a wall

And nothing more at all.

It can be broken down.

ASSATA SHAKUR

Contents

List of Illustrations ix

Preface xi

Introduction *1*

1 Constructing the Carceral Palimpsest *14*

2 Nobody Wants These People: Mariel Cubans
and the Specter of Mass Migration *29*

3 We Have Been Unable to Find Any Precedent:
Haitian Interdiction and Detention *64*

4 This Time, They'll Be Feet People: Central
American Wars and Seeds of Resistance *104*

5 Give Us Liberty, or We Will Tear the Place Apart!
Detention as Counterinsurgency *146*

6 Somos los Abandonados: Prison Uprisings
and the Architectures of Erasure *186*

Postscript: Writing about the Abuses against Us:
Detention Stories and Abolitionist Imaginaries *232*

Acknowledgments *247*

Notes *253*

Bibliography *293*

Index *315*

Illustrations

Visualization of US immigration detention
centers in DHS fiscal year 2018 *4*

Ronald Reagan 1980 campaign rally at Liberty Park, New Jersey *11*

Political cartoon criticizing Haitian deportations *27*

US Army photograph of National Guard
forces at Fort Chaffee, Arkansas *40*

Two gender nonconforming individuals grooming
in their barracks at Fort Chaffee *48*

Pro-US demonstration at Fort Chaffee *50*

Anti-Castro drawing by a Mariel Cuban detained at Fort Chaffee *51*

Cartoon published in the newspaper
La Vida Nueva at Fort Chaffee *57*

Portrait of an unaccompanied minor at the
Krome detention facility in Miami *75*

Poem and image from the Alderson federal
prison published in *No More Cages* *96*

Jesse Jackson visiting the Krome detention facility in Miami *97*

Associate Attorney General Rudy Giuliani
addressing the Congress of Corrections *112*

Protest against US intervention in El Salvador
at MacArthur Park, Los Angeles *121*

Hand-drawn map of the Caribbean Basin *127*

Protest against US intervention in El Salvador at
an INS detention center in Pasadena *133*

Child's drawing of "migra" after family's
immigration arrest in Seattle *148*

Haitian asylum-seeker sleeping on a cot at
the Krome detention facility *153*

Haitian men and women in the yard at the
Krome detention facility *154*

Sanctuary movement car caravan *164*

Map of sanctuary break-ins *182*

La Resistencia flyer advertising a demonstration against
the Immigration Reform and Control Act *213*

Vigil at the Atlanta federal penitentiary in solidarity
with indefinitely detained Mariel Cubans *215*

Cubans on the roof of the Atlanta federal penitentiary
during the 1987 Atlanta prison uprising *218*

Handwritten letter of Cuban demands during the 1987 uprisings *219*

Preface

I saw the resistance before I understood the darkness.

On May 1, 2006, I leaned against the window of my eleventh floor office in SoHo and looked down on a sea of people. It was "A Day without Immigrants," the largest general strike for immigrant rights in US history, within the largest general strike across the Americas in history, El Gran Paro Estadounidense. Conservative CNN commentator Lou Dobbs dubbed the day a "radical takeover" as hundreds of thousands marched in cities across the country, ranging from Los Angeles to the Miami suburb of Homestead—an unbeknownst future detention site for migrant children. In New York City, 12,000 people formed human chains in Manhattan, Queens, Brooklyn, and the Bronx. Organizers planned for the chains to form at 12:16 p.m. in symbolic opposition to the passage of a law on December 16, 2005, that further criminalized migration and allocated more funding for border wall construction. At 4:00 p.m., a large rally converged at Union Square and marched south down Broadway to the headquarters of Immigration and Customs Enforcement (ICE) at Federal Plaza. As the crowd passed, chants of "¡Sí se puede!" drew me from my desk. I waved and pressed my fist against the glass in a show of silent support, then went back to work in the large publishing house where I was employed. I admired the turnout, but it was not my fight.

A year later I would walk the same path the crowd had taken down Broadway to Federal Plaza, accompanying my husband for his check-in with ICE. He had received a "Notice to Appear" in the mail, scheduled on the same day and time as my master's graduation ceremony at New York University. It was a deportation order.

"More like 'Notice to Disappear,'" Andi joked. Then he stopped eating and sleeping, as if already disappearing. When the day arrived, he put on the suit we were married in and I a favorite blue dress, leaving my cap and gown behind. We arrived at Federal Plaza with a lawyer and our marriage certificate. The officer we met with lied and said Andi would not be detained that day. He told us to return to the waiting room while he arranged some paperwork. I began celebrating until our lawyer gave me a sharp look. He knew what I didn't. When we were called back into the small room, it was filled with officers. As they tore my husband from my arms, they rested their hands on their guns and cracked jokes with one another about getting beers afterward. Andi's bid for asylum had failed, and they sent him to a for-profit immigration prison in New Jersey. When I walked into the Elizabeth Detention Center the next day, I did not know I was entering the heart of US empire. Pressing my palm against the glass of the visitation booth in a gesture as useless as my silent fist, I recognized this had been my fight all along. Three months later, he was gone.

There was so much I did not know as a white, US-born citizen. I did not know what it meant to be illegalized, detained, deported. Nor did I know that I was not alone, that there were so many people fighting against the deportation machine and had been for decades. While Andi was detained, I met others in the visitation room. Spouses, siblings, parents, children, and friends who told of dead-end pleas to congressional representatives, of guards monitoring visits, and of ICE never answering the phone. Over time, through letters, visits, and the sharing of information, we pieced together what was happening inside. "Recreation," "medical," "library"—lies, we came to learn. We swore we would tell our stories, maybe even write a book together. But as individuals left the detention center, we never heard from them again, save from whispers. A failed business, a shuttered home, a husband imprisoned in Iran, a father's suicide in Colombia.

Two months into Andi's detention, I published an op-ed in a national newspaper. The next day, ICE made a decision on our case. Was it an act of retaliation? I will never know. Andi was soon deported. ICE let me drop off a suitcase but wouldn't tell me when Andi would leave—that would be a national security risk. His friend from inside called to tell me, "It happened. He's gone." Detention guards returned his suit, rumpled up in a bag, destroyed. When the friends I had made in the visitation room called and emailed, I couldn't bring myself to answer.

But I would soon find that joining the chain of affected family and community members, working to uncover the layers of history that built these prisons, and piecing together fragments of stories the state wants to destroy could be a way out of the darkness.

The continued expansion of the immigration detention system since 2007 paralleled my own path of loss and discovery. I entered graduate school that fall, and history became my refuge. I became a historian because I needed to find out for myself how our nation got to this point of mass incarceration. I became a historian because doing history—recovering testimonies, documenting, and storytelling—is its own form of organizing. And I became a historian because sometimes telling the stories of others is easier than telling your own.

In researching this book, I initially set out to learn why the first private prisons of the 1980s were immigration detention centers, but I found a much larger story. I discovered that for-profit prisons are but one layer of mass incarceration, itself a symptom of the underlying disease of US imperialism. In the fall of 2008, I interned with the Detention Watch Network in Washington, DC, mapping detention sites and collecting stories from affected communities. Late into Election Day, I danced with thousands behind the White House in a wave of hope that was quickly dashed as President Barack Obama soon took on the mantle of "Deporter in Chief." During my first few years of research, I sought a top-down understanding of how Reagan era policies of detention as deterrence won out. But as a pattern of lies and retaliation emerged, in both my historical research and my detention work in real time, I began to see the importance of documenting the story as told "from below." After many years of stumbling and learning to listen, I have come to understand why borders are constructed, the full spectrum of violence they inflict, and the need for abolition. Today, as the COVID-19 pandemic and climate change lay bare the fissures of global apartheid, no border or cage will salve what Martin Luther King Jr. has called the "triple evils of racism, economic exploitation, and militarism" in the United States.[1]

The year 2010 began with an earthquake in Haiti, signaling new patterns of hemispheric migration along old tracks. I spent that spring studying for my qualifying exams while preparing my hardship waiver—an application to waive my husband's ten-year bar on returning to the United States after deportation, imposed by immigration laws passed in 1996 under the Clinton administration. To win a waiver, you must document "extreme and unusual hardship" in the United States without your spouse. Soon after passing my exams with distinction, I received the rejection letter from US Citizenship and Immigration Services. It said the agency found my testimony "dishonest." My government called me a liar, and the system worked as it was designed to. I ran out of fight, and I fell silent.

In 2014, a new Central American migration crisis dominated the news cycle as the Obama administration resurrected the practice of family detention. I filed my dissertation. I filed for divorce. Questions at the end of these intertwining paths remain. What can be recovered? What never will be? In the end, I still don't know whom or what to blame for losing my marriage—the system? Myself? The stories shared in this book have been my most powerful teachers and healers.

It was seven years before I walked into a detention center again, this time to visit a stranger. I joined a national visitation network now called Freedom for Immigrants and began meeting with people detained at Adelanto. In the high desert east of Los Angeles and 160 miles north of the border, the city of Adelanto is a cross-section of mass incarceration in the United States, with an area population of 34,000 and prison population of 10,000 held in a remote cluster of state and federal prisons, a county jail, and a privately run jail and immigration detention center. The Adelanto detention facility is one of the nation's largest immigration detention centers with a capacity of 1,940, run by one of the world's largest prison corporations. Receiving its first contract from the Reagan administration in 1984 to detain immigrants, GEO Group is now a multibillion-dollar industry leader. By 2017, Adelanto had also become the deadliest facility, with three deaths in three months since the inauguration of President Donald Trump.

The #Adelanto9, as they would be known, were a group of nine male asylum-seekers from El Salvador and Honduras who had been detained at Adelanto for over a month since arriving at the US-Mexico border in May 2017. They had traveled with La caravana Viacrusis de Refugiados, a refugee caravan of Central American and Haitian migrants who began their journey in Guatemala the month before. Following in the footsteps of past caravans and organizing themselves along the way, their numbers had grown from 15 to 250 when they arrived in Tijuana on May 7. Fleeing violence and poverty at home, caravaneras traveled as a group to find safety in visibility, to raise public awareness of the dangers of the migrant trail, to protest restrictive Mexican and US immigration laws, and to demand the right to free passage. They received a legal orientation from cross-border advocacy groups in Tijuana, who warned them of injustices they would likely encounter in US detention.

The events that followed are modern-day manifestations of the central subject of this book—how intertwining histories of US imperialism, mass incarceration, and a resurgence of white nationalist state-making under the Reagan administration define today's US immigration detention system. Although the experiences of the Adelanto 9 cannot tell the full spectrum of trauma inflicted by immigration enforcement on individuals and communities, they illustrate forms of retaliatory violence now deeply entrenched in detention architectures: family separations; routine denials of due process, medical care, adequate nutrition, and communications with the outside; vast discrepancies between written standards and practices on the ground; and physical and psychic assaults.[2] However, this is also a story about the liberatory power of testimony.

When the Adelanto 9 arrived at the US port of entry to present themselves for asylum, Customs and Border Protection separated them from their spouses. Isaac's wife was immediately deported, while others were detained at the Otay Mesa facility in San Diego, one in violation of a government directive against the detention of pregnant women. The men were sent to Adelanto.

On the morning of June 12, the nine men refused to leave the table, where they had also refused breakfast. A letter lay on the table listing their demands—clean clothing and water, better food, medical care, religious services, fair bond amounts, and due process. They stated they would not eat until they could speak with a representative of Immigration and Customs Enforcement. For half an hour, guards employed by GEO Group, the private prison company contracted by ICE to run the Adelanto detention facility, ignored them. A guard ordered the men to eat or return to their beds for "the count." When Bladi, Julio C., Marvin, Isaac, Omar, Luis, Mateo, Julio V., and Alexander linked arms instead, a brutal assault began.

Male and female guards screamed at the nine in English, discharging a can of pepper spray at their faces, bodies, and genitals. The men huddled together to protect their eyes, but a group of guards converged, separating and striking them. They handcuffed the nine and threw them into the hallway against a concrete wall lined with plastic phone booths and then into the showers. When Omar refused, a female guard scratched his face and forearms and a male guard shoved him into the wall. Omar fractured his nose, losing one tooth and a gold crown on another. The guards forced the men under the water, laughing and yelling, "Hotter!" to intensify the scalding effects of the pepper spray. A civil rights complaint to the Department of Homeland Security filed by Omar's attorney, Nicole Ramos, equated this treatment to torture and stated, "The fact that those responsible for their care and custody were now laughing at them, *after beating them like animals*, humiliated and terrified the men."[3]

ICE immediately deported Julio V. to El Salvador and separated the remaining eight by placing them in solitary confinement. In the following days, guards and ICE officers taunted them with food and threatened them with deportation, transfers, and harm to their asylum cases.[4] An ICE officer came to photograph Omar's mouth and face, but Omar never received medical attention. Isaac, who worked as a journalist in El Salvador and served as a spokesperson for the group, relayed their plans to continue the hunger strike to the media: "We see that ICE lied to us. . . . ICE can do something to lower the bonds. . . . We feel that they tricked us, and we are going to continue because we aren't anyone's toys."[5]

Inside-outside organizing, a strategy prioritizing the leadership and knowledge of incarcerated people with support from collaborators on the outside, shaped what happened next. The day of the assault, Isaac dictated the Adelanto 9's grievances over the phone to the cross-border organizations Sureñxs En Acción and Pueblos sin Fronteras. Both groups had accompanied the caravan in Mexico and worked with Freedom for Immigrants to create a press release. Two days later, thirty-three women detained in another wing at Adelanto launched a hunger strike of their own. Their demands included better medical care and fair bond amounts, to be reunited with their children and families, and to be treated "like humans, not animals." Guards threatened them with pepper spray and segregation. The women also contacted Freedom for Immigrants, and we published both groups' statements online.[6]

On June 20, World Refugee Day, sixty faith leaders and community members traveled to Adelanto to visit people in detention, including those on hunger strike. We gathered at a local church where I shared with the group about my husband's deportation. A volunteer named Louis Watanabe also spoke. His Japanese American parents and grandparents had been incarcerated at Manzanar during World War II, just two and a half hours north of Adelanto up Highway 395 in eastern California. His grandfather R. F. Kado, who later became a renowned architect, built the internment camp's stone guardhouses and memorial site. Referencing the intergenerational trauma inflicted by overlapping forms of violence across histories of detention, Louis told us, "Adelanto is very personal to me."

I planned to visit Isaac that day, but when we arrived at the detention center, GEO Group and ICE shut down visitation and locked everyone out, including lawyers and families with children. They told us the lockout was due to our activism but told people inside it was due to their own misbehavior.[7] This sowed division among us on the outside—were our attempts of showing solidarity with migrants inside helpful, or harmful? ICE and GEO first denied the severity of their assault on hunger strikers as a "gross and regrettable exaggeration" but then admitted to it a few days later after the hunger strikers' side of the story was publicized in the media through inside-outside collaboration.[8]

Into the summer, conditions worsened at Adelanto, and a man from Senegal attempted suicide. Coordinated hunger strikes continued with up to fifty people participating, led by a coalition of Haitians and Central Americans— two migrant groups subjected to exceptional discrimination in the detention system since the Reagan era. Despite retaliation, community efforts to raise funds to bond hunger strikers out of detention prevailed, with many eventually winning asylum. Even more, media attention and advocacy surrounding the hunger strikes of 2017 prompted state-level reforms in California.[9] Yet Adelanto, with its abusive conditions, continues to operate. Hunger strikes have long been and remain a frequent occurrence at detention facilities across the country. Since the advent of the COVID-19 pandemic, rates of incidence have only increased.[10]

The story of the Adelanto 9 provides a small window into the vast complex of over 200 local, federal, and private facilities that has grown tenfold since the mid-1980s to imprison a record high of 55,000 migrants a day and 500,000 a year across the United States by early 2020.[11] Abusive detention conditions raise urgent questions about how this system came to be and why it continues with seeming impunity. The "divide and conquer" tactics that occurred inside and outside Adelanto are not uncommon. Rather, they define the US immigration detention system and reflect a decades-long pattern of raced and gendered punishment with a purpose—to terrorize and deter migrants, all while obscuring the inherent violence of borders themselves.

I used to believe that if everyone knew what was happening inside immigration detention, it wouldn't be happening. But now I am not so sure. Revelations of abuse fade in and out of public view, yet continue—simply exposing them is not enough. While this book does document horrific conditions inside detention, it also seeks, as it asks us all, to do more.

Media and archival production—history, in essence—is marshaled in the struggles traced in this book. Some of the central questions driving my research have concerned which stories are silenced, how, and why? While no historical narrative is neutral and is rather a constructed "bundle of silences," in the words of Michel-Rolph Trouillot, each is the result of a unique process. I follow scholars who interpret the erasure at work in official archives as technologies of the imperial state. As the confinement of bodies translates into the suppression of stories through a state-sponsored "prose of counter-insurgency," evidence of resistance forms an alternate archive.[12]

An analysis of White House and US government files from the Carter and Reagan administrations reveals that emergency, ad-hoc detention measures adopted in moments of perceived migration crisis played a central role in the rise of the detention system. Congressional appropriations and legislation providing for the system's expansion only followed from counterinsurgent enforcement practices first adopted on the ground in response to an alleged immigration crisis.[13] This book takes a top-down and a bottom-up approach—not to replicate the unequal power structures of knowledge production but to indict them. By elevating voices that have been lost within larger public discourses of Reagan era immigration and foreign policy making, this book reveals how migrant and community-level acts of resistance significantly shaped decision-making at the top levels of government.

Even less visible than the silencing actions of the state are the silencing effects of the trauma it inflicts. Scholarship across disciplines takes this into account in crucial ways, from the traumatological impacts of immigration enforcement on public health to attention to archival silences in the humanities.[14] Countless individuals impacted by detention whom I have met and worked with over the past decade have become ghosts—their stories, and many of their lives, lost. However, historians can work intentionally to account for and recover the losses. "To engage in war and refugee studies, then," writes Yến Lê Espiritu, "is to look for the things that are barely there . . . that is, to write ghost stories."[15]

If we look, ghosts are in plain sight, and the voices of those affected are all around us. Testimonies from detention, "hidden transcripts" of resistance, seek to make visible what the state actively seeks to obscure.[16] Immigration detention sites and the lives they render invisible may hide on the peripheries of US empire and public and political discourses, but working to reverse processes of erasure is central to our reckoning with the enduring xenophobia driving detention policies and practices today.

A note on terminology: except where indicated and where the legal distinctions matter, I intentionally collapse the terms *refugee, asylum-seeker,* and *undocumented migrant,* using them interchangeably in order to challenge the state's ongoing systematic denial of asylum-seekers and to argue for an expanded definition of *refugee* that includes undocumented and illegalized migrants. I also purposefully refrain from using the state-sanctioned terms *alien, detainee, deportee, inmate, prisoner,* and *riot,* unless where quoted, because of their dehumanizing intents and impacts. Here, I also offer the working definition of *refugee* provided by the University of California Critical Refugee

Studies Collective: "Refugees are human beings forcibly displaced within or outside of their land of origin as a result of persecution, conflict, war, conquest, settler/colonialism, militarism, occupation, empire, and environmental and climate-related disasters, regardless of their legal status. Refugees can be self-identified and are often unrecognized within the limited definitions proffered by international and state laws, hence may be subsumed, in those instances, under other labels."[17]

Detention Empire

Introduction

The detention of migrants remains one of the most inaccessible and misunderstood phenomena in US society. As a locus of US foreign policy and mass incarceration, it reflects the global dimensions of US war-making. This book zeroes in on the 1980s, a critical turning point when detention transformed in tandem with a larger transformation of US empire—through proxy wars and new forms of economic coercion and cultural hegemony—that appeared to make US state power less visible, yet it remained no less violent. The United States' embrace of counterinsurgent warfare abroad after World War II set the stage for this transformation, informing policing tactics and the rise of mass incarceration at home. In the 1980s, the Reagan administration adopted new, more punitive immigration enforcement measures in response to Caribbean and Central American migrations that have since fueled detention's growth.

The Mariel Cuban migration of 1980 was a galvanizing event for these transformations, ushering in a sea change in border policing and prison policy making. Symbolizing a confluence of threats facing the nation, Mariel occupied a central position in what I call the *Reagan imaginary*. Shaped by neoconservative politics, neoliberal economics, and long-standing mythologies of settler colonialism, the Reagan imaginary is a vision and strategy of white nationalist state-making. Serving as a blueprint for mapping new frontiers of imperial expansion and carceral landscapes, it still undergirds the false logic of US bordering practices today.

This book contends that immigration detention operates as a form of *counterinsurgency*, a strategy of preemptive warfare targeting those deemed enemies of the state.[1] Counterinsurgent, or counterrevolutionary, military and policing tactics have a long racialized history in the United States. The Reagan administration weaponized existing Cold War foreign policy and border enforcement trends but also forged news tools of exclusion in response to an envisioned "mass immigration emergency." Recurrent spectacles of Cuban, Haitian, and Central American migrations during a time of perceived crisis, themselves created and fueled by US Cold War foreign policy, migration controls, and media and public xenophobia, served to justify the Reagan administration's expansion of the detention system, obscure the impact of its foreign policies, and retaliate against and silence migrant voices and allied opposition.[2]

Not only did the administration frame the crisis in Cold War terms, but its calls to expand the carceral state through a globalized War on Drugs also reflected domestic political goals of enhancing law enforcement functions to contain the specter of Latin American mass migration. The administration's obsession with Central America and the Caribbean, often referred to as the United States' "third" or "fourth border" in Reagan speeches and policy documents, shows how this specter was defined as an anti-Black, anti-Indigenous, and heterosexist crisis of white nationalist reproduction. Displaced Cuban, Haitian, and Central American migrants—especially those racialized as Afro-Latinx or Indigenous or seen as hyper-reproductive, queer, or gender nonconforming—posed a direct challenge to the racial-colonial project of US state-building, their literal presence exposing its failures.[3] By failures, I mean the state's reliance on the commission of transnational violence in order to sustain itself.

Migrant lives, journeys, and voices speak to these failures. While asylum-seeking and illegalized migrants often testify to conditions in countries of origin, this book is primarily concerned with how voices from detention, and migration itself, speak to US empire. In line with the aims of critical refugee studies to center migrants as knowledge producers, this book traces how migrant testimonies counter the silencing effects of state violence. It concludes that borders and walls, and the lies that sustain them, cannot erase the wake of harm left in empire's path.

As the multitudes of violence set in motion by US imperialism—war and political violence; poverty via labor and economic coercion; race, sex, and gender-based violence; environmental degradation and theft of Indigenous land and sovereignty—manifest in scales of mass migration, detention exacts such violence on the scale of migrant bodies. The contemporary US immigration detention system emerged out of contestations over the presence of migrants and the truths they wield, a dialectic of resistance and retaliation.

This book's focus on asylum-seeking migrants from the Caribbean and Central America recenters the geopolitics of asylum and migrant detention itself within the transnational scope of counterinsurgent warfare and its role in the rise of carceral trends more broadly. While building upon longer histories of immigration enforcement as empire-in-action, the specific historical convergence of the Reagan administration's revanchist right turn and adoption of Cold War "low-intensity conflict" doctrine shaped new forms of white nationalist state-making. As these new expressions of state violence met escalating migrant solidarity resistance in the early 1980s, these contestations dramatically recast the US immigration detention system in the modern era.

In theory, immigration detention is a civil, administrative procedure distinct from the criminal legal system. Not subjected to punishment in a legal sense, migrants in detention are not "doing time." Instead they are suspended in it, awaiting deportation or release, which may take months or years. They may be undocumented, newly arriving asylum-seekers, or legal permanent residents targeted for removal for commission of certain crimes.[4]

In practice, detention looks and feels like prison, functioning within a larger context of mass incarceration in the United States. The increasing criminalization of migration itself since the 1980s, a phenomenon scholars label *crimmigration*, has melded the two systems together in ways that have made them nearly indistinguishable—from local law enforcement's cooperation with ICE to the building of "mixed-use" facilities. Immigration violations now make up over half of all federal charges, while many migrants now serve lengthy prison sentences for reentry before beginning the administrative detention and removal process.[5] Immigration detention has also become increasingly privatized in recent years, with 75 to 90 percent of migrants detained in corporate-run facilities.

As detention operates to systematically target, terrorize, and exclude, this book illustrates the relationship between race, gender, migration, and US empire. Migrant journeys and transnational solidarity networks point to this historical relationship, as collective forms of resistance to detention such as caravans, hunger strikes, and the Sanctuary movement reflect a larger critique of US foreign and immigration policies more broadly.

A declaration of the spring 2018 Viacrusis Migrantes caravan describes a different kind of migration crisis than articulated by US presidents, rooted instead in histories of US intervention in Latin America, systemic violence, and inequality. It states, "We hope to be an example of solidarity and struggle to the world," charging government corruption, gang violence, and violence against women, Afro-Latinx, and Indigenous peoples, environmental activists, and QTGNC (queer, trans, and gender nonconforming) communities with pushing people from their homes. Caravanera testimonies such as that of Honduran poet Héctor Efrén Flores place responsibility on the United States. "This caravan is yours, Mr. Trump," he wrote in 2018. "Borders are an invention of yours and yours alone."[6] Latin American migrant caravans have a longer

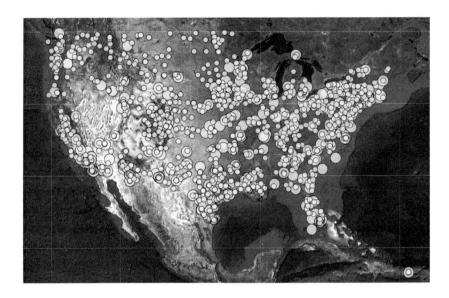

A visualization of US immigration detention centers in Department of Homeland Security fiscal year 2018 created by the Torn Apart/Separados project team led by Manan Ahmed as "a rapidly deployed critical data & visualization intervention in the USA's 2018 'Zero Tolerance Policy' for asylum seekers at the US Ports of Entry and the humanitarian crisis that has followed." The larger dots indicate facilities in use as of FY2018; the smaller dots designate facilities no longer in use. Courtesy of the Torn Apart/Separados Project.

history than commonly understood in US popular perception. Since the 1980s, the Central American peace movement and migrant solidarity caravans have raised sharp critiques of the state's role in persecution and displacement.

Overlapping episodes of violence across histories of detention inflict intergenerational trauma, but piecing them together also opens possibilities for forming new solidarities and *abolitionist imaginaries*—vision and praxis for building a future without detention. Through migrant and activist testimonies, media coverage, and government documents, this book explores the modes of resistance inside and outside detention that arose in response to what I call Reagan's Cold War on immigrants, and the modes of retaliation adopted by the administration in response. Set in motion against the larger backdrop of restrictionist narratives that attempt to normalize state violence and render immigration enforcement invisible, the dialectic nature of resistance and retaliation in US immigration detention is, at heart, a battle over truth. Acts of truth-telling in the face of state violence—from within spaces of detention and through inside-outside and coalition activism illustrating the intersections of oppression facing migrant and racialized groups—map alternatives to trajectories of US imperialism and prison doctrines embraced by subsequent administrations.

Reagan's Cold War on Immigrants

The history of immigration detention in the United States is characterized by recurring episodes of contested storytelling, an overlapping of memory and forgetting, uncovering and erasure as migration crises move in and out of public view. I conceive that iterations of detention over time may be described as a *carceral palimpsest*. In textual and architectural studies, the term "palimpsest" describes a reinscription of new writing or design practices over old ones. Meanwhile, old patterns are not entirely obscured but still visible.[7] Today's US immigration detention system sits atop entangled roots of settler colonialism, nativism, and war. Its implementation draws upon preexisting practices and spaces of incarceration. These historical foundations are the subject of chapter 1.

However, the Reagan administration laid new foundations—with lasting ramifications. "The cruelty is the point" is a popular refrain in response to escalating immigration enforcement since the Trump era, including raids, family separations, and revelations of widespread abuse in detention. This phrase refers to the specific injustices of the Trump administration's bald-faced xenophobia, but it also characterizes the emergence of a significant trend discussed in this book: a shift since the 1980s toward "attrition through enforcement"—an explicit policy weaponizing detention as deterrence.[8] In the post–civil rights era, Ronald Reagan became a central figurehead and architect of what Dylan Rodríguez calls white reconstruction. As governor of California, Reagan had developed a revanchist, or retaliatory, politics in response to rising social and labor movements. In the White House, the Reagan administration drew upon these prior battles to wage a new war on migrant rights.

I define Reagan's Cold War on immigrants as a suite of new, counterinsurgent enforcement measures adopted by his administration during its first term that cemented in place a globalized crimmigration regime. Hinging upon Cold War foreign policy aims and the administration's Mass Immigration Emergency Plan of 1982, these measures included the detention of asylum-seekers as a deterrent to migration, maritime drug and immigrant interdiction programs, the militarization of a more broadly imagined US border, and prison privatization. The narrative of this book spans the Reagan administration

(1980–88) but is not always linear. Chapters 2, 3, and 4 discuss Mariel Cuban, Haitian, and Central American migrant groups, respectively, to illustrate how dynamics of migration, resistance, and state retaliation shaped these new enforcement measures—each adding new layers to Reagan's carceral palimpsest. As a result, Reagan's war on immigrants normalized crisis as a mode of governing, cementing new detention structures in response to, and in anticipation of, crises of the US government's own making that today appear perpetual.

Reagan's Cold War on immigrants was a *total war*. Waged at home and abroad, Reagan's enforcement measures also blurred boundaries between military and civil society. Forged in the crucible of US military "low-intensity conflict" doctrine developed during the Cold War and reactionary domestic politics that justified military and carceral build-ups as defensive measures against imagined enemies, total war is a bundling of counterinsurgent, covert operations, psychological tactics, and public relations vying for hearts and minds.[9] Although the origins of low-intensity conflict doctrine lie in US engagement in Vietnam, the Reagan administration's revitalization of counterinsurgent warfare, especially in El Salvador, led to the US Army's official definition in the 1980s: "Low-intensity conflict is a limited politico-military struggle to achieve political, social, economic, or psychological objectives. It is often protracted and ranges from diplomatic, economic, and psychosocial pressures through terrorism and insurgency."[10] A key point here is the admission that counterinsurgent tactics are, in essence, state-sponsored terror. Although the state positions counterinsurgency as a response to a real or perceived threat—in this case, migrations and social movements seen as "insurgent" or challenging state power—the Reagan administration deployed its measures preemptively, with a goal of low visibility.

By the end of the 1970s, steep economic recession and post-Vietnam fears of national decline fueled a growing conservative counterrevolution that swept Reagan into office. Revolutions in Iran and Nicaragua in 1979 as well as increasing refugee flows in the wake of wars in Southeast Asia and Central America also stoked anti-communist and anti-immigrant sentiment.[11] Reagan's larger foreign policy vision ultimately rejected Jimmy Carter's emphasis on détente and human rights, aiming instead to revitalize Cold War nationalism and recapture US self-confidence supposedly lost in Vietnam. Reagan had the rhetorical ability to finesse the revanchist resentment of the late 1970s; indeed, few presidents are as known for their mastery of grand narrative and assertion of imagined community through the clear demarcation of enemies.

In the Reagan imaginary, the boundaries of border policing stretched well beyond the US-Mexico divide. Cold War foreign policy and migration trajectories were inextricably linked, and Reagan's foreign and immigration policies were mutually constitutive. The 1980 presidential election campaign coincided with the Mariel boatlift, during which 125,000 Cubans, as well as thousands of Haitians fleeing a repressive dictatorship and economic devastation, arrived in the United States over five months' time. The same year, US-backed civil wars that began in El Salvador and were continuing in Guatemala sent 500,000 and 200,000 refugees to the United States over the next five years, respectively.

Reagan made seemingly contradictory promises on immigration, which may explain why his administration is often mistakenly remembered as being soft on the issue. Reagan's ramping up of immigration enforcement efforts relied upon a much longer history of border violence against Chinese, Mexican, and other migrants, yet Reagan continued to deny the existence of such violence while shifting its modes and targets, using doublespeak and drawing selective attention to and away from the US-Mexico border to wage a broader border war. As Reagan courted migrant-hiring industries and the "Hispanic vote," he often spoke of a "peaceful" US-Mexico border. But amid a rising tide of nativism and right-wing extremism, Reagan "split the difference"—by promising immigration reform, including amnesty and a guest worker program, while turning focus to a new Caribbean Basin migration threat and counterinsurgent solutions. Before the 1980s, the Immigration and Naturalization Service (INS) saw its main enforcement purpose as cracking down on undocumented labor believed to compete with the US workforce. But as notions of crime and illegality continued to merge, INS enforcement priorities would shift as the Reagan administration resurrected older theories of policing while increasingly relying on preemptive tactics like raids, detention, and giving silent nods to vigilante violence in the borderlands.[12]

Despite Reagan's speeches depicting the United States as a "beacon of freedom" welcoming refugees, the Reagan imaginary was anchored and animated by a resurgent white nationalism. Immigration policy makers in his administration often referenced the era of national origins immigration quotas (1924–52) with admiration. Reagan's Associate Attorney General Rudy Giuliani was a key architect and defender of Reagan's new detention and interdiction policies. He lambasted the United States' acceptance of 800,000 legal immigrants in 1980, not seen "even during the great unrestricted tides of immigration between 1880 and 1921." He continued, "America simply cannot take all those who would choose to come here. That has been so since 1921 when we first established numerical limitations for foreign countries. With the state of our economy and our own responsibilities to the unemployed in the

United States, these ceilings are as important, probably more important than ever before."[13] Giuliani's telling of history both erases the era of Chinese exclusion (1882–1943) from the record and celebrates the national origins quotas that were designed to restrict immigration from everywhere but Europe—in effect, resurrecting a renewed vision of a white nation.

Although white nationalism shaped the Reagan imaginary, dog whistle politics in the post–civil rights era infused and shifted debates surrounding immigration in ways that would further shield the racist, revanchist sentiment behind new calls to halt immigration. In 1979, ophthalmologist and white nationalist John Tanton founded the restrictionist organization Federation for American Immigration Reform, or FAIR, which would blossom into a network of organizations and immigration policy "think tanks" that would enjoy exceptional access to policy makers in the 1980s, as evidenced by the prevalence of the federation's recommendations in White House documents.[14] Although politicians who championed immigration restriction in this era, like Senator Jesse Helms, were the "intellectual heirs" to eugenicist-restrictionists of the 1920s, they spoke of cultural assimilation rather than overt references to race.[15] Restrictionists also made humanitarian and environmental appeals from the left. Rhetoric produced by Tanton and his network, with many members boasting bona fide civil rights credentials, often touted a "pro-immigration" but "anti-illegal" stance and raised environmental conservation and reproductive rights—population control rooted in eugenicist thinking—as central themes. Such appeals have become entrenched in modern-day immigration debates, where those in favor of restriction often state the firm belief that it is "not about race."

Anti-Blackness and homophobia surrounding Cuban and Haitian migrants also converged with Reagan's dog whistle signaling on race, deviance, and crime that predominantly targeted African Americans, with xenophobia bolstering the administration's resolve to enhance the state's punitive functions.[16] Upon taking office, Reagan formed two task forces, on immigration and on violent crime, with Giuliani serving on both. The Task Force on Immigration and Refugee Policy's primary goal was to prevent "another Mariel" crisis. In the spring of 1981, counselor to the attorney general Kenneth Starr told the *Washington Post*, "It is absolutely clear that this administration would not tolerate a massive influx of the type we witnessed in 1980."[17] That summer, the attorney general's office rolled out the first of the Reagan administration's new immigration enforcement measures: the detention of asylum-seekers and the interdiction of Haitians on the high seas, both with the stated intent to deter future migrations.[18]

As Reagan era preoccupations with controlling borders, counterinsurgent approaches to prisons and policing, and a resurgent nationalism converged on the Caribbean and Central America, obsessions with Mariel Cuban criminality and curbing drug trafficking networks in Colombia, Cuba, Central America, and Miami all became justifications for boosting defense, carceral, and private sector spending and for extending law enforcement efforts abroad in a new, globalized War on Drugs. In the fall of 1981, President Reagan announced to the nation that "a wave of violent crime has engulfed our nation," and "just as a strong national defense is essential to protect us from our enemies in other lands, a strong domestic defense is necessary to protect us from our enemies within our own country."[19] Reagan's Task Force on Violent Crime proposed new drug interdiction efforts that fall, coinciding with the Haitian interdiction program.

As counterinsurgent military techniques initially developed in El Salvador "came home," they were mobilized to militarize drug and immigration enforcement efforts along the US-Mexico border.[20] Features of low-intensity conflict doctrine are apparent in the Reagan administration's massive militaristic build-up of border enforcement provisions alongside a growing cooperative network between US military forces and the Drug Enforcement Administration, the FBI, the CIA, and the INS. Ballooning INS budgets during these years benefited US Border Patrol and detention operations the most. The INS's construction of twenty-two new Border Patrol stations and four traffic checkpoints during Reagan's first term, outfitted with the latest surveillance technologies and used for cooperative antidrug and immigration operations, also reveals how the War on Drugs further accelerated border militarization and the enfolding of migrants into the criminal legal system.[21] The administration's anti-migrant offensive was further supported by Reagan's restoration of secrecy in intelligence activities as signaled by his pardoning of former FBI officials charged with crimes relating to the COINTELPRO infiltration of the Black Panther Party in the 1960s and by his signing of Executive Order 12333 in December 1981. In effect, the order legalized domestic surveillance "in support of national foreign policy objectives abroad" and created a pretext for harassing activists and members of the Sanctuary movement, discussed in chapter 5.[22]

Neoliberal economics was also a central philosophy driving the Reagan imaginary. Counterinsurgent warfare in Central America accompanied new free trade initiatives developed to curb migration from the Caribbean Basin. Characterized by a decentralized network of cronies and consultants, the Reagan administration developed a "trade and aid" plan known as the

Caribbean Basin Initiative to expand political and economic influence in the Caribbean and Central America and, in theory, counter communism and alleviate the conditions driving migration to the United States. Driven by a global trickle-down "locomotive theory" that US power would lead the world in economic recovery, the Caribbean Basin Initiative was a precursor to the North American Free Trade Agreement. These free trade agreements ushered in a new era of global imperialism.[23] Not only did the Caribbean Basin Initiative grease the wheels and provide cover for US direct and covert military intervention in the region, but it also highlighted a core contradiction: exploitative development and free trade programs that originated in designs to curb migration ultimately served to further displace people, creating a feedback loop of migration crisis.

The hyper-incarceration of Black and Brown youth in the War on Crime and subsequent War on Drugs in the 1970s and 1980s fueled another crisis of the US government's own making—prison overcrowding—which buttressed the rise of crimmigration. However, prison overcrowding and the anti-Blackness fueling it were not merely domestic phenomena. Immigration crackdowns also exacerbated the issue of "bed space" that served to justify carceral expansion. Patrisia Macías-Rojas identifies Reagan's Criminal Alien Program, an effort to purge local jails of immigrant offenders, as a key moment merging criminal and immigration systems.[24] Chapter 6 explores how the indefinite detention of Mariel Cubans throughout the 1980s played a central role in the passage of laws expanding criminal grounds for deportation and the establishment of private contract and mixed-use facilities for detaining "criminal aliens," soon becoming a boon to the emergent private prison industry.

In sum, immigration control became a thread tying together the Reagan administration's reassertions of US hegemony and white supremacy in its domestic, foreign policy, and neoliberal economic agendas. In addition to being a central theme of Reagan's Cold War rhetoric and proxy wars abroad, immigration was woven into domestic policing and prison policy making. Detention became a central mechanism in the Reagan administration's reassertion of state sovereignty over migrant rights.

Nations such as the United States wield categories of refugee status as a tool of empire. The US government's indefinite detention of Mariel Cubans and blanket rejection of Haitian, Salvadoran, and Guatemalan asylum applications throughout the 1980s reflected Cold War bias but also the white nationalist core of Reagan foreign policy making. Importantly, it was racialized and gendered threats of mass arrivals of *asylum-seeking* groups from the Caribbean and Central America, curious exceptions to "refugee-as-victim"

Republican presidential candidate Ronald Reagan gives a speech about welcoming refugees at Liberty Park, New Jersey, in view of the Statue of Liberty on September 1, 1980. Vic DeLucia. Reprinted with permission from *New York Times*/Redux.

tropes, that drove Reagan's embrace of detention as counterinsurgency. In this way, not only did prison and policing trends shape immigration enforcement, but migration itself transformed the landscape of mass incarceration in turn.

"My Words Are Like Seeds"

Cuban, Haitian, and Central American migrant experiences provide a clearer picture of the intersecting landscapes of resistance to Reagan that originated within and transcended detention sites. Inside-outside strategies, transnational coalition-building, and anti-racist and anti-imperial resistance to Reagan should be seen as both a continuation and a culmination in this era of crisis. The stories presented here are a continuation of longer histories of slavery, colonialism, migration controls, and forms of protest that paralleled other struggles for self-determination. However, resistance to Reagan also marked a culmination—defining a new era of public, transnational protest surrounding exceptional forms of discrimination and due process violations in detention—especially as escalating violence in detention reflected new expressions of US global power.

Ongoing contestations over the visibility of migrants, living testimony of imperial violence, shape detention's retaliatory features and functions. Detention spaces reflect these relations and their contradictions: extremes of heat and cold, sterile appearances with frequent outbreaks of disease. Medical and health emergencies go untreated but become opportunities to seclude and punish. Time is heavily regimented and disregarded; people are lined up and counted up to seven times a day beginning at 4:00 or 5:00 a.m. in a window-less environment where fluorescent lights and televisions blare through the night. Paperwork and security cameras carefully document official versions of events and misbehavior, while personal belongings and legal documents are routinely destroyed. Acts of solidarity and resistance are silenced through solitary confinement, transfers, and deportation. On the outside, investigative reporting and scholarly and legal documentation of detention's abuses have been mounting for decades, including through internal review, yet this reporting continually fails to be acted upon.[25]

As voices from detention go unheard, radical action becomes the only option. Flashpoints of resistance in immigration detention and political and community contestations outside during the Reagan era often played out as media spectacle. However, vying for visibility in the counterinsurgent landscape of detention and state surveillance can be life-threatening and may not always be the goal. I define resistance in detention, and beyond, as a range of efforts to hold the state accountable for its abuses and to counter state-inflicted trauma and its attendant silences.[26]

Chapters 2 through 6 open with snapshots of resistance from detention: a Mariel Cuban "disturbance" at the Fort Chaffee, Arkansas, military base in 1980; events leading up to Haitian-led hunger strikes at the Krome facility in Miami in 1981; a senator's report sharing Salvadoran stories from the El Centro detention facility in California in 1981; a 1984 Sanctuary movement caravan and INS raid in Seattle; and a two-week prison uprising in Atlanta and Oakdale, Louisiana, in 1987 led by Mariel Cubans—the longest in US history.

The Reagan administration faced mounting resistance to its new detention practices, and chapter 5 takes a closer look at how forms of resistance inside detention such as uprisings, hunger strikes, and suicides escalated securitization and retaliation enacted on migrants. As alternative visions posed by the Central American peace and Sanctuary movements sustained mass support, inside-outside activism pushed the administration to wage a counterinsurgent total war against its opponents.

Organizing is messy, rife with politics, white saviorism, and in-fighting as existing social hierarchies and the traumas of state violence reverberate through movement spaces. Advocacy on behalf of Cubans, for example, often took a pro-US and anti-communist stance. Much Haitian and Central

American advocacy, by contrast, was revolutionary, laying the suffering of migrants at the feet of US imperialism.

Historian Elizabeth Hinton argues that rebellions against prisons and policing are not inherently violent; they are instead a response to state violence.[27] Chapter 6 follows the interweaving trajectories of the US government's indefinite detention of Mariel Cubans leading up to the uprisings of 1987 and the Reagan administration's attempts to establish long-term and contingency detention sites in fulfillment of its Mass Immigration Emergency Plan. The Mariel Cuban uprisings were a culminating response to the exceptional forms of violence inflicted upon these Cuban migrants by the US government since their arrival in the United States. The uprisings were also a plea for the US public to hear the words of the incarcerated.

The impacts of war and imperialism abroad have crucial implications for the study of migrant detention and the rise of neoliberal carceral systems more broadly, not only for understanding the multilayered drivers of migration—where political, economic, and ecological violence are increasingly intertwined—but for recognizing the ways in which the globalization of the War on Drugs, cooperative new methods and technologies of surveillance, and counterinsurgent modes of warfare developed abroad return home to shape domestic policing and prison landscapes. The extraordinary violence experienced by Mariel Cuban, Haitian, Central American, and other migrants in detention and the afterlives of resistance and retaliation became embedded in new iterations of incarceration, revealing the lasting legacies of Reagan's Cold War on immigrants.

And yet, voices of resistance to US empire continue to grow in strength. The testimony of Alfredo, an Indigenous Maya speaking from sanctuary in Seattle in 1984, articulated his belief in the liberatory power of his words: "I know my words are like seeds in the ground, and later we will be able to harvest good fruit in the future. . . . There are certain things that unite all Guatemalans. All of us, Latinos or Indians, are poor, oppressed, and have the same problems: white, brown, barefoot, shoes on, sandals; we are all screwed."[28]

By design, the US immigration detention system works to render migrants invisible and to silence their voices. This book aims to bring their stories to light.

1

Constructing the
Carceral Palimpsest

Can we doubt that only a Divine Providence placed
this land, this island of freedom, here as a refuge for
all those people who yearn to breathe free?

Ronald Reagan, presidential nomination acceptance speech, July 1980

Categorical exclusions were embedded in the founding of the United States. Article I, Section 8, of the Constitution grants Congress the responsibility of determining a "uniform rule" for immigrants to become citizens, and the Naturalization Act of 1790 was the first law allowing for naturalization to citizenship. Yet this privilege was reserved only for "free white persons" of "good moral character," effectively excluding Native Americans, indentured servants, enslaved people, free Blacks, and Asians. Women's citizenship was determined by the status of their fathers or husbands. The Alien and Sedition Acts of 1798 established an early mechanism for the deportation of dissidents—people deemed "dangerous to the peace and safety of the United States"—and were shaped in a period of intense fearmongering over crime, poverty, revolution in France, and insurrections of enslaved peoples. Since the late eighteenth century, US government notions of "refugee" acceptance were contingent upon perceived benefits of acceptance versus denial and intimately tied to wars of imperial expansion. Perpetual exclusion of Native Americans and enslaved people of African descent, forcibly displaced yet never acknowledged as refugees, underlines how nations like the United States wield asylum as a tool of empire building.[1]

Systems of incarceration have always disproportionately targeted specific groups—based on race, most clearly, but also on gender, class, and ideology. Together, these markers of difference have also shaped immigration policy and detention practices. Intertwining immigration and carceral histories extend from the nation's origins as a white settler colony. As historian Kelly Lytle Hernández has shown, migrant detention operates within legacies of slavery and Jim Crow segregation, Native American removal, and imperial expansion tied together in a continuous and dynamic process of "mass elimination."[2] This chapter recounts the legal and cultural origins of Reagan's Cold War on immigrants, tracing how structural continuities and changes relate to rhetorical ones.

The historical foundations of migrant detention sketched below are not comprehensive, but they are chosen to emphasize the ways in which migration trends, crisis narratives, and carceral practices are interconnected with war, imperialism, and counterinsurgency. They also reveal the persistence of transnational solidarity movements against detention and deportation. In this, a recurring pattern emerges. As resistance to state violence shapes retaliatory detention practices in turn, this dynamic reinforces detention's alleged legitimacy. Exercises of state control over migrant bodies, denial, and erasure in detention can be read as empire-in-action. Prison camps are not exceptional, aberrations in US history; rather, they extend from the continued maintenance of a white settler nation—through the forced removal and disappearance of bodies deemed foreign and through the stories we tell that erase these histories.[3]

What constitutes immigration crisis, and for whom? Of Latin and Greek origins, "crisis" is defined as a turning point. It is helpful to think about the ways in which narratives of crisis have operated in media, public, and political discourse as decisive points to sustain the logics of immigration enforcement—but it is also appropriate to challenge these logics.

Experiences of forced migration and detention are singular emergencies, their traumas difficult to identify, voice, and write about. In the words of Simon, a Mariel Cuban migrant detained at Fort Chaffee, Arkansas, in 1980, "For me it was a terrible dream. You can't imagine anything."[4] These experiences are visceral—a "terrible dream," unimaginable, unknowable. In this way, an immigration crisis may be invisible to those not facing it firsthand. Indeed, carceral spaces function by design to silence the voices of those imprisoned.

While individuals and communities in transit or in detention experience a crisis in real time, narratives of immigration crisis that circulate in the public sphere (for example, in media and political debates) are often mere constructions, relying on long-standing ideas—myths—about who we are as a nation. As Dan Kanstroom argues, today's immigration enforcement regime is a "living legacy of historical episodes marked by ideas about race, imperialism, and government power that we have largely rejected in other realms."[5] Therefore, policy justifications that deem immigration a crisis, not for migrants *but for the nation itself*, declare bodies who do not have a "right" to occupy this land a threat to the body politic.

Narratives that cast migrants and migrant groups as threatening, or in more sympathetic accounts as victims, sort good from bad, deserving from undeserving, utilizing language that generalizes and amplifies characteristics marking them as Other. These narratives flatten and silence lived experiences in service of defining the nation and its bordering logics. Public debates over the US-Mexico border wall deflect attention from the inner workings of a much vaster network of immigrant prisons and a deportation apparatus that extends within and beyond the nation. As this book shows, immigration crises become opportunities—to define the contours of US empire, to strengthen border controls, and even to profit from the confinement of those subject to removal.

With state interests at stake, narratives of immigration crisis reflect a power struggle as the state uses rhetorics of war and counterinsurgency to silence dissent and to label rebellion as irrational and violent acts. These narratives work to discredit dissent and appear in official state documents and in mass media.[6] Migrants' lived experiences counter the crisis rhetoric constructed by nationalist states, while resistance to detention across time has revealed what is at stake at home and abroad.

Ultimately, immigration crises are a product of the inherent violence of borders themselves—not only as sites of lawlessness and mass death historically but also in their defined purpose to systematically exclude. As US courts and lawmakers continue to uphold the logic of immigration enforcement, these histories, like the mass of an iceberg under the surface, may be the hardest to uncover and to see.

The real crisis is not migration itself but the racism underwriting the rise of a global crimmigration regime. The real crisis has been the human cost.

Blueprints

During the era of explicit racialized exclusion in federal immigration law, 1882 to 1952, the targeting of Asian and Mexican migrant groups in particular drew early blueprints for detention practices and structures. Since the nation's founding, the United States' establishment of a legal right to exclude and deport originated in a white settler "right of conquest" with antecedents in English colonization, Native American removal, and fugitive slave laws.[7] Historians document how a patchwork of deportation practices and shadowy immigration detention sites arose in the mid- to late 1800s out of poor laws targeting Irish migrants, "medicalized nativism," and the criminal targeting of Asian and Mexican migrants, all contributing to early federal detention policy.[8] The passage of the Chinese Exclusion Act in 1882 ushered in a new era of federal bureaucratization of immigration enforcement.[9] Eliciting narratives of threat and contagion, US officials detained Asian migrants at Angel Island in San Francisco Bay in the 1890s and subjected Mexican migrants to quarantine and sterilization practices along the US-Mexico border. The pathologizing of migrant bodies mirrored broader narratives of scientific racism, eugenics, and social Darwinism in this era, centrally concerned with racial and social "fitness." This racism also justified Native American relocation and cultural annihilation, Jim Crow segregation and convict leasing practices in the South, and US Pacific and Latin American imperial expansion.

The advancement of racial capitalism through post-emancipation convict leasing in the US South also laid the foundations of today's prison-industrial complex. The passing of the Thirteenth Amendment and the abolishment of slavery, which allowed for the exception of "involuntary servitude" in punishment for crimes, gave new impetus to expand the practice of leasing incarcerated labor to private interests. As W. E. B. Du Bois noted in 1901, whites were determined after the Civil War "to restore slavery in everything but name."[10] The convict lease system operated from 1865 to 1923, where Black people made up the majority of those leased out and private contractors profited at much higher rates than governments. Ostensibly outlawed in the 1920s, coerced labor in imprisonment continues to this day.[11]

Early immigration detention efforts were transnational; so was resistance to them. The United States both coerced and cooperated with its neighbors to surveil and restrict Chinese migration from Mexico, Cuba, and Canada as new systems of migrant identification, border enforcement, and deportation were put into place.[12] However, migrants worked across borders and from within detention to subvert these systems for their benefit and survival.

Chinese exclusion sparked a movement for immigrant rights as the Chinese Consolidated Benevolent Association, or Six Companies, operated mutual aid networks in the United States, Canada, and China to launch civil disobedience campaigns and litigation against exclusion.[13]

This litigation culminated in a series of Supreme Court cases at the end of the nineteenth century that upheld the United States' right to detain noncitizens pending removal and formed two "foundational principles" of immigration detention in US law upon which the system still operates: the executive branch of the US government can exercise plenary (absolute) power to deport, and detention and deportation are administrative procedures rather than punishment or "imprisonment in a legal sense."[14] Together, these cases created administrative immigration detention in the United States as a new form of confinement within and alongside existing carceral systems.

The decade following World War I raised new ideological concerns as fears of political radicalism and communism in the wake of the Mexican and Russian Revolutions contributed to rising xenophobia and new calls for immigration restriction in the 1920s, or the "Tribal Twenties"—an era shaped by eugenics and a resurgence of the Ku Klux Klan. The creation of the US Border Patrol and the passage of the racially motivated National Origins Act, both in 1924, along with the passage of law in 1929 making unauthorized migration a misdemeanor, effectively drew a line around Europe as the only acceptable source of immigration and created a new category of "undocumented" immigrant.[15] Into the Great Depression of the 1930s, economic anxieties propelled the United States to deport one million Mexicans and Filipinos in the "decade of betrayal."[16] An estimated 60 percent of those repatriated were US citizens of Mexican heritage or Filipino Americans whose status was revoked upon the passage of the Philippine Independence Act in 1934 and the United States' subsequent withdrawal from colonial occupation of the South Pacific archipelago.

World War II ruptured the political, economic, and cultural fabric of the United States once again as the transnational detentions of "enemy aliens" during the war set new precedents and mapped a new geography of rightless detention. President Franklin Roosevelt's signing of Executive Order 9066 in 1942 gave the government broad authorities, justified by wartime, to designate areas from which "any or all persons may be excluded" and to relocate and incarcerate 120,000 Japanese Americans and Japanese foreign nationals at concentration camps across the western United States without due process.[17] This overlapping of citizen and noncitizen incarceration furthered structures and cultures criminalizing migration.

Constructing the Carceral Palimpsest

Japanese communities resisted their incarceration from the outset and challenged the racism of war hysteria in myriad ways. Two internment camps built on federally recognized Indian reservations in Arizona faced Indigenous resistance as well. Legal challenges culminated in *Yasui v. United States* (1943), *Hirabayashi v. United States* (1943), and *Korematsu v. United States* (1944).[18] The Supreme Court upheld the constitutionality of curfews, relocations, and Japanese incarcerations in a context of wartime emergency—a justification the Reagan administration would call upon in its re-formation of enforcement policy. Finally, Japanese detentions were a transnational phenomenon. The US government detained Japanese prisoners of war and community members on its archipelagic network of military bases and occupations in Hawai'i and Alaska and throughout the Pacific and even coordinated with twenty nations in the Americas to deport 8,000 Japanese Latin Americans to the United States to be detained as "illegal aliens" on military bases.[19] Together, these practices paved the way for the militarization and off-shoring of refugee management after the Vietnam War.

World War II also accelerated the gradual "Mexicanization" of immigration enforcement, as border policing technologies initially developed to target Asian migrants shifted onto Mexicans. Wartime cooperation between Mexico and the United States and production needs led to the Bracero Program, a series of diplomatic agreements that brought millions of Mexican guest workers to the United States between 1942 and 1964. During and especially after the war, however, the United States targeted Mexicans for removal, culminating in Operation Wetback and Operation Terror in 1954, a militaristic enforcement initiative of large-scale raids that resulted in the deportation of 1 million Mexicans. That year was also a high-water mark for detentions in US history, at half a million.[20]

Although the 1940s and 1950s marked an unprecedented expansion of wartime executive power and immigration enforcement technologies, the horrors of the Holocaust and a global refugee crisis created by World War II also led to the establishment of an international human rights regime, new categories of refugee law, and a scaling back of detention's use in the postwar era. Changes in immigration and refugee law after the war would appear to move away from the era of racialized restrictions, although protections afforded to displaced people around the world were applied unevenly and aligned primarily with Cold War politics.[21] In 1948, Congress passed the Displaced Persons Act, allowing for the United States to accept European war refugees beyond national quotas. That same year, the newly formed United Nations drafted a Universal Declaration of Human Rights, ushering in an era of international cooperation in refugee management. In 1951, the United Nations further defined the rights of "refugees" in international law but limited the definition only to those displaced by the war in Europe. In 1967, amid worldwide processes of decolonization, the UN expanded the definition to what it is today in the *Convention and Protocol Relating to the Status of Refugees*, defining a refugee as anyone who "has a well-founded fear of being persecuted for reasons of race, religion, nationality, membership of a particular social group or political opinion."[22] This definition is based on the principle of *non-refoulement*—not returning asylum-seekers to a nation where they may face persecution. Although the United States ratified the protocol, almost all refugees it admitted from the 1950s to the 1970s were fleeing communist nations.[23] It was not until the passage of the 1980 Refugee Act that US law would align with the UN's expanded definition, but even then it would not fulfill its promise.

The United States adopted "humane" immigration law and enforcement reforms in the 1950s, and it appeared that detention as a systematic practice would come to an end. The Immigration and Nationality Act of 1952, upon which today's detention and deportation practices are based, ended Asian exclusion and introduced a new system of preferential migration based on skills and family reunification. However, it maintained the race-based national origins quotas established in the 1920s and deemed those affiliated with anarchism or communism deportable. Just months after Operation Wetback, INS officials announced the closure of Ellis Island and a sharp reversal of detention policy to one of conditional parole, with only a "few but necessary exceptions" for those whose presence would constitute a "danger to the national security and public safety." The INS also announced a 100 percent reduction in detention rates, amounting to only four migrants allegedly being detained in 1955. The Supreme Court lauded this move, with Justice Tom C. Clark writing in 1958, "Physical detention of aliens is now the exception. Certainly this policy reflects humane qualities of an enlightened civilization."[24] Although federal detention numbers appeared to decline between the 1950s and 1970s, Jessica Ordaz shows how the US detention and deportation regime continued to expand during this time through the heightened policing of Mexican migrants in the southwest borderlands.[25] Again, state violence targeting migrants remained a continual backdrop.

In a new era of civil rights reforms, the 1965 Immigration Act effectively eliminated the national origins quota system, opening new immigration pathways from Africa, the Middle East, and Asia and leading to demographic shifts in subsequent decades. However, the new law also put a cap on Latin

American migration for the first time, creating a new appearance of immigration crisis by increasing levels of "undocumented" migration from the region—setting the stage for new contestations that would pave the way for detention's resurgence.

Turning Points

Transnational flows of US state violence continued to drive prison and policing trends in the postwar era—trends that both responded to and resulted from a growing international human rights regime and movements for self-determination. The origins of modern mass incarceration lie in the United States' embrace of counterinsurgent responses to freedom struggles in the 1950s to 1970s, which in turn introduced new economies, politics, and geographies to US prison landscapes.[26] Domestically, these struggles were the fight for civil rights and urban and prison rebellions; globally, these were Cold War conflicts, revolutions, decolonization, and resultant mass migrations. As these struggles ramped up into the 1980s, they introduced new rhetorics of resistance to state power—and of retaliation. Although the Republican Party would become the primary architect, and beneficiary, of the "backlash" politics largely credited for mass incarceration's rise, it is crucial to remember that US militarism and mass incarceration have always been bipartisan projects.[27]

From the vantage of the Global South, "Cold War" is a misnomer, privileging a US-centric perspective that downplays the extent of violence occurring globally throughout this era—violence the United States both instigated and remained largely incubated from. However, I retain use of the term in order to emphasize the central role of counterinsurgency in the transformation of US empire during this era, as expressions of state power transitioned from overt to covert.

Counterinsurgent warfare, defined as a series of allied military and civilian tactics responding to rebellion, has deep, racialized roots in the United States. Broadly characterized as a combination of tactics meant to defeat non-state, guerrilla, or revolutionary actors, counterinsurgent tactics can include surveillance, intelligence gathering, and infiltration; harassment and intimidation; ambush or preemptive strikes; economic, political, or psychological manipulation; or state-sponsored propaganda and media campaigns. While histories of European imperial violence also lent theory and practice to its development, it arguably originated in wars of US imperial expansion in the 1800s—against Native Americans, during the Civil War, and in the Spanish-American and Philippine-American Wars.[28] These encounters have in turn shaped domestic policing, especially after World War II when counterinsurgency became the US military's preferred mode of operation.[29]

As Jordan T. Camp argues, policing philosophies in the United States moved toward counterinsurgency in strategic response to the crisis of legitimacy posed by the civil rights movement and as Jim Crow capitalism gave way to neoliberalism.[30] Neoliberalism is an economic model of free trade, deregulation, and the privatization of government functions; a political philosophy privileging freedom of individuals over state power; and a mode of conduct favoring personal responsibility over social welfare. This ideology went hand in hand with the rise of counterinsurgency at home and abroad, especially in Latin America. Carceral studies scholars Stuart Schrader and Micol Seigel have shown how US engagements in global counterinsurgent warfare during the 1960s and in police training, riot control, and assistance programs abroad have informed the shaping of domestic retaliatory policing trends. In service of US economic interests, Seigel names the growing interdependence between state power, policing, and global capitalism as "violence work."[31] Extending Camp's theory of counterinsurgency from prison to transnational contexts, this book explores how US counterinsurgent operations and proxy wars abroad, and their attendant rhetorics at home, have informed and reinforced one another.

Racial hierarchies and wealth disparities between the United States and Latin American nations stemmed from colonial histories and continued to shape US foreign policy. Although the United States officially ended direct military intervention in Latin America in the 1930s, US power did not recede after World War II. Rather, the United States continued to exert extraordinary influence in the region through economic coercion, covert operations, military support, and low-intensity conflict doctrine to further US interests.[32] Dollar diplomacy, or direct economic investment, in Latin America was a critical component of US power during the early imperial period. After World War II, coercion continued through new notions of economic "development" programs. Touted as a weapon against communism and a salve for wealth inequality, aid has more often served as a vehicle of empire by accompanying counterinsurgent and military agendas.[33]

In 1946, the US Army founded the School of the Americas in the Panama Canal Zone and at Fort Benning, Georgia, to train Latin American militaries. CIA covert actions also backed violent coups in Iran in 1953 and Guatemala in 1954 to install US-friendly governments at devastating human costs—merely the beginning of such operations throughout the Cold War as behind-the-scenes US actions and investments stoked violence and political and economic instability throughout the hemisphere. To this day, the United States engages in ongoing historical erasure by denying that state-sponsored upheavals have been a prime driver of migration to the United States.[34]

The Cold War also reordered the domestic front. After World War II, neoliberal state and capitalist interests divested from US cities, plunging them into deepening poverty, segregation, and racial conflict. White flight suburbanization accompanied emerging oil, military, and aerospace industries in the US South and West to bolster a new region of rising importance dubbed the Sunbelt. Shifting prison economies and political cultures emerged from these new configurations, a precursor to the rise of neoliberal economics and a booming rural prison industry in the Reagan era.[35] By the end of the 1980s, the Sunbelt would incarcerate more people than any other US region, with immigrant incarceration helping fuel this trend.[36]

Inquiring into the transnational dimensions of freedom struggles during these decades reveals how migration has also contributed to the rise of the neoliberal carceral state. The fight against Jim Crow segregation was accompanied by broader identity, solidarity, and international rights movements of multiracial, Indigenous, student, women, queer, labor, environmental, anti-nuclear, and antiwar activism throughout the 1960s. In addition to political gains such as desegregation and the Civil Liberties and Voting Rights Acts of 1964 and 1965, these movements also opened up new spaces for naming and exposing the state's abuses and for demanding redress. Colleges and universities were key sites where students organized protests and where civil rights discourse influenced the rise of New Left academic scholarship, which cast a critical eye on histories of slavery, the Civil War, Reconstruction, and US imperialism. Communities affected by policing and immigration enforcement also led civil rights organizing, and prisons were key sites for the development of ethnic studies and anti-capitalist, anti-colonial liberation theories. Incarcerated people and students often worked together toward prison reform and abolition and to recover and weave together histories of oppression and resistance.

Nationalist movements, revolutions, and the European decolonization of Asia, Africa, the Middle East, and the Caribbean opened new possibilities for leftist internationalism as forty-five nations in Africa, twenty-two in Asia, and eight in the Caribbean gained independence between the end of World War II and 1977. Some transitions were peaceful, while others, like Vietnam, involved protracted global conflict and widespread devastation. Almost all were shaped by neocolonial ideological, military, and strategic contestations between world superpowers. As a new human rights regime emerged alongside these continuing hegemonic forms of power, those struggling for independence came to understand and articulate a common cause for freedom across national lines. Cuba's communist revolution, complete by 1959, drastically altered US-Cuba relations and drew focus to the Caribbean as a strategic Cold War battleground. Many on the left viewed Cuba as a model for anti-capitalist resistance and Black liberation.[37] Of course, these global solidarities gave the state further cause to surveil and retaliate against perceived enemies.

Although immigration detentions were down in this period, prison conditions continued to deteriorate. Social unrest reverberated through prison walls, especially as the state retaliated against and incarcerated movement leaders, most notably Black nationalists. In the 1950s the FBI drew upon counterinsurgent tactics to surveil and discredit social movements, and in 1969 the FBI's Counter-Intelligence Program, or COINTELPRO, worked to "neutralize," imprison on false evidence, and even assassinate Black Panther leaders. Between 1967 and 1972 there were forty-eight prison rebellions across the country, characterized by civil rights tactics, hunger and labor strikes, and solidarities across ethnic groups.[38]

Social and prison unrest peaking in the late 1960s and early 1970s presented a crisis of legitimacy for old orders of racial control, which were retooled rather than abandoned. The Republican Party adopted a new "Southern strategy" in 1968 of using racially coded language to maintain support throughout the South and emerging Sunbelt. Reactionary political *revanchism* was central to this process—defined as the utilization of scapegoats and a reliance on anxieties surrounding race, class, gender, nationality, and sexual preference to mobilize a populist, nationalist spirit of revenge and evidenced in the ways in which labor, civil rights, feminist, and socialist movements have been cast as enemies of the state.[39]

As Republican governor of California from 1967 to 1975, Ronald Reagan was a central figure responding to and shaping these political shifts. For example, Reagan supported gun control laws aiming to criminalize the Black Panthers, firing scholar-activist Angela Davis at UCLA for her communist affiliations, and retaliating against the 1968 Third World Liberation Front student strike for ethnic studies at San Francisco State University. These years shaped Reagan's philosophy on prisons as punishment and his anti-Black racism. After the 1965 Watts uprisings, Reagan concurred with the McCone Commission's conclusions that pathologized inner cities and identified state dependency, or welfare, as a key corrupting force behind urban unrest.[40] On the failings of the rehabilitative prison model, Governor Reagan asserted, "We must return to a belief in every individual being responsible for his conduct and his misdeeds with punishment immediate and certain. With all our science and sophistication, our culture and our pride in intellectual accomplishment, the jungle still is waiting to take over. The man with the badge holds it back."[41] Reagan would affirm this policy position as president, repeating neoliberal ideologies of individual responsibility in presidential speeches about crime—including this same phrase about the jungle with its clear racial overtones.

Global freedom struggles also informed new solidarities across movements for immigrant rights, prompting new forms of repression. The multiracial United Farm Workers movement originating in California in the early 1960s redefined farm labor activism, organizing strikes and international consumer boycotts to secure worker protections. However, debates over tactics and respectability politics plagued the movement, dividing workers and ultimately harming undocumented migrants by prioritizing the rights and dignity of documented immigrants and farmworkers. The visibility of the farmworkers' movement also fueled Reagan's revanchist, anti-union campaign for governor.[42] These contestations with rights movements helped shape the counterinsurgent, white nationalist contours of the Reagan imaginary.

New economic and social crises of the 1970s launched revanchist politics into the mainstream, shaping informal immigration enforcement trends that would also pave the way for the Reagan era. Processes of globalization, capital flight abroad, an oil crisis, and inflation—in addition to the political corruption of the Nixon presidency and the losses of the Vietnam War— fueled fears of national decline. In California, Governor Reagan proposed "law and order" solutions in line with President Richard Nixon and rising conservative power blocs across the Sunbelt. Immigration to California from Mexico and Central America increased in the 1970s due to agricultural labor needs, widening a growing wealth gap and stoking nativism.[43] As retaliatory crackdowns on immigrants emerged alongside US counterinsurgency campaigns in Latin America and Asia during the Cold War, Rachel Ida Buff argues that deportations became a form of "domestic and international counterinsurgency, enforcing the postwar global racial capitalist order."[44] The threat of deportation became another tool in FBI investigations and harassment of movement organizers, alongside the heightened policing of Chicanx and Latinx migrants under the pretext of curbing drugs and arms trafficking under Nixon's War on Crime.[45]

Refugees or Asylum-Seekers

The massive scope and devastations of the Vietnam War indelibly scarred US political and social life, reshaping subsequent US refugee politics. Growing public divisions over the war also help to explain the seeming paradox of immigration detention's return in the human rights era. The United States' acceptance of half a million refugees from Cuba between 1959 and 1973 solidified a status quo of anti-communist refugee politics, but new refugee patterns in the 1970s, specifically Soviet, Chilean (to a limited extent), and Southeast Asian, somewhat transcended the binary Cold War logic of prior US refugee acceptance.[46] However, the militarization of refugee camps in the wake of the Vietnam War, coupled with narratives of US benevolence, created a powerful new blueprint for the erasure of state power.

A proliferation of new terms such as "parolee" and "entrant" signifying refugee status (or non-status) after the Vietnam War further reflects the increasing ways the United States wielded or sidestepped refugee law under exceptional circumstances, often in alignment with its foreign policy aims.[47] In the 1970s, the United States' management of two refugee groups with different fates laid the groundwork for the reinscription of a detention regime: Vietnamese refugees and Haitian asylum-seekers. Note here the definitional distinction between "refugee" and "asylum-seeker," the first being a person already granted refugee status under US or international law and the second being a person in search of status. In subsequent chapters, I intentionally collapse these terms, using them interchangeably to argue for an expanded definition of the concept and to challenge the state's denial of refugee status for Cubans, Haitians, and Central Americans, especially as detention policy formation hinged upon the exceptional exclusion of these migrant groups. Here, however, the distinction is important. While Vietnamese refugees were accepted as "citizens in the making" by the United States and held on military bases during resettlement, Haitians were largely denied refugee status and held in jails, prisons, and detention centers (and later on military bases as well).[48] Although often cast as deserving and undeserving opposites, together they illustrate the range of spaces used to incarcerate noncitizens. In fact, the mobilization of this false binary is central to processes of erasure and denial; both groups experienced trauma, racism, and extraordinary state violence in spaces of incarceration.[49] The immense costs of US militarism borne by Vietnamese refugees have also been flattened and erased by "model minority" stereotypes of Asian Americans that misread silence as docility rather than trauma.

Constructing the Carceral Palimpsest

This political cartoon, originally published in the *Palm Beach Post* on February 2, 1979, and reprinted in an American Committee for the Protection of Foreign Born newsletter that November, critiques both the racism and the hypocrisy of INS blanket denials of Haitian asylum-seekers fleeing the US-backed totalitarian dictatorship of Jean-Claude Duvalier. Pat Crowley. Reprinted with permission from USA Today Network/University of Miami Special Collections.

The resettlement of Vietnamese refugees served as a critical turning point for refugee politics and detention landscapes, as the United States would again draw upon its archipelagic network of offshore power in its militarized management of refugee crises after the war. Between 1975 and 1992, the United States accepted over 1 million refugees from Vietnam, Cambodia, and Laos. The military's central role in the allegedly benevolent process of resettlement resulted in "militarized refuge(es)"—a term encapsulating the co-constitutive impact of militarism on sites of resettlement and on bodies.[50] As Jana Lipman writes, the benevolent framing of Vietnamese refugee camps "worked to displace the violence of war with a humanitarian operation as the dominant image of the military."[51]

By contrast, the United States' blanket denial of Haitian asylum-seekers reveals the anti-Blackness at the heart of the United States' return to systematic detention. The US government's incarceration of Haitians in jails and detention centers beginning in the early 1970s predated Reagan's official announcement of such a policy in 1981 and facilitated the criminalization of asylum-seekers. Advocacy for detained Haitians in the 1970s and early 1980s drew upon coalitions and tactics formed in decades of nongovernmental organizational support for refugees throughout the twentieth century as well as on more recent forms of protest in the 1960s and 1970s that paralleled other struggles for self-determination.[52] Advocates for Haitian migrants also called out the racism and hypocrisy of US support for the totalitarian dictatorship of Jean-Claude Duvalier.

In many ways, the Mariel Cuban migration of 1980 marked a convergence of domestic and foreign policy crises outlined above. The passage of the 1980 Refugee Act, just a few weeks before the Mariel boatlift began, appeared to be a high-water mark for human rights, adhering US law to the UN's 1967 refugee protocol for the first time. However, this moment of promise was quickly eclipsed by retrenchment in the Reagan era, a return to Cold War priorities, and an overall decline in refugee admissions.[53] Although the biggest champions of immigration restriction in the 1980s were those on the New Right, the revival and maturation of restrictionism in the 1980s was a bipartisan effort with voices on the left joining concerns over crime and economic competition. However, the 1980s was hardly a decade of consensus—the civil rights movement did not fade away, and many of its same alliances voiced increasingly loud resistance to Reagan's new detention policies.[54]

These voices included a growing World War II Japanese incarceration redress movement that culminated in Congress's establishment of the Commission on Wartime Relocation and Internment of Civilians in 1980. Those testifying in public hearings in the summer of 1981 used their platform to draw connections between Japanese incarcerations and broader histories of racial oppression. In 1983, the commission's report, *Personal Justice Denied*, found that racism and fear, rather than wartime necessity, drove Japanese internment policy. Although the Reagan administration largely opposed the commission's proposed Civil Liberties Act, calling for a national apology and reparation payments to survivors, it passed in 1988. A. Naomi Paik concludes, however, that the reconciliation hearings gave only a "pretense of listening," while redress "worked to obscure the continuing, indeed accelerating, deployment of racist statecraft at the very moment of the Civil Liberties Act's passage."[55]

Just as the nation was beginning to reckon with these histories, the Reagan administration was reinscribing a new carceral chapter.

2

Nobody Wants These People

Mariel Cubans and the Specter of Mass Migration

They are getting the worst ready to leave—the prostitutes and homosexuals, and the crazy people, too . . . like Castro taking out his garbage. They took everyone straight from the prison to the boat.

"Freedom Flotilla" boat crew member, Los Angeles Times, 1980

I can't say bad things about the people out there. They are not bad people. Do they know we are here?

Estanislao Menendez, Mariel Cuban imprisoned in Atlanta, 1983

Between April 21 and September 29, 1980, 125,266 Cuban refugees arrived in Key West, Florida, transported on US vessels from Mariel Harbor, Cuba, in what is now known as the Mariel boatlift. This exodus, sparked by many factors that included economic and political strife in Cuba and US-Cuban negotiations for family reunification, began under assumptions that the United States would accept 3,500 refugees. But shortly after Fidel Castro announced the opening of Mariel Harbor to US vessels wishing to pick up family members, the operation spiraled out of control and five months of mass migration ensued.

On the night of May 26, 200 of the 18,000 Cuban refugees housed at Fort Chaffee, Arkansas, walked out of an unlocked gate in protest against their detainment by the US government and the slow resettlement process being managed by the Department of Health and Human Services, the Federal Emergency Management Agency, and the Immigration and Naturalization Service. As they entered the adjacent rural community of Jenny Lind, armed residents on rooftops fired hundreds of rounds into the night sky. No one was harmed, and US Army officers in charge of camp security rounded up and returned the Cubans with little incident. Later that night, hooded Ku Klux Klan members appeared outside the fort carrying torches and signs reading "Kill the Communist Criminals," while a vigilante security patrol of armed Jenny Lind residents circled the camp in pickup trucks.[1]

Six nights later, on June 1, tensions flared again. An estimated 1,000 Mariel Cubans set fire to five army buildings and stormed the front gates, chanting "¡Libertad!" as they marched down Route 22 toward the small community of Barling. Arkansas state troopers fired over their heads and held them back with rifle butts and billy clubs just outside the town limits, while Cubans threw rocks, bottles, and pieces of concrete. Federal troops, unable to intervene due to the law of posse comitatus that dictated that military personnel could not arrest civilians, stood between state troopers and civilians yelling, "Don't hit them! Don't hit them!" After a couple of hours, the state troopers finally contained unruly Cubans within the camp, using clubs and tear gas. The "Fort Chaffee incident" left one Cuban dead, forty injured, and eighty-four jailed. One civilian and fifteen state troopers were also injured.[2]

Livid that federal troops had been unable to use restraining force, Governor Bill Clinton immediately called in the National Guard and summoned President Carter's aide Gene Eidenberg to demand tighter security at the refugee camp. The night after the disturbance, Clinton took Eidenberg on a tour of Barling and Jenny Lind in his car; he recalled, "It was well after midnight, but down every street we drove, at every house, armed residents were on alert, sitting on their lawns, on their porches, and, in one case, on the roof. I'll never forget one lady, who looked to be in her seventies, sitting stoically in her lawn chair with her shotgun across her lap. Eidenberg was shocked by what he saw. After we finished the tour he looked at me and said, 'I had no idea.'"[3] Clinton also recalled that there had been a run on handguns and rifles in every gun store within fifty miles of Chaffee, while Gun City in Barling sold T-shirts after the incident depicting crowds of Cubans through a gun sight with the caption "I survived the Cuban Rock Festival."[4]

The panic displayed by local residents at Fort Chaffee mirrored widespread panic expressed in local and national media reports. On May 26, coincidentally the same day as the initial disturbance at Fort Chaffee, *People* magazine quoted an INS officer claiming that "85 percent of the refugees are convicts, robbers, murderers, homosexuals, and prostitutes." This figure was a gross overestimate, but it fueled fear.[5] On June 7 White House press secretary Jody Powell further stoked Cold War anxieties and xenophobia by announcing that among the agitators were a "few hardened criminals" positively linked with Cuban intelligence efforts.[6]

Eidenberg reflected on the media's role in the incident: "I was in Chicago in 1968. What happened at Ft. Chaffee was a disturbance but it became a riot in the public mind. The national media defined the character of 127,000 Cubans. . . . People wandered off the base on a hot summer night to stretch their legs, they were scared, nervous, bored, but not about to take on the U.S. Army."[7] Lieutenant Francisco Bazán, stationed at Fort Chaffee during the disturbances, later recalled, "The majority who wandered off that night were not considered undesirables when the investigation was completed." He cited frustration with bureaucratic delays as the cause of the protests. He also added, "The locals were not very hospitable, and some had reason not to be. They did not feel adequately protected by their police, and they were being told daily by television, newspapers, and radio that these Cuban refugees right at their doorstep were potentially dangerous people." One Cuban man, Estanislao Menendez, did not condone the actions of the agitators who escaped that night but identified with their grievances, saying, "I was taught as a child to respect the law and the military. . . . I would never do what the others were doing. . . . But I can see there was a reason for what they were doing—throwing stones, running away—and the reason was that we were not free, and we did not know what was going to happen to us."[8]

It did not take long after the first arrivals of Mariel Cubans in the United States for reports of Castro purposefully infiltrating the boatlift with criminals and other social "undesirables" to begin circulating in the media. Overwhelmed, President Jimmy Carter's administration declared a state of emergency in south Florida. While roughly half of the arrivals were reunited with family members or resettled in the Miami area in a relatively timely manner, the other half were sent to one of four military bases across the country that served as temporary camps for processing—Eglin Air Force Base in Florida,

Fort Chaffee in Arkansas, Fort Indiantown Gap in Pennsylvania, and Fort McCoy in Wisconsin.[9]

The Fort Chaffee incident did not occur in isolation; resistance ranging from peaceful protests to hunger strikes and outright violence frequently punctuated the indefinite detention of Mariel Cubans that, for some, lasted for years. This specific incident, however, introduced the various actors involved in what would be called a growing national immigration crisis: displaced migrants, the mass media, local communities, camp administrators, and all levels of government officials. It also led to many questions: Where do migrants seeking asylum belong? Who should house them? Who should adjudicate their cases? Who has the right to exert control over their lives? Fort Chaffee provides a fitting beginning for an exploration of the "mass immigration emergency" that the administration of Ronald Reagan, who entered office in 1981, felt it inherited.

Straddling the 1980 election that marked Democratic losses for Carter and Arkansas governor Bill Clinton, the Mariel military detentions ushered in a monumental, punitive shift in the politics and architectures of asylum. Transnational anti-Blackness and homophobia surrounding a minority of the migration whom the United States subjected to indefinite detention underwrote this shift and facilitated narratives and policing practices that criminalized Mariel Cubans writ large.

Heightened xenophobia in this time period is indicative of the larger post-Vietnam rightward shift in US political culture that paved the way for Reagan's conservative counteroffensive—a confluence of resurgent white nationalism at home and reassertion of US empire abroad. Growing anti-immigrant sentiment melded with racial and gender anxieties as migrants seemingly posed a threat to the national body. Together, these larger national trends set the stage for "moral panic" surrounding migrants increasingly represented as dark, criminal, and sexually deviant that took on symbolic overtones resonating with larger narratives of national decline.[10]

This chapter details how Cuban life and resistance inside the camps, contestations over the closure of Fort Chaffee, and complex inside-outside politics galvanized Reagan's new policy of detention as deterrence. The perceived mismanagement of Mariel would continue to haunt defeated Democrats, shaping a bipartisan consensus on anti-immigrant policy making to the present day. Even more, the specter of mass migration would continue to color the Reagan administration's revanchist right turn—powered by the virulent rhetoric of white nationalism.

From Open Arms to State of Emergency

Large-scale migration to the United States from Cuba after the revolution of 1953–59 was not unprecedented. Since its diplomatic break with Cuba in January 1961 amid heightened Cold War tensions, the United States had adhered to a policy of granting entering Cubans immediate parole and hailing them as "freedom fighters" who had bravely escaped Castro's communist regime.[11] In September 1965 Fidel Castro announced the opening of Camarioca port in Cuba to Cuban Americans wishing to pick up relatives for immigration to the United States. Through mutual negotiations between Cuba and the United States, this began an eight-year "Freedom Flight" during which 268,000 Cubans entered the United States as legal refugees.[12] But the Mariel boatlift would introduce a new era of diplomatic warfare between the United States and Cuba—with migrants at the center.

Despite this precedent of Cuban migration, the Mariel boatlift of 1980 was a "nightmare" from official US perspectives. As Carter's chief of staff Jack Watson told *Life* magazine, "Castro, in a way, is using people like bullets aimed at this country."[13] The boatlift, in only six months' time and with far less notice, brought in approximately half of the number of refugees who came in 1965, greatly straining government resources. The *INS Reporter* concluded, "Never had there been such a massive wave of intending immigrants boldly arriving on our shores unannounced, unscreened, and uninvited."[14] The demographic composition of the Mariel Cubans differed from those who had emigrated previously, largely explaining this group's negative public reception. Whereas earlier exiles were mainly older, white, and upper- or middle-class Cubans seeking family reunification, Mariel Cubans were predominantly younger, male, and single.[15]

Even though Mariel Cubans were more educated than their predecessors on average, the racial and gender composition of this group contributed to their ultimate labeling by the government as "undesirables." An estimated 30 to 50 percent of the overall Mariel migration were Afro-Cuban, but they had divergent fates from the overall population: only 8 to 10 percent of Mariel Cubans who were processed in Miami and quickly resettled with family members were Black, whereas 75 percent of those detained long-term at Fort Chaffee or in federal penitentiaries were. Also, 70 percent of the boatlift were male. Although it is impossible to know the overall number of QTGNC (queer, trans, and gender nonconforming) Mariel migrants because of misreporting and the state's lack of record keeping, this group received a disproportionate amount of media attention.[16]

A confluence of political factors further distinguished Mariel Cubans from previous refugees, leading them to become one of the most stigmatized groups in recent history.[17] While the Carter administration's initial response to the boatlift aligned with the customarily receptive stance of the United States toward refugees from communist countries, rumors of Castro's aim to relieve Cuba of its prisoners and social undesirables quickly changed the administration's tune. Less than three weeks after the boatlift began, President Carter announced at a press conference on May 5, "We'll continue to provide an open heart and open arms to refugees seeking freedom from Communist domination, brought about primarily by Fidel Castro and his government."[18] At the same time, however, INS officers in Key West reported that Cuban migrants appeared "more hardened and rougher in appearance" than earlier arrivals, and stirrings of negative publicity began surrounding the Mariel exodus. The day after Carter's initial endorsement, he declared a state of emergency in southern Florida. A week later, a US State Department bulletin accused Castro's government of "taking hardened criminals out of prison and mental patients out of hospitals and forcing boat captains to take them to the United States." The bulletin concluded, "We will not permit our country to be used as a dumping ground for criminals who present a danger to society."[19]

The belief that Fidel Castro purposefully infiltrated the boatlift worked to Cuba's advantage by alleviating the embarrassment caused by unexpected and overwhelming numbers of Cubans trying to emigrate. As María Cristina García explains, the opening of Mariel was a rare "olive branch" extended to the Cuban exile community in the United States at a time of growing international criticism of Cuba's human rights record in the 1970s and economic crisis.[20] Although the reality on the ground was distorted both by the Cuban government's commitment to remaining ambiguous on the subject and by US media and bureaucratic responses to Mariel Cubans, the boatlift was also used strategically by Cuba as a homophobic nationalist campaign. Eyewitness accounts confirm that Cuban officials were releasing people whom Castro deemed *escoria* ("trash") or *lumpen*—so-called loafers, criminals, and mentally ill—from prisons and forcing them onto boats bound for the United States.

Fidel Castro remained fairly silent on the issue throughout the boatlift; however, in a May Day rally speech he attempted to shatter the notion that those wanting to leave Cuba were anti-communist dissidents. Castro used homophobic language to discredit refugees by saying, "The large majority of the people there were that kind: lumpen. Some limp wrists [*flojito*]." This elicited laughter from the crowd, and Castro continued, "Some shameless creatures who had been covering up." Castro concluded that those who would

Mariel Cubans and the Specter of Mass Migration

accept the refugees were "doing an excellent sanitation job."[21] State repression of homosexuality—particularly gender nonconforming and "passive" male homosexuality—was a well-documented aspect of Cuban society under the revolution, which championed the image of a masculine workingman. On June 14, Castro again spoke publicly against refugees in this vein, saying, "So we don't have to worry about losing a bit of soft tissue. We are left with the muscles and the bone of the people."[22]

Cuba did not cooperate with US efforts to obtain immigrant prison records, further complicated by the fact that many were jailed in Cuba for reasons the United States might not consider criminal, such as participation in the black market, homosexuality, or dissenting with the communist government. One young man, Manuel, who was detained at Fort McCoy, for example, said he was wrongly imprisoned in Cuba for merely being in the vicinity of a theft caused by hunger. When the boatlift began, Cuban officials came to the prison to interview him. They "became aware of my negative attitude towards the system, and they told me to gather my things."[23] He was then escorted to one of five buses leaving from the prison to Mariel harbor.

Oral histories describe Mariel Cuban efforts to secure exit permits and confirm the state's interest in purging Cuba of homosexuals. One young man, Antonio Conchez, "had gone prepared with an eye-catching outfit, my hair messed up and a little bit of makeup on my eyes and face. I also spoke with a fake voice, exaggerating my mannerisms so that they would be convinced that I was a homosexual." Another recalled seeing a poster while waiting for an exit permit that read, "Homosexuals, get out; scum of the earth, get out."[24] Others said they were threatened with jail time if they did not agree to leave the island. Cubans may have exaggerated their sexual orientations and criminal histories in order to leave the country, adding to misreporting in the United States, but this also reflects their agency as they used the Cuban state's homophobic discourse against itself for their own aims. Upon arrival, these confusions were compounded by the tension between the United States' acceptance of anti-communist refugees and its immigration policy barring homosexuals. At the time, homosexuality was still a potential ground for exclusion in US immigration law, which would not change until 1990.

Attempting to deflect and resolve these tensions, the Carter administration determined that Mariel Cubans did not qualify for refugee status under the 1980 Refugee Act, which had gone into effect just one month before the boatlift began. The new law promised to expand the definition of "refugee" in alignment with the UN's 1967 refugee protocol to any persons fleeing fear of persecution. Instead, the administration created a new category of *Cuban/Haitian* entrant (status pending).[25] It also established a Cuban-Haitian Task Force to deal with the unprecedented number of both Cuban and Haitian arrivals by sea in 1980, which remained in place into Reagan's first term. Detailed more in chapter 3, policy discussions lumping these two migrant groups together, despite divergent US foreign policies toward each nation and their disparate fates in detention, reveal how anti-Black racism animated both exceptional forms of discrimination against Haitian migrants and the criminalization of Mariel Cubans. Even though media and government sources often referred to Mariel Cubans as refugees, their temporary status of "entrant" justified their indefinite detention and signified they were not yet an accepted part of the nation.

The domestic political and economic climate in 1980 also played a large role in Carter's decision to sidestep designating Mariel Cubans as refugees. Over the previous decade, the United States had accepted hundreds of thousands of refugees in the wake of war and persecution, most notably from Vietnam and Southeast Asia, and in smaller numbers from the Middle East, the Soviet Union, Central and South America, and the Caribbean. Between 1978 and 1980 alone, 465,000 Southeast Asian refugees and asylum-seekers from Cuba and Haiti arrived in the United States. Reports that the US government had spent $400 million on processing and resettling Cuban and Haitian entrants by August 1980 aggravated "compassion fatigue" and sentiments that immigration burdened social services and increased job competition.[26] US citizens were reluctant to sponsor refugees in the economic downturn as Cuban entrants were seemingly pitted against refugees from other countries for resources and public sympathy, including 14,000 a month arriving from Southeast Asia who also met heightened racial resentment.

Racialized fears associated with crime, especially in Miami, compounded public racism. Following the acquittal of four white police officers implicated in the death of African American Arthur McDuffie, a three-day race rebellion broke out on May 18, 1980, in the predominantly Black Miami neighborhoods Liberty City and Overtown. At the time, 50,000 Mariel Cuban arrivals were camped at the Orange Bowl, furthering the city's tensions. Fitting into a longer history of urban rebellions against police brutality, the Miami uprising stood out as unusually violent in its targeting of white victims, with gruesome deaths on public display. One man, for example, was left to die in the street with his tongue and one ear cut off and a red rose in his mouth. With 18 dead, 350 injured, 600 arrested, and $100 million in property damage, it was the deadliest rebellion between the 1960s and Los Angeles in 1992.[27] By the fall of 1980, a spate of alarming media coverage attributed increasing crime and homicide

Mariel Cubans and the Specter of Mass Migration

rates in Miami to Mariel Cubans. The Miami police department allegedly tracked crime suspects on a white board using a red *R* to denote a Mariel Cuban. Research has disproven that African Americans or Mariel Cubans were responsible for rising crime rates in Miami, but the image stuck.[28]

In the increasingly complicated politics of exile, Cuban Americans were initially sympathetic to Mariel Cubans. In the early days of the boatlift, government agencies provided security and kept order at makeshift camps, and the local Cuban American community and charitable organizations raised funds to provide for migrants' welfare needs. As reporting of Castro's plan and Mariel criminality increased, however, many Cuban Americans took care to distinguish themselves from the new immigrants by calling them "Marielitos," a term that quickly took on pejorative connotations.[29] Nicasio Lopez-Puerta, a first-wave exile and Cuban American political leader, explained the conflict through this lens: "[Castro] tried to get the American people to turn against us by sending . . . his worst social beings to pollute the image we had so carefully cultivated. . . . I have relatives who came in from Mariel. I am aware of the suffering and the sacrifice. That's not new. What is new is that our relationships with other communities in Miami deteriorated, and xenophobia reared its ugly head."[30] After the Fort Chaffee incident, the Miami Cuban news outlet *Réplica* denounced those participating in the rebellion as not worthy of "the title of political refugees."[31] Such sentiments helped solidify divisions between deserving versus undeserving migrant groups in public discourse.

Shortly after the Fort Chaffee incident and at Governor Clinton's urging, the Pentagon granted federal troops the emergency power to use restraining force to contain Cubans within the four military bases across the country where they were being held, and the White House promised no more Cubans would be sent to Arkansas. However, as the boatlift drew to a close, Fort Chaffee became the consolidation site for 9,500 unsettled Mariel Cubans in the fall of 1980, where operational problems would continue. A total of 19,060 Cubans were processed through Fort Chaffee until the fort's closure in February 1982, when the Reagan administration sent 392 remaining Cubans, labeled as "antisocial," to several prisons across the country. There they joined 1,200 Cubans who were already imprisoned based on suspected felony charges. An additional 600 labeled "serious mental cases" were housed at St. Elizabeths Hospital in Washington, DC.[32] Many of them, still with indefinite legal status and unable to repatriate due to cold relations between the United States and Cuba, remained in INS or Bureau of Prisons custody for years, and some for well over a decade. These scattered, overlapping spaces of Mariel Cuban detention exemplify the emergence of Reagan's carceral palimpsest.

"Esos No Son Compatriotas Nuestros": Constructing Cuban Criminality

Imprisoned Cubans refused to accept their fates, resisting detention from the outset in myriad ways. Some began filing individual habeas corpus claims in 1980; several were decided in their favor, resulting in their release. Because of the sheer number of arrivals and because Cubans were un-deportable, the INS also relaxed its enforcement of determining exclusion based on homosexuality in September 1980. This unclear "don't ask, don't tell" policy led to a lack of data and media misinformation, but it also opened up spaces for migrants to maneuver within. As Mariel Cuban migrants, especially those who were queer or trans, were detained and segregated on military bases, they navigated these liminal spaces to affirm and demand respect for their identities. Yet a close look at local community interactions and life inside Mariel Cuban detention at Fort Libertad, Fort McCoy, Fort Indiantown Gap, and Fort Chaffee shows that as refugees sought to reclaim lives inside the camps, a pattern of retaliation emerged.

In the late spring of 1980, one month after the boatlift began, administrators at the makeshift camp Fort Libertad on Eglin Air Force Base in Florida noted "processing problems." Refugee grievances over slow out-processing and camp conditions resulted in a series of small-scale uprisings. An air force report on the disturbances, citing coordination difficulties between the military, FEMA, and volunteer agencies, described an "explosive situation" at the camp that could soon escalate into a "full-scale riot." In a coordination meeting, Major General Robert M. Bond asked, "What would Eglin and the AF look like if the nation were told that Air Police were guarding Cuban Refugees with barbwire, dogs, guns, fire trucks, and clubs[?] . . . We must remember the Air Police have limited jurisdiction for arrest and detainment. If refugees go over the fence, because of slow processing, we are going to let them go. . . . These people left Cuba because of the same conditions."[33] He also directed that civilian and "rent-a-cop" police officers be spoken to about their use of "tough talk and action" with refugees.

A week later, Cubans staged a hunger strike at Fort Libertad, which according to reports "spread throughout the entire camp" as a growing number of refugees participated. One of the strike leaders said he would not speak until he could meet with his political advisor. It is unclear whether this was someone inside or outside the camp, but his demand reflected Cubans' careful organizational strategies. Thirty Cubans issued a list of grievances, requesting to be released by four o'clock that afternoon "or else!" By 7:00 p.m.

Mariel Cubans and the Specter of Mass Migration

the demonstration turned into a confrontation, and several Cubans were injured. Follow-up Federal Control Center reports describing logistical and administrative breakdowns stated, "The perception of coming from an armed environment in Cuba to another prison camp in the United States can be quite explosive."[34] However, the reports ultimately blamed unrest not on detention itself but on the military police's lack of authority to intervene and make arrests, as well as on a lack of segregation between "problem groups" and "family groups." The list of groups identified as causing tensions included single men, criminals, political agitators, prostitutes, and homosexuals. Raising security questions, one report concluded, "I realize this is not our function as we are to process Refugees only, but from common sense something needs to be done immediately because the longer they are held the more these problems are going to occur."[35] Negative effects of long-term detention and growing resistance did not elude camp administrators, but their comments also pointed to the US government's broader ideological view of Mariel Cubans—whether vulnerable or criminal, they posed a national security threat nonetheless.

The Cuban-Haitian Task Force, formed by the Carter administration to coordinate resettlement efforts, including managing the camps as well as public relations, also weighed options for handling four "problem" groups that were hampering the resettlement process and receiving an outsized amount of media attention: the "criminal element," "unaccompanied minors," those with "mental illness," and "homosexuals." Under heightened public and official scrutiny, members of these groups experienced a range of segregation and punitive practices in detention that, in effect, blurred these distinctions to confirm their deviance, heighten their suffering, and prolong their detention times. Ultimately, Mariel Cubans' stigmatization and experiences of detention facilitated the broader criminalization of the entire migrant group within and beyond detention sites.[36] To obscure the political fallout from the migration, the Carter and Reagan administrations sought procedural and policy "solutions" ranging from transferring detention responsibilities to other sectors to a whole new approach to detention.

Presidential library holdings reveal that both the Carter and Reagan administrations monitored negative media coverage of Mariel carefully, and scholars have traced the astounding proliferation of narratives of Cuban deviance in US media. The *New York Times* and the *Washington Post* as well as local outlets near refugee camps in Miami, Arkansas, Pennsylvania, and Wisconsin ran stories almost daily relating to unrest at the refugee camps and crimes committed by resettled Mariel Cubans.[37]

A 1980 US Army photograph showing National Guard forces at Fort Chaffee, Arkansas, responding to a Cuban "disturbance" indicates the increasingly militarized and punitive nature of the refugee camp. Cuban Heritage Collection, University of Miami.

However, smaller and identity-based media showed a more nuanced range of responses to Mariel Cubans—from solidarity to hate. Interviews with Afro-Cuban arrivals in Miami and analysis of Black and Spanish-language media coverage reveal multiple and contradictory voices from the African American community. While some Black community leaders urged solidarity and warned of the "divide and conquer" narrative tactics of the white elite used against African American and immigrant communities, many African American op-eds and letters to the editor drew from "nativist perspectives." The recent death of McDuffie and subsequent uprisings in Miami exacerbated these tensions, as African Americans expressed racial resentment toward Cuban migrants they saw as white and privileged, especially in contrast to the US government's discriminatory treatment of Haitian migrants, and heightened fears that focusing resources on immigration would further Black inequality.[38]

Voices from Mariel Cubans themselves and Cuban Americans in Spanish-language media further reflected a range of empathy and division. While the established Cuban American community defended Mariel Cubans, editorials in *El Miami Herald* also eschewed those seen as troublemakers, using language affiliated with Blackness and crime. One editorial referred to the refugee tent city in Miami as the first "Cuban ghetto," while another decried the embarrassment of violent uprisings in the camps, claiming, "esos no son

Mariel Cubans and the Specter of Mass Migration

compatriotas nuestros [these are not our compatriots]."[39] In what Monika Gosin calls the "quest for worthy citizenship," Mariel Cubans and Cuban Americans alike emphasized narratives of deservingness, hard work, and sacrifice. In fact, divisions over Mariel served as a catalyst for the creation of the Cuban American National Foundation (CANF) in 1981, a right-wing, anti-communist organization that worked, among other things, to promote "legal" immigration accompanied by increased immigration enforcement.[40] CANF was formed under advisement from Reagan's national security advisor Richard Allen, who hoped the organization would be a public voice in support of US foreign policy in the Caribbean and Central America.

Some members of the Chicanx community distanced themselves from Mariel Cubans as well. A public statement issued by El Centro de la Raza in July 1980 declared, "We too feel a sense of pain for these Cuban emigrants. . . . But like other victims in our society who take the path of self-indulgence and antisocial behavior—such as drug dealers and pimps—our sympathy can only go so far. . . . History will measure the extent to which we contribute to the development of our people; not the extent to which we give handouts to lazy misfits." With its notable anti-Black reference to pimps and drug dealers, the statement went on to explain that Mariel Cubans should not be eligible for social services that were hard fought for by Chicano organizing and that wealthy Cubans and US corporations should "figure out what to do with them."[41] While not all organizing for Latinx and migrant rights excluded Mariel Cubans, they often found themselves eclipsed between left and right domestic politics.

In Arkansas, the national media's role in elevating narratives of Cuban deviance helped shape local concerns, while hate groups the Ku Klux Klan and the Federation for American Immigration Reform disseminated brochures and misinformation that inflamed anti-immigrant sentiment. The first 128 Mariel Cubans to arrive at the military base on May 9, 1980, received a mostly warm welcome. However, right before the refugees' plane landed, a retired marine dressed in KKK robes ran through the Air National Guard Station, yelling, "Don't let them Cubans in! Hoodlums! They're gonna come in here and get a free ride for everything!"[42] White nationalism and immigration restriction took on a growing affinity at this time, as indicated by the Federation for American Immigration Reform's dissemination of a booklet of anti-Mariel political cartoons in the early 1980s.[43] In February 1982, after the last Cubans were moved out of Fort Chaffee, the New York Times quoted Fort Smith mayor Jack Freeze as he recounted the experience: "People here decided they didn't want the Cubans before they saw them. The press had already said they were bad. I knew they couldn't be productive. There might be a Desi Arnaz or two out there, but mostly they were going to be killing one another."[44] This reveals how the preexistence of negative press surrounding Mariel Cubans helped shape local perceptions.

Fort Chaffee's recent use as a Vietnamese refugee resettlement camp also undoubtedly contributed to local compassion fatigue. A May 1980 *New York Times* article describing a picket at Fort Chaffee cited the economic recession as paramount. One unemployed mother carried a sign reading "What are they going to do now—relocate us Americans?" Another young man remembered that 50,000 Vietnamese refugees were detained at Fort Chaffee back in 1975, relating, "Everywhere you go there's a Vietnamese working now—at least one."[45] But local attitudes also softened toward Cubans due to the 2,000 jobs Fort Chaffee created for local residents. The false notion that immigrants pose a threat of job competition has been a long-standing argument against immigration in the United States; however, this perception of prison job creation foreshadowed the dynamics underlying the prison boom of the 1980s.[46]

Narratives of disease and sexual deviance circulating among local law enforcement were also elevated in the media and all the way to the White House. Media reporting highlighted the spread of tuberculosis, gonorrhea, and syphilis in the camps. A Fort Smith newspaper printed a rumor that twenty Cubans had raped a female police officer at Fort Chaffee, a story allegedly beginning with a local KKK member reporting the incident to Governor Clinton's office.[47] Similar stories abounded, reflecting perceived sexualized threats. After an uprising at the camp in April 1981 in which one Cuban was shot, the *Arkansas Democrat* ran an article that began, "Fort Chaffee—The insane who huddle under blankets are sedated lest they cut their wrists to get attention. Homosexuals swish along dusty streets in drag. Single young women bear children conceived in the American resettlement camp. These are the unwanted Cubans at Fort Chaffee." Republican governor Frank White, who unseated Clinton in 1980, sent this article to the White House relaying the "desperate need to resolve this situation" and demanding the camp's closure.[48]

In the process of sending refugees without sponsors to Fort McCoy, Wisconsin; Fort Indiantown Gap, Pennsylvania; and Fort Chaffee, Arkansas, interagency coordination between FEMA, the Office of Refugee Resettlement, the Department of Health and Human Services, and the newly formed Cuban-Haitian Task Force had attempted to distinguish and separate "problem groups" from the rest. A majority of unaccompanied minors were sent to Fort McCoy, while QTGNC migrants were unofficially sent to Fort Indiantown Gap. Despite xenophobic responses to resettlement camps

　　　　　　　　　Mariel Cubans and the Specter of Mass Migration

expressed by local communities, Mariel Cubans did receive some community support, especially in the boatlift's earlier days. KKK members demonstrated outside Fort Chaffee's fences, but so did those in support of Cubans receiving refugee status.[49] These contestations show how Cubans became symbols of very different views of how to protect and promote the US national body.

After the Fort Chaffee incident, Siro del Castillo, a Cuban American serving as associate director of human resources for the Cuban-Haitian Task Force at the camp, addressed detained Cubans. Reminding them of their conditional freedom, he stated, "Let's compare this waiting period with that of those Cubans who stayed in Cuba. . . . Let's have, as we said before, a little more humility and maybe a little gratitude. . . . Let's keep in mind that the behavior of each and every one of you who leaves the camp and the behavior of every one of you inside the camp, this is what will determine if the doors of Fort Chaffee are opened or closed to each and every one of you."[50] Castillo seemed to warn Cubans that the doors to joining outside society were open to them, but only if they acted more civilly and more "American." Complex refugee politics inside the camps and community contestations outside fueled divisive good-versus-bad migrant narratives and revealed the conditional dynamics behind Castillo's words.

Efforts to obtain sponsorship and resettlement for Cubans involved cultural training and expressions of heteronormative US values; by contrast, those who remained excludable were rendered invisible by continued detention. A statement by Nick Nichols of Carter's Cuban-Haitian Task Force exemplifies this dual nature of detention facilities as he legitimized their use: "The centers allowed the government to do a better job of identifying dangerous refugees and isolating them from the community. The second purpose was to encourage private citizens to sponsor the Cubans, thereby taking them off the government's hands." Although I discuss assimilation and incarceration/exclusion here as two "outcomes" of a refugee camp's purpose, they are not opposites. Rather, they are both forms of violence, albeit varying by degree, inflicted by the state.[51]

Some of the strongest support for Mariel Cubans came from the religious and QTGNC communities. With a lack of government funding, refugee resettlement required the help of private volunteer organizations to locate sponsors. The National Council of Churches, the Church World Service, and the Lutheran Immigration and Refugee Service coordinated with local organizations on the ground. The Lutheran Immigration and Refugee Service and the Church World Service created pamphlets promoting refugee sponsorship, and the Cuban-Haitian Task Force organized a "Sponsorship Awareness

Tour" in multiple cities across the country in 1980–81.[52] Many community members from churches, volunteer agencies, and local schools and colleges volunteered their time, money, and energies at the military bases, providing English lessons, trade classes, sports and recreational activities, and training in job interviewing and life skills.

Oral histories recount how US-Cuba student solidarity formations prior to Mariel and the queer community of Metropolitan Community Church in Philadelphia came to support QTGNC migrants at Fort Indiantown Gap. Three months before the boatlift began, Penn Law student Fernando Chang-Moy traveled to Cuba over winter break with Columbia University's Black Law Student Association. A Mexican academic introduced Fernando to Havana resident Eloy Gonzalez, who invited Fernando into the city's clandestine, "counterrevolutionary" queer scene. Three months later, Fernando's mother received a call from Eloy, who arrived with the boatlift and was camped at the Orange Bowl, needing a sponsor and a place to stay. She hosted Eloy and a few of his friends at her home in Miami before Eloy resettled in Philadelphia. From this friendship, Fernando was inspired to join "a liberal arm of lawyers" from the National Lawyers Guild who visited Fort Indiantown Gap to interview detained Cubans and facilitate their resettlement.[53]

Although no official data on homosexuality was collected, Cuban-edited camp newspapers La Libertad at Fort Indiantown Gap and La Vida Nueva at Fort Chaffee acknowledged queer and gender nonconforming groups, mostly in relation to education about sexually transmitted infections. Reflecting the camp's homophobic gaze, an interview with a Cuban named Tamayo in La Libertad related, "Problems which occur with the homosexuals are being controlled, since generally they keep to their own side of the area or around their barracks, or get sent to other areas. Here in America, homosexuality is not a crime, so it seems gays are enjoying their newfound freedom, perhaps in an exaggerated way, and causing problems by agitating straight men and families, who do not like their children to see or hear certain things."[54] This assumption of freedom, however, became increasingly problematic.

Mark Segal, activist and founder of the National Gay Newspaper Guild and the Philadelphia Gay News, was one of the first to learn of QTGNC Cubans at Fort Indiantown Gap through a friend at Metropolitan Community Church. Wanting to get the "scoop," Segal and a friend drove out to the heavily guarded camp. Segal wore a black Nehru shirt with cardboard in the collar, posing as a priest and telling US Army guards he was a representative of Metropolitan Community Church there to help "resettle the homosexuals." Looking disgusted, a guard directed them to two barracks. Segal recalls, "It was like a

Mariel Cubans and the Specter of Mass Migration

party was going on in that place. There were drag queens throwing material around each other, they were trying on makeup . . . even in captivity, in an Army base, they felt that freedom. It was amazing." Segal says when he revealed they were from a gay newspaper, "the whole place lit up. A gay newspaper! Gay people are here! And they all came running over . . . it was very festive and very loud. And about half an hour later we found ourselves surrounded by the Army with rifles drawn." They left with their camera and tape recorder. A few days later, Segal received a call from a general demanding the tape and film, but it was too late. "We were the first newspaper in America to report on the gay Cubans in Pennsylvania."[55]

Despite stories of solidarity and freedom, camp conditions continued to deteriorate. An internal Health and Human Services evaluation conducted by two medical officers who observed Fort McCoy, Wisconsin, for two weeks in August 1980 again highlighted "problem" groups. Known as the Kramer Report, it described horrific conditions at the camp including daily stabbings inspired by family feuds and "jealousy over the homosexual love affairs," criminal activity organized by the "Warhawks" gang, and the "most bleak" punitive section of the camp dubbed "P.O.W." because of its use as a prisoner-of-war barracks during World War II. The "special problem" of un-accompanied minors was most alarming—the report detailed a high rate of teenage pregnancy, a myriad of mental health concerns and suicide attempts, and a number of minors "unaccounted for . . . hidden in the men's barracks, where they are used sexually by others or paired with adults."[56] Briefly publicized then quickly repudiated by the government (although its reporting was never refuted), the document concluded that the unorganized and prisonlike conditions of the camp exacerbated these conditions and recommended the immediate transfer of minors to a safer facility.

Importantly, *both* humanitarian calls to protect vulnerable refugees *and* xenophobic anger over migrant deviance served to justify the institutional solutions the Carter and Reagan administrations sought in mitigating the media and political fallout of Mariel. By September, reports of INS officers detaining minors in a punitive area of Fort Indiantown Gap and a brutal handcuffing of minors to a fence at Fort McCoy inflamed public anger and local media, which labeled the camps a "keg of dynamite" and hastened the government's desire to consolidate camp operations.[57]

Indicating the rise of neoliberalism and growing trends in incarceration administration by the late 1970s, FEMA used various private contracts in Mariel processing and detention. In the activation of its four military camps, the Carter administration claimed it had a "a scarcity of enforcement assets," while administrators at Camp Libertad in Florida, for example, discussed how best to handle growing security concerns. They believed military personnel should be phased out in favor of civil and private sector "rent-a-cop" policing and also met service needs such as food, recreation, and medical treatment through contracts. Private contracting was desirable for three stated reasons. First, it was more economical; local food service hires could be paid three dollars an hour versus the US Air Force mandate of five. Second, private contracts could provide expertise where needed, such as in field medicine, where FEMA did not have the "technical competence to assess medical guidelines." And third, contracting was seen to have an added benefit of being "a good way to dump money on the local economy." The Federal Control Center concluded the purpose of contracts was "to relieve military costs from operations, management and support of all refugee function at Camp Libertad," recommending that the camp "expedite" contract implementation.[58]

As the Cuban-Haitian Task Force prepared to consolidate Mariel Cubans at Fort Chaffee that fall, it concurrently planned to transfer custody of all remaining unaccompanied minors to the Bureau of Prisons, which would contract with halfway houses in Denver and New Mexico to place what the INS labeled "50 hardcore juvenile criminals."[59] In a White House meeting in December, Gene Eidenberg also proposed transferring 500 Cubans with psychiatric problems to Bureau of Prisons facilities. Interestingly, both the INS and the Bureau of Prisons objected to the plan due to a lack of resources. The INS also rejected the idea of detaining Cubans at existing immigration detention centers in El Centro, California, and El Paso and Port Isabel, Texas. An INS official wrote, "These are low-level security operations designed only for administrative, non-criminal and short-term purposes. Detention of illegal, but non-criminal, aliens ranges from 1–10 days. Space in these facilities is extremely limited. We strongly discourage their use during the current crisis."[60] When Forts McCoy and Indiantown Gap closed that fall and Cubans were transferred to Fort Chaffee, eighty-four remaining juveniles at McCoy were moved into cabins at a nearby state park. In Pennsylvania, a local resident shared his reaction: "In this part of Pennsylvania a Cuban is mud. . . . There was dancing in the streets when local people heard the camp would be closed."[61] President Carter punted on the decision of where "problem" Cubans would ultimately go, but these dilemmas foreshadowed the Reagan administration's turn toward the use of prisons and private contracts for migrant detention.

La Vida Nueva

If I could choose a political party I would choose art.

Jorge, detained at Fort Chaffee, 1980[62]

While at capacity of around 19,000 Cubans in addition to army officers and camp administrators, Fort Chaffee became the third largest "city" in Arkansas. It was a truly transnational space; Cubans arrived with their own Cold War political educations and vocabularies.[63] Some had experienced the outside world and returned after their sponsorships broke down for a variety of reasons, including widespread reports of labor exploitation and mistreatment.[64] At first, people were fairly free to re-create Cuban social structures and cultural activities. They played sports and games brought from home such as boxing, baseball, and dominoes and followed Catholic religious practices. Single men, single women, QTGNC migrants, and families were housed separately, mostly by choice, and personal relations and the development of a black market based on cigarettes, blue jeans, and other commodities, including sex, was not regulated.[65] Cuban-edited camp newspapers and artistic expression offered space for Mariel Cubans to confront and contest their liminality.

Sylvia Gonzalez of the Cuban-Haitian Task Force noted that queer life in the camp was "freer" than in Cuba or the United States: "We have to impress upon them that homosexuality is not an accepted thing by Americans at large. . . . So once they've been assigned a sponsor, you'll see that the eyebrows tend to grow out and the make-up fades as they prepare for reality."[66] That gender nonconformity proved a liability outside the camp says more about the severity of discrimination across US and Cuban society, however, than it does about so-called freedom in detention. As queer and trans people in detention received increasing media attention, they were forcibly segregated at Fort Chaffee in separate barracks in an attempt to move them, as well as other "problem" groups, away from public visibility. Susana Peña argues that the INS's ambiguous policy on homosexuality inflicted a "fractured gaze" on detained Mariel Cubans, as "authorities had to see homosexuals in order to move them out of the media spotlight even as they claimed not to see the homosexuals in order to deny their existence to the media."[67] This uneven process of "seeing" and "not seeing" resulted in misreporting, distorted media narratives, and imposed segregation on detained QTGNC migrants.

Working against pervasive anti-Blackness and homophobia, sponsor organizations pressed Cubans to demonstrate a willingness to "fit in" with US

Two gender nonconforming individuals grooming in their barracks at Fort Chaffee, c. 1981. The American flag and magazine photos of women's bodies are displayed prominently, indicating Cubans' self-expression. Charles Lee Hughes Fort Chaffee Photograph Collection, University of Arkansas Special Collections.

society. Paula Dominique of the Church World Service told the *New York Times,* "There are people who call up and request a white, college-educated Cuban who speaks English. . . . We remind them that we're not a Sears catalogue." And David Lewis of the US Catholic Conference appeared on the *MacNeil/Lehrer Report,* saying, "If we pick up some facets of their personality which are possibly going to be a surprise to the sponsor, if José, as it turns out, is in fact wearing a dress, it's obviously very important that we discuss this issue with the sponsor."[68] Most sponsors preferred women, children, or entire families, but the majority of those held at Fort Chaffee were single young men. Almost three-quarters were Afro-Cubans or dark-skinned Cubans, many were unskilled or with low educational attainment, and 16 percent were reported to have spent time in jail in Cuba or the United States.[69] Efforts to increase Cubans' prospects for sponsorship included a variety of educational techniques and programs focused on the teaching of English, US cultural practices, and democratic values. Local high school students visited the camp for boxing matches and baseball games and gave presentations on the success of

Mariel Cubans and the Specter of Mass Migration

capitalism in the United States. The fact that men were encouraged to engage in masculine activities such as sports and discouraged from overtly expressing nonnormative gender identities in order to obtain sponsorship exemplifies camp efforts to prepare Cubans to become model citizens.[70]

The newspaper *La Vida Nueva*, authored in large part by Cubans and edited by the Cuban-Haitian Task Force, served as an educational tool and as a form of transnational media. The newspaper ran three times a week and provided updates on camp happenings and world news, health tips, lessons on US history and politics, and messages from the camp director, Barbara Lawson. The newspaper also took opportunities such as holidays to educate Cubans about US customs and values. On Thanksgiving in 1980, for example, the camp held a "Turkey Trot" race, served a Thanksgiving dinner, and published Lawson's message in *La Vida Nueva*: "On this first Thanksgiving, it is especially important to remember those first refugees, the pilgrims. . . . They had been able to overcome obstacles and . . . reach their proposed goal: freedom, just like millions of immigrants after them who triumphed over the barriers of language and culture. My prayer on this day of giving thanks is that we will soon have sponsors for each of you, so you can begin your new life in the U.S. as thousands of refugees have done before you."[71]

Cubans contributed to this effort to weave themselves into this Thanksgiving narrative of US immigration history. Ramón Valdes Hevia's piece in the Thanksgiving issue read, "We Cuban exiles, who have found freedom in this land of open arms, which opens the great gates of life, we join the Christian sense of this town commemorating the 27th of November. . . . I thank God for being in this land of freedom."[72] A group of older Cubans in the camp known as "the Abuelas" held a small pro-US demonstration to show what Thanksgiving meant to them, with signs that read "The Communism It's 'Cancer' for the Peoples," "Muera el Comunisma," "Hurrah U.S.A. Champion of the Straight Humans," and "Thanks to the American People!"[73]

However, the politics of exile were more fraught and uneven than *La Vida Nueva* acknowledged. After the demonstration, Fort Chaffee's former deputy director of public affairs Sylvia Spencer published a local op-ed claiming that the Abuelas' actions were staged. She asserted that pro-Reagan camp administrators had suppressed the actions when they were originally inspired, around the time of the Reagan-Carter election, because their visibility would help Carter. Then, she wrote, "several weeks after the election, American officials staged a 'spontaneous' demonstration of appreciation to the American people and compliant Cubans obediently paraded for television network cameras."[74] While clearly upset at Reagan's victory and the change of administration at

A group of older Cuban asylum-seekers, known as the Abuelos, holding a pro-US demonstration in the fall of 1980 at Fort Chaffee. However, some camp administrators alleged that the event was staged for pro-Reagan political purposes. Charles Lee Hughes Fort Chaffee Photograph Collection, University of Arkansas Special Collections.

Fort Chaffee, Spencer also used language that denied Cuban agency in the camp.

Despite Cuban efforts to combat negative stereotypes in the media and claim belonging in US society, and despite the fact that all but several thousand Mariel Cubans were resettled within two years of arrival, Cubans' prolonged detention at Fort Chaffee furthered the stigma of criminalization. As time went on, especially after consolidation and recurrent instances of unrest, the camp turned increasingly punitive. As the concentration of hard-to-sponsor Cubans increased, hopes decreased as they faced a lack of employment, boredom, and frustration. The longer they remained at Fort Chaffee, the lower their chances of obtaining sponsorship.

The experience of detention itself often hardened people and kept them from the doors to freedom. David Lewis of the US Catholic Conference explained a system of green, yellow, and red lights for profiling Cubans for

Mariel Cubans and the Specter of Mass Migration

An anti-Castro drawing by an unnamed Mariel Cuban detained at Fort Chaffee, c. 1980. Cuban Heritage Collection, University of Miami.

sponsorship to the *New York Times*. He noted, "There's no telling how many have crossed from green to yellow because of their experiences in here . . . but you know there have been casualties." Immigration guards carrying Mace and clubs had by this time taken control over a segregation area at the fort called Level II, where alleged fence jumpers and troublemakers were kept. The "stockade" was a place of solitary confinement for those accused of more serious crimes, and those labeled most threatening were sent to prisons to be detained indefinitely. Criminal acts were not the only cause of further isolation at Fort Chaffee; administrators also kept mentally ill patients considered "red" lights in a psychiatric ward and barred journalists from entering. The *Times* also cited accusations of negligence surrounding the October 1980 death of a twenty-three-year-old female patient with a history of seizures left alone in a seclusion area.[75] Over time, these architectures of exclusion would increasingly overlap and serve to render Mariel Cubans subject to indefinite detention invisible within the United States' network of detention centers, mental health institutions, and prisons.

"Nobody Wants These People": From Panic to Policy

As narratives of Cuban criminality reverberated locally and transnationally, heightened surveillance and policing of Cubans in communities of resettlement and modes of retaliation in detention reflected a broader, counterinsurgent turn in White House policy making. Symbolizing a specter of future mass migrations and a nexus of racial, communist, and criminal threats, Mariel Cubans at Fort Chaffee drove Reagan's Cold War on immigrants—including the criminalization of asylum-seeking and new policies of detention as deterrence.

In many ways, Carter served as an "invisible bridge" enabling the rise of Reagan. From the South himself, Jimmy Carter was a racial moderate who borrowed from Southern strategy rhetoric in his own campaigning.[76] By adopting diplomatic and humanitarian language to obscure the racism in US foreign and immigration policy, Carter played a central role in developing language surrounding migration and asylum-seekers that avoided race—a politics of denial that Reagan would double down upon.

Reagan's presidential campaign linked themes of national renewal with denunciation of an immigration crisis inherited from the Carter administration. The overarching importance of US-Cuba relations and the Mariel Cuban migration in the Reagan imaginary cannot be overstated. On the campaign trail, Reagan stoked Cold War divides, blaming Fidel Castro for flaming the revolutionary wars in Central America. Often invoking Dwight D. Eisenhower's "domino theory," Reagan's calls to stem migration from the Caribbean and Central America went hand in hand with halting "evil empire" Soviet-Cuban communist insurgency across the hemisphere.

Reagan's embrace of antigovernment conservatism and neoliberalism reveals the economic, political, and cultural dimensions of Reaganism. In his inaugural address on January 20, 1981, Reagan emphasized themes of rebirth and recovery, stating, "As we renew ourselves here in our own land, we will be seen as having greater strength throughout the world. We will again be the exemplar of freedom and a beacon of hope for those who do not now have freedom." He also famously asserted, "Government is not the solution to our problem; government is the problem."[77] Channeling policy issues through emotional and dramatic narrative to garner support through an appeal to shared values, Reagan often simplified or generalized conclusions about events in the process.[78] As will be seen, Reagan's revanchism relied heavily upon rhetorical strategies of gaslighting and outright lies.

Welfare and crime were also major themes of Reagan's campaign rhetoric, as he decried "welfare queen" government dependence and the dangers of criminal "predators," all with anti-Black racial undertones. This played well among disaffected whites. Some 22 percent of Democrats defected from their party to vote for Reagan in 1980; that number rose to 34 percent among white Democrats who believed civil rights efforts were moving "too fast."[79] Reagan's commitment to immigration enforcement rested within this context as policy discussions often conflated the issues of immigration and crime, allying with the restrictionist view that immigration posed a threat to public safety.

The Reagan administration also marked a sea change in prison philosophy, confirming a shift away from rehabilitative models toward punishment as the primary goal of incarceration. As president, Reagan's position on prisons reflected views shaped while he was governor of California, as indicated by an internal memo from the attorney general in the fall of 1981: "The time has arrived for a major policy statement on prisons . . . along with a clear statement of our philosophy that prison is aimed at achieving the purposes of punishment, deterrence, and protection of society, and putting rehabilitation into its proper context—namely, as a hoped-for result, but not one which can be expected nor one as to which there are any systematic methods of achievement."[80]

When Reagan echoed this policy shift in a speech announcing the administration's new War on Drugs in the fall of 1982, he touted a "new political consensus" that "utterly rejects" the prior view that expensive government programs could remedy "poor socioeconomic conditions" believed to be a root cause of crime. Instead, he argued, "the American people are reasserting certain enduring truths. The belief that right and wrong do matter, that individuals are responsible for their actions, that evil is frequently a conscious choice, and that retribution must be swift and sure for those who decide to make a career of preying on the innocent."[81] The Reagan administration's view of Mariel Cubans would reflect this hard-line stance.

Mariel Cuban detention at Fort Chaffee was so contentious in Arkansas that it became the central issue during the gubernatorial election of 1980. Republican candidate Frank White used Fort Chaffee against incumbent Bill Clinton, saying that Clinton had not "stood up" to the White House and had passively accepted the refugees. White promised to empty Fort Chaffee within a year and aired commercials showing Cuban unrest at Fort Chaffee to assist his win in November.[82] At a conference at the University of Arkansas at Little Rock the following spring, Frank White and Hillary Clinton sat down together to discuss the election. She stopped short of calling the television ads racist but noted that all the refugees in them were Black. "It was not fair or accurate, but it was very effective," she said. "Voters kept asking why Bill Clinton let the Cubans in. . . . I think a political campaign has come down to a 30-second war on television."[83] A White House memo in June 1981 concluded, "It is the opinion of the Governor, his political advisors, and those of us who have analyzed the 1980 election that Governor White was elected solely on the basis of this issue."[84]

On a national level, the Carter-Reagan race echoed these themes. Extensive media coverage of the Mariel boatlift made immigration an issue the incoming administration could not ignore. On the campaign trail, Reagan denounced Carter's handling of the boatlift and promised to "get tough with Cuba." Once in office, Reagan sought ways to retaliate against Cuba and restrict contact with Fidel Castro by imposing new sanctions and a travel ban and even adding Cuba to the United States' list of countries sponsoring terrorism—all moves that prolonged the detention and indefinite status of Mariel Cubans as Cuba continued to refuse repatriation.[85]

Reagan began taking immediate steps to combat the imagined combined threat of crime, drugs, and immigration. In March, he formed the President's Task Force on Immigration and Refugee Policy to chart a new course on immigration enforcement, led by Attorney General William French Smith and Associate Attorney General Rudy Giuliani.[86] One of the task force's initial questions concerned the extent "border enforcement of US laws [should] be integrated, i.e., regarding immigrants and refugees/drug traffickers/smugglers."[87] Reflecting on this mission, Reagan highlighted the prominence of Fort Chaffee in his diary: "Bill Smith came in with a task force report on immigration. Our 1st problem is what to do with 1000's of Cubans—criminals & the insane that Castro loaded on refugee boats & sent here."[88] Reagan had already adopted the dominant yet incorrect view of the Mariel boatlift.

Closing Fort Chaffee was a top priority for Reagan, but where would the administration send the 5,200 unsettled Cubans who still remained there in early 1981? The White House described its dilemma regarding the fort's closure, saying that "political obstacles prevent a solution" and "political commitments prevent its use."[89] Chief of Staff James Baker and Vice President George H. W. Bush both expressed their commitment to solving the problem to Governor White. Baker wrote to White in May 1981, "Your problem at Fort Chaffee is receiving priority attention at the cabinet level. Nobody wants these people. As you pointed out, the Reagan Administration did not admit

Mariel Cubans and the Specter of Mass Migration

them." On June 3 Bush wrote, "I have your letter on the undesirables at Fort Chaffee and have been pressing the system for an answer. Your concern is widely shared but by no one as strongly as me.... This is a high priority matter in the Administration. As soon as I can report progress on the undesirables, I will be in touch."[90] Both letters reveal political solidarity with White while affirming the government's dehumanization of Cubans. Cuban welfare did not factor into the administration's proposed solutions.

Reagan moved quickly to explore alternatives to Fort Chaffee and to establish new policies to criminalize migration more broadly, especially as US communities reported problems with Cuban resettlement. Law enforcement agencies in Miami and La Crosse, Wisconsin, for example, attributed rising crime rates to resettled Cubans.[91] More often, however, these originated in suspicion, minor scuffles, and community complaints. At a conference in June 1981, the INS seemed to reverse its prior reluctance to detain Cubans and Haitians. In her notes from the meeting, Alina Fernandez of the Cuban-Haitian Task Force recorded that an INS representative said the agency was open to conditional parole, but only if a national detention facility was first established. She wrote, "INS encourages local law enforcement to prosecute the entrants and try to establish a criminology, then INS can take the case."[92] While appearing minor, this note reveals efforts to establish a new procedural flow—a shift from "catch and release" to detain and release—and the criminalization of asylum-seeking as a new rationale for immigration and local law enforcement collaboration, as well as detention.

In the summer of 1981, Reagan's Task Force on Immigration released its recommendations that would change the course of detention policy. Under the heading "Contingency Planning," the task force advised the identification of suitable facilities "to hold 10,000 to 20,000 people" in the event of an immigration emergency like Mariel and to "plan for activation of the facilities on short notice, but maintain the facilities on an inactive basis." And under "Enforcement Options," it proposed to "detain undocumented aliens upon arrival pending exclusion or granting of asylum. This requires facilities with a capacity of 5,000–10,000 assuming more rapid exclusion hearings and high apprehensions."[93] These recommendations marked three important new strategies the Reagan administration would adopt to assure the exclusion of unwanted immigrants: the use of the specter of another Mariel to legitimize more permanent detention facilities, the use of detention as a deterrent to illegal immigration, and the detention of asylum-seekers upon arrival.

These strategies contrasted sharply with the Carter administration's stated intent for detention, at least as it claimed. In 1979, INS commissioner Leo

Castillo told the House of Representatives that the purpose of immigration detention was not to punish migrants but to ensure their appearance for expulsion hearings and to provide for their welfare.[94] As chapters 3 and 4 discuss, this was already problematic because of abusive conditions facing Haitian, Mexican, Central American, and other migrants in existing detention sites. The Reagan administration stating that punishment was now official policy, however, opened a new door for detention's expansion. When Attorney General Smith delivered Regan's new policy recommendations to the House in July 1981, he claimed, "The problem has been out of control for years. . . . Detention of aliens seeking asylum was necessary to discourage people . . . from setting sail in the first place."[95] In October, Reagan asked Congress to grant the administration "emergency powers to keep unwanted immigrants off U.S. shores." This authority would exempt the government from all environmental laws, aiding in the construction of difficult-to-place detention centers.[96]

A week after announcing the Immigration Task Force's new recommendations, Smith addressed the Houston Chamber of Commerce. He elicited a settler colonialist view of US history to defend the administration's new policies, framing immigration as a white nationalist project. The first two priorities, Smith said, were stemming "illegal immigration" from across the southwestern border and from arrival by sea, conflating asylum-seeking with illegality. He continued, "Throughout the process of developing our new proposals, we have remembered well that American history has been the history of immigrants. On this day nearly four centuries ago, Christopher Columbus first set sail for the New World, beginning the greatest wave of migration the world has ever seen." However, "The immigration issues we face today are very different from those we have confronted in our past." Smith then lauded the most racially restrictive era of immigration policy in US history, the 1920s to the 1970s, when national origins quotas favored emigration from Western Europe, and noted that "the percentage of our population that was foreign-born has declined every decade." But now, Smith claimed, "we have lost control of both the number and the type of persons entering the United States." The story Smith told was one celebrating a white settler nation and the restoration and maintenance of it through the "new beginning" of the Reagan era.[97]

Closing Fort Chaffee and finding an alternative for Mariel Cuban detention, however, became increasingly difficult as one state after another refused to accept or detain the remaining Cubans. Texas state representative Buck Florence said that he did not want Cubans moving to Texas because "they urinate in public and are prone to masturbation."[98] Governor Harry Hughes

A cartoon drawn by Enrique published in the November 1, 1980, issue of the newspaper *La Vida Nueva* at Fort Chaffee. A woman approaches a man frozen in ice, asking in Spanish, "Did it take me long, dear?" Not only referencing cold weather, the cartoon expresses Cubans' frustrations with long processing times at the camp and feelings of uncertainty. Cuban Heritage Collection, University of Miami.

of Maryland declared his "most vigorous opposition" to a proposal to build a detention facility in Bainbridge, and the mayor of Port Deposit stated, "There is apprehension here and a few people have become so alarmed as to say, 'Oh, I have to buy a gun.'"[99] Illegalizing asylum-seekers yet again, Attorney General Smith noted that Cuban and Haitian "release into Florida adversely affects the local community; Governor [Bob] Graham and the Congressional delegation urge dispersal of the illegals to other areas of the country." He called for the expansion of other facilities to "meet a possible immigration emergency."[100] In August 1981, the *New York Times* reported that there were "720 refugees left at Fort Chaffee, Ark., most of them classified as 'antisocial,' and, according to Federal officials, no one wants them."[101] As negative publicity continued, options for the transfer of Mariel Cubans grew slimmer.

The US government even considered relying on its imperial strength for a potential solution. An idea to return Cubans through the US military base at Guantánamo Bay, established in 1898 when the United States took control of Cuba from Spain, circulated in government and in the media.[102] The notion to rely on militarized, offshore sites to resolve the Fort Chaffee crisis speaks to the legacies of US empire. It also foreshadowed a new Reagan era strategy and the future use of Guantánamo Bay by the Bush Sr. and Clinton administrations to detain Cuban and Haitian asylum-seekers in the 1990s. An internal White House memo noted that using Guantánamo Bay "would avoid the domestic political costs of continuing to hold them within the United States; getting undesirable Cubans out of the U.S. would be viewed as an Administration victory." However, this solution was untenable given US-Cuba relations. The White House and the State Department later denied reports that the administration even considered Guantanámo.[103]

In an interview in December 1981, Reagan alluded to the administration's plans for expanding immigration detention structures. When asked about Mariel, he replied, "In 1980—the administration then was caught by the great exodus from Cuba. . . . No planning had been made for that. We're also looking at available sites and facilities for a detention center for those who are apprehended and are illegal aliens, who will probably be returned." He also admitted problems "finding [a site] that the inhabitants of the State would be willing—you'd be surprised how difficult it is to find some State that wants it."[104] These statements reveal an important transformation that occurred within the administration; the refugee "resettlement camp" had become inseparable from the "detention center" for "illegal aliens."

That same month, after rejecting Fort Drum, New York, as a possible relocation site for Mariel Cubans, the Office of Management and Budget made an "eleventh hour" decision to transfer full responsibility for Cuban detention at Fort Chaffee from the Department of Health and Human Services to the INS.[105] This prompted the administration to briefly consider a pitch for a private contract facility in Glasgow, Montana. The *New York Times* opined that the unsettled Cubans remaining at Fort Chaffee "have become more important as political symbols than as individuals" and cited a letter from Frank White to Health and Human Services that stated, "I don't need to tell you how important it is to the Republican Party and to my own political future that these people be moved."[106]

However, passing off the political hot potato of Cuban detention ultimately led the administration to arrive at the most expedient solution available, in coordination with the Bureau of Prisons. As a White House proposal outlined,

"Termination of Ft. Chaffee operations is the major priority at this time. . . . If greater speed is required . . . [an] alternative would be faster and millions of dollars less expensive. . . . Our proposal will permit Ft. Chaffee to be closed sooner and can be implemented at less cost."[107] The proposal recommended that Cubans from Fort Chaffee be transferred to various Bureau of Prisons facilities instead of to Glasgow, Montana. This recommendation became a reality. As Fort Chaffee closed and the last Cuban disappeared into the prison system in February 1982, Justice Department officials legitimized the decision, claiming, "It's cheaper to keep them there" and that it was an "interim solution."[108] It was also the least visible, and therefore least politically costly, solution.

The legacy of the Reagan administration's handling of Fort Chaffee was the criminalization of Mariel Cubans and the buildup of a more permanent immigration detention system that led to the unprecedented use of private contract facilities beginning in 1983. In March 1982 the attorney general's office described a foreseen need for detention: "A very real possibility exists for other major movements of illegal entrants from Central America and the Caribbean into the United States during the next several years. A new permanent detention facility would allow the Department to enforce its illegal alien detention policy more equitably nation-wide."[109] This specter would dramatically reshape immigration enforcement in the coming years.

Legacies of the Long Mariel Crisis

The *New York Times* presciently commented in 1980 that "the plight of the Cubans at Fort Chaffee may be the beginning rather than the end of a problem of national and international proportions."[110] Indeed, a long Mariel crisis would extend for years—and for some Cubans detained indefinitely, decades.

In a series of recorded interviews in 1981, Fort Chaffee director Barbara Lawson expressed her frustrations with the media and the Reagan administration's treatment of Cuban refugees. Asked by a journalist if she had witnessed the same public reluctance to welcome refugees when she worked with the Red Cross in Vietnamese resettlement, Lawson replied, "I think we had a lot more guilt in those days." Complaining about the nation's right turn, she said, "I don't like to hear the United States of America talk about Guantánamo Bay and sending people back to Cuba like we're a bunch of Nazi fascists, and that's what it's getting to. There is a real swing towards conservatism . . . this attitude of send them back, shoot them when they get off the boat." As a camp administrator, it seemed Lawson's hands were tied in influencing policy decisions. Experiencing retaliation from the administration herself, she continued, "They've already called me up and said, 'Look, Barbara, you talk too much down there.' . . . I get fired, and nothing happens for the Cubans. Right? So who wins? . . . Are we gonna keep people forever? That's the issue. Do you warehouse people, or do you provide some kinds of services so that we can release them into our country? That's the bottom line."[111] Lawson's comments point to the ways in which Mariel became a pivotal moment for detention policy making.

Immediately after the closure of Fort Chaffee in 1982, Reagan officials worked on new plans to detain asylum-seekers while the problem of indefinite detention of Mariel Cubans still remained. Reagan wrote in his diary, "What to do with 3000 jailed Cubans. Castro infiltrated with the Mariel refugees. These have criminal records and history of mental problems. They are truly violent and were evidently released from prison and hospitals in Cuba just to be dumped on us. A judge threatens to release them from our jails and turn them loose on society. The problem—as yet unsolved is how to return them."[112] Indeed, the Reagan administration would take a combative stance toward the courts as legal battles over the rights of detained migrants would continue throughout the decade. A handwritten note by James Cicconi, special assistant to James Baker, from that same month in 1982 stated three points: "Pres. is committed to at least a degree; predicting new refugee flows from Caribbean (result of Cent Am prob & Cuban activs as well as econ diff); Throw newly arrived refugees into prisons for processing?"[113] The following chapters discuss the continued tying together of Caribbean and Central American migration in the Reagan imaginary and how this suggestion of targeting asylum-seekers from the Caribbean and Central America for detention quickly became standard procedure.

By this time, the image of Mariel Cuban criminality was well entrenched in law enforcement, US media, and popular culture, from political cartoons to the 1983 film *Scarface*. A public opinion poll conducted in 1981 revealed that Cubans were the least favorable migrant group in the country, with 78 percent of whites and 73 percent of African Americans polled saying they would "discourage" their entry. Iranians and Iranian students were second, with Haitians and Vietnamese tied for third.[114]

In addition to almost 3,000 Mariel Cubans whom the US government subjected to indefinite detention since their arrival with the boatlift, around 3,000 more would be arrested and re-incarcerated in the first few years after resettlement—mostly as a result of heightened policing and surveillance nationwide. Even though no more than 1,000 Mariel Cuban arrivals had been

Mariel Cubans and the Specter of Mass Migration

determined to have committed crimes in Cuba, the false belief that 40,000 had spent time in prison in Cuba continued to circulate among police departments across the country. In the fall of 1982, a story in the *Columbus Dispatch* reported that "the 'Marielistas,' a society of Cuban criminals who came to this country on the 'Freedom Flotilla,' might be organizing in Columbus.... Street informants have told police that four tattooed men, described as homosexuals, were combing the streets buying weapons" and that the gang had orchestrated the theft of forty cars in Miami that were later seen being driven by Cuban police. When the reporter confronted the police officer pushing the story with an FBI refutation of it, he waffled: "Do you mean we made an ass out of ourselves?"[115]

Rumors or no, this perception drove the Reagan administration to pour new resources into enforcement on local to federal levels, tying together criminal and immigration enforcement. As part of his announcement of a new War on Drugs in the fall of 1982, Reagan claimed that "massive immigration, rampant crime, and epidemic drug smuggling have created a serious problem" in south Florida. The administration moved to centralize federal immigration and drug enforcement efforts through FBI, DEA, and Coast Guard cooperation and encouraged federal-local cooperation through the creation of the South Florida Task Force.[116] In 1983, the INS worked with Florida's Dade County and the Cuban-Haitian Task Force to compile a database to track Cubans and Haitians, shared with law enforcement officials across the country. And congressional testimony by an unnamed former Cuban intelligence officer in 1984 asserted the belief among law enforcement that 3,000 Mariel Cubans were "secret agents of Castro who had been spying on fellow exiles and running a vast underground network for addicting Americans to cocaine in a Castro-inspired plot to spread social decay among the people of the United States."[117] However, it has since been revealed that anti-Castro Cuban Americans in the United States and the CIA were more involved in the crack cocaine trade than any Castro conspiracy.[118] In reality, the majority of Mariel Cubans who were arrested, re-detained after resettlement, and deemed "excludable" were charged with such crimes as theft, minor drug offenses, and, most commonly, INS parole violations.[119]

By the decade's end, even the Cuban American National Foundation had incorporated "lessons" from Mariel in its immigration policy recommendations. As CANF grew in political influence, it often furthered narratives of good versus bad immigrants and reform measures accompanied by increased enforcement. In line with its anti-Castro stance, CANF warned of the need to mitigate the negative fallout of mass migration in the event of democratic regime change in Cuba. A CANF report concluded, "Such large-scale move-ments present public health and safety and economic concerns, as was demon-strated by the experience of the 1980 Mariel Boatlift. To avoid a repetition of that experience, the Commission calls for a coordinated Federal-State-local plan." It recommended interagency and intelligence cooperation, fully funded immigration enforcement contingency plans "before a crisis occurs," and "continuous monitoring of potential threats."[120]

Meanwhile, litigation by and on behalf of Cubans continued. Between 1981 and 1985, 300 Cubans had been released because the INS did not have criminal evidence against them. Some 2,500 more won their release from the Atlanta penitentiary due to a probation system set up in response to a ruling by US district judge Marvin Shoob. Considered a key adversary by the Reagan administration, Judge Shoob would continue to rule that Cubans had the right to due process and to know why they were being detained and a limited right to counsel. The Eleventh Circuit, however, overturned Shoob's rulings. Judge Robert Vance, siding with the administration's right to detain Cubans indefinitely, claimed that Shoob had "poached on the prerogatives of the executive branch."[121] In November 1982, 1,000 jailed Cubans filed a class action lawsuit challenging their indefinite detention and asserting that mi-grants should have due process rights, but it did not succeed. US government counsel Douglas Roberto said, "If the attorney general determines they are a danger to society, he doesn't have to let them out." In 1986, the Eleventh Circuit upheld the indefinite detention of Mariel Cubans in *Garcia-Mir v. Meese*.[122]

Asylum claims can also be a powerful site of resistance. One such claim was that of Fidel Armando Toboso-Alfonso, who arrived with the Mariel boatlift and was paroled into the United States in 1980. But in 1985, the INS re-detained him and terminated his parole for possession of cocaine—deeming him de-portable for this crime of "moral turpitude." In response, Toboso-Alfonso filed a political asylum claim based on the 1980 Refugee Act's protection of members of "a particular social group"—in this case, homosexuals. The INS argued such a persecuted group did not exist, but Toboso-Alfonso demon-strated that Cuban police kept a file on homosexuals, thus documenting a decade of discrimination he had faced in Cuba before arriving in the United States. In 1990, the court found he had indeed experienced persecution in Cuba for being gay, and Toboso-Alfonso won his freedom. *Matter of Toboso-Alfonso* was the first successful asylum case defining homosexuals as a per-secuted group, therefore effectively challenging the United States' Cold War refugee paradigm. The United States repealed homosexuality as grounds for inadmissibility in immigration law in 1990 in response to mounting demands for gay rights. In 1994, Attorney General Janet Reno established this ruling as a new precedent for refugee/asylum cases, ultimately shaping a new QTGNC immigration and refugee politics in the United States.[123] Today, such asylum cases are a powerful challenge to the prolonged detention of queer and trans migrants and have secured the release of many, effectively saving lives.

As the long Mariel crisis persisted, the boatlift would continue to haunt politicians and subsequent administrations. In Arkansas, Bill Clinton regained the governorship in 1982 after giving Frank White a taste of his own medicine. While running again, Clinton criticized White for not handling the refugee situation at Fort Chaffee as promised, telling the Associated Press that closing the camp was to Reagan's credit and that White "didn't kick the Cubans out as soon as he got elected."[124] Continued attempts by the United States to repatriate Mariel Cubans throughout the 1980s, discussed in chapter 6, would play a central role in the Reagan administration's plans to build prisons and alleviate overcrowding. The indefinite detention of Mariel Cubans would recede from public view until Cuban-led prison uprisings in 1984 and 1987 spurred new forms of state retaliation, with the question of their indefinite detention remaining legally unresolved until 2005.

Cubans were not the only immigrant group to be detained en masse during this time. However, the size and scope of the US immigration detention system grew exponentially after the "crisis" of the early 1980s that began with the Mariel Cuban migration and continued as Haitians and Central Americans increasingly sought refuge in the United States. Mariel became a key symbol of the specter of future immigration emergencies for the United States, and narratives surrounding the urgent need to contain the threat of foreign—racialized, queer, and deviant—bodies became a counterpart of Reagan's renewed white nationalism. As the next chapter shows, retaliatory policies outlined by the Reagan administration in response to Cuban and Haitian "boat people" marked new US immigration enforcement practices that remain firmly in place today.

We Have Been Unable to Find Any Precedent

Haitian Interdiction and Detention

You can imagine that if we risked our lives by leaving our country on sailboats and planes it was in order to find a haven on the soil of America. . . . Why are you letting us suffer this way, America? Don't you have a father's heart? Haven't you thought we were humans, that we had a heart to suffer with and a soul that could be wounded?

"Unhappy Refugees of Enclave VI," Fort Allen, Puerto Rico, November 1981

On October 9, 1980, a United States Coast Guard plane conducting a routine search discovered over 100 Haitians marooned on Cayo Lobos, a deserted Caribbean island the size of a football field. With nothing but an unmanned lighthouse and a few abandoned buildings for shelter, the island lay twenty-five miles off the coast of Cuba and within jurisdiction of the Bahamas. The Coast Guard alerted the Bahamian government of the Haitians' presence and dropped food and medical supplies on the island by air. When the Coast Guard's cutter *Dallas* landed on Cayo Lobos to administer medical examinations on October 20, Haitian boat captain Claude Pierre said a storm had forced the migrants ashore, including twenty-five women with several among them pregnant, after they left Haiti on September 22 for Miami. Six passengers died before their arrival on the island, and five had starved since landing.[1]

The stranded Haitians found themselves at the center of an international "jurisdictional squabble" between Haiti, the Bahamas, the United States, and the United Nations High Commissioner for Refugees. According to Bahamian prime minister Lynden O. Pindling, his government was willing to release the migrants to the UN High Commissioner for Refugees but only on the condition that "the United Nations and the United States would accept full responsibility for all illegal aliens in the Bahamas, estimated to number 20,000 to 40,000."[2] Finally, after the Haitian government expressed it would take the migrants back but could not transport them, Bahamian police officers landed on the island on November 11 in an attempt to evacuate them. Starving but not wanting to return home, the Haitians turned the officers away with knives, sticks, and bottles. Claude Pierre protested, "I can't go any place but Miami. . . . We lost everything in Haiti. They will beat us up, kill us, put us in jail. It is a decision between life and death."[3] The next day, the director of Miami's Haitian Refugee Center, Reverend Gérard Jean-Juste, landed on the island in a CBS helicopter and advised the Haitians not to return to Haiti, suggesting instead that the United States would accept them. The Bahamian police officers soon returned, this time wielding clubs and tear gas, and the weary migrants submitted to going back to Haiti on November 16. President Jimmy Carter's assistant for intergovernmental affairs Gene Eidenberg, claiming the president and his administration were unaware of the situation until the *Miami Herald* brought it to their attention only days before the Bahamians' attempted evacuation, said, "I'm outraged. . . . The White House is looking into the question of how this situation was allowed to occur."[4]

In the wake of the Mariel Cuban boatlift that had taken place that summer, media images of desperate Black refugees evoked little public sympathy. After the *Miami Herald* editorial board called for the US public to show compassion towards Haitians stranded at Cayo Lobos, angry letters to the editor reflected the xenophobia of the time. While some citizen letters laid blame on Haitian dictator Jean-Claude "Baby Doc" Duvalier, Albert Harvey of North Miami Beach wrote, "You stated that Americans sitting in the comfort of their secure homes cannot be smug about the inhumanity to the Haitians on the island of Cayo Lobos. However, we are not secure, smug, nor comfortable in our homes anymore. We have lost faith in our government to protect us from violent crime, inflation, unemployment, and the loss of American pride."[5] Other letters also reflected economic anxiety and racism linking Black migrants to crime, and one writer even suspected communist Cubans had infiltrated

Haitian boats. Earlier that month, Florida citizens had elected Ronald Reagan president, and a hotly debated anti-bilingual measure passed in Dade County.

In the spring and summer of 1980, Haitian boat arrivals in southern Florida sharply increased in untimely parallel with the Mariel Cuban boatlift.[6] In March, the same month the 1980 Refugee Act went into effect, the Immigration and Naturalization Service signed an agreement with the Bureau of Prisons and the US Public Health Service to detain migrants in Bureau of Prison facilities. Because it was signed in Miami and required at least one Creole interpreter at each facility, the agreement was clearly designed to target Haitians.[7] Once in office, President Reagan took unprecedented measures to restrict Haitian migration through a policy of interdiction on the high seas. By executive order and diplomatic agreement with Haiti in September 1981, Reagan directed the US Coast Guard to patrol the waters between Haiti and Florida and intercept refugee vessels. INS officers on board would then interview Haitian migrants, bringing to the United States those found to have credible asylum claims and returning to Haiti those found excludable.[8] The Coast Guard began patrolling the Windward Passage off the northwest coast of Haiti on October 11, making its first interdiction on the night of October 25. The leaking Haitian boat sank shortly after its fifty-seven passengers were transferred to the cutter *Chase*, which took them all back to Port-au-Prince.

The very next morning, in "wretched symmetry," as the *New York Times* described it, the bodies of thirty-three Haitians who had drowned when their small boat capsized washed up on the shores of the resort community of Hillsboro Beach, Florida. According to the INS, it was the worst accident of its kind since the agency began processing Haitian boat arrivals in Florida in the early 1970s. Governor Bob Graham called the event "a human tragedy which has been waiting to happen," while a Coast Guard spokesman in Miami said, "It's what we were hoping to avoid" through the new interdiction policy. Thirty-four survivors from the shipwreck were apprehended and sent to the Krome North detention facility in south Miami, joining a thousand other Haitian migrants who had been detained for months.[9] After the drownings, the National Association for the Advancement of Colored People, which had previously labeled the policy of interdiction a "barbaric assault on human freedom," sent a fact-finding team to Miami to interview INS officials, survivors, and Haitian nationals. NAACP executive director Benjamin Hooks sent a telegram to President Reagan demanding a meeting with him and urging the president "to rescind the interdiction order which has been applied in a discriminatory manner towards Haitians fleeing their country."[10] Meanwhile, relatives of those detained and civil rights activists continued to demonstrate on the streets outside of Krome, chanting, "Hey hey, USA, stop supporting Duvalier" and drawing international attention to the detention center.[11]

In the 1970s, the INS began using detention and informal punitive measures to deter Haitian boat arrivals in southern Florida and expedite their exclusion. These measures, including the Carter administration's short-lived Haitian Program, predated Reagan's official policies of interdiction and detention as deterrence. As Haitian migrants drew upon existing exile solidarities and anti-racist and anti-imperial mobilizations to wage inside-outside resistance to detention, their increasing visibility drew both public empathy and ire. Ultimately, however, the continuity of an anti-Black undercurrent running through the Carter and Reagan administrations enabled Reagan's revanchism as the Carter administration denied its racist treatment of Haitians and foreign policy hypocrisies through diplomatic, economic, and humanitarian rhetorics that shielded the US government's growing use of informal immigration enforcement practices from mounting criticism.

If Fort Chaffee was a site representative of the experience of detained Mariel Cubans, Krome North exemplified the experience of Haitians who made it to US soil—but Cuban and Haitian experiences were not equal. As Jana Lipman explains, "While the Cuban refugees entered in far greater numbers and received far greater media attention, the US policies that developed in this moment to monitor, process, and control Haitian refugees created the more enduring legal and political precedents."[12] Krome was first established as a nuclear missile site in the 1960s in response to the Cuban missile crisis and then used as a housing unit for soldiers. It reopened in 1980 in response to the Mariel boatlift and the Carter administration initially detained Cubans and Haitians there, but separately. The government housed Cubans at Krome South in the summer of 1980 at a cost of $300 per day per person, before re-settlement or transfer to military bases. Haitians were housed in much worse conditions on the swampier side of the property at Krome North, at a cost of only $27 per day per person.[13]

Disparate Cuban and Haitian detention conditions reflected both racial bias and the Cold War protocol of receiving Cubans as anti-communist political refugees and rejecting Haitians as economically driven "illegal immigrants." The procedures and outcomes of their adjudication also followed different paths. As deportation from the United States was not an option for Cubans, it was a reality for Haitians. Haitians who set out for the United States without a visa most likely faced one of the scenarios described above: denial on the high seas, detention, deportation, or death. As a migrant group, Haitians stand out as being overwhelmingly denied refugee status in the United States. Between 1972 and 1980, out of approximately 50,000 Haitians who sought asylum in the United States, only 25 succeeded. And during Reagan's first term, from September 1981 to March 1985, not one of the nearly 3,000 Haitians intercepted by the Coast Guard was found to have a valid asylum claim, and not one was taken to the United States for adjudication.[14]

While acknowledging the complex histories of each migrant group and their disparate treatment, it is crucial to consider the ways in which US officials and media narratives *imagined* these groups together.[15] Despite their contrasting contexts, Haitian "boat people," much like Cubans, became central figures in US immigration and foreign policy making. Although Cubans could not be deported and Haitians had to be, per Reagan doctrine dictate, both groups served to justify new forms of detention and measures criminalizing migration. Moreover, the Mariel Cuban migration was a catalyzing event, changing the course of immigration policy making in the Reagan era with tragic consequences for Haitian and Central American migrants who were already being detained at higher rates than other migrant groups.[16] Mariel also informed the creation of the Coast Guard's interdiction program that targeted Haitians alone.

Cuba and Haiti share histories of US colonialism and military occupation. The US government lumped Cubans and Haitians together in a shared "Cuban/Haitian entrant" status in 1980, in immigration policy discussions (in Carter's creation and Reagan's continuation of the Cuban-Haitian Task Force, for example), and in media narratives describing the influx of dark-skinned "boat people" from the Caribbean, melding both groups together in the public mind. Also, both groups' shared experience of detention, albeit in different facilities, furthered their criminalization. The parallel spikes in Cuban and Haitian migration in 1980 remained a key symbol in the Reagan imaginary with its heightened focus on the Caribbean as geopolitical strategy and migration threat. Knowing what the political costs of "boat people" had been to Carter, Reagan entered office ready to tackle what his administration had labeled "the worst immigration problem imaginable."[17] In his diary on July 16, 1981, Reagan wrote, "The Haitians and the criminal Cubans Castro sent us mixed in with the refugees [are] our 2 greatest problems."[18] Here, he describes detained Haitians and Cubans together as two aspects of the same "crisis."

In all, this facile collapsing of two Black migrant groups in some contexts and the US government's unique discrimination against Haitian migrants in others illustrate the anti-Black racism driving Reagan's new immigration

Haitian Interdiction and Detention

enforcement measures. Haitians have suffered some of the detention system's most extreme injustices. Continuity between the Carter and Reagan administrations' treatment of Haitians enabled the Reagan administration to wage a broader war on migrant rights as liberal human rights discourses gave way to neoliberal rhetorics of personal responsibility, punishment, and denial. Once in office, the Reagan administration used the tools at hand to move these trends even further to the right—and to expand US imperial reach into the Caribbean Basin in order to stem migration.

This chapter's focus on Haitian migrants shows how the legal justifications sought and established by the Reagan administration for Haitian detention, deportation, and especially interdiction relied on prior foundations yet marked a new extension of executive authority beyond US borders to affirm state sovereignty over migrant rights. This expansion of executive power, in turn, cleared the way for cementing the subsequent layers of Reagan's carceral palimpsest. The Haitian case also illustrates the mutually constitutive relationship between migration and foreign policy. As the desire to stem Haitian migration shaped US foreign and economic policies toward the Caribbean Basin and compelled the United States to support totalitarianism, asylum and detention in turn became foreign policy tools. Although political and economic conditions in Haiti intertwined to displace migrants, Associate Attorney General Rudy Giuliani forged diplomatic relations with Haiti to de-link politics from economics in order to justify interdiction and systematically deny Haitians asylum. Migration control was also an impetus for the Reagan administration's neoliberal "trade and aid" Caribbean Basin Initiative.

As Haitians and their collaborators resisted interdiction and detention, the Reagan administration moved swiftly to defuse case backlogs and media attention. In the end, these contestations served to shape the human rights versus revanchist rhetorics of the immigration debate, ultimately normalizing crisis governmentality and detention as a tool of migration control.

"We Came Here to Save Our Lives"

Contestations over the United States' distinct and discriminatory treatment of Haitian migrants throughout the 1970s foreshadowed showdowns over Latin American foreign policy and migration in the 1980s; even more, they paved the way for Reagan's right turn.

Haiti holds a unique position in US history and imagination. Its status as the first "maroon republic" in the Americas, gaining independence from France through anti-colonial slave insurrection in 1804, has long prompted the disdain of Western nations. Haiti's economy, hobbled by debt and colonial coercion since independence, is the poorest in the Western Hemisphere and sustains one of the world's most inequitable distributions of wealth. Most recent in line, the United States has exerted imperial influence, economic exclusion, and even direct military occupation of the nation from 1915 to 1934 in the name of promoting regional stability. US occupation opened an early path for Haitians to migrate to the United States beginning in 1915, but the United States directed most Haitian migration to Cuba and the Dominican Republic as contract labor. Beyond this exploitation, as a Black nation, "Haiti, like Africa, had been fixed 'textually' since the nineteenth century," as J. Michael Dash argues. US popular culture has reflected fear of and a fascination with Haiti, which is "suggestive of mystery and carnality," including mythologies of Vodou, zombies, and contagion.[19] At the same time, however, the United States has viewed Haiti as an important Caribbean ally, especially as an ideological bulwark against communism after the Cuban Revolution.

When the election of François "Papa Doc" Duvalier as president of Haiti on a Black nationalist platform in 1957 quickly turned into a brutal dictatorship, people and capital fled the country. Mirroring trends in Cuban migration, earlier Haitian emigrations were of the professional classes, with New York City a destination hub. Dash writes that by the 1960s, "the belief that Haiti had simply lapsed into savagery . . . acquired great currency." Popular depictions of the nation, like in Graham Greene's 1966 novel, *The Comedians*, reduced Haiti under Duvalier to "a land of obscurity, barbarity, and *voudou* drumming."[20] This context gave rise to a complicated politics of exile, as some worked from the United States to destabilize Duvalier, while others, fearfully reminiscent of US occupation and wishing to ally with African Americans to combat broader racisms during the civil rights era, hesitated to criticize Haiti's leadership.

When François Duvalier's son, Jean-Claude "Baby Doc," came to power in 1971, Haiti's manufacturing sector improved, but poverty and government corruption, repression, and persecution remained rampant. Official terror was coupled with lawlessness in the countryside, where government officials subsisted on practices of extortion and land dispossession at the hands of the Tontons Macoutes, private security forces. Although the United States was generally more tolerant of Jean-Claude's leadership, many US citizens sharply criticized Haiti's oppressive regime. Even so, when Haitians with less means began arriving in southern Florida by boat, US government and media messaging surrounding these new arrivals often framed Haitian migration as a threat to US sovereignty and a carrier of contagion, especially amid a tuberculosis scare.[21]

Anti-Black racism conjoined with US foreign policy in the Nixon administration's determination that Haitians were "economic migrants" rather than "refugees." Despite all evidence of the Duvaliers' ongoing brutality, the United States looked the other way when it came to Haiti's human rights violations, seeing Haiti instead as a crucial Cold War ally—strategically situated, mineral rich, and a counter to communism in the Caribbean. Responding to domestic xenophobia and calls for increased immigration enforcement, the INS turned to a set of informal enforcement practices to support the US government's denial of Haitian asylum-seekers, including detention, family separation, denial of work permits upon release, and discriminatory interviewing and processing procedures.[22] Discriminatory processing included the use of hasty, informal exclusion hearings, which are hearings determining the admissibility of someone who arrives at a US port of entry, resulting in blanket asylum denials. The INS began detaining Haitians in local Florida jails, as well as in prisons and immigration detention centers in Port Isabel and El Paso, Texas, and elsewhere. The INS separated husbands and wives, sending Haitian women to a federal prison in Alderson, West Virginia. Despite the agency's assertion during the Mariel boatlift in 1980 that its detention centers in Texas were meant only for stays of one to ten days, already by 1974 human rights groups were documenting Haitian detention lengths of months and more.

From the outset, grassroots resistance to Haitian detention adopted tactics to publicize these hidden practices. Resistance was coalitional, drawing support from religious organizations as well as from labor and civil rights–era movements. According to Carl Lindskoog, advocacy responses grew quickly out of exile activist networks that had formed in the late 1950s and 1960s. From beyond the Haitian community, the National Council of Churches of Christ and labor organizations lent their support to found the Haitian Refugee Center in Miami in 1973 and the Rescue Committee for Haitian Refugees in New York in 1974.[23] These organizations launched litigation against discriminatory Haitian processing as well as powerful critiques of US foreign policy hypocrisies.

In March 1974, the American Committee for the Protection of Foreign Born alerted its members, "There is an emergency! Haitian refugees coming here risk their lives. . . . On arrival, instead of receiving their legal rights as refugees, they are jailed for 'illegal entry.' More than 100 have been incarcerated since September; 50 of them held in isolated Port Isabel, Texas."[24] Some 200 demonstrators, including clergy and labor unions, had staged a protest the month before, and American Committee general counsel Ira Gollobin litigated successfully for Haitian asylum hearings to allow documentation and witnesses for the first time. The American Committee urged readers to write to their elected representatives and local newspapers to raise awareness about Haitian detention and the need to protect migrant workers.

The death of a Haitian man named Turenne Deville, who killed himself in a Miami jail on the eve of his deportation, sparked more protests that spring. Friendship Baptist Church held a funeral service for Deville and published his testimony. It detailed time he spent imprisoned in Haiti and his escape to the Bahamas and then to Miami. "In Haiti's jail, there is no food, no water. One must drink his own urine," he wrote. "Many stacked in one room; if sick, no medicine, no doctors, no shower to take baths. Neither friends nor parents can come to visit you. Once there, one must be distorted. I can't go back." A statement of solidarity after Deville's testimony read, "We the Black people of the Model City area and all concerned human beings of Dade County, do hereby declare that our Black Haitian Brother Turenne Deville, is now and forever . . . a citizen of Dade County."[25]

Activism on behalf of detained Haitians drew comparisons across repressive governments and spaces of confinement while predicting INS retaliation. The US Committee for Justice to Latin American Political Prisoners in New York published a flyer that read, "The most recent attempt to deport 10 Haitians, which resulted in the suicide of Turenne Deville, is a test case for the U.S. government. It is a test case to see if all the Haitian refugees in this country can be deported without an outcry from the American people. We are here today to say that we will not let the US government get away with this."[26] The US Committee for Justice called for solidarity between Haitians and Chileans, as both groups faced persecution at the hands of US-backed dictatorships, and the United States labeled both economic migrants rather than refugees. The committee also warned that practice would soon become policy. After the Deville protests, the INS began a "series of dragnets" in Brooklyn, New York, arresting Haitians working in a factory and at barber shops without papers. York College's Black student magazine *Spirit* opined that it was an act of retaliation, calling it "a clear attempt to intimidate the Haitian community into silence." One Haitian activist responded, "This is not the time to be silent. This is the time to stand up to the government. If we retreat now Immigration will intensify their raids."[27]

Despite legal victories for Haitian asylum-seekers in 1976–77 that secured parole and work authorizations for many, the INS adopted new retaliatory procedures to expedite asylum cases in response to an increasing number of arrivals and growing public xenophobia. Inside detention, conditions deteriorated. A letter to the American Committee for Protection of Foreign

Born written on behalf of forty-six Haitians in El Paso in 1977 revealed they had been detained there for fifteen months. Detailing their intent to apply for asylum and the persecution they and their family members had faced in Haiti, they wrote, "Every one of us almost have that same political problem." They pleaded, "We ask you please to show this letter to the rest of the peoples to help us in that great danger we in now." They wrote that they did not come to the United States to look for jobs. Rather, "we came here to save our lives. If the president in Haiti is over for a democratic one the immigration can send us home right away. We wait for your answer."[28] But the Haitian Program—an agreement struck between the INS and the State Department in 1978—reinstated detention and the denial of work permits for Haitian arrivals and expedited exclusion hearings, increasing in number from an average of 5–15 per day to 100–150.[29]

In December 1978, Reverend Gérard Jean-Juste of the Haitian Refugee Center, who was the first Haitian ordained as a Catholic priest in the United States, discovered an egregious case of family separation. During a routine visit to the West Palm Beach city jail, he found an eight-year-old Haitian girl, Rosalene Dorsinvil, sobbing alone in a cell. She had been imprisoned there for two weeks since arriving on a boat with her father, who INS sent to a detention center. Neither the jail officials nor the INS claimed responsibility, and after several hours of negotiation she was released to Jean-Juste's custody. Chairman of the American Committee Paul Lehman and Antoine Adrien of the Haitian Fathers in New York stated in a press release, "The callous and cruel imprisonment . . . could have continued indefinitely if a priest had not accidentally heard her sobbing. Such flagrant disregard, not only of the refugee law (the Protocol Relating to the Status of Refugees) but of the most elementary human norms, cannot be attributed to a mere bureaucratic 'error' by local authorities. It is part and parcel of a new harsh policy toward Haitian refugees."[30]

In protesting detention as a violation of international human rights, Haitians also protested detention conditions as a form of environmental racism. Shortly after this incident, seventy Haitians detained in the Immokalee and Belle Glade jails went on hunger strike. A press release by the Rescue Committee for Haitian Refugees announced, "The Haitians are protesting the contaminated, bad-smelling water, poor food, and one set of clothing—when laundered and until their clothes are dry, the Haitians have to lie around naked in a chilly room—all of which have resulted in skin diseases, respiratory ailments and other illnesses."[31] Not only does detention itself serve to criminalize migration, but it also creates public health crises that, in turn, contribute to public xenophobia.

Double Standards

As Cubans and Haitians arrived in Miami side by side during the 1980 boatlift, it became increasingly difficult for the US government to "hide the politics of asylum." Gil Loescher and John Scanlan argue that the INS adopted a "series of reinforcing practices" to facilitate Haitian asylum denials and deny the foreign policy double standard driving them. In a congressional hearing in 1976, Miami's INS district director defended this double standard, saying, "We feel that any relaxation of the rules could produce a flood of economic refugees from all over the Caribbean."[32] To the agency, Haitian migrants symbolized a larger specter of mass migration and an imagined need to hold the line. In addition to detention and family separation, legal observers at Miami's Seventy-Ninth Street processing center recorded another "reinforcing practice" in July 1980—discriminatory INS interview procedures. In their report, the observers argued that the "mechanics" of intake interviews with Cubans and Haitians revealed the "crux" of the problem: "The subjective attitudes and perceptions of INS agents conducting the interviews so strongly infect the procedures as to make 'equal' treatment impossible." When discussing Cuban entrants, INS agents were quoted as saying, "It's impossible to live in Cuba," "People starve in Cuba," and "Castro has eliminated all freedoms in Cuba." In contrast, one agent said of Haitians, "These people are poor, ignorant peasants without a political thought in their minds," while another said, "They come here because they're starving—and our asylum laws don't recognize people who are starving."[33] Importantly, agents referred to both groups as "starving," but since only one was starving due to communism, only one group's migration could be political.

Cuban-Haitian Task Force records reveal that the Carter administration was aware that this double standard would appear outwardly racist, yet it remained committed to its tacit support for Haiti's dictatorship and incarceration of Haitian asylum-seekers. Although Carter sent ambassador to the UN Andrew Young to Haiti in 1977 to announce Carter's commitment to human rights, international NGOs and watch groups reported widely on the frequency of human rights violations under Duvalier's regime. Refugees and advocates frequently called Carter out on the racist treatment of Haitians, pointing out that the Haitian Program was especially hypocritical given Carter's stated human rights priorities.

In 1979, the State Department sent a study team to Haiti to investigate migration from the island and whether Haitians faced persecution upon return. While the team's report acknowledged that "Haiti has a long history

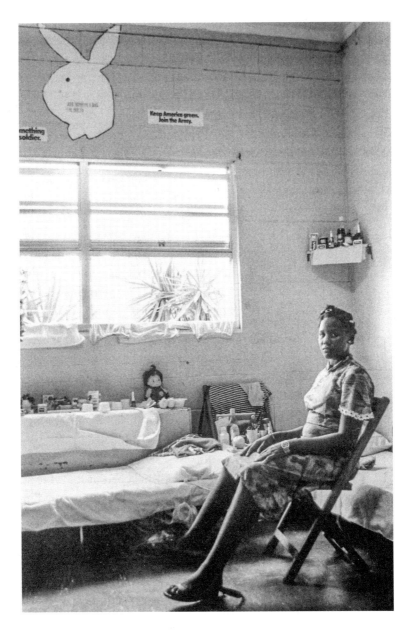

Portrait of an "'unaccompanied minor'—child who arrived in US without her natural parents" at the Krome detention facility in 1980. On the wall is the Playboy bunny logo and the caption "Keep America Green. Join the Army," indicating the facility's prior use as a military barracks. Used by permission of Michael Carlebach. Special Collections, University of Miami.

of authoritarian rule with many periods of instability and the most serious types of human rights abuses," it claimed that eighty-six Haitians interviewed after deportation all said they had left for economic reasons. The report also stated there was no evidence of persecution upon return "except for organizers," who faced fines and imprisonment. To confirm the economic conditions, the report surveyed the northwest region of Haiti: "The primary launching point for outmigration, is illustrative of the squalor which is the lot of the majority of Haitians. There, homes are mud huts without electricity or adequate sanitation. . . . Inhabitants are exposed to malaria, tuberculosis, and other diseases." In highlighting these conditions, the report confirmed popular imagery of Haitian pathology. Finally, the Carter administration relied on humanitarian language to claim that Haitians were treated justly. When Victor Palmieri of the Cuban-Haitian Task Force announced in June 1980 that Cuban and Haitian entrants would be permitted to remain in the country for six months, with benefits, and that they could apply for permanent residency after two years (twice the waiting period for regular "refugees"), he claimed this was, in part, inspired by long-term advocacy on behalf of Haitians and the administration's desire to establish an "equitable and humane immigration policy" for the two groups.[34] Such concessions are but one example of how humanitarian logics can serve to paper over institutional state violence.

The same week the Mariel boatlift began, Judge James L. King heard arguments in *HRC v. Civiletti*, the class action lawsuit against the Haitian Program. Haitian testimonies of persecution in Haiti refuted the State Department's report. The *Miami News* relayed the story of Solivece Romet, who was "held by the Tonton Macoutes for four days during which he was forced to stand in a 2 by 3 foot cell. Beaten repeatedly . . . he developed a speech impediment. After escaping to Florida in a sailboat, he was detained by the Immigration and Naturalization Service. INS was trying to deport him on the grounds that he was an economic immigrant."[35] However, a flood of negative media reporting on the "boat people" arriving on Florida's shores seemed to drown out these voices. Reporting depicting Haitians as disease carriers stirred public anxiety, such as an article in the *Palm Beach Post* detailing Border Patrol agents' fears that Haitians would transfer tuberculosis and exotic skin diseases to them during processing and others linking Haitians' impoverished living conditions and "voodoo" practices to venereal disease and mysterious illnesses resistant to antibiotics.[36]

During the Mariel boatlift, Cuban and Haitian migrants stoked public and media anxieties over race, crime, and a perceived immigration emergency—all serving to justify the use of detention. But advocacy in their favor, led by Cuban and Haitian exile communities, African American civil rights groups, and other human rights, legal aid, and faith-based organizations, also attracted positive media coverage. However, support for Haitians was more sustained and widely publicized than support for Mariel Cubans because of the networks of resistance against Haitian exclusion that had already formed by this time and because of the complex politics of exile surrounding Cuban migrants, as discussed in chapter 2. Judge King's 1980 decision in *HRC v. Civiletti* declared the Haitian Program unconstitutional and found that Haitians had not been given due process, marking the first major win for Haitian refugees in the court system. In a powerful indictment of INS mistreatment, King stated, "It is beyond dispute that some Haitians will be subjected to the brutal treatment and bloody prisons of Duvalier upon their deportation. Until INS can definitely state which Haitians will be so treated and which will not, the brutality and bloodletting is its responsibility." Rebuffing the official narrative the INS and the federal government had been trying to establish throughout the decade, King determined that Haitians' "economic situation . . . is a political condition."[37]

King's ruling and Carter's subsequent promise of equal treatment for Cubans and Haitians highlight two important trends that would carry into the Reagan era and beyond. First, despite King's judgment that Haitians should not be deported without a chance to pursue political asylum and his recognition of racial bias in INS memos describing Haitians as a threat to the social and economic well-being of Miami, the ruling did not grant legal status to Haitians and instead merely ordered the INS to follow the principles of due process. This would become an increasingly familiar theme into the 1980s as the INS would continue to ignore court orders to provide migrants due process. And second, public and internal pressure during an election year, brought by media coverage of the injustices facing Haitians and the Congressional Black Caucus's criticism of US foreign policy, moved Carter to respond. After the ruling, the administration outwardly condemned earlier discrimination against Haitians, and its granting of a temporary "Cuban/Haitian entrant" status was, in part, an attempt to redress King's decision.[38] However, when the boatlift ended in October, this status effectively expired. Haitians who remained in detention with their asylum cases backlogged and those who continued to arrive after the October 10 cutoff date no longer qualified for this status and were subject to deportation.[39] Cubans, on the other hand, could avail themselves of the 1966 Cuban Adjustment Act to obtain permanent resident status. In sum, while the state appeared to respond to public and internal pressure, it often did so superficially in ways that played to liberal values such as promises of equal treatment but in practice came up empty.

When Reagan took office, there was a backlog of 11,000 Haitian asylum cases pending in the immigration court system. Only 5,200 Cubans and 2,000 Haitians remained in detention; the vast majority of Cubans had been released and resettled into society, and Haitians arriving before October 10, 1980, were paroled and living in the community while awaiting exclusion hearings.[40] Although those still in detention made up a small percentage of original arrivals, they would continue to garner media attention. For example, nationwide coverage of disturbances surrounding Haitian detention at the Krome North facility in Miami mirrored coverage of disturbances at Fort Chaffee, Arkansas, and other military bases where Cubans were held.[41]

Echoing the political fallout of Fort Chaffee, Florida governor Bob Graham petitioned the White House for more funding in 1981, citing terrible conditions at Krome and stating that it was a public health risk—not for its residents but for nearby communities. Eventually, the government granted $5 million for improvements, most of which went toward security enhancements to make it more suitable for long-term detention. Graham even sued the US government to move Haitians out of Florida. A brief filed on behalf of Graham in the case reads, "Krome North detainees are being released, indeed 'dumped,' by Defendants into Florida without proper medical screening, thereby creating a grave risk of a public health disaster. . . . The resulting overcrowded and squalid conditions in Little Haiti have created a severe public health hazard. . . . The unsanitary conditions and improper garbage disposal in Little Haiti have led to extensive rat infestation." The brief emphasized the costs of these impacts as well as "crime problems" and "urban decay" with clear racial undertones.[42]

Early Reagan administration policy making took shape within this oppositional climate, affirming xenophobic responses to Haitian migration. While policy discussions fixated on threats posed by Cuban and Haitian migrant groups and on stemming migration from the Caribbean more broadly, they also emphasized the need to stop Haitian boat arrivals and streamline Haitian case backlogs in particular to expedite deportations. To justify developing new enforcement measures and to quell dissent, the administration needed first to create new legal spaces in which to exert executive authority over immigration enforcement and then to maintain that Haitians were economically driven "illegal" immigrants rather than political refugees in alignment with US foreign policy goals. The Reagan administration quickly went to work to develop the world's first extraterritorial maritime interdiction program.

Haitian Interdiction: "A New and Important Beginning"

Reagan's Task Force on Immigration had two main goals: first, to launch a contingency plan in the event of another Mariel-type migration, and second, to curb "illegal" immigration at its source. The Reagan administration's plans for Haitian interdiction addressed both of these as it mobilized the specter of Mariel to justify the extension of executive authority onto the high seas in times of crisis. Records show that even though policy makers questioned the legality of such an extraordinary new measure, the administration adopted the Haitian interdiction program as an emergency measure nonetheless. In its efforts to justify interdiction, the attorney general's office drew upon not only the immediate crisis of Mariel but also prior foundations of crisis governmentality laid during the early Cold War.

The task force addressed the priority of stopping unauthorized Haitian migration by sea immediately. In March 1981, Chief of Staff James Baker reported to Reagan that an estimated 1,500–2,000 Haitians were arriving in south Florida per month and updated the president on the task force's work: "In the view of Justice, there is no clear legal authority to take persons without valid visas on such boats back to the country of their origin, even though that country is willing to receive them and there is no evidence of potential persecution. Your Task Force is looking at these issues (including contingency plans in the event of another major influx) on a priority basis."[43] Already, the administration was exploring the possibility of turning back Haitian boats and investigating the legal authority of the executive to do so.

In a report for the task force's policy group in April, the attorney general's Office of Legal Counsel confirmed the lack of legal precedent for interdiction but instead cited the 1952 Immigration and Nationality Act (INA) and an early Cold War Supreme Court decision to suggest that such executive power already existed in the realm of foreign relations. The office wrote: "We have been unable to find any precedent for such an operation. Nor have we found any example of the President's using inherent executive authority to regulate immigration in the years before Congress first enacted extensive immigration legislation." However, it posed two possible legal justifications for interdiction in "broad statutory provisions coupled with the President's implied powers under Article II of the Constitution."[44]

The first and more substantial justification, the report argued, invoked statutory power based on the "flexibility" of sections 1182(f) and 1185(a)(1) of the INA, which state, "Whenever the President finds that the entry of any aliens or any class of aliens into the United States would be detrimental to the interests of the United States, he may by proclamation, and for such period as he shall deem necessary, suspend the entry of all aliens or any class of aliens as immigrants or nonimmigrants, or impose on the entry of aliens any restrictions he may deem to be appropriate," and, "Unless otherwise ordered by the President, it shall be unlawful—(1) for any alien to . . . attempt to . . . enter the United States except under such reasonable rules, regulations, and orders, and subject to such limitations and exceptions as the President may prescribe," respectively.[45] Given the INA's post–World War II and pre-global refugee protocol context, this amounted to a resurrection of early Cold War xenophobia—this time marshaled for Haitian exclusion.

The report's second justification underlined the implied constitutional power of the president to exclude migrants as supported by the 1950 Supreme Court decision *Knauff v. Shaughnessy*, which states, "The exclusion of aliens is a fundamental act of sovereignty. The right to do so stems not alone from the legislative power but is inherent in the executive power to control the foreign affairs of the nation."[46] Thus, the president could reassert latent constitutional power to "make a finding that the entry of all Haitians without proper documentation is detrimental to our interests and issue a proclamation suspending their entry." Furthermore, "to protect the United States from massive illegal immigration," the president "may act to return the boats with Haiti's permission as an exercise of his power in the field of foreign relations."[47] The Office of Legal Counsel's report also anticipated possible counterarguments to these claims in the principles of *non-refoulement* in international law and in the possibility of third parties (Haitians and advocates) challenging interdiction in the district court of Florida. Ultimately, the office proposed legislative reform to resolve the question of executive authority in interdicting Haitian vessels.[48]

The administration's subsequent immigration enforcement proposals, including legislative reform, all hinged upon the alleged need for expanding executive authority in the wake of Mariel and in the face of a perceived Latin American immigration emergency.[49] When Attorney General William French Smith announced the administration's new and complementary sets of enforcement practices—the detention of asylum-seekers and Haitian interdiction—in July 1981, he singled Haitians out as an example group. Addressing the House, Smith claimed, "The detention of aliens seeking asylum was necessary to discourage people *like the Haitians* from setting sail in the first place" (emphasis added).[50] But then, the legal justification put forth by the administration to establish Haitian interdiction was copied directly from

Haitian Interdiction and Detention

plans it mapped out to respond to a "Mariel-type" scenario, including a memo discussing US complicity with Cuba's closed-door policy.[51] Beyond double standards, detention and interdiction measures adopted as contingency planning in the event of another immigration emergency *like Mariel* and as a deterrent to illegal immigration *like that of the Haitians* collapse the opposing contexts of US-Cuban and US-Haitian relationships, revealing a mechanism for the expansion of US power. Not only did this have tragic consequences for Haitians, but it also legitimized the expansion of US executive authority in immigration enforcement on the high seas, allowing for "anti-smuggling," "anti-communist," "anti-drug," and later "anti-terrorist" efforts across contexts.

The administration's outline of the interdiction program made several recommendations for legislation:

1. To prohibit bringing undocumented aliens to the U.S., and to strengthen existing authority for the interdiction, seizure and forfeiture of vessels used in violation of our laws.

2. To authorize the President to direct the Coast Guard to interdict unregistered vessels and to assist foreign governments that request such assistance to interdict on the high seas their flag vessels, suspected of attempting to violate U.S. law.[52]

It also sought to find "additional resettlement opportunities for Haitians in Western Hemisphere countries" and to "secure the cooperation of the Haitian government in restraining illegal immigration of its nationals to the U.S. and accepting the return of Haitians attempting to enter the U.S. illegally."[53] As indicated, the interdiction program was targeted entirely toward Haitians.

Handwritten marginalia in White House records reveal hesitations but ultimately a consensus over interpretive maneuvering of immigration law. A second internal memo from the Office of Legal Counsel in August 1981 discussed the further use of loopholes found in the Immigration and Nationality Act to assert state sovereignty over the liminal spaces of migration on the high seas. Citing sections of the INA that delineate migrants' rights to asylum claims and exclusion hearings, the memo stated that noncitizens are entitled to exclusion and deportation proceedings but only if they arrive "by water or by air at any port within the United States" and are "within the United States" (8 U.S.C. § 1221 and § 1251). Asylum claims may also be filed only by those "physically present in the United States or at a land border or port of entry" (8 U.S.C. § 1158[a]). The memo reasoned, "Since the interdiction will be taking place on the high seas, which is not part of the United States, 8 U.S.C. § 1001(a)(38), none of these provisions will apply." Furthermore, "since the section delegates to the President the authority to exclude entirely certain classes of aliens, we believe that a return of the Haitians can be based on the Coast Guard's power to enforce federal laws."[54] In the margins, White House legal aid J. Michael Luttig wrote in response, "This is quite a leap. How does Coast Guard enforce fed laws in non US or Haiti waters. The presumption here is that there is an attempted entry. Aren't we stopping them before we know. . . . They have to get here before they can be rejected." Luttig pointed out an important inconsistency in this justification: although the INA would not apply on the high seas in terms of migrants' rights to request asylum or deportation hearings, the authority given to the executive as implied by the INA would apply in justifying interdiction practices.[55]

However, Luttig's subsequent notes reveal how the administration got around these questions by framing interdiction as an effort to enforce Haitian immigration laws rather than US ones—again showing a remarkable extension of US power. He wrote, "We'd specify that only Haitian law of immigration being enforced (it's ok) . . . What when everyone claims asylum? Interview all. Decide pretty much on spot. 10–15 minutes each. Logistics: Ship to Guantanamo Bay, Cuba or Miami, or stay on ship . . . no juris to do it, all must rest on Exec. authority—no rules in area is point."[56] Luttig also confirmed the use of the INA's authorization of the president to determine whether a migrant group would prove "detrimental to the interests of the United States" by writing, "This can be framed to read in interest of US to foster and continue good relations with Haiti."[57] Two important conclusions can be drawn here. First, the Reagan administration's Haitian interdiction program was tenable because it was unprecedented. There was no clear language in the Constitution or US law and no jurisdiction over the high seas that barred the extension of executive authority into this extralegal space to restrict immigration. Second, interdiction was further justified under the purview of the president's command over foreign policy, even as the administration acknowledged, "Politically—we are enforcing laws which we have said are repugnant."[58] Allying with Haiti in this manner in order to halt the flow of Black migrants to the United States sparked immediate criticism and ongoing resistance, as explored below.

On September 29, 1981, President Reagan signed Executive Order 12324 and Proclamation 4865 establishing the Haitian interdiction program, coupled with an agreement signaling Haiti's cooperation.[59] Although immigration

           Haitian Interdiction and Detention

control has always been a transnational endeavor, the inception of the Haitian interdiction program marked the first time in US history the government extended legal authority (through executive order and proclamation) beyond its borders to halt the flow of migration. The interdiction program provided for refugee claims to be adjudicated on board intercepted vessels by a team of State Department members, an INS representative, and a Creole interpreter. This offshore practice effectively sidestepped US immigration law as previously practiced by taking adjudication out of the hands of immigration judges.[60]

Ultimately, the administration justified Haitian interdiction through the specter, not the reality, of mass migration. In October, the White House also submitted a proposal to Congress for legislation to permit the president to "declare an immigration emergency" for up to a year in response to "the actual or threatened mass migration of visaless aliens to the United States." Citing the 1980 "Cuban Flotilla" as a portent of future immigration crises, the proposal claimed existing emergency legislation under the International Emergency Economic Powers Act was unsatisfactory, as it "probably would not authorize such procedures as those designed to expedite exclusion and asylum claims, the detention of aliens pending deportation proceedings, and the interdiction of aliens coming to the United States."[61]

The lasting impacts of Mariel Cuban and Haitian migrations are seen in the legislative proposals' attempts to further consolidate executive power by restricting judicial review. The proposed legislation would grant power to the attorney general to transfer migrants to different detention facilities without any court authority having the ability to review the decision, exempt the government from environmental laws in setting up detention camps (a roadblock the Carter and Reagan administrations had already confronted), grant the US government authority to board foreign vessels without the consent of the foreign country (in direct violation of international law), and curtail noncitizens' access to courts via asylum cases being adjudicated entirely within the INS, without chance for judicial appeal.[62] The White House's exact proposal was not introduced in Congress, however, as it hoped a concurrent filing of a "Simpson-Mazzoli" immigration bill would affirm these powers. Immigration reform would not come until the 1986 Immigration Reform and Control Act. Even then, many questions surrounding these operations would remain unresolved, left instead in the hands of discretionary INS practice.

Reflecting on the Immigration Task Force's new policies in his memoir, Attorney General Smith lauded Haitian interdiction as an appropriate administrative response to an envisioned broader Latin American migration crisis. Referencing the Mariel migration, he wrote, "We took firm but fair steps to curb illegal immigration by sea from the Caribbean. . . . The 1980 Mariel boatlift brought 125,000 Cubans to the beaches of South Florida. Most of them were seeking a better life, but also coming aboard were criminals and mentally ill people expelled from Cuban prisons and asylums by a hostile and cynical dictator. The effects on some U.S. communities had been devastating."[63] Here, Smith extrapolates the perceived negative impact of the Mariel migration onto the potential impact of Haitians to justify the interdiction program and references Cubans and Haitians jointly as indicative of a larger immigration crisis. Smith then identified the Caribbean and Central America as a region of primary concern, conflating Cuban migration with illegality: "The pressure to migrate from the Caribbean basin is not limited to Cuba. Political instability and poverty throughout this critical region drive illegal immigration, and these pressures could increase in coming decades. Increasing numbers of illegal immigrants have arrived by land and sea, from all the Central American countries."[64] This reveals the administration's prediction that migration would only increase in the coming years, a consistent fear driving policy making. Smith also blurred distinctions between migrant categories and the economic and political drivers of migration—a distinction the Reagan administration would ironically fight hard to maintain in order to justify Haitian deportations. Here, however, Smith does so in service of rejecting Caribbean and Central American migrants in totality. Reflecting on Reagan's new policies, Smith concluded, "Together, the interdiction program and the policy of detention represented a new and important beginning."[65]

In a 1982 article for the *INS Reporter*, Rudy Giuliani echoed Smith's defense of the Haitian interdiction program, offering an apology: "The plight of the Haitians is particularly tragic. In their homeland they face poverty and hunger. . . . The United States unfortunately cannot throw open its doors to all the poor of Haiti, any more than it can to all the poor of the world."[66] Neglecting the possibility that Haitians could claim political asylum, Giuliani's statement also denies a longer history of US responsibility for Haiti's economic and political instability.

The Caribbean Basin Initiative:
"An Alternative to Would-Be Migrants"

They are bluffing. How come when the Polish came, they know
why they came. When the Chinese came, they know why they
came. And why don't they recognize the Haitians who come here?

Capois, Haitian detained at Brooklyn Navy Yard, July 1982

Rudy Giuliani played a central role in reinforcing Reagan's new interdiction
and detention policies, leading efforts to maintain a relationship with Haiti
that would deny the existence of political oppression under Duvalier's regime
and justify Haitian deportations. In this way, Haitian migration to the United
States shaped the administration's foreign policy toward Haiti, more so than
foreign policy dictated migration patterns. The Reagan administration continued yet strengthened prior policy by increasing military and economic aid
to Haiti and honing a neoliberal agenda called the Caribbean Basin Initiative
(CBI) with a stated, specific intent to stop migration flows from the Caribbean
and Central America. Couched in humanitarian language and with bipartisan
support, the CBI advanced a new kind of economic imperialism while the
Reagan administration moved to conduct its foreign policy aims away from
public scrutiny, in the private sector.

Granted, Reagan's return to a hard-line Cold War foreign policy stance
led to the admission of refugees fleeing communism. The administration's
decision to halt deportations to Poland provides one example of how foreign
policy shaped immigration policy. As the State Department recommended to
the attorney general in December 1982, "In view of the policy of the United
States toward the Government of Poland . . . the Department of State believes the 'non-enforcement of departure' policy for Polish nationals should
be maintained. . . . The U.S. and its Allies have taken a number of concerted
steps to convey to the Polish authorities the seriousness with which we view
their continual denial of rights."[67] Due to US opposition to communist rule,
Polish nationals were provided blanket relief from deportation with a stated
intent to send a message to the Polish government.

The Department of Justice applied a similar view to Cubans, as evidenced by the public outcry and corrective measures taken after a Cuban
stowaway named Andres Rodriguez-Fernandez was returned to Cuba in
January 1982—the first Cuban deported since Fidel Castro came to power.
The deportation sparked protests by Cuban Americans and press coverage;

meanwhile, the White House rushed to find explanations.[68] Internal memos on the public relations disaster demanded that the Department of Justice explain why the stowaway was returned. Even without knowing the contents of Rodriguez-Fernandez's asylum application, it is clear the administration saw the deportation of Cubans, and transparency in the asylum process, as perilous. As Giuliani stated to Smith, "This was an extremely sensitive case involving the first involuntary return of a Cuban to Castro's Cuba and contact with Cuba to request such return. It generated predictable outrage within the Cuban-American community and provided Castro with propaganda material."[69] The attention given to the Cuban stowaway case at the highest levels of government and the administration's concern over transnational press coverage indicate the importance of maintaining a hard line against Cuba.

In stark contrast, while publicly maintaining that Cubans were refugees, the Reagan administration went to great lengths to refute Judge King's ruling and reestablish the narrative that Haitians were not refugees but economically driven "illegal" immigrants. Haitian accounts and international criticism continued to reveal dire living conditions in Haiti under Duvalier and the confluence of economic and political factors. The story of "Michel," held in a federal prison in Otisville, New York, in November 1981, demonstrates the relationship between political and economic conditions in Haiti. Sharing his testimony in a documentary film, he says, "There is a link between political and economic problems. The reason that Haiti has political problems is because it is a poor country. The economic problems caused the political problems. I'm suffering, I can't eat, I need to go to school—I can't, school is so expensive. If I say this they will beat me up. If I write this and say that I can't eat, that I don't have any shoes, if someone in the government hears me, they say I am against the government."[70] That same month, Reverend Jean-Juste of the Haitian Refugee Center protested the Reagan administration's plans to detain Haitians at Fort Drum, New York. Commenting on conditions in Haiti to the *New York Times*, he stated, "We have a hellish situation in Haiti. How come Mr. Reagan wants to back up this Government that has been there for 24 years and keeps getting worse?"[71] The Reagan administration, however, took an even harder line than Carter in refusing to acknowledge the political dimensions of Haiti's troubles.

Reagan's foreign policy objectives toward Haiti borrowed from those of past administrations while also moving sharply rightward—to support friendly right-wing authoritarian regimes at all costs in order to contain communist adversaries.[72] Only one month into office, Reagan wrote in his diary, "A call in evening reported a boat load of Haitians approaching our shores.

Haitian Interdiction and Detention

I'm all for opening the doors to refugees from totalitarianism but this is more complicated. These are just people who believe they can have a better life here. They are in fact illegal aliens. We'll have to deport them but it's a long & complicated business due to our own laws."[73] Although appearing as a private musing refusing to acknowledge that capitalist dictatorships could produce refugees, presidential diaries are also a mediated source, always in public view. While revealing the extent of Reagan's commitment to this policy stance, it can also be read as an attempt to absolve US complicity in the Haitian government's repression against its citizens.

Reagan's anti-communist commitments coupled with continued public pressure to curtail Haitian migration pushed the United States to foster even friendlier relations with Haiti. When Reagan appointed Ernest Preeg as the US ambassador to Haiti in the spring of 1981, Preeg's primary task was to stop Haitian migration to the United States.[74] The best way the US government saw to do this was to provide aid to Baby Doc Duvalier's "democratic" regime.

Rudy Giuliani became the key spokesperson in the Reagan administration tasked with upholding the rationale that Haitian migration was strictly economic. Giuliani visited Haiti in March 1982 and received a personal promise from Duvalier that returning Haitians would not be persecuted, as stated in the United States and Haiti's exchange of diplomatic letters from the fall of 1981 instituting the interdiction program. Giuliani articulated the Reagan administration's Haitian policy in his testimony in a New York court case in April—namely, that Haitians were not political refugees and were not subjected to persecution by Duvalier's regime upon return to Haiti.[75] After the *New York Times* reported on his testimony, Giuliani received a letter from a citizen criticizing his defense of Haitian interdiction. "You will have to answer the country at some point for bad advice if not downright lies—Beware," the author warned.[76]

To help prove that Haitians were economic migrants, the Reagan administration also granted military and economic aid to Haiti to stem further migration, including deputizing the Haitian Navy. After his trip, Giuliani thanked US Coast Guard liaison officer Louis Casale for his efforts in helping set up Haitian-run patrols, writing, "The assistance being provided to the Haitian Navy by the Coast Guard is vital if the Haitians are to develop a capability for maintaining patrols. We believe this is an extremely worthwhile undertaking and appreciate the professional and sensitive manner in which it has been handled by you and the other Coast Guard personnel."[77] There are conflicting reports of how much assistance the United States actually provided in return for Haitian cooperation in the interdiction program. In 1983, Giuliani appealed to the State Department's Agency for International

Development to support the Haitian Red Cross's "attempts to assist Haitian migrants who return to Haiti.... We believe that projects such as this are vital for humanitarian reasons and to help mitigate the causes for mass migration from Haiti to the United States."[78] Here, Giuliani claimed migration control was a humanitarian effort.

In addition to supporting a self-sufficient Haitian Navy to aid in halting future migration, the administration asked Congress to increase aid to Haiti to alleviate the economic causes of migration. However, rather than addressing the root causes of migration, the Reagan administration's vision of private sector solutions for Haitian uplift was more for the benefit of US corporate interests. Reagan and the Congressional Black Caucus (CBC) did agree on trying to improve human rights conditions in Haiti, and in 1982 Congress passed the Mica Amendment, which stipulated that aid to Haiti was contingent upon cooperation both in halting migration to the United States and in improving human rights in Haiti. As Millery Polyné explains, Haitian exile politics that arose in the 1960s alongside "modernization" theory and civil rights struggles against racism created complex circumstances that at times allied Haitian and African American visions of pan-Americanism—yet at other times, "African Americans were forced to negotiate and at times stifle their political affiliations and beliefs." The CBC's seeming compromise shows how influential African Americans have "chosen to work as stewards of the government and capitalist structures in order to uphold US interests (such as promoting democratic government in the hemisphere and providing foreign aid), but have also challenged the ways Washington contradicted those same political ideals."[79] This difficult position of US politicians who claimed to support migrant rights would continue to frustrate activists, who increasingly resorted to working outside structures of government to advocate for migrants in detention.

The Caribbean Basin Initiative was another trade, assistance, and private sector plan aiming to expand political and economic influence in the Caribbean and Central America and, in theory, counter communist influence in the region and alleviate the conditions driving migration to the United States. Reflecting both domestic and foreign policy goals, Reagan promoted the CBI not only as serving US business interests but also as an alternative to direct military action—constituting, in effect, a form of indirect imperialism. Enacted through the 1983 Caribbean Economic Recovery Act, the CBI was a program of direct foreign investment that included trade preferences, economic assistance, and tax incentives to generate growth in the region through private sector investment and trade.[80] Only the president could grant beneficiary status, and each country had to meet certain conditions: no communist countries were eligible (the CBI explicitly excluded Cuba) nor any country that failed to prove it was cooperating effectively in combating drug trafficking or that gave preference to commodities from a developed country other than the United States. While CBI's proponents touted it as a "multilateral" program created in consultation with twenty-seven participating countries, in reality it reflected US preferences and political aims—especially its aims to curb migration.[81]

Reagan's plans for the CBI built upon those of a group spearheaded by Florida governor Bob Graham during the Carter administration called "Caribbean/Central American Action." Convening in the spring of 1980, Carter addressed the group: "We have before us an exciting and extremely important new enterprise . . . a coming together of two concerns: first, our shared concern about the vital importance of the entire Caribbean region— that concern and interest has been growing lately—and secondly, a recognition that friendship on a people-to-people basis must be the foundation for any progress." He went on to describe the United States' "unselfish" interest in protecting the Caribbean and Central America from threats posed by Cuba through increasing aid, World Bank development programs (loans), and humanitarian programs in the region. He ended by emphasizing three core values: dignity, development, and democracy.[82]

This intention would grow under the Reagan administration to become the Caribbean Basin Initiative, and the administration stated its political motives in much blunter terms. The program originated in a visit between Jamaica's new conservative prime minister Edward Seaga and Reagan in January 1981. Seaga had defeated socialist leader Michael Manley in 1980 and would forge close ties with the Reagan administration in the coming years. After the meeting, Reagan remarked on Jamaica's turnaround, musing that it could serve as an anti-communist "model" in the Caribbean. The administration soon created the US Business Committee on Jamaica to advise private companies on investing the region, comprising twenty-three CEOs and chaired by David Rockefeller at the request of Secretary of State Alexander Haig. The United States then urged Canada and Venezuela to form similar committees.[83] In keeping with the Reagan administration's preferences for operating through a decentralized network of private interests and consultants, CBI drafters also worked closely with the Caribbeana Council, a private organization founded in 1977 to promote "grass roots, self-help programs" that had as its goal "a free enterprise development of the Caribbean." With financial backing from Citibank and Coca-Cola, among others, the Caribbeana Council's founder served in the Reagan administration and worked with Reagan's National Security Council to build energy and agriculture connections between the United States and top-level CBI participants Canada, Mexico, and Venezuela.[84] With the United States at the helm, these four countries agreed, after some pushback from Mexico, to contribute funds to the program.

As White House policy makers developed plans for the CBI in 1982, they anticipated roadblocks. Memos reveal motives behind the initiative and rhetorical tactics employed in promoting it. They recognized "trade and aid" would be a hard sell to the US public and Congress during a time of economic recession and that the CBI might draw more global criticism of Reagan's foreign policy hypocrisies, concluding that Reagan would need to promote it as a security shield against the twin threats of migration and political subversion. An early memo to the CBI's primary architect, US trade representative William E. Brock, considered problems the CBI would face on Capitol Hill, acknowledging it was "a bad time for a program like CBI, but if it must go ahead now because of strategic considerations, then the President must present it as a package required in the interest of national security." The memo recommended that Reagan and Haig be the program's visible proponents.[85] Expecting opposition from interest groups, protectionists, commodity groups, and labor, another early memo suggested, "Present the Free Trade Area [where most opposition will happen] in the form of Presidential negotiating authority, whereby the President designates beneficiaries based on his finding that such countries are proceeding in a direction consonant with U.S. policy goals (e.g. making progress towards a sound emigration control policy; towards establishing a suitable investment climate, perhaps including a bilateral investment treaty)."[86] Notable here is the listing of migration control as a primary selling point.

Notes on Reagan's speech drafts for promoting the CBI to the Organization of American States and the US Congress in 1982 also reveal complex politics and the high-level presence of Haitian detention in policy deliberations. While themes in Reagan's speech to the Organization of American States emphasize hemispheric unity, for example, a memo to Chief of Staff James Baker noted "one problem":

> The speech cites the refugee flow as one reason the CBI is needed. It goes on to talk about the Caribbean countries in a spirit of brother-hood. . . . The issue of the Haitians presently being detained will *no doubt* be raised in response. I can envision pictures of Haitians behind barbed wire at Krome North being used as examples of how we treat our "neighbors." We must take some action before the speech to

address the problem of Krome resembling a prison camp, or else we will not only face the symbolism of it from our own press, but from Soviet/Cuban propaganda arms as well.[87]

Immediate and ongoing resistance to Haitian detention undoubtedly lent to this prediction, but likely so did longer histories of US Cold War enemies pointing to the Achilles' heel of domestic racism. The Reagan administration soon claimed that conditions at Krome were improving; in reality, they were only further securitized. Meanwhile, Reagan emphasized the importance of the CBI as a bulwark against communism and migration.

A list of talking points prepared for Congress in support of the CBI wove together race, xenophobia, trade, and national security interests. The first talking point mentioned Mariel: "There is a potential catastrophe in the Caribbean Basin. If we do not act boldly and soon, we will see more Cubas, more Mariels, more boat people. Vital U.S. interests are at stake: denial of our military facilities to our adversaries; critical resources like bauxite and oil; vital sea lanes including the Panama canal. Over half our total imports and exports pass through the Caribbean." On the issue of migration, CBI drafter Brock claimed erroneously that "illegal immigration" had cost the United States $1 billion in the past three years. Talking points for Congress further argued, "Development gives an alternative to would-be migrants, thus relieving one pressure on the U.S. job market," and concluded with a reassurance that private sector economic uplift was of vital security interest. "We recognize how tight the budget is, but our security won't wait."[88] As the Reagan administration became increasingly embroiled in Central America, it would continue to promote the CBI as a key strategy and alternative to military options in the fight against communism in the region, and in El Salvador in particular; however, the CBI served to both propel and shield US military objectives.

The range of diplomatic and economic efforts taken by the US government to stabilize Haiti and curb migration unintentionally drew further attention to the reality of economic and political oppression facing migrants fleeing Duvalier's Haiti. Mounting criticism and instability would eventually depose Duvalier in 1986, replaced after several interim years by democratically elected Jean-Bertrand Aristide. As Alex Stepick concludes, "Ironically, an immigration policy that began with the fear of criticizing the friendly regime of Duvalier eventually contributed to its demise."[89] Even though policies developed by Reagan administration officials seeded new forms of resistance and undermined their own plans, ideological commitments only strengthened their resolve.

"Let Our People Go"

After the "Cuban/Haitian entrant" status expired and Reagan took office, the INS resumed a beefed-up version of Carter's Haitian Program—in direct refutation of Judge King's prior ruling that the program was racist and discriminatory. Viewing judges such as King as enemies, the Reagan administration sought to aggressively defend and uphold its enforcement measures on all fronts.[90] These moves were met with a new wave of inside-outside activism, critical public opinion, and ongoing legal actions demanding justice for Haitians.

During the summer of 1981, around the time the president's Task Force on Immigration released its recommendations, the INS shifted its practice of regularly releasing Haitians to detention without parole. As the Krome North facility in Miami overcrowded, the INS transferred Haitians to at least seventeen other detention sites—military facilities, local jails, and federal prisons—across the country in New York, West Virginia, Kentucky, Texas, Louisiana, Missouri, and Puerto Rico. The INS also resumed mass hearings of upward of forty Haitians at a time, often behind closed doors and without legal access. These efforts to expedite deportations generated strong voices of dissent that criticized the United States' double standard of accepting Cubans and rejecting Haitians, its tacit approval of Haiti's dictatorial regime, and egregious detention conditions. Groups supporting Haitians outside detention ranged from churches; African American, civil, and human rights organizations; radical feminists; public interest lawyers; and some state and local officials, who continued to be a thorn in the Reagan administration's side, especially as resistance gained public visibility.

While not monolithic, the Congressional Black Caucus, the NAACP, African American journalists, and Reverend Jesse Jackson lent angry voices from the Black community, framing the treatment of Haitians as a transnational civil and human rights issue. Many African Americans, even if torn over the fight against communism, related the United States' complacency toward Duvalier's human rights violations to oppression they felt in the United States. Congressman Walter E. Fauntroy articulated the CBC's position: "We, as black people, want to make it clear that we understand the connection between the treatment of Haitian refugees and the regard for which this administration may have for black people at home." He stated that the CBC would "stand with our Haitian brothers and sisters in their quest for simple justice and will be taking the issue to every forum and community available to us." Criticizing Reagan's interdiction plan and the deportation of Haitians, CBC chair

Shirley Chisholm stated, "The return of refugees to their country, given the gross and consistent pattern of human rights violations, makes a mockery of International Human Rights Day."[91] As mentioned above, the CBC did support US aid to Haiti, but Chisholm made it clear that aid should not be conflated with support for Duvalier.

Advocating racial solidarity, organizations such as the NAACP and the Southern Christian Leadership Conference adapted language and tactics of the civil rights movement to highlight Reagan's racial prejudice toward Haitians. After the Haitian migrant drownings in Hillsboro Beach, Florida, the NAACP sent a legal team to Miami to investigate their deaths and also detention conditions. Head of the team George Hairston then reported on the NAACP's commitment to activate "the large network of NAACP branches nearest the centers to monitor all activities and provide as much comfort to the refugees as possible."[92] The NAACP Youth Council also appealed to President Reagan to reconsider his mistreatment of Haitian refugees. In a 1982 telegram, the council wrote, "We . . . detest the illegal incarceration of the Haitian Refugees. We are registered voters and we are taxpayers. . . . As far as we can see our foreign policy is biased. . . . We demand a stop to the illegal deportation of our brothren [sic]. Therefore, we sincerely call for a stop to the illegal incarceration of the brothren, the Haitian Refugees. We demand a stop to illegal deportation hearings. Mr. President 'LET OUR PEOPLE GO!'"[93] Racial identification evoked African American sympathy for the plight of Haitian "boat people" as Black civil rights leaders in the United States recognized a familiar struggle in the Haitians' efforts to secure the right to due process.[94]

Religious leaders and organizations had long played a leading role in advocacy for detained Haitians. The National Council of Churches, the Haitian Refugee Center, and other advocates forwarded reports to the Organization of American States from Krome and Fort Allen, Puerto Rico, where the Reagan administration began detaining Haitians in the summer of 1981. The organization subsequently launched one of its first probes into US human rights violations. INS commissioner Alan Nelson commented, "The International Human Rights Law Group will try to use this as a forum to publicize their position that Haitian asylum applicants are being denied due process."[95] In the fall of 1981, as the Haitian interdiction program began, Bishop Edward McCarthy and forty-four other Dade County clergy protested outside of Krome, expressing their "moral outrage" over its concentration camp–like atmosphere. "I re-read the inscription on the Statue of Liberty before coming here this morning," McCarthy said. "I don't think we could look her in the eye." Also that fall, the INS sent sixty-nine Haitian women to the federal prison at Alderson, West Virginia. The Alderson Hospitality House, a volunteer organization formed in 1976 to support and house women released from the prison, issued a newsletter decrying the transfer of Haitians to the remote region and the conditions they faced. Margaret Loudon wrote, "Even though this prison and the others scattered around the U.S. could provide healthier and less crowded conditions, it provided a smokescreen for a more decent solution. . . . I wondered how the INS hoped to protect the Haitians' rights to due process . . . in this area. I am confused at the logic that denied parole with its safeguards and puts the Haitians in prisons at a tremendous cost to taxpayers."[96] Loudon also pointed out that while the United States looked the other way on Haiti's human rights violations, US companies made $130 million a year in Haiti developing mineral resources.

The radical women's collective *Off Our Backs* and its feminist publication of the same name, founded in 1970, also stated their solidarity with political prisoners and detained migrants in Haiti and with resisting dictatorship and US imperialism. The collective formed a Creole-speaking Women's Task Force for Haitian Political Prisoners, whose members visited the women detained at Alderson and took an inside-outside approach to publishing the voices of Haitian women experiencing violence and retaliation in detention and to supporting them across facilities as they waged hunger and labor strikes. In a series of articles in 1982, *Off Our Backs* drew connections between histories of women's resistance against slavery and colonialism, the Haitian revolution, resistance to US occupation of Haiti, and women factory workers and farmworkers subjected to gender and sexual exploitation and discrimination. The publication also called out the Reagan administration's hypocritical treatment of Cuban, Salvadoran, and Haitian migrants in particular as "inhuman and unjust" and "the establishment and operation of concentration camps" by the INS as "a blatant violation of human rights."[97]

Off Our Backs detailed conditions of Haitian confinement in women's own words as they recounted horrific instances of reproductive violence and retaliation in detention. This included pregnant women systematically given injections to induce abortions upon arrival in Miami; Haitian and Cuban women held in "extreme isolation" at Alderson, deprived of physical contact and information; and wages of $10 a month for laboring in the prison's mattress factory, compared with $200 a month paid to incarcerated citizens.[98] Haitian women at Alderson also experienced retaliation in the form of restricted phone and visitation access for trying to communicate with the outside world. INS officers routinely harassed them, encouraging them to return to Haiti voluntarily and to find lawyers to expedite the exclusion process. In response, the collective formed the Washington-Alderson Link, an "information link between those doing national support work for all Haitian refugees."[99] The Washington-Alderson Link worked to share information across detention sites and with Haitian Americans living in Miami, New York, and Montreal, advising the women not to accept INS-recommended legal counsel and instead opt for group efforts of resistance.

The publication also provided sharp critique of the prison's infantilizing and humanitarian posturing toward Haitian women, creating space for stories of suffering and resilience. One April 1982 article was written by visitor and medical anthropologist Lani Davidson:

> They call them girls. They call the building in which they are imprisoned—a dank brick structure encircled by a 15-foot chain link fence—a cottage. Cottage 26. They say they are proud when "their girls" walk unescorted over to the cafeteria, when they say "I love you" in the hallway after English class, when they call their unit supervisor "Mommy." Countering this were Haitian women's testimonies of "common anguish." One woman speaking anonymously shared, "Life is getting worse and worse in here. The only time we get out of here is to eat, to go to chapel once a week, and to the doctor's—if they say our complaint is valid. We can't call anyone except relatives and no one can call us."

Davidson also reported grave health and mental health crises in the prison, including suicide attempts, nervous seizures, bleeding lips and bruises, depression, weakness, fatigue, and hospitalizations. "Many refuse to eat," Davidson wrote. "Boredom is one of the worst facets of women's lives here."[100]

However, these testimonies also revealed the women's resilience, such as in prayer services they led in their dorms, "accompanied by music played through paper-covered hair combs and songs written during the many long hours of anxiety and pain," and in a "home-fashioned beauty salon" run by a visitor named Renee who washed women's hair in a laundry sink. Davidson recounted the women saying, "We know we're not criminals. . . . We know who the real criminals are. We are not idle people, or stupid like they told us in Miami. We have our hands and our bodies and our minds. We are strong. In the death that they want us to have so much, we know life. You tell them they can never take that away from us."[101]

Far from the infantilizing narratives of the prison that appeared in the media and even from advocacy groups, detained Haitian women were organized and politicized, utilizing group tactics of hunger strikes and sit-ins

```
I can't escape it. I run up the hill
to work up a sweat "Bon Jour! Hello!"
Elles Disent.

I slow up, smile and wave "Bon soir
mes amis!" Je dit avec une sourire.

I see the police staring--move on--she
is smiling, arms folded, staring out
from snowy white curls. Our grandmother
guard says move on.

And I leave them their smiles torn to
grimaces, clenched teeth, fists, fight-
ing wailing, crying out to heaven for
help crying for help.

And I feel their cries in my blood it
rings in my eyes I turn to look back at
them and see only the police stare.

What can we do?
What is happening?
I don't know

What price do we pay for this demented
freedom?
                    A Sister in Alderson
```

Pauline Guillermo

This poem and image published in the *No More Cages* newsletter by the Women Free Women in Prison Collective express US-citizen solidarity with Haitian refugees held at the Alderson federal prison in Kentucky. Vol. 3, no. 6 (October/November 1982). Special Collections and University Archives, W. E. B. Du Bois Library, University of Massachusetts Amherst.

to resist their detention. The Off Our Backs task force coordinated across detention sites to amplify the women's demands. One article recounted a spate of hunger strikes, sit-ins, and INS retaliation in the spring of 1982. In response to rumors they would be transferred to Central America, women organized hunger strikes at Krome and Alderson that April. In a letter detailing the reasons for their strike, the women at Alderson wrote, "Are we not human beings like all other human beings? Just because we fled our country . . . Or is it because we're black? They don't treat refugees from other countries like this." They also pointed out, "We know that if we go back we will disappear within the blink of an eye. We have two clear examples of that already." The letter described two cases of individuals who agreed to "voluntary departure" and were returned to Haiti but whose families never heard from them again. "It is absolutely impossible for us to go back there," the letter continued. "Instead of going there to find death and have our relatives not even know where we are killed, we prefer to die here." Simultaneously at Krome, forty-one

Haitian Interdiction and Detention

Civil rights activist Jesse Jackson speaks to a guard during a tour of the Krome detention facility in Miami on December 30, 1981, after the quelling of a hunger strike during the Christmas holiday. Jackson's visit brought media attention to conditions at the facility. Mark Foley. Reprinted with permission from AP Photo.

women staged a hunger strike and "sit out" and were joined by several men through the fence separating them. After sleeping outside for five days, several were hospitalized and one force-fed intravenously. Protesters on the outside staged a May Day demonstration, and supporters in California joined the hunger strike as well. The article concluded, "A negative consequence is that surveillance and other security measures have been stepped up at Krome and Alderson."[102] Such a ramping up of abusive detention conditions, resistance, and state retaliation would continue to escalate in the Reagan era.

Civil rights activist Reverend Jesse Jackson was one of the most prominent voices leading the charge against Reagan's treatment of Haitian migrants. In the spring of 1980, Jackson organized a march of 1,000 people to a hotel in Miami where the INS detained 60 Haitian women and children who had arrived by boat. He arranged a series of rallies in support of Haitian refugees in Miami and Washington, DC, in 1980 and 1981, culminating in a massive march in coordination with the NAACP and other religious groups in front of the White House in December 1981.[103] Taking a coalition approach, Jackson also gave a series of spirited sermons and wrote opinion pieces in newspapers nationwide. Jackson went beyond framing the issue as solely a domestic civil rights one; his speeches and writings were highly critical of US imperialism. At a rally in Miami in 1980, Jackson stated, "There is room in the United States for Cubans trying to escape oppression. There is for Haitians trying to escape oppression." As 98 percent of Haitian migrants were Catholic, Jackson even appealed to the pope to support the Haitians as he did Polish immigrants.[104] In an opinion piece titled "White House Discriminates against Haitian Refugees," Jackson wrote,

> Polish refugees, Soviet Jews and Nicaraguans, just to mention a few, are welcomed because they suit the Cold War foreign policy needs of the Reagan Administration. . . . To admit that the Haitians are escaping political repression would be to admit that the United States is party to the oppression. The refusal to consider Haitians as political refugees as well as economic refugees is consistent with the racist nature of U.S. immigration policy. . . . Until all the Haitians are released, I am urging concerned people everywhere to wear red ribbons. The red ribbons will spark interest and conversations. . . . It will also show you care.[105]

Together, religious and African American communities had a powerful voice. In an op-ed, executive director of the US Catholic Conference's migration and refugee service John McCarthy called the treatment of Haitians "a terrible disaster, a scar on our nation—the first time this sort of thing happened since the start of World War II, when we did it to the Japanese. . . . I can't tell you why they are doing it. But I don't see any white faces among the detainees."[106] Drawing upon history and moral authority, such critiques connected experiences of racism across migrant groups and across time. In 1982, Jackson and the US Catholic Conference, with Miami mayor Maurice Ferré's support, proposed that Haitians be released to sponsors organized by the Catholic Conference. In response, INS commissioner Alan Nelson advised the White House to reaffirm its detention and interdiction policies: "It should be emphasized that the administration is unified" on these policies and "considers them effective and essential in gaining control of our borders."[107] Jackson's coalition again raised the issue of Haitian detention at the twentieth anniversary of the March on Washington in 1983.

Adding to mounting media attention, legal action presented the most successful challenges to the US government's treatment of "boat people," but the Reagan administration fought to limit litigation's effects. Administration officials, well aware of the dangers litigation posed to their policies, labeled lawyers and judges sympathetic to Cubans and Haitians as adversaries. William French Smith detailed ongoing efforts to release Cubans and Haitians from detention through litigation in his memoir: "An equally continuous program to release them was conducted by a group of immigration lawyers. They were aided by a federal judge, who, in my opinion, was indifferent to society's concerns. This judge—in order to impose his own system of values—determined to invade the province of the executive branch and in effect perform the functions of the INS. He was finally reined in by the United States Court of Appeals, thereby preventing even more people from being released to prey upon the public."[108]

Smith depicted the court system as a hindrance to the executive branch's authority to enforce immigration law and spoke of migrants in detention as an indisputable public threat. Smith referred here to the back-and-forth battles of *Louis v. Nelson* and then *Jean v. Nelson*, which began as a class action lawsuit in June 1981 to prevent the deportation of ninety Haitians and expanded with the backing of the Haitian Refugee Center. In June 1982, Judge Eugene P. Spellman found that the INS had violated the Administrative Procedures Act and granted an injunction that halted all Haitian exclusion proceedings without legal representation.[109] The Reagan administration successfully appealed the decision, with the Eleventh Circuit ultimately concluding that Haitians had not been treated discriminately. Further, the court found they had no rights under the Constitution while applying for asylum during exclusion hearings, and the president and attorney general had the authority to discriminate against a migrant group based on their national origin, especially as "a foreign leader . . . could eventually compel us to grant physical admission via parole to any aliens he wished by the simple expedient of sending them here and then refusing to take them back." This statement was a clear reference to the Mariel migration.[110] Litigation filed on behalf of detained Haitians and Salvadorans would continue throughout the decade, and while much of it succeeded in gaining procedural rights, it also served to prolong detention times and strengthen the administration's resolve to expand executive authority over migrant processing.

The Reagan administration drew upon revanchist politics and Reagan's experiences battling labor and civil rights movements of the 1960s and 1970s as governor of California to launch an offensive against migrant rights. In the fall of 1981, Mike Horowitz, general counsel for Reagan's Office of Management and Budget (OMB), pointed out the "budget crisis" the INS faced in processing Haitian refugees. He argued that legal action on their behalf by the Haitian Refugee Center further escalated costs as case backlogs required more detention time: "Administration policy is to warehouse them in detention facilities and then to exclude them after hearings, including determinations on asylum claims. Unfortunately, a small coterie of Haitian defense lawyers has contrived to tie the exclusion process up in knots, preventing their exclusion and transportation back to Haiti." Horowitz was referring to the well-known Haitian defense lawyers Ira Kurtzban, Ira Gollobin, and others. "The cost rises with every day and every boatload," he warned, and he continued to identify legal actions as an adversarial "political strategy" aiming to legalize all Haitians in the United States.[111]

Proposing a solution to a "bottleneck" of Haitian asylum cases, Horowitz invoked Reagan's experience as governor of California:

> The present procedural tangle reflects a *managerial problem* similar to that faced in California during the President's term at Governor when . . . the California Welfare Rights Organization adopted a calculated "spring offensive" to frustrate Governor Reagan's welfare reform by tying up the administrative hearing process—and temporarily succeeded. The state broke the offensive by using modern case management techniques, increasing hearing personnel, and providing full and speedy due process for all claimants. I believe that many of the same techniques can be brought to bear to solve the Haitian problem.

Interestingly, Horowitz proposed providing Haitians with the government's own lawyers. With the backing of INS commissioner Alan Nelson, who had served as a welfare official in California during Reagan's governorship, Horowitz proposed that the administration "concentrate its resources on the exclusion process." He reasoned that even though it was agreed upon that "the courts have overstepped their bounds in these cases," only "by giving the refugees all the due process in the world—and fast—can we avoid our problems with the courts, and spare ourselves the budgetary and political problems involved in massive detention centers."[112] Initially, Attorney General Smith rejected this proposal based on his ideological commitment to Haitian exclusion. Later, his office did work to locate lawyers for Haitians detained at Fort Allen, Puerto Rico, under a judge's order to provide them due process, and internal debate continued.

Ultimately, public attention generated by case backlogs, activism, and court actions on behalf of Haitians did not result in effective challenges to detention and interdiction policies. Instead, these battles prompted a new range of counterinsurgent responses to resistance and strengthened the administration's commitment to expedite Haitian exclusion.

The Mass Immigration Emergency Plan

Haiti, my home, misery surrounds me
It grows along the alleys, the gutters
Crawls on the fences, the railings
In our hunger, in our suffering, in this darkness
We deceive each other
It's a dog-eat-dog world
Looking for a way out is no sin
To Miami, we are coming to look for a life.

"Le Grand Voyage," Farah Juste

US Cold War foreign policy would seem to call for a dichotomous view of Cuban and Haitian arrivals as refugees and "illegal" immigrants, respectively. However, pervasive xenophobia and racism enveloping Cuban and Haitian migrants cast Caribbean "boat people," and soon to include Central American "feet people," as a combined threat in the Reagan imaginary. The resurgent white nationalism accompanying Reagan's election and surrounding Mariel Cubans in custody who could not be effectively deported, as well as Haitians awaiting exclusion proceedings, reveals the ways in which anti-Blackness underwrote a punitive shift in detention policy that was then mobilized against subsequent migrant groups. As this chapter has shown, the extraordinary forms of violence and discrimination targeting Haitians since the 1970s paved the way for Reagan's detention and interdiction policies, as Carter-era rhetorics of humanitarianism gave way to counterinsurgent responses to those deemed threats to the nation.

Affirming the widespread xenophobia surrounding Cuban and Haitian migrants, William French Smith recalled, "The problem of where to locate detention centers for the Mariel boat people was extremely difficult. No one wanted one in his own backyard, and the reaction of politicians to proposed sites in their areas was strong."[113] Public anger against the presence of Cubans and Haitians revealed the racism reflected in politicians' refusals to accept proposed detention sites in areas throughout the country. In one example, Texas senator John Tower reacted with outrage against the transfer of Haitians to Big Springs. In a call to the White House, he complained, "You have tripled the black population of Big Springs, Texas, and not even advised me in advance." An internal White House memo noted, "Unfortunately, the problem is compounded because Big Springs, Texas, is in the District of Congressman

Charles Stenholm," making it "an altogether monumental disaster" for congressional relations.[114] Political considerations weighed heavily in the search for detention space as the White House increased its efforts to find expedient solutions.

Policy discussions culminated in Reagan's 1982 Mass Immigration Emergency Plan—a contingency plan for Mariel-type migrations that required the location of additional, permanent detention facilities. The plan also served as a blueprint for subsequent detention policy. Referencing the political fallout of Cuban and Haitian migrations, it also mapped out preemptive measures in anticipation of increasing Central American migration, discussed more in chapter 4. Couched in the larger context of Reagan's promises for renewed wars on crime and drugs, immigration detention policy centered on the anticipation of future emergencies and shortages of prison space.

The attorney general's office outlined this crisis in March 1982, calculating that the federal prison system was "17 percent over capacity. . . . If Cubans/Haitians are excluded, FPS is 7.6 percent over capacity. . . . A new detention facility which can be expanded easily is consistent with the Administration's Mass Immigration Emergency Plan."[115] The proposal provided for separate detention facilities for Cubans and Haitians, but both groups served to legitimize detention in different ways: for Cubans, indefinite detention, and for Haitians, the detention of asylum-seekers. As the administration continued its contempt for litigation and public protest against Haitian interdiction and detention, it saw case delays caused by litigation as further justification for long-term detention facilities.

The Mass Immigration Emergency Plan, drafted in August 1982, clearly referenced Fidel Castro's role in the Mariel boatlift in its stated purpose of ensuring the US government "will be prepared to deal promptly and effectively with any sudden, illegal, large-scale immigration effort, including any effort that is deliberately generated and politically inspired by a foreign government." It outlined five phases of operation: the Ready Phase, including the use of CIA/FBI intelligence, surveillance, threat analysis, and congressional, local official, and media liaisons; the Interdiction Phase; the Landing Phase, including initial custody, processing, and screening; the Movement/Detention Phase, allowing for the movement of up to 10,000 detained migrants at a time; and the Exclusion Phase, providing for either deportation or resettlement.[116]

Despite growing resistance, even from within the administration, these emergency response measures were incorporated—and normalized. When Mike Horowitz of the OMB advised the administration to concentrate resources on expediting Haitian exclusion hearings, he also advised against a

Haitian Interdiction and Detention

long-term detention policy. He wrote, "The present policy is the worst of all possible options. We create inhumane and politically unpopular quasi-concentration camps, and produce a new fugitive class of undocumented aliens." In March 1982, after the closing of Fort Chaffee, the OMB viewed the immigration crisis caused by Cubans and Haitians as mostly resolved. Under the heading "Cuban-Haitian Detention Needs Have Changed," the OMB stated, "Many believe that interdiction has been an effective deterrent. . . . Thus Haitian detention needs in the future are unlikely to require long-term custody." On the closing of Fort Chaffee, the OMB argued, "An INS detention center that offers neither community resettlement nor institutional care is not an appropriate long-term custody solution for the Cubans." The OMB also questioned the management capabilities of the INS and argued that expanded detention capacity might only encourage longer detention stays. Finally, regarding future immigration, the OMB determined that "the uncertainty in El Salvador and other Caribbean countries poses a threat of new groups of entrants, however it should be noted that U.S. refugee and immigration policy is oriented to orderly entry processed from refugee camps or Consular offices overseas not to housing entrants here in detention centers."[117]

Over a year later, in June 1983, the General Accounting Office raised similar concerns about the unnecessary costs of detention, including the human cost. A GAO report, *Detention Policies Affecting Haitian Nationals*, found that long-term detention of Haitians was quite costly, at forty-nine dollars a day, and pushed for alternatives: "INS will, undoubtedly, be faced with the continuing choice of either paroling aliens or keeping them in detention for substantial lengths of time. The cost and the adverse humanitarian effects of long-term detention do not make it attractive as a normal way of dealing with undocumented aliens seeking asylum. GAO believes that INS should work to achieve better alternatives than the extremes that detention and parole now offer."[118] Yet, the Reagan administration insisted on searching for solutions that included increasing detention capacity. Stigmas of crime and contagion surrounding Cubans and Haitians also served to meld immigration detention and prison systems together through interagency cooperation in Reagan's War on Drugs. As the next chapter shows, Central America was intimately connected to the Caribbean in the Reagan imaginary—as a Cold War battleground, in plans for the Caribbean Basin Initiative, and as a new source of migration crisis. Patterns of detention practices, asylum denials, and growing resistance would play out in much the same way as the United States' treatment of Haitians, yet on an even larger and more visible scale.

4

This Time, They'll Be Feet People

Central American Wars and Seeds of Resistance

¡En el nombre de Dios, ayúdanos! [In the name of God, help us!]

Banner at the El Centro Detention Center, 1983

In late October 1981, one month after Reagan issued his executive order launching the Coast Guard's Haitian interdiction plan, a staff member from Arizona senator Dennis DeConcini's office traveled to the El Centro detention center in the Southern California desert to report on the Immigration and Naturalization Service's administration of the camp and the conditions faced by people detained there. DeConcini's aide took a tour of the facility, ate a meal in the cafeteria, listened to stories in the recreation yard, and sat in on three deportation hearings in which "about 50 total aliens were deported within an hour."[1] His report highlighted grave problems at the facility: overcrowding, poor sanitation, lack of proper nutrition and basic necessities, limited access to medical care, reports of physical abuse, and case backlogs that lengthened stays. Senator DeConcini forwarded the "appalling" fifty-page report to Attorney General William French Smith, concluding, "Regardless of the reasons for these people being in the United States, they deserve to live in healthy and humane conditions while they await evaluation of their petitions to remain in this country. If my staff person's report is essentially correct, they are not receiving the minimum level of care consistent with humanitarian principles."[2] The attorney general responded to DeConcini's office five months later with a seventeen-page refutation of the report, claiming that many of the issues raised in the report were false, while others were being corrected by the INS.[3]

DeConcini described the facility as a "refugee camp" and his aide's report labeled it a "detention center," while the INS considered it a "service processing center which entails processing aliens, holding them for about three days max, then deporting them back to their country." However, as the aide's report noted, "There is a slight problem. This was formed as a processing center five years ago when the volume of aliens coming into this country was minimal. Now it is out of control and they are carrying more than what they can handle. There are aliens that have been in this camp for almost two years."[4] In fact, the El Centro detention center was long entrenched in the US carceral palimpsest. According to Jessica Ordaz, it was built in 1945 by migrant labor using discarded materials from a World War II internment camp, and it operated for decades as a detention site for unauthorized Mexican migrants.[5] By the early 1980s, the El Centro facility was responsible for all deportation proceedings of migrants apprehended in California, Nevada, Washington, Arizona, and Utah, with only two San Diego judges hearing about 700 cases a week, often ruling on 20 at a time.

On his tour, DeConcini's aide saw that while the administration building was under construction for expansion, the INS had no plans to improve other facilities. First, he visited the maximum security area, where those being disciplined or labeled "mentally disturbed" were held two per room in ten-by-ten cells with no sinks, toilets, or electricity and "a horrible smell of human waste." Next, in the "holding tank," over twenty arrivals waited in a room for upward of ten hours without food or drink. In the infirmary, where no medical doctors were present, a man "had some type of wound (which looked like a bullet wound) on his chest, and who was complaining of chest pains. The nurse gave him aspirin." Director Harry Malone relayed there was no funding for "medical attention, especially mental cases." The barracks each held 200 bunk beds with one water cooler and one color television, but they were closed during the day, confining people to the scorching hot recreation yard. The grounds, all dirt, had only a twenty-by-twenty aluminum-covered patio to shade the 600–700 people in detention. DeConcini's aide saw men "sitting around the ground playing with rocks, smoking cigarettes, and leaning against a fence talking." When he asked Malone what recreation consisted of, Malone replied, "You're looking at it."[6]

According to the report, 85 percent of the people held at El Centro were from El Salvador, with more Salvadorans deported each month than all other nationalities combined. Following Salvadorans in number were Guatemalans, Mexicans, Cubans, Costa Ricans, and a small number of Asians, Pacific Islanders, and South Americans. The State Department estimated that by 1984, around 500,000 Salvadorans, one-tenth of the country's population, had entered the United States without papers.[7] While DeConcini's aide visited the recreation yard, a hundred men between sixteen and thirty years old surrounded him, emotional and eager to share their experiences of migration and life at El Centro. One man from El Salvador said "his brother and cousin were in this camp about 6 months ago, and were deported back to El Salvador. He showed me a letter from his aunt from El Salvador stating that his brother and cousin were executed and their bodies were found just 2 miles from the airport."[8] The *New York Times* also reported a story from El Centro claiming some who had been deported "had been murdered as they disembarked at the Comalapa airport in San Salvador, the capital, on Christmas Day," which sparked a hunger strike at the facility.[9] DeConcini's aide concluded that people detained there "seemed to be humiliated and stripped of their dignity. I heard their testimonies, and watched them share some tears from emotional experiences they had encountered in their plight for freedom. Just being there and . . . seeing their relief that people outside the compound care for them, drained me emotionally."[10]

Over that summer, the Manzo Area Council from Tucson, Arizona, had begun providing legal aid to Salvadoran migrants at El Centro and raising money to pay bonds for their release from detention. This intervention gained media attention. Around the time of DeConcini's aide's visit—which itself indicated a growing amount of congressional concern over detention conditions and rising violence in Central America—press reports charged that living conditions at El Centro were inadequate and that INS officers' use of undue force inflicted psychological damage upon migrants. Malone reported receiving threatening phone calls at home, with one citizen calling him the "bastard of Buchenwald," referring to a Nazi concentration camp. However, when El Centro, usually closed to visitors, invited the press in for an open house in the spring of 1981, the *Los Angeles Times* reported that the detention site appeared "immaculate and meticulously run." The newspaper concluded, "It is the presence of Salvadorans, who human rights groups claim should be accorded automatic asylum here because of war in their homeland, that has brought controversy to Malone's camp." Malone told the reporter, "We're a political football in the middle of the whole Salvadoran thing."[11]

Although Salvadorans raised public alarm because of their prolonged detention and the foreign policy dimensions of their circumstances, these conditions at El Centro were not new. Conflicting media reporting and DeConcini's aide's ignorance of El Centro's longer history, including abusive conditions that had primarily targeted Mexican migrants over the past several decades, illustrates how the violence of border enforcement had already become normalized—enabling the ramped-up abuses of the 1980s.[12] As overlapping episodes of violence and erasure both characterized US imperialism and were foundational to the carceral palimpsest, Reagan would rely on these foundations to employ new tactics of erasure in his Cold War on immigrants at home and abroad.

Salvadorans at El Centro were not passive recipients of mistreatment, as the report of DeConcini's aide seemed to indicate. Rather, their experiences of migration and confinement sowed the seeds of a growing transnational, solidarity politics of resistance and inside-outside organizing that raised public awareness about detention conditions. Salvadorans would ally with other migrant groups to resist their detention and lead a series of hunger strikes at El Centro between 1981 and 1985. On the outside, Central American refugees, many of whom had been formerly detained, played a leading role in forming solidarity groups to help document detention conditions and raise their visibility in the media. While ongoing resistance created mounting pressure from within detention, outside civil disobedience and activism opposing Reagan's Central American foreign policies gained traction.[13] Religious organizations formed another growing arm of resistance, culminating in the highly visible Sanctuary movement, discussed more in chapter 5.

Akin to the US government's wholesale rejection of Haitian appeals for political asylum due to its support for Duvalier's regime in Haiti, Salvadoran and Guatemalan asylum denials were rooted in US support of their right-wing governments in civil wars throughout the decade. Like Haitians, Salvadorans and Guatemalans faced long-term detention, delays, and due process denials in pursuing their asylum claims. They also partnered with legal aid and human rights organizations to litigate against the administration's policies and practices. In all cases, the US government labeled them "economic" migrants rather than refugees and denied that Haitian and Central American migrants faced persecution upon their return. In the case of El Salvador,

Reagan's anti-communist commitments pushed the administration even further than it had gone with Haiti to cover up the reality of state violence that subsequent investigations have confirmed were genocidal in level.[14] By 1983, Salvadorans occupied 30 to 35 percent of detention space on any given day, held predominantly at Port Isabel and El Paso detention centers in Texas and at El Centro in California. INS commissioner Alan Nelson predicted, "Every indication is that this trend will continue."[15]

In addition to the sharp increase of Cuban and Haitian arrivals in the United States in 1980, a third and even larger exodus from Central America seemed only to confirm the Reagan administration's fears of communism spreading across the hemisphere. One of the loudest saber-rattlers of this "Reaganaut" worldview was Secretary of State Alexander Haig. White House aide Michael Deaver recalled, "It certainly had a good effect on me. It scared the shit out of me . . . scared the shit out of Ronald Reagan, too."[16]

This chapter explores how US interventions in Central America came home as the Reagan administration developed a range of counterinsurgent tactics to wage total war against those deemed enemies within and without. Such tactics included launching military aid, training, and covert operations in Central America; merging border surveillance, intelligence, and policing operations; retaliating against migrants fleeing right-wing death squad violence and allies decrying it; pursuing the Caribbean Basin Initiative, a neoliberal agenda to curb migration and further US interests in the region; and a propaganda campaign of denial and disinformation.

These counterinsurgent measures were informed by Cold War low-intensity conflict doctrine, characterized by Timothy Dunn as "employed in a preemptive or preventive fashion, to forestall the development of outright armed conflict." These measures also had a psychosocial component of "maintaining social control over targeted civilian populations."[17] By striking first, the Reagan administration could control the story by deflecting blame, propelling narratives of communist threat and leftist subversion to deny any role in so-called war. This included outright lies refuting the United States' role in genocidal violence that disproportionately targeted poor, Indigenous, and Afro-Latinx communities. Laying blame for human rights abuses on the Left, the administration also wielded detention and the US asylum system, including the 1980 Refugee Act, against Central American migrants. At the intersections of Reagan's wars against enemies at home and abroad, migrant detention itself was a crucible of counterinsurgent warfare. Indeed, detention capacity and contingency planning for a mass immigration emergency remained a core preoccupation of immigration policy makers during Reagan's first term.

Border Militarization in the War on Drugs

In 1961, the US Navy turned over its air station at Port Isabel, Texas, to the INS. Known as the corralón by people detained there, Port Isabel became a Border Patrol academy and immigration detention site. But the facility also had a lesser-known function—the United States Agency for International Development's Public Safety Program also used Port Isabel as a training site for the International Police Academy, based in Washington, DC, which taught anticommunist counterinsurgency methods to police officers from Latin American countries in the 1960s and early 1970s. Subjects taught at the academy, in league with the CIA, included interrogation techniques, bomb handling and manufacture, terrorist devices, and assassination weapons. One graduate of the International Police Academy was El Salvador's Roberto D'Aubuisson, labeled the "godfather" of the country's right-wing death squads and nicknamed "Blowtorch Bob" for his interrogation techniques during the civil war. The Public Safety Program also worked in El Salvador in the early 1970s training the National Police in "security investigations." Chillingly, ten years later many people fleeing El Salvador's brutal death squads were imprisoned in the same Texas facility where D'Aubuisson attended class.[18]

Port Isabel's overlapping functions point to the relationship between transnational flows of US state violence and domestic prison and policing trends. The global dimensions of Reagan's War on Drugs and merging of interagency enforcement efforts in the militarization of the US-Mexico border exemplify this.

Reagan's renewed commitment to combating the combined threat of crime, drugs, and immigration through the War on Drugs resulted in the administration extending domestic law enforcement efforts abroad through its drug and immigration interdiction policies. At the same time, it imported low-intensity conflict military techniques inherited from Vietnam and further developed in El Salvador in its militarization of drug and immigration enforcement efforts along the United States' southern border—including the Caribbean Basin and Central America, a region Reagan often called the United States' "third" (and sometimes "fourth") border.[19] The Reagan administration even recruited from domestic anti-migrant and white nationalist elements, many of them Vietnam veterans, to become covert foot soldiers in Central America and along the US-Mexico border.[20]

Border militarization occurred against a longer historical backdrop of violence targeting Mexican migrants in the US borderlands and within a domestic context of growing public anxieties over race, immigration, and crime since the Vietnam War that fueled Reagan's revanchist politics.[21] Scholars have shown how President Lyndon B. Johnson's War on Crime and President Richard Nixon's War on Drugs in the 1960s and 1970s were political and racial projects. As Nixon's counsel and Watergate coconspirator John Erlichman famously admitted in the 1990s about the War on Drugs, "We knew we couldn't make it illegal to be either against the war or black, but by getting the public to associate the hippies with marijuana and blacks with heroin, and then criminalizing both heavily, we could disrupt those communities."[22] These domestic law enforcement efforts also had immigration impacts.

Despite low immigration detention numbers throughout the "humane" era of immigration reform in the 1960s and 1970s, the INS's Operation Wetback of the 1950s left a lasting legacy of migrant policing and detention operations—including raids and public order policing, a culture of hate, and a growing "hydra of caging options"—that Reagan would revitalize.[23] In the 1980s, this legacy would converge with the ways in which transnational counterinsurgent warfare influenced domestic policing trends throughout the Cold War to galvanize Reagan's new security state, in effect fueling crimmigration and buttressing global capitalism through covert violence.

The late 1960s and 1970s saw a heightening of crimmigration trends, facilitated by the 1965 Immigration and Nationality Act's capping of migration from Latin America for the first time. This limited "legal" immigration paths, creating more unauthorized migration as growing labor demands continued to draw migration to the United States, while fueling notions of "Latino threat" as the public called for increased policing of immigrants. The concept of the "criminal alien" has a long history, notably in the Border Patrol's preference for this term over "wetback" in the 1950s, which agents thought too sympathetic.[24] In 1968, Congress established a separate court to try migrants for unlawful entry—expanding potential for arrests, detention, and deportation.[25] Both the INS and local police were conflicted, however. In the 1970s, migration from Mexico became increasingly affiliated with drug trafficking and organized crime, but Border Patrol efforts faced resource limitations. While many local law enforcement agencies bought into long-standing false notions linking immigration and crime rates, they also found that undocumented migrants were more often the victims of crime and that local police cooperation with the INS led to public distrust, risking public safety. Even more, immigration control stretched policing resources thin. In the era of Nixon's War on Crime, police forces tried to resolve this by also referring to the threat of an "alien criminal"—usually depicted as an undocumented Mexican. These long-standing notions were a precursor to the federal government's

Central American Wars and Seeds of Resistance

establishment of an official "criminal alien" category through the 1986 Criminal Alien Program.[26] The policing of Mexican migrants did not prompt immediate detention expansion, mostly because their detention was not long-term, but it did contribute to swelling local and county jail capacity in the late 1960s and 1970s.[27] In California, contestations heightened as the rising radicalism of Chicanx and labor rights movements met an upsurge of racist attacks on migrants and of vigilante "border watch" groups, further fueled by resentful Vietnam veterans and white nationalist organizing.[28]

By the end of the 1970s, the US public seemed to agree that crime was the country's largest domestic problem, an argument Reagan and the Department of Justice would continue to make. Gallup polling indicates that since 1968, the public's perception of crime rates was at its highest between 1980 and 1982, with 48 percent of those polled expressing fears of violent crime in their own neighborhoods and that crime rates were only increasing—despite the violent crime rate actually declining in the United States in the early 1980s.[29] In hoping to fulfill a renewed commitment to more punitive measures in line with Nixon's War on Crime that spurred prison population growth since the late 1960s, the incoming Reagan administration immediately faced a manufactured "crisis" of prison overcrowding. Before the 1980s, few new prisons had been built in the United States since before World War II, and facilities were increasingly pressured by growing incarceration numbers. During his presidential campaign, Reagan promised to expand the federal government's role in combating street crime, a role traditionally taken on by state and local governments. The incoming administration also faced lawsuits and demands from corrections unions to alleviate conditions caused by overcrowding. As these conditions worsened, politicians elected on "tough on crime" platforms found themselves in a bind, lacking the prison space to back up their promises. The immediate solution was to increase funding to improve existing prisons and build new ones.

Again, Rudy Giuliani became a key spokesperson in the Reagan administration driving this message and recommending more interagency cooperation. As associate attorney general, Giuliani oversaw all federal enforcement responsibilities, including the Criminal Division, the FBI, the INS, and the DEA. Addressing the 1981 Congress of Corrections, Giuliani dubiously claimed that crime rates were at an all-time high in US history. Expressing the urgency of the moment and reiterating Reagan's punitive position, Giuliani stated, "We cannot afford to engage in philosophical discourse. We do not have the luxury of making leisurely studies of the roots of crime while people in the streets are being murdered, robbed, assaulted, and raped in record

In a keynote speech to the Congress of Corrections in Miami in the fall of 1981, Associate Attorney General Rudy Giuliani announced the recommendations of the president's Task Force on Violent Crime, including increasing federal law enforcement budgets. Subject Files of Rudolph W. Giuliani, NARA II, College Park, MD.

numbers."[30] He then described the recommendations of Reagan's Task Force on Violent Crime, which followed the same timeline as the Task Force on Immigration. The task force's priorities were to address the immediate "crisis" of prison overcrowding and to locate ways to expand federal law enforcement roles and ramp up funding. While Giuliani cited determinate sentencing laws and mandatory minimums as causing overcrowding, he also noted the imprisonment of Mariel Cubans as contributing to the crisis. Of course, overcrowding could be relieved by revoking mandatory minimums, but this was not an option in the Reagan imaginary. Instead, the task force recommended expanding the use of federal property for prison building and interagency training, to which military agencies would contribute. Giuliani concluded by emphasizing the need to develop a wider range of facility types to address the "diverse problems" the country was now facing. Further reflecting on the intersections of Reagan's wars, Attorney General Smith justified increasing the Justice Department's policing budget in 1981 by arguing the department was "the internal arm of the nation's defense."[31]

After Giuliani appeared on several television news programs in 1982, including ABC's *Nightline* to discuss "crime in America," the Department of Justice received a number of letters expressing overwhelming support for

Central American Wars and Seeds of Resistance

his message to the nation conflating immigration and crime in his call for prison building and harsher sentencing. On the whole, the letters reflected how political and media rhetoric played into the nation's racial anxieties. Some conveyed extreme racism and white nationalism not worth repeating; in fact, one was so egregious that someone wrote a note to Giuliani at the top: "The Executive Branch needs to realize this." A letter from a child named Paolo read, "Congratulations for announcing that there is a shortage of prison cells. I do not feel bad for these inmates. Keep up the good work." Another written by a retired veteran called for curbing migrant rights and stepping up deportations: "May I commend you for your thoughts on ALIENS on the television show. . . . They are already claiming their rights. I say as a taxpayer and a veteran that they have TOO MANY RIGHTS. This may be a free country, but not that free for them!"[32] Whether or not these letters represented a true cross-section of public sentiment, federal law enforcement budgets began to soar once Reagan entered office.[33]

A return to immigration raids and public order policing in the early 1980s—largely a retaliatory response to growing migrant rights efforts— also contributed to prison expansion needs. In Los Angeles, for example, lawsuits by the Mexican American Legal Defense and Educational Fund in the 1970s curbed police cooperation with the INS, which the Los Angeles Police Department sidestepped in the 1980s by using drug and gang activity as a pretense for heightened community policing. As Max Felker-Kantor argues, the LAPD "repackaged" a 1950s theory of public order policing (or "broken windows" policing) to target immigrants in their daily lives, such as at street vending and day labor sites. Growing rates of undocumented Central American arrivals seemed to confirm the LAPD's rationale of restoring public order.[34] Articulated most famously by social scientists George Kelling and James Q. Wilson in 1982, "broken windows" policing is preemptive in nature; by its logic, policing minor crime prevents major crime. However, this form of policing has more often resulted in heightened racial profiling and the hyper-incarceration of Black and Brown youths.[35] Yet it remained influential; Rudy Giuliani would propel broken windows policing further in New York City during his time as mayor in the 1990s.

The early Reagan administration brought an upsurge in immigration raids, too, which critics likened to the days of Operation Wetback.[36] An INS week-long operation in the spring of 1982 called Project Jobs was particularly brutal, targeting undocumented laborers at job sites in nine US cities—Chicago, Dallas, Denver, Detroit, Houston, Los Angeles, Newark, New York, and San Francisco—resulting in 4,900 arrests nationwide and 800 in Los Angeles alone. While the arrests represented forty-four nationalities, 87 percent were Mexican. An informal poll by the *Los Angeles Herald Examiner* found that 80 percent of callers approved of the operation. Despite public approval and the INS lauding the operation as a success, Project Jobs also received a backlash of criticism, including from US and Mexican political leaders. US senator Alan Cranston (D-CA) claimed that in a country still steeped in recession, Reagan was using undocumented workers as "scapegoats for the administration's failed economic policies."[37] Los Angeles representative Edward Roybal, himself of Hispanic heritage, sent Reagan a telegram urging investigation of abuses during the raids, including racial profiling, arrests and detention of pregnant women, and the INS's failure to inform those arrested of their rights. INS commissioner Alan Nelson replied that any allegations of racial profiling were "unfounded."[38] The Hispanic-serving American GI Forum also complained to the INS about increasing raids under the Reagan administration. "As usual, the children will be the victims of these actions by the INS," the forum wrote. "They will be coming home from school to find that their father or mother are not coming home." The INS again replied with denial, writing, "INS does not make a practice of separating family members, or of depriving children of their parents."[39] As will be seen, the growing visibility and criticism of "routine" INS operations likely also contributed to the INS's shifting priorities in the 1980s to interagency cooperation and new forms of detention.

Project Jobs also swelled detention capacity. Graphs charting detention capacities at five INS service processing centers show a spike in daily detention numbers at the Brooklyn, New York, facility caused by Project Jobs when the facility exceeded its capacity of 224 to a peak of 479. The graph notes, "During Project Jobs, additional detention space was made available. Indicates Potential."[40] As the Reagan administration remained committed to viewing immigration as a criminal issue, its new detention policies placed an additional strain on prison overcrowding. Looking to the US Southwest in the spring of 1982, the Bureau of Prisons sought to erect a new federal correctional institution in Phoenix, Arizona, reporting, "Detention of . . . immigration detainees plays a role in overcrowding. . . . Significantly more overcrowding will likely result from the present Administration's focus upon increased federal prosecution of violent and narcotics offenders." New INS facilities were also sought in the same region due to "a significant increase in alien apprehensions and a concomitant need for detention space. . . . INS must compete with other Federal, state and local entities for limited jail space."[41] Undocumented immigrants and criminal offenders were thus seen as two sides of the same coin.

Reagan's ramping up of immigration enforcement efforts relied on a longer history of violence against Mexican migrants that enabled the INS to dismiss the violence of raids, family separations, and deportations as nonexistent. Reagan also continued to deny the actuality of US violence in the borderlands, all while shifting its modes and targets, using doublespeak and drawing selective attention to and away from the US-Mexico border to wage a more broadly imagined border war. As Reagan courted free trade relations with Mexico, the right-wing Hispanic vote, and migrant-hiring industries, he emphasized the United States' strong relationship with Mexico, a Cold War ally, and spoke often of a "peaceful" US-Mexico border. In a 1983 speech to the National Association of Manufacturers, for example, Reagan used Mexico as a foil to illustrate the larger threat posed by Central America. Referring to Mexico as "a country of enormous human and material importance with which we share 1,800 miles of peaceful frontier," Reagan simultaneously decried leftist revolutionaries in Central America waging a "revolution without frontiers" that threatened US foreign trade. From their new base in Nicaragua, Reagan argued, "Soviets and their own Cuban henchmen" would spread their influence first to El Salvador. These enemies, Reagan concluded, want to "tie down our attention and our forces on our own southern border and so limit our capacity to act in more distant places" such as the Caribbean Sea and Central America, which "constitute this nation's fourth border."[42]

Indeed, Reagan articulated these combined threats facing the nation through his renewed commitment to a globalized War on Drugs. This further enveloped immigrants into the growing incarceration trend of the early 1980s as the administration subsumed its intertwining goals of intercepting migration and drug trafficking under the broader threat of communism and political subversion in Latin America. As Timothy Dunn asserts, nowhere was federal and local law enforcement as linked under the Reagan administration as it was in the War on Drugs.

Once in office, Reagan supported the passage of the Department of Defense Authorization Act of 1981, which loosened restrictions on military and civilian law enforcement cooperation. The DOD Authorization Act's changes to the law of posse comitatus, which was originally established in 1879 to prohibit the deputizing of military personnel to assist in domestic law enforcement, were particularly tailored to allow for new forms of cooperation of federal and local officials in immigration and drug enforcement. By adding a new chapter to the posse comitatus statute titled "Military Cooperation with Civilian Law Enforcement Officials," the DOD Authorization Act allowed for the military to assist civilian law enforcement agencies in "monitoring and communicating the movement of air and sea traffic," in providing military bases to be used for law enforcement purposes, and in the sharing of information and "expert advice."[43]

The administration moved quickly to integrate cooperation between military and civilian drug and immigration enforcement efforts to address immigration, crime, and the drug trade, as evidenced in the 1982 Miami Action Plan. The international dimensions of the plan are notable, as the administration viewed Miami as ground zero in waging its drug war. The action plan began by describing the "deplorable situation" in southern Florida and the need for interagency cooperation: "Many pressures have been created for Miami and the entire state of Florida by immigration policies of the prior Administration, which enabled tens of thousands of Cuban and Haitian citizens to enter the United States. . . . Significantly, violent crime in metropolitan Miami rose. . . . In addition, Florida has become a nexus for international drug trade operations. . . . This Administration has given a high priority to the prompt and strong implementation of the recent amendments to the Posse Comitatus Act."[44]

Blaming the Carter administration, the plan attributed rising violent crime rates to the Cuban and Haitian migrations of 1980 and drug trafficking in equal measure. By 1983, the notion of a Cuban drug trafficking conspiracy had become widespread. In November 1982, four senior Cuban government officials (one of them an alleged organizer of the boatlift) were indicted by a grand jury in Miami on charges of conspiring to use Cuba as a safe haven while transporting drugs from Colombia to the United States. The case against the Cuban officials had scant evidence, built around two witnesses: an informant named Juan, who was a Colombian national and protected federal witness, and a former Cuban intelligence officer who claimed Cuban involvement in the drug trade was a deliberate attempt to destabilize US society. In 1983, Vice President George H. W. Bush repeated this unfounded claim during a visit to Miami, helping to cement combined threats of migration and drug trafficking in the public mind.[45]

The points of the Miami Action Plan included increasing federal-state cooperation to manage prison populations and alleviate overcrowding and stepping up drug and immigration interdiction efforts. In his 1981 address to the Congress of Corrections, Giuliani also lauded South Florida's interagency and federal-local law enforcement cooperation in responding to the Mariel migration. The Bureau of Prisons stepped in, Giuliani explained, to help Dade County deal with prison overcrowding due to Mariel Cubans. "Rather than litigate the question of whether the federal government has

Central American Wars and Seeds of Resistance

any technical legal liability for those entrants who had found their way into the Dade County Jail," Giuliani related, the Department of Justice was working with Florida officials to "solve this problem, which affects all of us."[46] As part of the administration's narcotics enforcement strategy, the Miami Action Plan also outlined support for "a foreign policy that vigorously seeks to interdict and eradicate illicit drugs," which included "the use of herbicides overseas."[47]

As perceptions of illegality and crime fueled growing enforcement trends targeting undocumented Mexican and more recently arriving Cuban and Haitian migrants, this backdrop would merge with new technologies and tactics of counterinsurgent warfare, together forming a new arsenal against Central American asylum-seekers and their allies. As Greg Grandin argues, unchecked vigilante violence in the US-Mexico borderlands was also a form of counterinsurgency, allowing Reagan to keep exclusionists happy while claiming to support humane reforms. This violence was in large part fueled by radicalized veterans returning from Vietnam, whom the Reagan administration also recruited in its covert wars abroad. One prime example of the cycles of US counterinsurgent violence is right-wing Vietnam veteran Thomas Posey's creation of the paramilitary group Civilian Matériel Assistance, which bypassed congressional restrictions to funnel aid and military training to Contras in Nicaragua and right-wing death squads in El Salvador. Growing to thousands of members across the United States by 1985, Civilian Matériel Assistance also operated as a domestic hate group, inflaming anti-communist white nationalism and organizing border watch groups to harass migrants and Sanctuary movement activists. Grandin concludes that by routing backlash through foreign policy, Reagan's deflections amounted to "a highly volatile game Reagan and his 'cowboys' were playing, one that could continue only as long as the frontier remained open."[48]

"This Is One You Can Win"

Revolutionary wars in Guatemala, Nicaragua, and El Salvador killed a quarter of a million people between 1974 and 1996.[49] The sheer number of Central American migrants fleeing war and seeking refuge in the United States during the 1980s—an estimation of over 1 million—embodied the stark failures of US foreign policy and attempts to exert control over the region through counterinsurgent warfare. Cold War ideology and US-supported attempts to preserve the privileged position of local oligarchs against leftist uprisings furthered violence in each country. In 1979 in Nicaragua, socialist revolutionary Frente Sandinista overthrew US-backed right-wing dictator Anastasio Somoza. The US government subsequently aided "Contra" rebel groups against the socialist Sandinistas throughout the 1980s, going so far as to initiate an illegal arms trade with Iran to fund Contra counterinsurgents in Reagan's infamous Iran-Contra scandal. In El Salvador, US-trained right-wing death squads fought against the Marxist-inspired Farabundo Martí National Liberation Front (FMLN), comprising rural peasants, unions, religious organizations, teachers, and students. In Guatemala, where civil war had been ongoing since 1960, the US-backed military government took near total control in the 1980s, terrorizing Indigenous Maya and Ladino groups who led leftist resistance in the countryside.

The incoming Reagan administration deployed a host of tactics to legitimize US interventions in Central America and wage an ideological counteroffensive at home. While the following discussion is not comprehensive, these tactics included appropriating human rights and ethnic struggles to accuse Sandinistas and leftists of ethnocide, enlisting exiles and interest groups to propel public disinformation campaigns, shielding militant motives and furthering private business interests through the Caribbean Basin Initiative, and playing up fears of an impending refugee crisis. Throughout, the perceived threat of Cuba loomed large.

As civil wars spread across Central America, the stakes couldn't be higher in the Reagan imaginary, or for a rising, anti-interventionist Central American peace movement. From the outset, the incoming Reagan administration viewed the civil wars of Central America as theaters in the Cold War, part of a larger East-West global struggle between communism and capitalism. At the center of this contestation, geographically and ideologically, stood Nicaragua, seen as a new hemispheric base for Soviet-Cuban influence and subversion. Flipping the script, Reagan argued that the Sandinistas, and leftist insurgency more broadly, posed the greatest threat to human rights by spreading communism and thereby limiting "individual liberty"—never mind the Contras' use of indiscriminate killings and torture. The Reagan administration not only viewed genocide perpetrated by US-backed death squads against Indigenous people with disdain and disregard, but instigated it and used it to formulate retaliatory lies against Sandinistas and the Left at large. This emboldened a new leftist internationalism, as a transnational solidarity movement arose out of the growing presence of refugees and exiles in the United States since the 1970s and as possibilities of armed resistance played out in real time.[50]

In March 1980, the civil war in El Salvador intensified as government-supported assassins killed Archbishop Óscar Romero at his altar a day after he called for Salvadoran soldiers to obey God's orders and stop oppressing the Salvadoran people. In December, five members of the Salvadoran National Guard murdered four US Catholic missionary women, jolting the US public into awareness.[51] After Reagan's election, violence against Indigenous people in Guatemala and El Salvador only escalated.

Purging long-standing CIA and State Department policy advisors and regional experts and replacing them with "fledgling hawks," Reagan's camp entered office determined to reverse Carter's policies, which it considered naïve and ineffective.[52] A strengthening of the Soviet Union throughout the late 1970s also primed the administration's anti-communist stance. Drawing inspiration from a number of sources, Reagan's transition team of Latin American policy advisors outlined a global anti-communist "rollback doctrine" and identified Central America as a place where the United States could salvage a forceful foreign policy lost in Vietnam. An influential 1980 document written by the Committee of Santa Fe of the Council for Inter-American Security took an extreme position, declaring that "WWIII is almost over" with the United States "everywhere in retreat." Invoking the Monroe Doctrine and labeling Latin America as the United States' "exposed southern flank," the Santa Fe Committee recommended a strong ideological and economic response to civil wars in Central America, including direct military intervention to unseat Fidel Castro if necessary.[53] Reagan's foreign policy advisor and ambassador to the UN Jeane Kirkpatrick affirmed this position, asserting that the United States must stop trying to force its allies to institute human rights reforms. She strongly supported US military aid to El Salvador's government, even if it meant backing death squad activities and selling arms to Contras in Nicaragua.[54] Upon inauguration, the Reagan administration restored military aid to Argentina, Brazil, Chile, El Salvador, and Guatemala, despite their ongoing human rights violations.

While the United States had exerted imperial influence over Central America for nearly a century, its importance lay not in its natural resources or strategic location but in its potential as an ideological battleground. The Reagan administration focused on El Salvador in particular as a prime testing ground for its new militant Cold War policy. By 1981, guerrillas in El Salvador were on the defensive, and the US-backed government appeared ascendant. Secretary of State Alexander Haig, considering Central America a "strategic choke point," told President Reagan, "This is one you can win."[55] Although Reagan's advisors reasoned that political fallout would be minimal, the reality of 1 million displaced migrants, the majority of them Salvadoran, could not be easily ignored by the administration or the US public.

Seeing Central America as a symbol of a larger clash between superpowers committed the Reagan administration to military victory in the region. When Reagan entered office, El Salvador's civil war was inflicting up to 500 civilian casualties a month. The administration's support for 17,000 US-trained and US-supplied army and security forces against 4,000 rebels seemed like a safe bet, but when the war soon stalemated, it began pouring economic and military aid into El Salvador at an astonishing rate. During Reagan's first term, military aid to El Salvador rose to an average level per *day* what it had been per year between 1950 and 1979, reaching over half a million dollars. El Salvador's military grew from 10,000 soldiers to 50,000, and the United States also assigned twenty new military "trainers" to the region as well as $20 million for CIA covert operations. Salvadoran soldiers, Nicaraguan Contras, and Argentinian support forces received special training in North American camps, mainly in neighboring Honduras.[56] The war in El Salvador escalated, and although the United States approved the reelection of President Jose Napoleon Duarte's Christian Democratic Party in the spring of 1982, the better-organized right-wing ARENA Party led by Roberto D'Aubuisson strong-armed its way into the ballot box. US efforts were failing, but the Reagan administration continued to back D'Aubuisson and his party's right-wing death squad affiliates.[57] Also in the spring of 1982 in Guatemala, dictator José Efraín Ríos Montt rose to power in a coup, ramping up the government's genocidal campaign against the Maya people.

Despite the administration's Cold War rhetoric, large portions of the US public initially opposed Reagan's hard-line stance in Central America. Reagan responded with gaslighting—a rhetorical tactic of denial and emotional manipulation. Secretary of State for Human Rights Elliott Abrams circulated a memo in 1981 urging the need for an ideological tack: "We will never maintain wide public support for our foreign policy unless we can relate it to American ideals and to the defense of freedom. Our ability to resist the Soviets around the world depends in part on our ability to draw this distinction."[58] White House efforts to shape public opinion included couching its goals in Central America in broader Cold War moralistic terms and redirecting attention to Cuban-Nicaraguan threats. Co-opting the language of global freedom struggles, Reagan and his supporters repeatedly characterized the spread of communism as a "new colonialism" in the Western Hemisphere. Often likening US-backed Nicaraguan Contras and Salvadoran counterinsurgents to freedom fighters, Reagan claimed communist aggression was the sole cause of human rights violations and refugee displacement. While denying histories of

Thousands showed up at MacArthur Park in Los Angeles on April 18, 1981, to protest US intervention in El Salvador. Paul Chinn. Herald Examiner Collection, Los Angeles Public Library.

oppression and realities on the ground outright, these narratives also denied agency to Central American people.

In efforts to sway public opinion, in February 1981 the State Department released a white paper, "Communist Interference in El Salvador," supposedly based on nineteen recovered guerrilla documents. The paper identified El Salvador's civil war as a "textbook case of indirect armed aggression by Communist powers" and asserted that Fidel Castro and the Cuban government played a key role in unifying a Salvadoran communist guerrilla front.[59] Although the US press mostly accepted the white paper as truth, the *Wall Street Journal* reported that its author admitted to using extrapolated statistics and to "mistakes and guessing" on the part of the intelligence analysts translating guerrilla documents.[60] The white paper only furthered public dissent, as indicated by the proliferation of a bumper sticker reading "El Salvador is Spanish for Vietnam."[61]

Appropriating Indigenous and ethnic struggles, the Reagan administration also manipulated and misreported violence to charge Nicaraguan Sandinistas with racism, ethnocide, and repression, all while remaining silent on violence perpetrated by right-wing forces. For years, the administration would point to the alleged mistreatment of the Miskito people in the controversial Navidad Roja, or the Red Christmas of 1981. It began when Reagan signed a directive in December 1981 authorizing the United States to build a paramilitary army of Nicaraguan exiles; one month later, the Sandinistas forcibly resettled 8,500 Miskito Indians from their ancestral coastal lands, displacing 10,000 more. Two stories emerged, that the incident was driven either by historical ethnic tensions or by a CIA plot. But as Mateo Cayetano Jarquín argues, "Reality is capacious enough for both perspectives."[62] There remain conflicting accounts of the level and timing of CIA involvement, but Sandinista-Miskito relations broke down at this point, contributing to escalating violence. Scholars conclude that contemporary narratives lacked understanding of the complex, multiethnic history and landscape of Nicaragua's "Mosquito" coast, home to 10 percent of the country's population, predominantly Indigenous and Afro-descendant, who had remained geographically, economically, and culturally isolated since independence from Spanish rule. As Roxanne Dunbar-Ortiz witnessed during her work for the United Nations during the wars, the larger problem was long-standing anti-Indigenous sentiment on all sides, as well as the Sandinistas' inheritance of Anglo-American imperialism, underdevelopment, and labor exploitation—fallout from Somoza's regime.[63]

As Reagan seized upon the Christmas exodus to decry Sandinista human rights abuses, a narrative pattern emerged through a stream of White House reporting and public declarations inflating and repeating examples of leftist violence, often relying on oversimplification and falsified evidence. The White House published a series of digests on Sandinista human rights violations in collaboration with the Heritage Foundation, the centrist human rights organization Freedom House, and others. In addition to describing Miskito concentration camps, labor union repression, and persecution against Jews and Christians, this reporting repeatedly defined oppression as an inherent characteristic of communism with statements such as, "Sandinistas have implemented a policy of Indian ethnocide that is generated internally from their own Marxist ideology and racist attitudes. When the Indians resisted, [Sandinistas] began an escalated program of counterinsurgency that continues unabated."[64] More outrageous instances of disinformation included a press conference held by CIA deputy director Bobby Ray Inman during which he pointed to a photograph of a baseball diamond in the northeast region of Nicaragua as proof that a permanent Cuban military base was being built, and Haig's use of a 1978 photograph of burning corpses from a Somoza-era bombing of civilians in Managua that he claimed were Red Christmas atrocities. "The administration was that brazen," Dunbar-Ortiz concludes. "Even when corrections were printed, the lies created a kind of populist genocidal

Central American Wars and Seeds of Resistance

logic, in which 'exaggerations' were then acknowledged, but people assumed there must be some core of truth to the charges nonetheless."[65]

Of the Reagan administration's many acts of erasure, its complete dismissal of a series of civilian massacres in El Salvador between 1981 and 1983 may be most egregious. In December 1981, the Salvadoran Army brutally killed nearly a thousand civilians in the village of El Mozote. Other such massacres occurred in Sumpul, El Junquillo, El Calabozo, and Las Hojas. At Las Hojas, national forces killed sixty families—almost all Indigenous children, women, and the elderly.[66] María, a survivor of El Mozote, testified, "By about noon, they had killed all the men, and the soldiers were coming in to take the young girls to the hillside to rape them. They were taking the young girls away from their mothers and beating the mothers and they took their children away." María found a place to hide before escaping, while soldiers killed remaining women and children.[67] After El Mozote, US ambassador Deane Hinton refuted FMLN's accounts airing over the radio. The administration's anti-Indigenous sentiment was clear. When FMLN issued another report of state-sponsored torture, confirmed by testimonies and 175 autopsies performed by the Christian Legal Aid office, National Security Council staff member Robert M. Kimmitt dismissed it as "legal propaganda" and mocked, "We . . . have marveled at the lucid English and well-presented arguments the humble guerillas of El Salvador were able to muster."[68] Meanwhile, foreign correspondents witnessed and reported on atrocities firsthand. "The massacre of El Mozote consolidated my own view that U.S. involvement in the Salvadoran conflict was criminal," wrote Mexican journalist Alma Guillermoprieto. "The State Department as a whole made every effort to discredit what I had seen with my own eyes."[69]

Although the US embassy conducted an investigation at the time, gathering refugees' testimony that confirmed these accounts of the violence, the US government maintained that evidence of these massacres was false until forensics uncovered proof of El Mozote ten years later, in 1992. Recent testimony by Stanford political scientist Terry Karl also confirms that a US military attaché was near El Mozote and well aware of events. A Commission on the Truth for El Salvador conducted in 1992–93 further confirmed the asymmetry of civil war violence and Reagan rhetoric, finding that 85 percent of deaths were perpetrated by US-backed state forces.[70]

The Reagan administration enlisted religious and community leaders to its cause, including evangelical missionaries and businesses with long-standing presence and influence in Central America, including right-wing Cuban and Nicaraguan exiles. A cache of correspondence in White House papers reveals the many public interest groups and industries invested in Reagan's Central American foreign policy, including offers for public relations help. Themes of morality are woven throughout, with narratives often revealing political and economic motives. After making an "informative visit" to El Salvador hosted by US ambassador Thomas R. Pickering, Moral Majority founder Jerry Falwell sent a telegram to Reagan. He promised to continue speaking publicly in support of military aid to the region and to work "within conservative groups to heal any breaches that may exist." The Jewish Institute for National Security Affairs worked to publicize Sandinista support for the Palestinian Liberation Organization, a talking point Reagan would emphasize to further discredit the Nicaraguan government as anti-Semitic. The president of the Diesel Automobile Association pitched his assistance in creating "a dramatic and realistic program of grass roots capitalism" in the region with an "Enterprise Corps" to counter the "collective action" promoted by the Left and "symbolize what's possible under democratic capitalism."[71] Viewpoints in favor of Reagan's policies were also interspersed with opposition to his moral crusade. Opposition often came from anti-interventionist and religious organizations, who also maintained a growing presence in Central America since the 1960s—but rooted in notions of solidarity and liberation theology.[72]

The administration even formed new "grassroots" interest groups to support its policies. By 1983, the White House had created the Outreach Working Group on Central America, led by Elliott Abrams, to combat a perceived "liberal media establishment" and serve as a mouthpiece to disseminate information and generate media in support of Reagan's policies in the region. The working group's list of over 100 organizations receiving weekly briefings included large corporations like Exxon, Proctor and Gamble, General Motors, Dow, and US Steel and interest groups like the American Legion, the American Legislative Exchange Council, the Cuban American National Foundation, Freedom House, and multiple Zionist organizations.[73] Citizens for America, a conservative organization formed by Reagan's "kitchen cabinet" of California business leaders, also began producing a series of "fact sheets" on Central America. Its first "Reality Report" made a series of distorted claims: that the USSR and Cuba had "50 times as many military advisors" in the region as the United States; that the Sandinista government had committed human rights abuses against Jews, Christians, and Indigenous peoples; that El Salvador's leftist FMLN had no support from the Salvadoran people and that El Salvador "desperately wants and needs the help of the United States to survive"; and that Reagan sought a "non-military solution to the problem."[74]

Central American Wars and Seeds of Resistance

In addition to infusions of disinformation in public discourse, the United States' direct invasion of Grenada in the fall of 1983 also garnered public support for US intervention against the spread of Cuban influence in the region. When Cuba sent civilian and military personnel to help develop Grenada after its Marxist People's Revolutionary Government came to power, the Reagan administration believed it to be a new base for Soviet armaments. Reagan told the National Association of Manufacturers that year, "With Cuba at the west end of the Caribbean, Grenada at the east end . . . it isn't nutmeg that's at stake in the Caribbean and Central America; it is the United States' national security."[75] When an attempted coup sparked political chaos in Grenada, the United States used military force to remove Cuban presence in the name of protecting US medical students on the island and preventing another Iranian hostage crisis. By calling it a rescue mission rather than an invasion, Reagan skirted the War Powers Act requiring congressional approval, and US forces invaded the island in late October. Although clumsily planned and executed, causing nineteen US, forty-five Grenadian, and twenty-four Cuban deaths, Operation Urgent Fury ended in a few days with US control of the nation.[76] The invasion remained divisive—official narratives celebrated the "restoration" of democracy while others called it "subjugation"—but it ultimately resulted in the expulsion of Cuban presence from the island nation, a victory for Reagan's anti-communist agenda as wars in Central America raged on.[77] Discussed more in chapter 6, Grenada would also spark new debates and negotiations surrounding Mariel Cubans and US-Cuba prisoner exchanges.

The Caribbean Basin Initiative in Central America

Intertwining US trade and security interests not only propelled the Grenada invasion but also inspired Reagan's Caribbean Basin Initiative, a trade pact through which El Salvador would receive the lion's share of funds. Proposed during a time of economic recession at home and growing resistance to US hegemony in the region, Reagan sold his Central American "Marshall Plan" as a humanitarian bulwark against communism and an alternative to military means. As with Haiti, "trade and aid" became an integral part of Reagan's low-intensity war in Central America, ultimately restructuring and expanding US power in the region while exacerbating violence.

As Reagan prepared to pitch the CBI to the Organization of American States and ask Congress for $350 million for the program's first year, a White House memo revealed the political and economic incentives behind Reagan's wars in Central America. "Cuba is exploiting the problems of the Caribbean, has won one new base (Nicaragua) and threatens to get others in Central America," it read. "We must respond to the economic crisis and the security threat in a comprehensive way. Our response will have costs, but they will be far less—financially, politically, socially—than allowing the development of a string of hostile states or major social upheavals on our border." Citing the Mariel migration and the costs already incurred by "illegal" immigration, the memo stated the CBI's ultimate goal: "To put as many countries as possible beyond the reach of Cuba. Access to our market is the key proposal." The plan outlined creating tax incentives for US investors in the region and earmarking the largest share of funds for El Salvador "to deal with the acute and immediate crisis."[78]

On February 18, 1982, Reagan unveiled the CBI in a defining speech to the Organization of American States that would set new terms of US economic power in the hemisphere in motion under the auspices of free trade. Rhetorically masterful and passionately delivered, Reagan's alternating refrains of hemispheric brotherhood and anti-communist xenophobia mirrored the shielding of US economic aggression through humanitarian terms. After opening by asserting, "We are all Americans," Reagan pointed to Central America on a map and warned, "A new kind of colonialism stalks the world today and threatens our independence. It is brutal and totalitarian. It is not of our hemisphere but it threatens our hemisphere and has established footholds on American soil." To illustrate the human rights abuses of communism, Reagan quoted poetry written by wheelchair-bound Cuban political prisoner Armando Valladares: "I am being held incommunicado. . . . I have not seen the sun in six months." He then implicated Nicaragua in Cuba's scheme to spread communism across the Americas, describing it as a "platform for covert military action" where arms were being smuggled to guerrillas in El Salvador and Guatemala. He listed Sandinista human rights abuses against Miskito Indians, free trade unions, and the media and condemned the "determined propaganda campaign" aimed at misleading the public "as to the true nature of the conflict in El Salvador." Reagan asked, rhetorically, why bother with Central America? In reply, "We must help because the people of the Caribbean Basin and Central America are in a fundamental sense fellow Americans. Freedom is our common destiny." Alluding to refugees fleeing communism as equal parts victim and threat, Reagan added, "The refugees in our midst are a vivid reminder of the closeness of this problem to all of us."[79] Well-received by member states, Reagan's speech set the tone, talking points, and narratives in support of the Caribbean Basin Initiative while also mapping out new frontiers of empire.

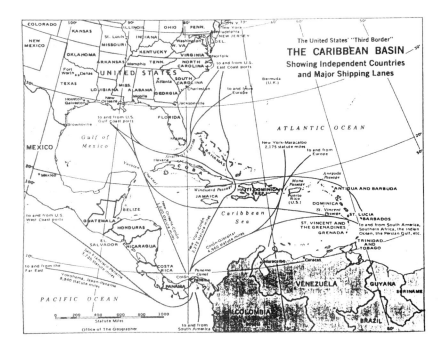

A hand-drawn map found in Reagan administration Caribbean Basin Initiative planning documents illustrates the United States' "Third Border" in the Reagan imaginary, with major shipping lanes. Note that Reagan's imagining of the Caribbean Basin included El Salvador, despite it bordering the Pacific Ocean rather than the Caribbean Sea. WHORM Subject Files, Ronald Reagan Presidential Library, Simi Valley, CA.

After Reagan delivered a similar pitch to Congress that echoed anti-communist and humanitarian themes while more openly promoting US interests, dissent came from a range of special interests and industries that felt threatened by the CBI. Reagan allies and foes alike also expressed broader security and human rights concerns. Personal letters written by Reagan in response show his commitment to the program but also how he played both sides, ultimately setting up a false choice between militarism and economic hegemony. Illinois senator Charles H. Percy wrote to Reagan recommending "that the Cuba issue, the El Salvador crisis and U.S. national security interests not appear to be the principal driving forces motivating the Initiative."[80] Similarly, Reagan's friend and filmmaker Douglas Morrow wrote to him that the CBI seemed too aggressive, with its foreign policy aims too obvious. The pro-immigrant American Friends Service Committee wrote, "Appearing at this time of increased tension, [the CBI] has been criticized as an attempt to divert attention from suspicion of United States attempts to destabilize or overthrow governments in the region."[81] To those opposing US military aid to El Salvador, Reagan touted the CBI as an alternative and a program of humanitarian uplift. To allies not wanting the United States to show its hand too clearly, Reagan assured them that military aid would continue, with CBI investments serving as a "security shield."[82]

Reflecting the political climate of the time and broader support for Reagan's neoliberal turn, the Caribbean Economic Recovery Act ultimately received bipartisan support. Congressional members roundly supported the CBI's free market initiatives, as well as its logic connecting economic security to curbing migration at its source. The CBI also won over Reagan skeptics, assuaging growing concern regarding the administration's increasingly militant policies. New York Democratic representative Robert Garcia called it a "symbolic stand" against the administration's policy of increased militarization.[83]

Allocation of CBI funds aligned with hemispheric hierarchies and US foreign policy priorities. Initially, CBI drafters proposed more than a third of total funds, $128 million, for El Salvador. Even though this drew criticism and Congress brought the total down to $75 million, El Salvador still received more than any other country. Congress also awarded $10 million to Guatemala, proving it willing to overlook ongoing human rights violations.[84] Assessments of the program's first two years of operation, 1984–86, report poor performance as the CBI was criticized mostly by business and government leaders in recipient countries. In effect, the CBI ultimately served US interests by forcefully pressing smaller Caribbean nations into trade dependencies with the United States and wresting control from its wealthier allies, including the United Kingdom. Five years later, many small Caribbean nations were still mired in debt, with higher unemployment rates, lower purchasing power, and a widening gap between import costs and export profits.[85] Ultimately, the CBI served to legitimize Reagan's Central American foreign policy—fitting within broader histories of "development" efforts wielded by the United States against the spread of communism while charting a new course for imperial expansion in Latin America.[86]

Despite the humanitarian framing of Reagan's economic initiatives, the United States doubled down on its investments in counterinsurgent warfare in Central America. After a visit to El Salvador in 1983, Jeane Kirkpatrick applauded the country's "legitimate democratic government" yet sounded the alarm that more military aid was needed to defeat guerrilla forces that in reality were fragmented and disorganized.[87] Reagan echoed this sentiment in an address on Central America to Congress in April, which he said he convened not "to resolve a crisis" but "in the hope that we can prevent one." Likening the Soviet threat in the Caribbean to that posed by Nazi Germany during World War II, Reagan asked for more support as "democracy is beginning to take root in El Salvador." Internally, however, a memo from Lieutenant Colonel Oliver North conceded, "It is generally agreed that at present the war is being lost." In addition to requesting more military aid, North expressed a continued commitment to opting for modes of counterinsurgent warfare "to do militarily almost anything, with nothing, forever."[88]

"If Central America Falls, We Are Going to Be Flooded with Refugees"

The refugee crisis created by US interventions in Central America also took on symbolic overtones in the Reagan imaginary, with migrants often reduced to pawns—or worse—in US political and public discourse. Refusing to give in, the administration continued to hide its role in contributing to violence in the region by maintaining the lie that communist agitation was the sole cause of migrant displacement. Indeed, animating xenophobia and manipulating refugee narratives was a centerpiece of Reagan's disinformation campaign. Mirroring its co-optation of human rights and freedom struggles in Central America, the administration manufactured and amplified narratives of immigration crisis by simultaneously comparing and contrasting refugee groups, with new refugees fleeing war in Central America portending an even greater threat to the nation than so-called boat people. In September 1982, Elliott Abrams told a Miami audience, "It is Communist rule that has caused the greatest refugee flows of recent years. We can, therefore, have a very firm notion of what the expansion of communism to El Salvador and Guatemala would mean. It has the potential to create a Southeast Asian refugee crisis right here on our doorsteps."[89] At a fundraising dinner in Mississippi in 1983, Reagan spoke of the consequences of a failed foreign policy in Central America. He warned that the result would be "a string of anti-American Marxist dictatorships" and "a tidal wave of refugees. And this time, they'll be 'feet people' and not 'boat people' swarming into our country, seeking a safe haven from Communist repression to our South. We cannot permit the Soviet-Cuban-Nicaraguan axis to take over Central America."[90]

This message reverberated among Reagan's staunchest supporters in government. Secretary of State Alexander Haig warned Congress to "just think what the level" of Central American migration to the United States might be "if the radicalization of this hemisphere continues with the only alternative a totalitarian model. . . . Why, it will make the Cuban influx look like child's play."[91] The Department of Defense also saw communism and migration as looming national security threats. General Ernest Graves warned that if all nations in Central America became communist dictatorships, there "would be a flood of refugees and illegal immigrants larger than any we have experienced to date."[92] Republican senator Jesse Helms sounded the same alarm with comments such as, "If Central America falls, we are going to be flooded with refugees."[93] Arizona state representative Tony Abril wrote to Reagan of the need to stop communism from advancing in Central America—an issue he recognized as intimately tied to immigration. "We cannot rid ourselves of the ants unless we rid ourselves of the ant hill," he wrote.[94] Abril's racist reduction of migrants to pests that must be exterminated, a common theme in xenophobic imagery and rhetoric across US history, verges on genocidal.

Internal policy discussions also reflected the gender and racial dimensions of the administration's definition of a Central American migration crisis. "Immigration Notes" circulated by the Department of Justice in the spring of 1984 relayed comments from a meeting of "top demographers" studying Central American population dynamics to provide background information for field staff on the causes of "illegal" migration from the region. According to the notes, principal speaker Dr. Michael Micklin said "we should be concerned" by the increasing volume of migration from the region, "not only for humanitarian reasons" but because "growth rate is explosive; fertility is high and mortality is low (in comparison to birth rate)." Interestingly, Micklin also identified ecological strains caused by the disequilibrium of land distribution and deforestation for cattle exports, primarily to the United States. He concluded that it was important to "disentangle political reasons from demographic/ecological causes."[95] Not only did such reporting support the INS's rejection of Salvadoran and Guatemalan asylum applications based on the argument that migration was economically driven, but it was also based in another long-standing xenophobic trope—fears that high birth rates among Latin American migrants would overtake US society.[96]

Although Reagan's policies at home and abroad affirmed xenophobia, he faced a dilemma. As the White House prepared to release a paper titled "Central America: The Refugee Crisis," it acknowledged the "two-edged sword" of addressing public support for restrictive immigration policies at the same time Reagan hoped to win reelection and the Hispanic vote. "Polls show the refugee issue to be one which is very exploitable and should be exploited," one memo reasoned, but "our reasons for concern revolve on the issue of

Hispanic refugees." It relayed that the authors "tried to produce a paper that would in no way be xenophobic." To walk this line, the paper emphasized anti-communism rather than race, distinguishing between deserving and undeserving refugees. It referenced the costs of the Mariel migration: "Should Central America fall to Communism, experience indicates that a flood of people would pour out of the region." It then discussed past contributions of refugees fleeing communism to the United States, especially Cubans. However, the paper concluded, "we must distinguish between the steady, if strong, streams of immigration, such as those that carried our ancestors to America, and sudden mass migrations which inevitably result with the establishment of Communist governments. Such migrations . . . [are] dangerously straining to our country."[97] While the Reagan administration still refused to acknowledge that right-wing authoritarianism could produce refugees, its emphasis on communism helped to serve "exceptional" immigrant narratives that enabled Reagan to continue courting the Hispanic vote.

After three years of White House assertions that communism was the root cause of violence in El Salvador, President Reagan appeared on television in May 1984 to announce that the United States was still holding the line. Eliciting Eisenhower's domino theory and xenophobia, he said, "Right now in El Salvador, Cuban-supported aggression has forced more than 400,000 men, women, and children to flee their homes. . . . Concerns about the prospect of hundreds of thousands of refugees fleeing communist oppression to seek entry into our country are well founded." Reagan acknowledged a link between US foreign policy and immigration yet refused to acknowledge the United States' hand in exacerbating the violence. He continued, "What we see in El Salvador is an attempt to destabilize the entire region and eventually move chaos and anarchy toward the American border. . . . If the communists can start war against the people of El Salvador, then El Salvador and its friends are surely justified in defending themselves. . . . This is not only in our strategic interest, it is morally right."[98] Positioning US interventions in Central America as defensive rather than offensive, Reagan rationalized increasing military aid to El Salvador as a necessary and moral component to winning a broader global war against the threat of communism—and stopping migration to the United States.

By selectively labeling the border as peaceful or chaotic and migrants as "refugees" fleeing communism or "illegal" immigrants, Reagan continued to manipulate narratives to serve political ends. Seizing the moral high ground by appropriating the language of human rights and Indigenous struggles for self-determination—thereby erasing legitimate grievances—was a key part of the process. Reagan again invoked these elisions in an oft-quoted speech in West Germany in 1985. Addressing the crowd during a military ceremony, Reagan asserted, "Today freedom-loving people around the world must say: I am a Berliner. I am a Jew in a world still threatened by anti-Semitism. I am an Afghan, and I am a prisoner of the Gulag. I am a refugee in a crowded boat foundering off the coast of Vietnam. I am a Laotian, a Cambodian, a Cuban, and a Miskito Indian in Nicaragua. I, too, am a potential victim of totalitarianism."[99] Meanwhile, as Reagan's wars in Central America came home to roost, mass resistance mounted inside and outside of detention.

Seeds of Resistance

> If returned to the San Salvador airport, I am sure
> I wouldn't even make it to my house.
>
> *Anonymous, detained at El Centro, 1985*

In the fall of 1981 in Southern California, the *Los Angeles Times* reported on a group of churchwomen who began protesting at a privately contracted site detaining Salvadoran women and children in Pasadena. Their signs read "No More Deportation" and "Save the Children" while they blocked INS vans from leaving the facility with their bodies on several occasions.[100] Two years later, thirteen-year-old Mayra arrived at the same Pasadena facility with her family. They fled El Salvador after her father, a teacher, faced threats. Well aware of the Cold War politics shaping the war at the time, Mayra recalls seeing US and USSR military forces in the country and bodies hanging from trees on her way to school. In transit to the United States, her family lost contact with cousins; Mayra still does not know their whereabouts. Traveling in a truck across the border, they were apprehended in Arizona and sent to a Border Patrol facility that was "like a house." For two weeks, she and her mother were separated in different cells before being sent to Pasadena, where, with her aunt and uncle's help, her family obtained a lawyer and pursued an asylum case. The family stayed for two months in the converted home, and Mayra volunteered in the kitchen. She remembers bars on the windows and a "huge room with bunk beds" where men were held separately.[101] She also remembers frequent protests outside the facility. Although her family's asylum case dragged on for years, Mayra and her family were "lucky ones," able to adjust their status through her mother's employer by the early 1990s. She now works as a high school aide, still in Southern California.

Near a pile of dummy corpses and a chain-link fence, churchwomen protest US intervention in El Salvador at an INS detention center in Pasadena detaining mostly women and children asylum-seekers from El Salvador, November 11, 1981. Michael Haering. Herald Examiner Collection, Los Angeles Public Library.

Throughout the 1980s, Central Americans who fled thousands of miles to the United States to escape civil war, repression, and economic devastation spurred a decade-long controversy over the government's asylum policies. The US asylum system was an extension of Reagan's counterinsurgent warfare in Central America—with the denial of state-sponsored violence a central feature.

Mass detention and deportations of Salvadoran and Guatemalan migrants further reflected the political, anti-Black and anti-Indigenous dimensions of Reagan foreign policy making. Unlike Salvadorans and Guatemalans, who encountered asylum denial rates of 97 percent and 99 percent throughout the 1980s, respectively, the United States granted refugee status to nearly 80 percent of Nicaraguans fleeing the Sandinista government by 1987.[102] However, Nicaraguan arrivals were starkly divided by class, ideology, and race. Those accepted were generally of higher socioeconomic status, pro-capitalist, and conservative, affirming Reagan and his Latin American allies' Cold War messaging. These refugees also presented another opportunity for Reagan to court the "right" Hispanic vote while furthering divisive immigrant narratives that served to erase those who were detained, denied refugee status, and deported: Salvadorans and Guatemalans fleeing right-wing death squads, but also a smaller percentage of impoverished migrants, more often Afro-Latinx or Indigenous, from Nicaragua's coastal regions fleeing violence stoked by the CIA-backed Contras.[103]

At odds with Reagan's claims were the testimonies of Salvadoran and Guatemalan migrants in the United States describing violence at the hand of national police forces rather than communist rebels. In 1982, Robert Tomsho reported Border Patrol agents noticing an upsurge in apprehensions of migrants they labeled "OTMs" or "Other Than Mexicans," most of whom were from El Salvador or Guatemala. While the Border Patrol and the INS at this time had been focused on apprehending Mexicans who were returned to Mexico within one or two days, Central American migrants, especially if applying for political asylum, required lengthier detention stays. As Tomsho met more migrants from El Salvador and Guatemala, he noted, "They were not people who joked about being sent home. Some told me they were certain it would mean death." Many of their stories were like those of Juan, who found refuge in a San Francisco church after making the long journey from El Salvador to a Guatemalan refugee camp and then to Tijuana, Mexico, where he paid a smuggler to take him across the US border. Juan claimed his numerous scars were from being captured and interrogated by Salvadoran National Guardsmen who raided a refugee camp near San Salvador, where he worked as a medical student. During his capture, the guardsmen accused him of aiding communists and guerrillas and exposed him to a variety of interrogation and torture techniques, including covering his head with a leather mask, hanging him from the ceiling by a rope around his waist, and giving him electric shocks.[104] Despite such testimonies, the United States consistently subjected Salvadorans and Guatemalans to detention, asylum denial, and deportation throughout the decade—a fate often ending in death.

When the Carter administration established an exceptional legal status for Cuban and Haitian boat arrivals, sidestepping the asylum process provided in the 1980 Refugee Act, it set a precedent the Reagan administration would build upon for its own purposes. This time, instead of disregarding the 1980 act, the Reagan administration wielded it to enact systematic erasure against Salvadoran and Guatemalan migrants who sought asylum from US-backed right-wing violence. The administration also invoked a Cold War category of Extended Voluntary Departure (EVD)—a temporary stay of removal proceedings—to sift out "exceptional" status refugees from undeserving "economic" migrants. In line with Reagan, the State Department and the INS buttressed these legal tools with outright lies.

As the administration denied the reality of Salvadoran and Guatemalan state violence disproportionately targeting Indigenous people, migrants arriving in the United States were living testimony of US foreign policy failures. Reagan's Central American wars reverberated in US detention. After visiting El Centro in 1981 to report on conditions at the facility, Senator DeConcini's aide relayed several Salvadoran migrants' stories. One man pointed to a recent untreated bullet wound, while another said, "Death is a part of life in El Salvador. It's normal to see a burning decapitated body in the middle of the street. If you are a college student or a professor or are related to one of them or if you are a member of Archbishop Romero's people, consider yourself *dead!*" He then showed the aide his INS intake form: "On a certain question it asks, 'Did you leave your country because of repression?' It was answered 'no.' . . . I asked him who marked 'no' on the question and he said the border patrol agent."[105] Such practices, it would be proven, were routine. As Reagan's war on truth permeated detention spaces and the asylum system, cycles of US state violence sowed the seeds of transnational resistance.

Reagan's diffuse propaganda efforts were met by a "counter public" of dissent led by Central American refugees and exiles, growing into one of the most powerful social movements of the 1980s. At the end of the Reagan administration, historian and peace movement participant Van Gosse argued that Reagan's "signal victories in terms of funding the war and massaging public opinion" had been "sabotaged by the realities the Central Americans themselves construct."[106] Under a banner of leftist anti-interventionism, the Central American peace movement in the United States grew to over 2,000 organizations by the mid-1980s. Roberto Lovato asserts that Salvadoran refugees "with the ability to turn poetry into politics . . . deployed their incredible stories of war, tragedy, and overcoming to inspire hundreds of thousands of North Americans to join their struggle."[107] Solidarity networks had been forming across Central America since the 1960s, against the backdrop of the Cuban Revolution and international decolonization and rights movements. These networks also fed into the peace movement, including thousands of US church people who staked a growing missionary presence in Latin America where they learned liberation theology, which would later inspire much of the Sanctuary movement—a branch of the Central American peace movement dedicated to shielding migrants from detention and deportation.[108] Gosse argues the "unnoticed seeding of church people well-informed about daily disappearances and torture" in Central and South America raised awareness of human rights abuses throughout the 1970s and developed an ethos of people-to-people contact.[109]

In the 1980s, a loose but nimble coalition of refugee organizations, leftist anti-interventionists, academics, and religious organizations—with a broad range of their own politics—employed an army of tactics to challenge Reagan foreign policy. Amid Central America's revolutionary civil wars, solidarity in the 1980s took on a broader understanding of the stakes, moving beyond human rights to leftist internationalism. While many focused on the primary goal of ending US military aid to Central America, immigration detention and asylum politics became key sites for refugee collaboration and resistance.

Having the largest presence in the United States, Salvadorans began organizing solidarity efforts in San Francisco in the mid-1970s. The Committee in Solidarity with the People of El Salvador (CISPES), one of the peace movement's most prominent and radical grassroots organizations, grew exponentially in the early Reagan years. CISPES issued a monthly newspaper called *El Salvador Alert!* and organized actions across the country, including vigils at detention sites; caravans to Fort Bragg, North Carolina, to denounce the training of Salvadoran officers; and a May 1981 demonstration in Washington, DC, with over 100,000 in attendance. Predating CISPES but less widely influential in the United States was the Network in Solidarity with the People of Guatemala.

Waves of North American visitors to Central America in the 1980s transformed the movement through firsthand witnessing. Tens of thousands of people went to Nicaragua and El Salvador to work in coffee fields and accompany communities facing persecution. Sanctuary movement religious leaders like Renny Golden, along with many others, spent one month a year in El Salvador to stay connected and apprised. Efforts of the Central American peace movement culminated in a Pledge of Resistance, a civil disobedience and legal protest pledge signed by thousands that some credit with preventing direct US military intervention. Van Gosse recalls that when activists delivered the pledge to Craig Johnstone, deputy assistant secretary of state for Inter-American Affairs, Johnstone "appeared sobered" that so many US citizens would resist their government.[110] Johnstone was often tasked with replying to, and refuting, a barrage of letters, telegrams, and petitions from CISPES, Americas Watch, Amnesty International, university professors, and other community groups sent to Reagan protesting US aid to El Salvador and Nicaraguan Contras, accompanied by phone calls, constituent delegations, pickets, and sit-ins.[111]

In the United States, solidarity groups provided mutual aid to migrants and worked to raise the visibility of detention conditions in the media. In 1980 in Arizona, the Manzo Area Council coordinated with a coalition of sixty local churches to form the Interfaith Task Force on Central America after encountering Salvadoran migrants in the desert. Manzo was one of the first grassroots organizations legally certified to assist migrants under the Carter

Central American Wars and Seeds of Resistance

administration. Volunteer Lupe Castillo recalled that in 1979, a man from El Salvador appeared in Manzo's office with a still-bleeding bullet wound, asking for help avoiding deportation. Castillo said, "That really dramatized the problem for us."[112] In June 1981, the Interfaith Task Force made a loan to immigration attorney Bruce Bowman in California to cofound El Rescate with Salvadoran asylum-seeker Alicia Rivera. With volunteers, they worked at their small Los Angeles office providing legal services and helping to secure food, clothing, jobs, and housing for migrants. El Rescate also trained volunteers to assist Salvadorans detained at El Centro and educate them of their rights. Rivera spoke of her work: "One man died in the immigration detention camp in El Centro, and the authorities kept his body for 15 days. His family had no money to send for it. We publicized the case and got money to send the body back. . . . We try to do anything that needs to be done."[113]

Meanwhile, in Edinburg, Texas, a group of clergymen, nuns, laypeople, and professors formed BARCA (Border Association for Refugees from Central America). Shortly thereafter, attorney Lisa Brodyaga founded the nonprofit law office Proyecto Libertad in response to abuses against Central American migrants she witnessed at the Port Isabel detention facility twenty miles east of Edinburg on the Gulf of Mexico. Proyecto Libertad was the first law office in the United States dedicated to fighting for legal rights for imprisoned Central American refugees.[114] On this growing web of responses to detention, Robert Kahn writes, "Other lawyers and religious groups opened law offices to represent refugees imprisoned in Miami, Florida; El Centro, California; and Florence, Arizona. When the INS opened new prisons in Houston and Laredo, in Texas, and in Oakdale, Louisiana, prison projects sprang up to represent refugees there too. When refugees gained access to legal representation, it increased pressure on the entire INS system."[115] These groups allied with migrants in detention to wage legal battles against the system's abuses. They also published accounts of their witnessing in mainstream media as well as in religious and Sanctuary movement newsletters and brochures that circulated around the country and across borders.[116]

As testimonies of abuse in detention, due process denials, and death upon deportation circulated in the public sphere, resistance to Reagan mounted. Demands for due process in detention took the form of recurrent hunger strikes and legal challenges, while a campaign for the Reagan administration to grant Extended Voluntary Departure to Salvadoran migrants gained broad public support, even from within Congress. However, defying the promises of the 1980 Refugee Act, the State Department and the INS wielded asylum law not to extend Salvadorans blanket relief but blanket denial.

In order to defend its overall rejection of refugee status for Salvadorans, the US government continued to deny that they were subject to persecution upon deportation. In June 1984, the ACLU Political Asylum Project, with support from congressional members who opposed Reagan's policies, gave the US House of Representatives and Elliott Abrams a report on human rights abuses inflicted on over 100 Salvadorans after deportation. By this time, the Human Rights Commission of the Catholic Archdiocese of San Salvador also estimated that 30 percent of those deported had been murdered. Despite such reporting, the administration denied there was any evidence of such executions. Abrams told the subcommittee, "Obviously we do not believe these claims or we would not deport these people."[117]

The stated purpose of EVD as established in the early 1960s was to provide migrant groups facing crisis conditions in their home countries temporary relief from deportation. However, EVD had long been used as a preferential Cold War tool granted almost exclusively to migrants fleeing communism—revealing how "crisis" is defined along political lines. In service of its foreign policy aims, the Reagan administration extended EVD to Polish nationals, and then to Nicaraguans, while continually denying EVD to Salvadorans despite public and congressional pleas on their behalf.[118] Although the 1980 Refugee Act had the potential to counter the Cold War discriminatory treatment of migrant groups, the Reagan administration used the new provisions of the act instead as a tool of deflection and exclusion.

Rather than providing Salvadorans blanket relief through EVD, the INS deployed individual case review through the 1980 act, in adherence with the United Nations' 1967 *Convention and Protocol Relating to the Status of Refugees*. As Wendy Brown argues, the application of human rights law to effect exclusion is a hallmark of neoliberal governance, under which "law becomes a medium for disseminating neoliberal rationality," ultimately serving processes of de-democratization.[119] In effect, the INS pointed to the law to claim that individuals had equal access to the asylum system while denying applications systematically on a case-by-case basis.

In January 1981, the city of Portland, Oregon, appealed to state governor Victor Atiyeh and the Reagan administration to halt Salvadoran deportations through EVD status, writing, "Reputable sources have reported that the massive slaughter of people in El Salvador are of genocidal proportions. Therefore, it is cruel and inhumane for the United States Government to deport individuals to a country where they are likely to be subjected to unconscionable human rights violations."[120] This plea invoked the *non-refoulement* (non-return) principle in international human rights law, which the United

States ostensibly ascribed to. However, the State Department responded, "The responsibility for establishing a well-founded fear of persecution rests with each applicant."[121] Further, it issued a directive to the INS in April 1981: "The granting of blanket voluntary departure for Salvadoran nationals now in the United States is not warranted at this time," with a statement by the under secretary for Political Affairs: "We find it difficult to accept the thesis that the majority of Salvadorans now in the United States departed their country only to seek safe haven. Most traveled through third countries before entering the United States." The directive concluded with the "consensus" that "most Salvadorans in the United States migrated here for economic reasons or to avoid civil strife and are not subject to persecution upon their return."[122]

Members of Congress repeatedly petitioned the government to limit military aid to El Salvador, even trying to pass legislation to grant EVD to Salvadorans throughout the decade. In June 1981, Congress passed a resolution seeking investigation into US aid to El Salvador, which the administration strongly rejected, opposing "any country-specific resolution which restricts the President in the conduct of foreign affairs."[123] The State Department and attorney general's office repeatedly rejected EVD, citing the 1980 Refugee Act as justification, as well as the government's position that Salvadorans were economic migrants who could find safe haven in Mexico instead and whose asylum claims were predominantly "frivolous." The administration also claimed EVD would be a "pull factor" encouraging "line-jumping," or more mass migration.[124] Two years later, the State Department issued a guidance statement in response to eighty-eight members of Congress who appealed for EVD for Salvadorans, maintaining the same position. Representative Bruce Morrison repudiated the State Department's position, tallying out of 1,139 applicants over four months' time in 1983, only 61 were granted asylum while 1,078 were deported. "Upon their return to El Salvador," he wrote, "many of these refugees met with calamities ranging from simple custody to torture and murder." He quoted an officer from the Salvadoran Army as saying, "The dangers faced by all . . . in El Salvador is greatly enhanced for those who are returned to El Salvador after being deported" and claimed that an estimated one out of five people deported was killed upon return.[125]

Paradoxically, the Reagan administration refused to extend blanket relief to Salvadoran migrants in the name of alleged fairness yet applied blanket denial through the same means. The State Department maintained publicly that it treated all asylum-seekers equally, but at the same time it instructed the INS to view Salvadorans as economically driven migrants. As one step of the asylum process, immigration judges were supposed to send an I-589 form to the State Department for its "advisory opinion" on each case. However, for Salvadoran cases, the INS instead attached a form letter to each I-589 saying the State Department did not believe the applicant would be persecuted in El Salvador, without any reference to the specific details of each case. While immigration judges had the authority to overturn these advisory opinions, only one judge out of a sample of 10,000 Salvadoran cases from 1981 to 1986 was found to have done so—evidencing a broader trend of court deference to executive discretion.[126]

Politics of denial and acts of gaslighting played out even within the Justice Department. In March 1982, INS spokeswoman Beverly McFarland told the *Miami Herald*, "In terms of the large detention of Haitians, you may see a very similar detention of Salvadorans in a very short time as soon as we find space for them. . . . Because thousands and thousands of them are pouring across the border from Mexico as the situation in their country worsens." In damage control, Rudy Giuliani quickly issued an internal memo to the INS stating the need to publicly correct McFarland's statement. Giuliani asserted that McFarland was incorrect in saying that the INS would "soon target El Salvadorans for detention as well and are looking for space to put them in. . . . Our detention policy, as you know, is to be even-handedly applied regardless of an alien's race or nationality."[127] Giuliani's assertion was untrue on multiple counts: first, there was mounting evidence of the INS and the State Department's discriminatory treatment of Salvadorans, and second, the attorney general's office was formulating its Mass Immigration Emergency Plan at that very moment. Giuliani soon appealed to Congress for funds to expand immigration detention capacity. He explained the strain on space had resulted from apprehensions of "other than Mexican nationals" in the Southwest, citing a steady increase of Border Patrol arrests of Salvadorans from 2,400 in 1977 to 15,900 in 1981.[128] A State Department paper from the same time also explored converting a former air force base as a possible INS detention site, identifying "Emergency Detention Needs" in western and southern regions where facilities operated at capacity in detaining 176,000 migrants in the prior year. The paper noted that "the overall instability of the Caribbean Basin, and the many thousands of El Salvadorans in refugee camps in Mexico and other countries, have, and will, escalate our detention needs beyond current capacities."[129]

Despite INS claims of fairness, Salvadorans and their allies told of a much different reality facing them in detention. The Fifth Amendment's due process clause requires that migrants in detention be made aware of their rights: to be represented by a lawyer (at their own expense), to a hearing to determine their deportability with the potential of obtaining a bond for release, to apply for political asylum, and to request voluntary departure.[130] Growing media coverage of violence facing Salvadorans at the border and in detention included reports that INS agents were coercing Salvadoran migrants into signing I-284 voluntary departure agreement forms against their will or without their knowledge that signing the form would waive their rights. The *New York Times* relayed the story of a Mr. Mendoza, apprehended at the border in Chula Vista, California. When he told an immigration agent he left his home because he was on a "death list" in El Salvador, the agent responded that unless he agreed to return home immediately, he would "spend a year or more in jail and would 'suffer a lot,'" so Mendoza signed the I-284.[131] The United Nations High Commissioner for Refugees sent the State Department a telegram demanding an investigation of these allegations and conditions facing Salvadorans in detention, to which the INS replied that agents did "not threaten or coerce illegal Salvadorans into accepting voluntary departure or deprive any individual in the United States from applying for asylum."[132] These words indicate how the INS had already illegalized Salvadoran migrants. Politics and practices of denial would continue throughout the decade, becoming firmly embedded in the culture of detention operations.

In 1982, a group of church and legal aid organizations sued the INS for denying Salvadoran migrants due process. The court filed a preliminary injunction in the case of *Orantes-Hernandez v. Smith*, finding that the INS did indeed violate Salvadorans' due process rights by engaging in a "pattern and practice of coercing" migrants to waive their rights and that this pattern "extended to detention centers, where their access to counsel and information about their rights was severely restricted."[133] In one Salvadoran woman's testimony in the case, INS agents at El Centro had forced Valium down her throat and guided her hand to force her to sign an I-247 form, waiving her right to seek asylum. Judge David Kenyon reprimanded the INS attorney, "You don't treat people like that. I wouldn't do that to the worst criminal who came into this courtroom."[134] Although Kenyon issued an injunction ordering the INS to follow proper legal procedures, attorney Robert Kahn documents how INS officers failed to comply and systematically violated the terms of such injunctions.[135]

Legal battles against rights violations made some progress throughout the 1980s, many of them originating in habeas corpus petitions filed by and on behalf of detained Cubans, Haitians, Central Americans, and Mexicans.[136] Preparing itself for the growing battle against detention, the Reagan administration established an Office of Immigration Litigation in 1983. Despite the limits of legal challenges, such challenges did slow down the deportation process and secure some rights for the detained—especially as legal aid groups utilized inside-outside strategies to amplify voices from detention in the courtroom. A 1984 INS directive limiting the use of solitary confinement, for example, was a direct response to testimonies of abuse in the *Orantes* case.

Continuing abuses and acts of retaliation in detention reveal the more insidious ways the INS undercut the promises of the 1980 Refugee Act through a range of counterinsurgent responses to migrant demands for justice. In 1985, the launch of an estimated 300-person hunger strike led by 15 migrants from multiple countries at El Centro revealed that conditions had only deteriorated since Senator DeConcini's aide's visit. Jessica Ordaz's analysis of the El Centro hunger strike concludes the men organized using a transnational solidarity politics that had developed over decades of war, revolution, migration, and resistance. Ordaz writes, "Collaborating was essential for the men to organize and make their grievances heard."[137] During the strike, El Rescate, CISPES, and other local organizations supported hunger strikers from outside the facility, relaying information through prison walls and to the media. Eighty-four hunger strike participants signed onto a letter detailing their grievances, including a shortage of bathroom facilities, fourteen-hour-long outdoor exposures to the desert heat, and the frequent use of solitary confinement as a form of punishment.[138] The hunger strikers also detailed the INS's systematic curtailing of their due process rights.

The INS responded with denial—and violence. The largest hunger strike in the facility's history ultimately ended within a week as a militarized Border Patrol Tactical Unit descended on the facility and assaulted a core of remaining strikers from Cuba, China, Honduras, and El Salvador.[139] The Department of Justice formed the Border Patrol Tactical Unit—a special forces team trained in riot control, surveillance, and counterterrorism techniques—in 1984 as part of the War on Drugs' strengthening of interagency cooperation. One of the unit's main functions was to assist in putting down prison uprisings that were growing in frequency in the early 1980s. After the strike, the INS retaliated against migrant organizers by transferring them to other facilities, restricting access to lawyers, and blaming outside agitators—tactics explored further in chapter 5. Escalating battles between detained migrants and the Reagan administration over abusive detention conditions would continue, changing the course of detention practices.

Orantes-Hernandez v. Smith was not resolved until 1991, when the court's initial injunction was made permanent with stipulations requiring due process for Salvadoran migrants, as well as improved detention conditions. In a rare admission, the US Department of Justice signed a consent decree that it had violated its own laws and the Geneva Convention in over 100,000 Salvadoran cases across the 1980s. However, with no enforceability or retroactive recourse, the decree has rung hollow. And, as a majority of Salvadoran asylum cases ended in deportation and an uncounted number of deaths, silence remains a prevailing outcome of Reagan's wars in Central America.[140]

"A Mariel-Type Scenario"

In the end, Reagan's wars in Central America left a lasting impact of transnational cycles of violence and generational trauma, especially on the thousands of Salvadorans and Guatemalans in the United States subjected to blanket detention and deportation. The trauma endured by Central American migrants, in combination with the Reagan administration's ongoing denials that never "legally confirmed" this trauma, yielded a chain of historical silences. As Salvadoran scholar Leisy Abrego writes,

> There is the silence that is the large void in generations of children of Salvadoran immigrants growing up in the United States being denied access to our own histories. There is the silence that was filled by others who did not know how to understand us and so used stereotypes and imposed their own experiences to make sense of who we are. And we continue to reproduce the silences when we do not know, cannot locate, have never been told of the structural, political, and economic sources of our collective pain, or of our collective resilience.[141]

As the next chapter explores, testimonies that combat the silencing effects of US state power played a central role in resisting Reagan's foreign and immigration policies and in the Sanctuary movement—the largest collective resistance to detention in US history.

Although the Reagan administration denied any role in exacerbating violence in Central America, it continued projecting warnings of future immigration emergencies. This language of crisis was couched in Cold War terms, blaming communist agitation for migrant displacements, but it also reflected the white nationalist contours of US xenophobia. The hauntings of Mariel Cuban, Haitian, and Central American migrations prompted new policies of systematic immigration detention, interdiction, and militarization of the US-Mexico border. These counterinsurgent responses to a perceived nexus of immigration, drug, and criminal threats in Reagan's global War on Drugs reflected low-intensity conflict doctrine in their reliance on increased cooperation between law enforcement capabilities and a focus on preventative measures to deter future migrations. This logic would continue to drive carceral buildups and expand the geographies of US border enforcement, fueling a Latin American migration crisis of Reagan's own making.

As a key geographic region in the Reagan imaginary, the Caribbean and Central America were tied together in myriad ways: as racial and communist threat; as Cold War geopolitical strategy; and as an economic development project through the Caribbean Basin Initiative, a neoliberal proving ground for exploitative free trade agreements and private contracting. Reagan's counterinsurgent wars in Central America, accompanied by the CBI, set in motion increasing cycles of violence, spurring migration and resistance that prompted increasing state repression in return. A precursor to the 1994 North American Free Trade Agreement, the CBI proved to have limited success in uplifting Caribbean economies, especially small, newly independent nations. Instead, it primarily benefited the United States—foretelling a new trend in global imperialism.[142]

The CBI also showed how the expansion of free trade in the hemisphere was intimately tied to counterinsurgent warfare and migrant displacement. As narratives championing the free movement of capital were coupled with securitization against the free movement of people, the CBI exposed a devastating irony. In effect, free trade agreements rooted in xenophobic designs to stop migrant flows from Latin America displaced migrants through economic and direct aggression—further fueling the detention and deportation apparatus. Elana Zilberg argues that Reagan era policies resulted in the creation of "neoliberal securityscapes" that served to enforce global capitalism. Spaces of detention, meanwhile, beget new generations of transnational violence—such as through circulations of the Los Angeles–originating Salvadoran Mara Salvatrucha gang—decried by politicians yet itself a product of hyper-policing of migrant youth, incarceration, and deportation.[143]

Reagan's Mass Immigration Emergency Plan drew a through-line from Mariel to El Salvador to inscribe detention as counterinsurgency across the US Sunbelt. The plan, although inspired by one instance of mass migration, continued to serve as a blueprint for detention building, as makeshift and "temporary" detention solutions became the standard.[144] In the spring of 1983 the attorney general's office set out to expand its contingency plan to the southern border: "The current Mass Immigration Emergency Plan is, in some instances, tailored specifically to a Mariel-type scenario," Giuliani explained to INS director Alan Nelson. But now, Giuliani continued, the attorney general has "requested we develop a similar plan for use on the Southern land border."[145] Giuliani then directed the INS and the Bureau of Prisons to work together to identify "contingency space": "As you know, record numbers of undocumented aliens are being apprehended. . . . Facilities are operating at or near capacity. . . . It is important, therefore, that we quickly identify any land . . . upon which temporary tent facilities might be established. . . . Given the emergency nature of the problem," the project must be completed "as soon as possible."[146] In sum, these layerings of migration crisis and response laid the foundations of Reagan's carceral palimpsest.

The preemptive logic of the Mass Immigration Emergency Plan also extended to stifling domestic dissent. In 1987, amid revelations of Reagan's Iran-Contra scandal, *Miami Herald* reporter Alfonso Chardy broke the story of a highly classified government plan developed three years earlier called "Rex84." Authored by FEMA director Louis O. Giuffrida and National Security Council liaison Oliver North, Rex84 was a scaled-up contingency plan for suspending the Constitution in the event of a wide-scale crisis—specifically, nuclear war, nationwide civil uprisings, or mass migration—sparked by a US invasion of Central America. Here, migration and civil unrest were positioned alongside nuclear war as existential threats to the nation and the planet, but not US aggression itself, revealing a logic that positioned US war making, border enforcement, and carceral buildup as defensive rather than offensive measures.

According to Chardy, Rex84 originated in a thesis Giuffrida had written as a student at the US Army War College in 1970. Giuffrida's thesis advocated for martial law and recommended preparing "relocation camps" for millions of "American Negroes" in the event of a national uprising of militant Black nationalists. In 1971, Giuffrida left the army to head California's Specialized Training Institute under Governor Reagan, training state authorities in paramilitary and counterterrorist tactics for police to employ during civil disturbances. Ten years later, Rex84 involved a series of highly classified trainings relying on interagency cooperation and a "fabled scenario" of mass migration, including detention of up to 400,000 undocumented immigrants.[147] Rex84's origins in civil rights–era battles and its targeting of immigrants and US citizens alike for mass arrests, while alarming, also reveals the anti-Black roots of Reagan's detention policies and the tenor of counterinsurgent measures the administration would soon launch against the Sanctuary movement.[148]

Give Us Liberty, or We Will Tear the Place Apart!

Detention as Counterinsurgency

One cannot tell the story of a crime without
telling who, how, and why it is committed.

Alejandro, in sanctuary in Rochester, New York, 1985

On July 4, 1984, a van and several cars pulled into the parking lot of Plymouth Congregational Church in downtown Seattle. The van had a large sign on its side reading "Sanctuary Caravan." When five Guatemalan refugees disembarked, a crowd of 500 cheered. Twenty-three-year-old "Alfredo" wore a bandanna over his face. He hoisted his infant daughter into the air and waved his straw hat at the crowd. Once inside the church, he removed the bandanna. Described in the *Seattle Post-Intelligencer* as a "short, slender Guatemalan Indian dressed in jeans and tennis shoes," Alfredo told the crowd, "I come from a lot of sadness but your presence gives me strength." He recounted his last memories of Guatemala, where "dogs [were] eating the corpses of Guatemalan Indians slain by the army." Another refugee, Mario Castillo, was a medical student fighting for workers' rights. He said, "The police captured and tortured me. I still have the signs of torture on my body."[1]

Reverend John Fife of Southside Presbyterian Church, who had accompanied the caravan along with Quakers and Unitarians all the way from Tucson, Arizona, read the Declaration of Independence and called the US government "powerless" for denying asylum to the persecuted. Seattle mayor Charles Royer was also in attendance. He said, "As a public official, I cannot condone violation of the law, but I can express my concern and compassion for those compelled to break it." After the event, the five refugees went to live in sanctuary in two Seattle area churches. The public car caravan had maintained a number of ten to twenty vehicles during the entire trip. Soren Sorenson, who drove the van, told a reporter they almost had a run-in with an INS patrol car between Los Angeles and Fresno. When the reporter asked the INS for comment, a spokesperson dismissed the entire thing as a "media event."[2]

In January 1985, shortly after Reagan's reelection, the Justice Department fought back. Orchestrating a nationwide crackdown, federal agents made a spate of arrests resulting in a seventy-one-count indictment against sixteen Sanctuary movement leaders. Meanwhile, INS agents arrested over sixty migrants named as coconspirators.[3] The INS arrests included seven in Seattle: two Salvadoran sisters-in-law named "Elba" and "Pilar Martinez" along with their five children, aged eight to eleven. Exactly two years before, Pilar had entered sanctuary at Seattle's University Baptist Church under this pseudonym and began sharing her story. In El Salvador, Pilar had been working with a Christian base community to provide medical aid to refugees. She had also befriended Jean Donovan, one of the four US missionary women killed by Salvadoran National Guard members, and witnessed Archbishop Óscar Romero's assassination in 1980. Pilar was imprisoned, handcuffed to her five-year-old child, Milagro, tortured, and raped by members of the National army. Narrowly escaping from a truck transporting them to a mass grave site, Pilar and Milagro traveled to the United States in search of asylum. Elba soon joined Pilar in Seattle, after the "New Underground Railroad"—the Sanctuary movement network—arranged for her transport from the US-Mexico border. Speaking from sanctuary, Pilar testified:

> I knew that I had to tell the world about the things that had happened to me and about El Salvador. . . . When you hear the helicopters and planes flying overhead and you look up and see that they are American planes and helicopters you know who is behind much of what is happening to our villages and people. And yet in many ways North Americans are the hope for El Salvador. It is only through your actions

A drawing of an immigration officer by one of Pilar's children, labeled "migra," after the arrest and detention of Pilar and Elba's family in Seattle in January of 1985. University of Washington Libraries Special Collections, University Baptist Church Sanctuary Movement Records, 5346–001, B9.

that your government will stop funding the military in my country and thereby end the atrocities.[4]

When INS agents raided Elba and Pilar's apartment, they shouted at the women and children and refused to give them privacy as they dressed. The INS detained the family for several days before releasing them. Elba told the press that an agent tried to make her sign a paper she did not understand and swore at her when she refused. University Baptist Church pastor Donovan Cook, also named an unindicted coconspirator in the Sanctuary trial, expressed concern over young Milagro's detention, as she still carried physical

Detention as Counterinsurgency

and psychological scars from her imprisonment in El Salvador at age five. Cook said, "Having to experience this trauma again is unconscionable—unthinkable." After Pilar's release, she became even more of a public figure. At a vigil in front of Seattle's federal building with Mario Castillo, both wearing bandannas over their faces, she told a crowd of 150 she was sure her arrest was an act of retaliation for her activism. On the prospect of being deported, she exclaimed, "If they're going to kill me, let them do it here. If they deport us, death is what awaits us, us and our children." Mario added, "We owe our lives to the Sanctuary movement," while his three-year-old daughter held a sign reading "Sanctuary to protect lives."[5]

In the summer of 1985, a "Freedom Caravan" carried Pilar and others on a speaking tour through nine cities in Idaho and Montana, where she appeared in twelve newspapers and on four radio shows and gave three presentations on television. Despite Pilar's public testimonies, Elba and Pilar refused to testify in the high-profile Sanctuary trial that year—to do so would reveal their true identities. Even though federal prosecutor Donald Reno offered the sisters-in-law permanent residency in the United States, Pilar asked, "How can I . . . knowing this means death for my family members?"[6]

As cycles of US state violence converged in detention spaces, this chapter connects case studies of Haitian and Central American migrant solidarity resistance with modes of state retaliation to illustrate how detention operates as counterinsurgency. Dynamics of resistance and retaliation within detention also reflected a broader dialectic between transnational social movements and state violence. As Heather McCarty asserts in her analysis of prison resistance in the 1960s, "Prisoners blended the culture of outside social movements from which they came with the particulars of the prison."[7] The mass mobilizations against mounting immigration enforcement efforts in the 1980s discussed here—orchestrated from within detention, through inside-outside coalition building, and in the broad civil disobedience of the Sanctuary movement—also set the stage for future contestations. Tracing this dialectic illustrates how resistance served to reinscribe counterinsurgent forms of retaliation in detention operations.

Flashpoints of resistance to Reagan's Cold War on immigrants were trans-local—simultaneously local and transnational—using a range of tactics adopted from social movements, war, and revolutions abroad and forged during the long era of civil rights and decolonization.[8] Migrants wielded their bodies and voices to resist in myriad ways, explored here through recurrent hunger strikes led by Haitians at the Krome detention facility in South Florida and at Fort Allen, Puerto Rico, and through Sanctuary movement "speech acts" testifying to the impacts of US wars in Central America.

How did the Reagan administration and the INS respond to growing resistance? Mounting protests did not just target specific conditions and human and civil rights abuses in detention but also connected them to Reagan's foreign policies to challenge the logic of detention itself. In the first years of the Reagan administration, detention operations fell under the sole purview of the INS, but in the face of mounting opposition, the administration adopted a range of retaliatory responses: disregarding detention rules and guidelines, responding to protest with physical and psychological abuse, transferring detention responsibilities to the Bureau of Prisons and the private sector, and merging cross-agency operations to control migrant bodies and wage legal, media, and covert attacks on activists, legal aid groups, and Sanctuary movement members.

INS and FBI clandestine operations borrowed from low-intensity conflict doctrine to intimidate and prosecute those deemed enemies of the state—especially Black and Indigenous migrants and leftist allies. A key aspect of low-intensity conflict doctrine is the increased use of surveillance, intelligence gathering, and covert operations. This was seen not only in the US government's interventions in Central America but also in its view of Salvadoran migrants as potential "terrorists." Together, this merging of retaliatory and preemptive tactics amounted to total war against Reagan's opponents, coalescing a culture of secrecy—and impunity—in detention management.

Hunger Strikes: "Until We Reach Our Goal"

> Yes, I am angry, because this is an injustice. I came here
> without any papers; that means I have a problem. If I have a
> problem, you're not supposed to push me away, to put me in
> jail. You can put me in jail for a while, but not for a year.

> *Michel, Haitian detained in Otisville, New York, November 1981*[9]

As Haitians detained at the Krome facility and at Fort Allen wielded their bodies and voices to demand justice, their resistance caused operational problems for detention administrators. On the outside, supporters worked to amplify their communications to the outside world. Allies also built coalitions, framing their protests against detention in anti-racist and anti-colonial terms,

Detention as Counterinsurgency

especially at Fort Allen. Although the Reagan administration would not be deterred, voices from detention continued to break through.

Demonstrations, uprisings, hunger strikes, violence, medical and mental health crises, suicides, and attempted suicides continued to plague detention operations, which administrators openly connected to mental health needs. Problems exacerbated by prolonged detention in "short-term" facilities were exemplified by Haitian detention at Krome and at Fort Allen. During the Mariel boatlift, the former missile sites Krome I and II south of Miami were outfitted to process and temporarily hold up to 1,000 Cuban and Haitians, separately.[10] Krome South, used primarily to detain Cubans, transitioned in October 1980 to become a temporary detention site for unaccompanied Haitian minors, who were then transferred to the Greer-Woodycrest Home in upstate New York. Krome continued to serve as a main hub from which Haitians were transferred to other facilities. Operational problems akin to those experienced by military administrators housing Cubans in the wake of Mariel abounded, on perhaps an even greater scale, in Haitian detention. And, as with Cuban refugees, Haitian unrest garnered negative media publicity that became a central concern for administrators.

In the summer of 1980, the State Department hired journalist Larry Mahoney to be the "chief spokesman—more often apologist—for Krome." After a year, however, Mahoney quit in frustration. In a whistleblowing exposé published in the *Miami Herald Tropic*, he explained he was no longer able to "cover for the indignities my government countenanced." Mahoney began his piece by asking, "Did you hear the one about the PR man's hell? It is having to represent tobacco companies or the Union of South Africa. At Krome, though I wasn't defending lung cancer or apartheid, it was not an easy job to explain how such an institution had come to exist in the United States." He detailed a nightmarish scene of barracks "still festooned with spray painted Mickey Mouses and raunchy GI graffiti" and refugees "living in giant, flapping blue-and-red striped circus tents. . . . The press was not allowed free access to these compounds. It was part of my job to keep it that way." Tasked with looking for positive stories and hosting limited, special tours for journalists, Mahoney befriended unaccompanied Haitian children detained in Krome South after Cubans were transferred out in the fall of 1980. "My basic strategy was to start by apologizing for Krome, then to point out that if the refugees from such a backward country were turned loose in the streets, they would be victimized; in short, that the Kromes were set up for their own protection."[11]

On that first Christmas of 1980, a "burly and black" local radio DJ named Hugh Ferguson arrived in a Santa costume to distribute gifts to the children.

The guards, most of whom were Cuban, according to Mahoney, were hostile and would not allow Ferguson inside. "*No* one sees the children," one guard said, and insults were exchanged. "I'm gonna kick your ass," another guard said to Ferguson. The children were eventually allowed to meet Santa in the parking lot to receive their gifts. As Santa Claus left, Mahoney thought to himself, "If they are treating *us* that way, imagine how they must be treating the Haitians." In the end, Mahoney wrote about the moment that broke him— seeing the humiliation of an old Haitian man named Daniel, a conga drum player and a frequenter of Palm Beach in the 1950s, as a French television crew filmed him eating a meal from a plastic tray with a juice box. "I had seen inhumane treatment of innocents, frightened children, chilling indifference—and occasional brutality—by guards. But nothing quite affected me the way I was affected by one proud old man's loss of dignity. I turned away and wept." When Mahoney's boss, Sylvia Gonzales of the Cuban-Haitian Task Force, asked him to write a speech "gently smoothing over the realities of what Krome was" for a United Nations function that following summer, he resigned.

On September 3, 1981, around 600 Haitians detained at Krome protested the conditions of their detention and broke down a chain-link fence at the facility while chanting, "Give us liberty, or we will tear the place apart!" They also hung a banner made out of a bedsheet on the fence that read, "It is either freedom or death!" Ninety-eight people temporarily escaped the compound until order was restored with tear gas. After the disturbance, INS officials transferred a number of Haitians determined to have been "troublemakers" in the uprising to a federal correctional facility in Otisville, New York.[12] Agitation outside of Krome also grew during this time; Haitian residents and community supporters staged demonstrations and marches, calling international attention to "beating by guards, poor medical treatment for camp inmates, assaults against women inmates, and the imprisonment of children in the camp," in the words of Reverend Gérard Jean-Juste of Miami's Haitian Refugee Center.[13]

Security problems continued to mount at Krome. On Christmas Day, a group of men led a hunger strike at the camp. Two days later, after a rumor spread that several had fainted from hunger, 500 Haitian Miami-area residents outside of Krome threw stones and bottles and stormed a facility gate while chanting "liberté, liberté" in the first confrontation between guards and outsiders. Inside, thirty contract guards and eight INS supervisors were unable to control 150 people who knocked down a fence and escaped. Outside, county and local police officers used clubs and tear gas to disperse the crowd, while demonstrators set fire to the surrounding Everglades underbrush as they fled

Detention as Counterinsurgency

A Haitian asylum-seeker uses a sheet and blanket in a seeming attempt to obtain privacy and solace at the Krome detention facility, 1981. Used by permission of Gary Monroe. Duke University Digital Repositories.

the scene. Afterward, witnesses said the INS guards and Miami-Dade police officers had used unnecessary force in subduing the crowd, and nineteen Haitians who were identified as leaders in the hunger strike were transferred to Bureau of Prisons custody. Directly underneath the *New York Times'* reporting on the hunger strike, a second headline, "Brief Disturbance at Ft. Chaffee," described an altercation between Cuban refugees and federal officers that occurred on the same day as the unrest at Krome.[14] The Youth International Party newspaper *Overthrow* also reported on the hunger strikes that fall, urging solidarity with refugees and concluding, "The Haitians are our brothers and sisters and they are fighting for their lives. We who are in the belly of the beast should learn from them and help them all we can."[15]

After the Christmas hunger strike, prominent civil rights leader Reverend Jesse Jackson visited Krome, toured the facilities, and met with Reagan administration officials. He warned that his coalition was planning a protest with 5,000 supporters and would lead increasing mass mobilizations. Reminiscent of the US government's counterinsurgent monitoring of Black activists in the 1960s and 1970s and referencing past unrest with racial undertones, INS commissioner Alan Nelson wrote to Associate Attorney General Rudy Giuliani of the need to monitor Jackson. He instructed, "Be sure he understands the

Haitian men and women talk to each other through the fences at the Krome detention facility in 1982. Used by permission of Michael Carlebach. Special Collections,
University of Miami.

difference between a peaceful protest demonstration and one that leads to
'rushing the barricades.'"[16] Internally, Giuliani commented on Jackson's coalition, "The statements of this group are largely inaccurate and extremely
one-sided," and he directed the FBI to investigate "outside agitators."[17]

Giuliani also deployed a US Marshals special operations group to investigate Krome and restore order, including efforts to reclaim the narrative. The
group's investigation concluded that frustrations and lack of proper access
to recreation fueled the unrest, and Haitians at Krome "had only despair,
hopelessness and rumor to report to friends, relatives, supporters and the
press."[18] The group recommended forming a new security plan, improving
recreational facilities, streamlining all statements and press releases through
Miami's INS public information officer, and establishing a system for briefing
influential community members on detention policy through the creation of
a liaison committee. Alan Nelson also wrote to the Department of Justice's
director of public affairs after the strike, "Both national and international
media, as well as the Miami press, radio and TV, have descended aggressively
upon Krome, which has required a concerted effort to simply respond to

Detention as Counterinsurgency

their requests for tours, interviews and information about the reception and detention of Haitians coming illegally to this country."[19] *Newsweek* called Krome a "bleak place," while the *Miami Herald* labeled it "inexcusable as a temporary-detention facility," and even more so "in a context of indifference in which 'temporary' translates to 'indefinite.'" The *Herald* also identified "emotional abuse" inflicted upon Haitians by the trauma of family separation in INS practice. As fifty-three-year-old Jeanne Joseph, unable to see her son Gustave, who was also detained at Krome, told the newspaper, "We have left the fire, and jumped into Hell."[20]

In hopes of reducing pressures inside the facility, the INS spent over $900,000 on improvements to Krome over the next year while transferring Haitians to seventeen locations throughout the United States and to Fort Allen, Puerto Rico. Officials claimed that overcrowding was the sole reason for these transfers, but Haitians and advocates maintained that transfers were a form of punishment intended to separate Haitians from legal aid.[21] The INS also separated family members from one another. The *Washington Post* reported the story of Samid Gay and his son, who were sent to Fort Allen, while his wife and daughter remained at Krome. The INS refused to recognize their common-law marriage. Such stories prompted Representative Robert Garcia (D-NY) to visit Krome and open a congressional investigation into family separations.[22] The "improvements" made at Krome largely consisted of enhanced security measures, which, together with continued efforts to cover up and deny mistreatment, only exacerbated the problems inherent in long-term detention that administration officials were already well aware of.

When Haitian transfers from Krome to Fort Allen began in August 1981, resistance from within and beyond the fort's fences exploded from the outset. The Carter administration had briefly held a smaller number of Cubans and Haitians at Fort Allen during the Mariel boatlift. Even then, San Juan mayor Hernán Padilla strongly opposed the transfer, arguing in the fall of 1980 that Carter's unilateral decision to use Fort Allen was "further evidence of the colonialistic attitude which the Federal government all too often exhibits towards Puerto Rico."[23] After a legal battle, Reagan's Department of Justice came to a new agreement with the Puerto Rican government that Fort Allen would be used to detain up to 800 Haitians for a period of one year. Governor Carlos Romero-Barcelo agreed on the condition that no Haitians would be resettled in Puerto Rico except for those with immediate family members on the island. Seventy miles from Puerto Rico's capital city, Fort Allen's main air-conditioned facilities remained empty while the INS erected tents for the Haitians' arrival.[24]

Even though facilities at Fort Allen were "nicer" than Krome, many Haitians felt that Puerto Rico was not part of the United States and likened the experience of being transferred to being deported. For example, three men attempted to jump out of an airplane taking them from Miami to Fort Allen in November 1981. After the incident, a representative of the Puerto Rico Bar Association attempted to visit the camp, but when he was barred from speaking to refugees, they angrily shook the fences and shouted.[25] When transfers began, the bar association issued a resolution repudiating the detentions, stating, "The involuntary confinement within Fort Allen's wire fence constitute[s] an infamous and shameful expression of dehumanization and racism, and unfair discrimination for political reasons." The bar association also called for the immediate release of "our Caribbean brothers."[26]

On the same day the attorney tried to visit the camp, nineteen women signed an open letter to the INS, declaring, "Why among all nations that emigrate to the United States have only the Haitians known such suffering? Since we arrived on American soil, we have been mistreated. . . . Now we cannot stand it any more. It is too much. If we have not been freed by the end of November, a good number of us are going to commit suicide. Because we have sworn to die in the United States." The letter, signed by the "Unhappy Refugees of Enclave VI," was relayed to the *New York Times* by the Inter-regional Council for Haitian Refugees.[27] In addition, 200 women at Fort Allen threatened a hunger strike. The feminist collective Off Our Backs worked to coordinate communications across multiple detention sites and to support Haitians on hunger and labor strike. The collective published an expanded version of the women's letter, along with reports that several women at Fort Allen had repeatedly attempted suicide by eating glass. The women's letter challenged the US government, asking, "Do you think that in acting that way you dissuade us from our purpose? Do you think that you are thus morally destroying us? You are wrong. We shall always be what we are." It concluded defiantly, "We are Haitians, proud great grandchildren of Toussaint Louverture, the greatest hero of the Black race. . . . We are a courageous people: it is a gift that we hold from these deep roots. He was called Louverture (the 'opening') because he opened new ways. The same is true of us, because we search for life wherever it is to be found, until we reach our goal." Calling upon their lineage in an unfinished Haitian revolution, the women's demands articulated visions of Afro-Caribbean, anti-imperial solidarity.[28]

In December, after INS officials erected fencing topped with barbed wire to separate Haitians by gender, 200 people knocked the fence down and threw rocks. The Border Patrol flew in 100 agents the next day to help restore order.

Dr. Jean-Claude Bajeux, director of the Inter-regional Council for Haitian Refugees, called the situation a "tinderbox that can go off at any moment."[29] On April 4, 1982, Haitians staged a sit-down, refusing to return to their compounds or engage in work in protest of camp conditions and slow processing. The sit-down lasted until April 15, when the protesters returned to their enclaves voluntarily after negotiating with an attorney from the inter-regional council. The INS reported it was prepared to "quell the disturbance by other means" and performed a search to locate and confiscate contraband.[30] In August, a twenty-four-year-old Haitian named Prophete Talerant hanged himself in a bathroom. He had been at Fort Allen for a year with a deportation order, awaiting appeal. The INS reported, "The Haitian population at Fort Allen is tense but no violence in the compound at this time. The detainees have refused to allow INS to remove the body and we have not forced the issue yet."[31] When a fifty-year-old man named Innocent died of a heart attack at Fort Allen the winter before, a group of Haitian men had refused to release his body and held a small group of officers, interpreters, and contract guards hostage for several hours. One man told the press that Innocent's real cause of death had been despair.[32] Administrators noted that "hostile" activities seemed to escalate during holidays.

Mental health emergencies further plagued Fort Allen, especially in cases of prolonged detention and isolation that experts agreed amounted to psychological torture. US attorney Joel Hirschhorn, hired to determine the sincerity of Haitians at Fort Allen who wanted to return home, noted that "Haitians considering themselves as not having been well received in the United States, are broken hearted and have broken spirit" and no longer had the strength to "stick it out."[33] Dr. Bajeux claimed, "The torture is not that they are tortured. . . . It is that they are doing nothing. They tell me, 'I am like an animal.' They don't understand why they've not been picked and others have been released. . . . They have a feeling of bad luck."[34] A report on the "extremely serious" mental health conditions at Fort Allen and Krome North by the Department of Health and Human Services noted an "alarming increase" in psychiatric visits and entrants with psychiatric illnesses. Among the conditions observed were frequent headaches, "feeling crazy," and depression with ideations of suicide—symptoms all beginning at the point of incarceration. They also commonly observed "a non-psychotic dissociative phenomenon of depersonalization in which the 'mind' separates from the body and sees the body as something almost inanimate and passively acted upon by events. This, I have been told, is not an uncommon phenomenon in prisoners of war"—evidencing overlapping likenesses between traumas of war, migration, and the psychic dimensions of counterinsurgent detention. The report concluded that "situational depression" stemmed from feelings of isolation, timelessness, confusion, and lack of information. Suggestions for alleviating these conditions included avoiding "dehumanization" by not forcing Haitians to wear uniforms, not subjecting them to unnecessary handcuffing (such as during transfers), and not making them "subject to arbitrary, often confusing, and contradictory commands."[35] Despite these recommendations and the "civil" designation of detention, however, these INS practices continued—in fact, they are part of detention's very design.

As psychiatric and medical emergencies abounded, the INS continued to violate its agreements for providing humane and basic care. Per an agreement between the United States and Puerto Rico, those at Fort Allen found with mental illness were supposed to be transferred back to Krome, but many never were. Medical emergencies and reproductive violence continued. The Centers for Disease Control and medical professionals were confounded when Haitian men spontaneously began experiencing gynecomastia, a swelling of breast tissue, at several detention sites in the fall of 1981. While the condition subsided, this medical mystery, likely caused by changes in diet and the administration of antipsychotic drugs, subjected the men to dehumanizing testing and scrutiny, further fueling narratives of Haitian pathology.[36] When a woman at Fort Allen gave birth to a stillborn child, Off Our Backs charged that the INS was in direct violation of its agreement not to transfer pregnant women at all and to instead release them from Krome.[37]

Although more supportive of Reagan than of Carter, San Juan mayor Hernán Padilla again spoke out against the use of Fort Allen before Haitians arrived, citing reasons that indicated a mixture of self-determination and xenophobia. In July 1981, he spoke of the negative impact Haitian detention would have on the community and on Puerto Rican–US relations due to "unpopular" Reagan administration economic policies that amounted to "unfair and discriminatory treatment being accorded our island."[38] However, in January, Padilla wrote to the US attorney general with a new critique:

> Initially, many Puerto Ricans were opposed to the Federal government transferring Haitian refugees to Fort Allen. However, as the first group arrived here in early August of last year, the Puerto Rican people were able to view first-hand the political, economic and social plight of these people. Gradually, the public mood became more receptive. . . . There has been a greater public awareness of the living conditions which exist at Fort Allen. Aided by reports from visitors

Detention as Counterinsurgency

to the facility, as well as by the local news media, the public image of Fort Allen today is one of a Federal government-sponsored prison or concentration camp, with severe environmental problems and living conditions not suitable for human habitation.

In response, Giuliani promised improvements and admitted that "Fort Allen was never intended to be a long term solution to the Haitian problem."[39] This exchange points to the administration's mounting dilemma as local communities connected the impacts of US imperialism to detention itself—with Puerto Rico, given its colonial positionally, especially attuned.

Indeed, public opinion in Puerto Rico warmed to Haitians as coalitions mounted resistance to Fort Allen outside the facility. Some support for Haitian resettlement in Puerto Rico came from planters seeking a new labor source, while others—they or their ancestors themselves having migrated to Puerto Rico by boat in the past—drew parallels between migration experiences, racism, and US oppression across the Caribbean.

Citizens United in Support of Haitian People was a coalition led by activist Ana Livia Cordero, students and professors at the University of Puerto Rico, teachers' and workers' unions, the bar association, and interfaith religious leaders who organized protests across the island, petitioned the United Nations, and staged a "caravan-march" to the fort in December 1981. Inés Muñoz, widow of an ex-governor, wrote an op-ed titled "Concentration Camps in Puerto Rico No" and joined the march. Carrying black flags signifying mourning, the caravan of vans and buses departed from the university on the morning of December 12, 1981, collecting signatures and offers of refugee sponsorship along the way. At Plaza de Juana Díaz, the group stopped to stage theatrical and musical performances of protest, and at dusk the caravan marched to the fort with torches and serenaded refugees behind barbed wire with congas, singing in Spanish and Creole.[40]

Puerto Rican opposition to Haitian detention at Fort Allen also took literary forms. In several fictional short stories, author Ana Lydia Vega reflected on Fort Allen and urged solidarity with Haitians. In "La Alambra," Puerto Ricans are stunned by the walls of the fort: "We looked. We had lost the habit of asking, and to whom. . . . It gave the impression that it had always been here." Upon the fort's closure, the story's characters are left with a guilty conscience.[41] Mounting dissent led to Fort Allen's closure, but like the Haitian interdiction program, it illustrates the Reagan administration's increasing attempts to off-shore and obscure its detention dilemma. It also foreshadows the use of Guantánamo Bay, Cuba, as a detention site in the 1990s and beyond.

While ongoing acts of resistance continued to build pressure from inside detention, on the outside, translocal networks strengthened, opposing US imperialism and a growing detention system as news of unrest and horrific conditions across detention mobilized public sympathy.

Sanctuary: "I Wish to Put the Truth in Your Hearts"

In 1983, the University of Washington newspaper published "Tales of El Salvador," stories shared by migrants living in sanctuary at University Baptist Church in Seattle. "Oscar," the most recent arrival, had been a soldier in the Salvadoran army, "literally taken off the streets, shoved into a uniform, and sent to boot camp." He said his training led by two North American advisors included "torture techniques and other methods for extracting information from the civilian population." After taking part in a series of campaigns in which members of the army kidnapped civilians from their homes, tortured, raped, and murdered them, Oscar and three other soldiers escaped into the mountains and then to Guatemala and northward. "Lydia," living in sanctuary with her four-month-old child, had helped organize a labor union in El Salvador. Shortly afterward, "three of the organizers were killed, one of whom was found beaten and mutilated. He was missing his lower jaw." She fled to the United States after her husband was killed on his way to work. "Have you ever seen the movie *El Salvador: Another Vietnam*?" she asked the congregation. "If you have, you have seen my husband. He is one of the many bodies in the film. I didn't know this, and was watching the movie for the first time when I saw his body and started screaming."[42]

Storytelling—the public mobilization of firsthand accounts of state violence and migration—became a central tactic of the Sanctuary movement. Acts of public witnessing by migrants and those who accompanied them on their journeys moved audiences and sought to hold the state accountable for its abuses abroad and in detention. Although much scholarship on the Sanctuary movement gives primacy to US actors and public opinion theory, Héctor Perla shows how Central Americans were "purposive actors" in the formation of the peace movement, mobilizing transnational activism and *testimonios* to name and expose the state's abuses, inspiring tens of thousands of North Americans to join them in opposing US policy.[43] Also writing on the central role of storytelling in the Sanctuary movement, Susan Bibler Coutin asserts that "re/membering" has been a necessary counterpart to the dismemberment of civil war by revealing commonalities "in the violence of war, poverty, crime, exile, emigration, criminalization, and deportation."[44]

Detention as Counterinsurgency

As the largest mass mobilization of civil disobedience against detention and deportation in US history, the Sanctuary movement became highly visible by the mid-1980s, especially as the media turned favorably toward movement leaders and their actions. Yet, Sanctuary was not without internal tensions. Histories of the movement reveal the fraught and fractured politics of resistance as participants questioned the limits of liberalism and debated whether to operate within existing frameworks of compassion, human rights, and electoral politics or to instead push imaginatively beyond them to challenge the logics of US foreign policy and border enforcement in their entirety. Often obscured in the Manichaean struggle between the Sanctuary movement and the US government were the millions of lives affected on the ground. Although Sanctuary and solidarity attempted to center Central American voices in their movements, which themselves were often migrant-led, white saviorism and US-centric perspectives from all sides more often prevailed. Decades later, there remains a dearth of Central American voices in public and academic discourse on the wars due to US violence, trauma, and bias, yet they continue to gain strength.[45]

More than 100,000 US citizens were mobilized in the larger 1980s Central American peace movement, of which Sanctuary formed the largest and most visible arm.[46] Organizational resistance most often began locally, in communities whose members experienced or witnessed the direct impact of migration and US detention practices. Faith-based activists like Dominican sister Renny Golden made up a large contingent of the movement, galvanized by notions of compassion, solidarity, and, for many, Latin American liberation theology, compelling them to work to end US interventions abroad. Golden recalls that although a background of feminist activism and prison work at Harvard Divinity School in the 1970s informed her vision of Central American solidarity, the killing of four US nuns in El Salvador in 1980 is what radicalized her. She remembers her moment of conviction while participating in a Chicago vigil for the slain missionaries. Walking in a circle with candles and reciting litanies in the freezing cold, she stopped and said, "I think the injunction is to pray for the dead, but fight like hell for the living."[47]

The concept of sanctuary was as old as the Bible. In US history, it was invoked in the establishment of the Underground Railroad for people escaping slavery during the nineteenth century and again during the Vietnam War when churches and universities sheltered draftees seeking to avoid military service. However, a Quaker named Jim Corbett living in Tucson, Arizona, came up with the idea of invoking the concept in defiance of US immigration law when he tried to help a man named Nelson from El Salvador get out of detention in the spring of 1981. Corbett was part of a local coalition of churches expressing solidarity with Central American refugees after witnessing a growing number of migrants dying in the desert, being detained, or reportedly being killed upon deportation.

After hearing of Nelson's detention, Corbett solicited advice from the Manzo Area Council, which had been helping detained migrants since the 1970s. He learned Nelson needed to sign a G-28 form designating legal counsel in order to prevent his deportation without a hearing. When Corbett went to the Santa Cruz jail to have Nelson sign the form, he met two more men from El Salvador. He went to the Border Patrol office to get more G-28 forms, but when he returned the warden told him, "Oh, you wanted to see those guys? The Border Patrol took them twenty or thirty minutes ago. They're all gone. And there's no way to know where they went."[48] Corbett and a friend then drove to the El Centro Detention Center in California hoping to find Nelson. When Corbett arrived at El Centro, the detention center had no record of Nelson. A detained man there who knew Nelson, however, said he had already been deported to El Salvador—even though he had signed a G-28 form. When an INS superintendent saw that Corbett's friend was recording the conversation, he locked the doors and demanded the tape recorder. After Corbett lectured him about refugee rights, the superintendent let them go.

Enraged, Corbett began writing "Dear Friend" letters to Quaker meetings and individuals across the country explaining the injustices facing Salvadoran refugees. Stories similar to that of Nelson's "kidnapping"—the INS tearing up G-28 forms and enacting disappearances and deportations on the spot before anyone could intervene—spread.[49] In addition to raising bond funds to free Salvadorans and Guatemalans from jail, Corbett argued that if the US government was violating its own laws, US citizens should violate immigration laws as well. In his first letter, he stated, "Active resistance will be the only alternative to abandoning the refugees to their fate." Alluding to the Quakers' participation in the Underground Railroad that helped people escape slavery in the South in the 1800s, Corbett wrote, "The creation of a network of actively concerned, mutually supportive people in the U.S. and Mexico may be the best preparation for an adequate response. . . . A network? Quakers will know what I mean."[50]

This is how Sanctuary began, as religious and legal aid groups raised money to bond people out of detention and worked with Salvadoran and Guatemalan migrants to prevent their detention and deportation. At its height, the movement grew into a network of 500 churches with tens of thousands of supporters across the United States, Mexico, and Canada operating a "New

Underground Railroad" that moved and sheltered migrants between congregations and safehouses by the middle of the decade.[51]

Tucson's Southside Presbyterian Church, led by Reverend John Fife, became the first officially declared "sanctuary" church for Central American migrants, in coordination with churches in California's East Bay, Los Angeles, Seattle, and Long Island, New York. Prior to Sanctuary, Fife had participated in the civil rights movement in Alabama in the 1960s and in ministry on a Native American reservation in Arizona. In the 1970s, he helped lobby Exxon and General Motors to divest from South Africa, recognize Black unions, and desegregate their facilities.[52] In Tucson, Fife collaborated with Manzo and Jim Corbett's growing network of migrant assistance. On the movement's decision to "go public," Corbett said, "By keeping the operation clandestine we were doing exactly what the government wanted us to do—keeping it hidden, keeping the issue out of the public view."[53] Fife recalled, "We got a very clear and direct message from INS and the border patrol, delivered from an INS attorney to one of the paralegals who was working with us. It said, 'Look, we know what Corbett and Fife are up to. You tell them to stop it, or we'll have to arrest them.' . . . The conclusion we came to is the only other option we have is to give public witness to what we're doing."[54]

On March 24, 1982, the second anniversary of the assassination of Archbishop Romero in El Salvador, Fife hung two banners outside of Southside Presbyterian that read in Spanish, "This is a sanctuary for the oppressed of Central America" and "Immigration: do not profane the sanctuary of God." To a crowd of reporters in front of the church, he introduced "Alfredo," a Salvadoran refugee wearing a bandanna over his face to protect his identity. Speaking in Spanish to eight television cameras, Alfredo thanked Christians for helping him get to Tucson without being caught by the INS. The *Tucson Citizen* labeled him "one of the most publicized undocumented aliens here ever." Jim Corbett appeared that night on the *CBS Evening News*, calling Salvadoran deportations "a clear violation of international law and of the most fundamental standards of human decency. Yet the US government is telling us that it is the victims who are illegal."[55] The day before the declaration, Southside Presbyterian delivered a letter to Attorney General William French Smith stating, "We are writing to inform you that the Southside Presbyterian Church will publicly violate the Immigration and Nationality Act Section 274(a). We have declared our church as a 'sanctuary' for undocumented refugees from Central America. . . . We believe the administration of the law to be immoral, as well as illegal. . . . Obedience to God requires this of all of us."[56] Sanctuary quickly blossomed into a highly

Sanctuary movement car caravans transporting migrants to safe houses across the United States adopted strategies of visibility and traveling together for the dual purposes of raising awareness and protection against retaliation from the INS and law enforcement. Reprinted from "Sanctuary: A Justice Ministry," published in 1985 by the Chicago Religious Task Force on Central America with permission from Renny Golden. Courtesy of Special Collections at the Claremont Colleges.

visible national movement, mobilizing 70,000 US citizens within the first three years of its operations.[57]

Sanctuary did not always have a clear organizational structure; further, the movement was often fractured by ideological splits over leadership, tactics, and charges of white saviorism—the centering of white, North American, or more privileged actors in organizing efforts. Lacking the hierarchical, centralized command structure of more traditional political organizations, Sanctuary congregations were largely autonomous and minimally coordinated nationally by the Chicago Religious Task Force on Central America (CRTFCA), which took over after the movement grew so quickly it became unmanageable for the Tucson group. Soon, political and ideological divides arose between Chicago and Tucson. Chicago's primarily female leadership, for example, criticized the male-dominated culture of Tucson Sanctuary, some describing Fife as "cocky" and an "ego guy" and Corbett as "patriarchal." Furthermore, as CRTFCA cofounder Renny Golden recalls, "Chicago took the position that we had to stop US intervention. Tucson took the position that we really had to show compassion for refugees." While not entirely a Protestant/Catholic divide, Golden characterizes many participants from Protestant denominations as more "liberal" compared with "radical" Catholics like herself and Jewish participants who spent more time in Central America. This helped inform a more radical stance, in line with organizations like the Committee in Solidarity with the People of El Salvador and with a liberation theology that urged the need for historical and systemic analysis of the source of migrant suffering: US state violence. Golden says, "Those two positions should not have been incompatible, and in spite of our differences, we really held it together for the sake of refugees." The growing number of refugees shaping the movement's actions also helped raise political consciousness.[58]

Movement along the "New Underground Railroad" often began with coordination between the sanctuary of Our Lady of Guadalupe Catholic Church on the Mexican side of Nogales and Sacred Heart Church in Nogales, Arizona, visible from the border.[59] Migrants would make the short journey from one church to the other and take refuge at Sacred Heart, where "conductors" Tony Clark and Mary K. Espinosa welcomed them. At first, Fife and Corbett flew refugees to designated sanctuary cities, but as numbers increased, a pattern emerged and a highway relay system became possible. Then, as Ann Crittenden describes it, "the new underground railroad was, more than anything, housewife chauffeurs driving station wagons and compact cars, carrying their charges from McDonald's and Roy Rogers to overnight stops in church basements. The final destination was often a garage apartment near a small church in a university community."[60] A network of West Coast churches also worked, with some success, to pressure airlines to stop deportation "death flights" from Los Angeles.[61]

Debates arose within the movement over publicity and storytelling tactics. As Tucson prioritized giving sanctuary to those in need, Chicago sought out those whose stories were more politically conscious. Other participants expressed fears of being too openly critical of the US government and drawing retaliation. A rift occurred when Chicago refused to accept a Salvadoran sergeant on the Underground Railroad because of optics and safety concerns. Golden says, "Our point was that we had Iowa housewives driving refugees from one point to another point" and didn't want to put them in jeopardy; the movement needed some criteria. When 100 movement participants gathered to iron out conflict, Golden remembers some calling CRTFCA members "commies" and accusing them of using refugees for political purposes. Corbett took the microphone and silenced the room by saying, "Would he or she who is without an ideology, cast the first stone?" Golden clarified Chicago's stance: "If you're accusing us of trying to stop US intervention, you're correct. If you're accusing us of using refugees to do that, you're incorrect. It's simply presenting the truth of the suffering."

The INS seized upon fractures within the movement, issuing media talking points discrediting Sanctuary, charging the movement with being exclusionary and using refugees for political purposes. Turning the movement's criticisms of the US government back onto itself, the INS alleged, "Most leaders of the 'Sanctuary' movement freely acknowledge that their motivation is to change U.S. foreign policy toward Central America. In effect, this is an admission that they are using the Central Americans in 'sanctuary' as pawns." The INS continued, "Sanctuary people are also screening people they are bringing in," pointing out that "no individual from Poland or Nicaragua or Ethiopia or Vietnam or Afghanistan has been sheltered by the movement." The INS used migrant stories as well—to refute Sanctuary's claims. A media relations guide issued by the INS included sketches of two stories lacking names or context, one of a Salvadoran man who claimed in his initial asylum application that he had deserted the Salvadoran army and was on the government's death list but whose story changed when he took the stand during his deportation hearing. Another sketch described "one woman who tells a frightful tale of torture and rape in public" but who "privately has admitted that she came to the U.S. to visit her sister."[62] The INS's dismissals of asylum claims during this time as "frivolous" and of kinship ties as "fraudulent" evidence an ongoing suppression of truth and flattening of the complexity of migrant lives.

At the center of Sanctuary mobilizations were the physical presence and testimonies of migrants in sanctuary spaces. Migrants in sanctuary often spoke to congregations during church services in "speech acts" designed to make their stories visible—in direct refutation of the Reagan administration's attempts to erase and deny their truths. Most hid their faces with bandannas for anonymity while simultaneously politicizing their bodies and voices to challenge US foreign policy. Public events and sanctuary caravans like the one arriving in Seattle in July 1984 created media spectacles across the country. University Baptist Church in Seattle was the seventh congregation to declare sanctuary in the country and the first in the Northwest. Led by Reverend Donovan Cook, the church maintained a "vigorous schedule of speaking engagements, a newsletter, symposiums, conferences and media coverage." These efforts aimed to reach "small-town America" where diversity and immigration issues were much less visible. In Ashland in southern Oregon, for example, "Sandra" told a congregation, "I have a chance to reach North Americans in their homes, and denounce the war-like policies of Reagan

Detention as Counterinsurgency

that oppress our people," while "Armando" added, "I feel free in this place to express what is happening in Guatemala. In Guatemala, one cannot protest. Nobody is speaking right now because they are afraid to die." Testimonies often involved refugees revealing parts of their bodies to audiences to show evidence of torture—scars, acid burns, bullet wounds. At an event at Seattle Central Community College, Mario Castillo showed the scars on his body from an acid attack by police forces in Guatemala to an audience of 150. "We need your help," he said. "I know you can help us if you want to."[63]

The selective storytelling and visibility tactics of the Sanctuary movement have been critiqued as contributing to divisive "good" versus "bad" immigrant narratives that have, over time, caused harm to migrants already marginalized by race, class, gender or sexual orientation, and religion.[64] Some scholars of Sanctuary have concluded that the movement's actions and narratives, including the use of selective storytelling, have often served to reproduce the very "exclusions it has sought to dismantle."[65] Refugee stories often emphasized Indigenous and campesino or farmworker identities but also Christian, heteronormative, and familial themes; those whose stories might not resonate with US audiences, such as those who were queer or trans, often went unheard. Trauma and fear of retaliation also silenced many more—in effect, mirroring the effects of US state power projected abroad. Many refugees in sanctuary experienced it as isolation, usually staying in a small room inside a church such as a rectory, unable to go out in fear of being picked up by the INS. Some even likened it to the experience of detention. Movement leaders were aware of these issues, such as during efforts to coordinate Elba Martinez's travel from Mexico to Seattle to be reunited with her sister-in-law Pilar. Suffering from depression and fear, Elba did not wish to enter public sanctuary, making some organizers less willing to help. Corbett and Fife debated encouraging her to go public given her "good story," but Corbett resisted: "There's no way we can convert people. . . . We just want to do instrumentally good things."[66]

More radical critiques of the Sanctuary movement emerged from Sanctuary participants themselves. Alejandro Rodriguez reflected on his experiences in Rochester, New York, in 1985:

> It is as if sanctuary were just another way of importing cheap labor
> into the U.S., without any of the social or religious objectives which
> give authority to sanctuary and justify its existence. . . . I hope to be
> able to expand and deepen the work until this movement becomes
> more aware of itself and its people, with a real expression of its historic
> roots. There is little real worry about the family, and little vision of

the work directed in solidarity with the people who are truly suffering repression. This manifests itself when you ask for a message without content. . . . The sanctuary movement must take the next step, which is a historic step: to forge an anti-investment solidarity movement.[67]

Rodriguez's words point to several ways in which refugees often viewed and experienced sanctuary as problematic, or even objectifying. First, stripping away the movement's religious or political "objectives" revealed the lived and material realities for migrants in the United States—as laborers. Second, Rodriguez was critiquing the lack of migrant voices and leadership in the movement, which, he argued, would lead to a more holistic understanding of the causes and continuation of oppression. Finally, by urging Sanctuary to become an "anti-investment solidarity movement," Rodriguez asked US audiences to "divest" from complicity in empire in all its forms.

Rodriguez's testimony appeared alongside others in a self-reflective booklet produced and disseminated by the CRTFCA called *Sanctuary Perspectives*. While almost all migrants interviewed expressed gratitude and agreement with the movement, their testimonies also urged movement members to see Sanctuary as a process—a way to provide an ideological education and to center migrant voices and needs. In sanctuary in Tacoma, Washington, Rumalda and Francisco Domingo affirmed Rodriguez's views, adding, "Give the refugee more participation in the committee meetings at their sanctuary in order to inform them about how the movement is doing. We assure you that this would help a lot more." Some spoke of the difficulties in sharing their stories. One person in sanctuary at Montclair Presbyterian Church in Oakland offered, "We agree with our congregation over the issue of sanctuary, except in that they would like us to speak publically about our case but we are worried about our children and other relatives and prefer not to talk about it." Speaking from Dallas, another added, "We often have only a few minutes to get our ideas across." The Hernandez family in Olympia, Washington, shared their biggest challenge: the "incredulity and hardness of the American people. It is impossible for you to imagine how much I wish to put the truth in your hearts and take off the blindfolds that keep you from seeing."[68]

When church leaders decided their church would become a sanctuary, their entire congregation became aware of the Central American issue. The movement's religious orientation, its calling on history, and its compelling refugee stories drew people from across political lines. Congregants at Central Presbyterian Church in Ohio, for example, explained why they voted for their church to join Sanctuary. Robert DeMass, who was a student at Kent State during rising activism in the 1960s, did not oppose the Vietnam War. This time, "I made my decisions on the basis of being a Christian rather than on being a patriot." William Clarke, an electrical contractor who voted for Reagan, said, "I'm the last person in the world to be advocating civil disobedience." But, "we look down on those churches in Germany that allowed Jews to be rounded up after they knew what would happen to them. . . . By offering sanctuary, we can at least stop supplying these death squads with their victims."[69] Another movement participant related, "It was incredible to hear Salvadorans talk about their horrible experiences. I had always heard about people far away, but they had never been 'real.' This hit me like a bomb. When I realized that I could make a difference, I jumped all over it, and my life changed."[70] Many US citizens, especially students and those involved in church missionary work, witnessed atrocities in Central America firsthand. When University of Washington engineering student James Hogg returned from a "fact-finding" mission to El Salvador, where he was detained by National forces, interrogated, and questioned for being a communist sympathizer, his story received much media attention—likely due to his positionality as a white male US citizen. Hogg reported seeing US helicopter pilots and men in suits who claimed to be from the US embassy on an air force base. Corroborating migrants' claims, he said, "When they tell us Americans are not flying these missions, they're not telling the truth."[71]

US citizen Sanctuary participants acknowledged political fissures and difficulties in gathering resources but also how meeting refugees radicalized them by making them see the importance of political education in their communities. After sheltering migrants and "having had many rounds with the INS," the Lutheran church in Tucson broadened its mission beyond helping Central American refugees to educational efforts to support "the undocumented and oppressed in general," even specifying plans to expand solidarity work in South Africa, Namibia, Mexico, and Honduras. Meanwhile, Presbyterian church participants in Oakland reported shifting their ideology to embrace liberation theology. Members of University Friends in Seattle recounted their actions, including using the church's property as collateral to start a bail program to bond out twenty refugees by 1985, starting a woodworking cooperative to employ migrants, signing the Central American peace movement's Pledge of Resistance, and helping refugees move on safely to Canada.[72] Participants also shared challenges they still faced: overcoming fears of breaking US law, confronting right-wing views in local media and US Latinx communities, and remedying the ongoing silencing and psychological impacts of war and migration traumas on refugees.

Sanctuary gained greater visibility through Reverend Jesse Jackson's 1984 presidential bid and public relations tour to Central America and the Caribbean. The CRTFCA's central mission was to "inform, educate and activate people on the conditions in Central America and the plight of refugees." In its first few years, it coordinated refugee movement and housing, distributed 50,000 sanctuary manuals, and organized three national caravans of refugees. In Chicago, Jackson declared his campaign headquarters, Operation PUSH (People United to Save Humanity) and the National Rainbow Coalition, an official sanctuary. He was the only presidential candidate who made challenging US foreign policies in Latin America central to his platform while also unifying opposition to militarism, environmental racism, and nuclear buildup with advocacy for universal health care and worker, gay, and migrant rights.[73] Forgoing preparations for the Democratic National Convention, Jackson went on a five-day Central American tour in June 1984. He was accompanied by seventy-five journalists and met with officials in Panama, Honduras, Costa Rica, Nicaragua, El Salvador, and finally Cuba, where he successfully negotiated with Fidel Castro for the release and return of Cuban and US citizen political prisoners.[74]

Jackson was present at the commissioning of one of the CRTFCA's refugee caravans, the Freedom Train, in Los Angeles, and received refugees at the PUSH offices at the end of the caravan in Chicago in September 1984. Jackson gave a speech pleading for cross-movement solidarities:

> If Americans had protested against sending troops to Vietnam soon enough, our country could have avoided its longest and most tragic conflict since the Civil War against slavery. If Americans had offered Sanctuary to the victims of fascism soon enough, the Holocaust might have been avoided. If Americans had remembered their commitment to human rights, our citizens of Japanese descent would never have been carried off to the very concentration camps where Salvadoran and Guatemalan refugees are now imprisoned awaiting deportation and certain death. We must stand up for what is right, and we must do it in time, this time. In joining the nationwide sanctuary movement, we are at the same time challenging it to widen its vision and open its heart, to find ways to extend protection to all the victims of American policy abroad, including refugees from apartheid in South Africa and from misery and social injustice in Haiti.[75]

Here, Jackson globalized and historicized the plight of Haitians and Central Americans, connecting them to other groups victimized by US imperialism.

In response to the arrests of two Sanctuary movement leaders in 1985, the CRTFCA organized a mock public "Trial of Truth." The trial was performed in Chicago in November 1985, with the last line of the performance read by all: "We will not be silenced."[76] Together, Jackson's campaign, CRTFCA actions, and the tactics of the Sanctuary movement designed to make migrant experiences visible illustrate the coalescence of a broader coalition of resistance to Reagan.

On the whole, the press treated the Sanctuary movement favorably but featured white US citizen leaders more prominently and cast the movement as a primarily domestic battle. Narratives of conscience combated anti-immigrant sentiment, and mounting criticism of US foreign and immigration policies placed further pressure upon the Reagan administration. Sanctuary's religious designation placed it in the realm of untouchable for authorities. Regarding the movement's visibility, Corbett acknowledged, "The media are not interested in the indigenous martyrs of Central America, but they are fascinated with the willingness of U.S. citizens to go to some slight risk in order to help refugees evade capture."[77] In August 1982, *People* magazine ran a six-page hagiographic story about Corbett smuggling a Salvadoran couple with three children to a safe haven, as "no pain or weakness or uncertainty showed on his face. The fact that he was about to commit a federal crime troubled Jim Corbett not at all."[78] Such outsized coverage of the movement's white male leadership left uneven impressions and detracted from how much of Sanctuary's work was migrant and women-led. Renny Golden describes Corbett as a saintly, "gentle and brilliant" Quaker but expresses dismay at some of Sanctuary's lost opportunities to foster broader solidarity beyond Central America, acknowledge domestic racism, and give migrants more of a voice in movement leadership. "We had in many ways a bully pulpit," she says.[79]

There were also great moments of joy, such as when the CRTFCA organized a twenty-eight-car caravan in 1984 escorting the Guatemalan "Excot" family from Chicago to Washington, DC, and then to a Benedictine monastery in Vermont to live in sanctuary. Along the way, the group held rallies in several cities. Upon their arrival in Vermont, the family was greeted by a crowd of 500 and a celebration in a barn, where their hosts played music and performed a Greek circle dance around the family. A priest who hid Mr. Excot in Guatemala City three years earlier was also present. "It was really beautiful," Golden remembers, feeling a sense of victory when the story was publicized in the *New York Times*. "There was no longer an underground railroad." Excot told the *Times* he was a farmer, threatened by the Guatemalan government for teaching villagers to read. Sharing mixed feelings about the family's arrival in the small town of Weston and likely longing for home, Mrs. Excot said, "I am very, very happy, and it's perhaps the saddest day of my life."[80] Mrs. Excot also shared her family's story in *Redbook* magazine. "This testimony had a great impact on many people, especially women," Mr. Excot said, concluding, "It seems our voices are being listened to."

Media attention surrounding Sanctuary seemed to taunt immigration enforcement efforts and angered politicians like Arizona senator Barry Goldwater, who pushed for the INS to prosecute defiant churches. Although the FBI and the INS had been monitoring the Sanctuary movement from the very beginning, the INS hesitated at the prospect of invading churches.[81] Internal communications dismissed both the legitimacy of the movement and concern over migrant lives. Instead, INS director Alan Nelson asserted the movement was "at base a foreign policy disagreement between the churches' view of present conditions in El Salvador and the U.S. Government's assessment of those conditions." Nelson told PBS's *Frontline* that Sanctuary activists were "well-meaning," but "many of them will admit what they are really doing is opposing the president's policy in Central America." He also noted, "Legally we can enter churches, private residences, theaters, schools and similar institutions with court-ordered search warrants."[82] But how would it look if INS officers began storming churches? In 1982, INS assistant general counsel Bill Joyce said, "We're not about to send investigators into a church to start dragging out people in front of television cameras."[83] Tucson Border Patrol chief and thirty-five-year veteran Leon Ring was also hesitant to act, remembering a public outcry in the 1970s over Border Patrol agents arresting several undocumented women as they left church on a Sunday morning. Since then, Border Patrol agents had an unwritten rule designating churches as hands-off.[84] This would soon change, however, as mounting pressures moved the administration to retaliate.

Controlling Migrant Bodies

> I am not here to hold any man's hand. It is my camp, and
> those who are hired will soon learn how I want it run.
>
> *Cecilio L. Ruiz Jr., INS assistant district director at Port Isabel*

During and after the Mariel Cuban boatlift in 1980–81, the Cuban-Haitian Task Force warned of the ill effects of militarized, long-term, and punitive immigration detention practices. Mental health experts also noted the detrimental effects of long-term detention. Camp administrators at Fort Chaffee, Arkansas, noted that "the lack of alternatives for these people could develop into a sub-stantial security problem.... Staff consensus—including that of psychologists and psychiatrists—is that both their mental health and ability to adapt to life in the United States would be enhanced if placed in locations/situations with other than a refugee camp atmosphere."[85] As the Reagan administration resolved to keep refugee populations separated from the US public in increas-ingly punitive conditions, these problems only worsened.

In 1981, the attorney general's office stated, "The Government, and espe-cially INS, finds itself in a Catch-22 situation where, no matter what action it takes, someone sues to prevent it." For example, the INS was simultaneously being sued by Florida governor Bob Graham "to prevent resettlement of Haitians in South Florida" and by the Haitian Refugee Center "to require parole of Haitians in South Florida." The attorney general concluded, "To say the least, it is difficult for INS to know what it can and cannot do."[86] In March 1982, the Department of Justice began exploring new options for shifting detention responsibilities, "prompted by problems related to housing the Cuban and Haitian entrants and the need to formulate an effective long-term detention policy."[87] The growing pressures and visibility of prolonged Central American detention also contributed to the administration's search for detention solutions.

In their deliberations, the administration sided with public assent. Weigh-ing a decision to transfer the responsibility of long-term detention to the Bureau of Prisons (BOP), the attorney general stated, "INS has no expertise in this area and has housed long-term detainees in sub-standard conditions. Until BOP ... provide[d] assistance to INS at Krome, the facility was a dis-grace." But in response to one of the "cons" of a BOP transfer, "the stigma of holding aliens in penal institutions could create a negative public reaction," the office wrote, "This may be true to some extent. On the other hand, the change might be publically viewed as a positive step motivated by concern for the aliens' welfare, which is what it is. Many ... are currently held in actual penal institutions without any great public outcry." Refugee policy and management discussions were often couched in such humanitarian terms in this era, serving to obscure and deny detention's harms. Also, the attorney general's office argued the stigma surrounding "penal institutions" would be reduced after the transfer as migrants would be held in "facilities called something like 'Immigration Detention Service Centers' managed by a sepa-rate section of BOP."[88] These discussions of the responsibilities of detention operations highlighted a seeming contradiction: concern over political and public fallout due to detention's "stigma of criminalization" on one hand, and the recognition that a large segment of the public did not seem to oppose current detention practices on the other.[89] Over time, this contradiction faded as laws criminalizing migration served to normalize Reagan's detention policies. Meanwhile, resistance continued.

Parallel to the question of who should be responsible for the planning, construction, and operation of detention facilities was the question of who had the authority, and what were the best methods, to control the potentially "explosive" detention population itself. Interagency collaboration between the INS and the BOP in this endeavor had already been established in the case of Haitian detention, strengthening further in response to recurring unrest. After the 1981 Christmas hunger strike and disturbance at Krome, for example, the INS invited two BOP officials to bring their expertise to help manage Krome for the duration of one year "to establish professional operations at Krome and train INS personnel."[90] As noted above, the administration touted this as a great success. Such cooperation reflected both an affirmation of the administration's turn toward long-term detention and the further conflation of civil detention and criminal imprisonment. Three procedures carried out by INS officers in particular—transfers, segregation, and isolation (solitary confinement)—had the stated intention of protecting migrants but were more often used as disciplinary measures of retaliation against acts of dissent. Vast discrepancies between official rhetoric and on-the-ground realities in detention reveal the overriding priority of keeping migrants in detention under control and out of sight.

Although the frequent transfer of migrants between facilities was highly criticized by detention's opponents and even challenged in court, the INS maintained that transfers were made only to relieve overcrowding and were made in migrants' best interests. Testifying to a House subcommittee in June 1982, Arthur C. Helton of the Lawyers Committee for International Human Rights cited numerous reports of abuses and human rights violations experienced by Haitian migrants in detention. Helton criticized the transfer of immigrants to inadequately equipped facilities in remote locations, where they had no access to family, friends, or legal counsel. Opposing the construction of new detention facilities and Reagan's detention policies on the whole, Helton concluded, "It is hard to believe this is happening in the United States of America."[91] When Haitians were transferred to BOP facilities in Big Springs, Texas, and Lexington, Kentucky, in July 1981 to relieve overcrowding at Krome, Congressman Larry Hopkins of Kentucky and Senator Lloyd Bentsen of Texas expressed opposition from their constituencies, rooted in racism and xenophobia. Rudy Giuliani reassured them, "This action, and the other transfers which were recently made, is being taken in the interest of the health and welfare of the detainees. There is no long term plan to use Bureau of Prisons facilities to house Haitian undocumented aliens. These are well-behaved people who have posed no disciplinary or security problems at Krome North. Those who would be held . . . will be segregated, for their own protection, from the prison population."[92]

Giuliani's assertions were untrue. The INS often targeted Haitians who were identified as agitators or "troublemakers" for transfers, and the attorney general's office did approve of BOP facilities as a long-term detention solution. Also, Giuliani's use of humanitarian claims to placate public xenophobia is as revealing as his lie.

Giuliani's insistence that protection was the main purpose of segregation, like transfers, contradicts the punitive and harsh conditions migrants actually faced. The INS 1980 "Standards for Detention" state, "Administrative segregation should be used to protect detainees from other detainees." The standards also provided that each facility grant each person the right to a "healthful place in which to live," including basic medical care and "the same right to bodily integrity as if he or she went to a community hospital facility," as well as access to recreational facilities, equipment, and outdoor exercise.[93] According to warden George Rodgers at the Ray Brook BOP facility in Lake Placid, New York, however, Haitians were restricted to their dormitory and a small fenced-in area of blacktop they used to play soccer, while incarcerated citizens played softball and had the freedom to walk around the fifty-five-acre facility grounds.[94] Arthur Helton's June 1982 House testimony also cited inadequate recreational facilities and INS failures to provide access to medical care. In one case, a man named Albetre Mauclair died after sustaining an injury during a soccer match and no doctor was available for his request for medical treatment.[95] The frequent denial of recreation and medical care, among other failures to comply with official detention standards, became a common complaint that continues in immigration detention to this day.

On paper, the INS mandated that solitary confinement, or "administrative detention," be used sparingly and only in cases where people needed protection. In practice, the INS frequently used it to retaliate against those who resisted, revealing another way civil detention and prison operations had become indistinguishable. Isolation is an inherently punitive measure; scholars and practitioners have long documented the detrimental effects of solitary confinement on mental health, especially on asylum seekers who have experienced past trauma.[96] Fort Chaffee's "Joint Security Plan" of 1980 stated,

"Certain aliens within the camp will not conform to the established rules and will require confinement in administrative detention, a stockade or a federal correctional institution." The plan listed behavior that could be detrimental to others and thus merit administrative detention, including "non-criminal harassment," "badgering," and "instigation."[97] This allowed for looser interpretations—a logic that if migrants didn't "conform" to rules, the INS could break them in return. In August 1981, a Haitian man detained at Ray Brook in New York lay down in front of a truck in protest of his detention and was placed in solitary confinement for his action. After accusing another man, Bernaivil Elisnord, of encouraging Haitians to hunger strike, the INS placed him in isolation. There he remained for eight days, allowed to leave his room only twice for fifteen minutes of exercise and a shower.[98]

In 1984, the INS directed that administrative detention was "in no way meant to be punishment, it is administrative segregation only," and should be limited to a maximum of seventy-two hours.[99] This policy was in keeping with the 1980 detention standards, yet it was systematically violated. Jessica Ordaz's study of hunger strikes at El Centro shows how the INS retaliated against detained Salvadorans, especially, due to their leading role in organizing acts of protest. Use of solitary confinement, or la loba, and tactics of bodily control were characterized by both physical and psychological abuse. Water Chu, a participant in the 1985 hunger strike at El Centro, related that INS guards taunted strikers by forcing them to sit in front of full plates of food, daily. Before the INS planned to force-feed the hunger strikers (a practice the UN Human Rights Commission has equated to torture), a local pastor named Alex William Koski used his life savings, about $26,000, to bail them out of detention. Acts of retaliation also had a public relations angle, as the INS attempted to discredit hunger strikers in the media. As Ordaz shows, despite the men being "experienced organizers and politically conscious," given their backgrounds, regional INS commissioner Harold W. Ezell told the media, "Their so-called demands are really so much baloney. . . . The conditions at the center have been inspected over and over. . . . The inmates are living in a correctional facility, [not] the Conrad Hilton." INS district director James B. Turnage Jr. also asserted, "This certainly is not a spontaneous demonstration" and blamed the Sanctuary movement by adding, "This has been staged by outside managers."[100] Akin to Giuliani's response to hunger strikes at Krome and the Reagan administration's broader dismissal of rights movements as communism, laying blame on outside agitators worked to delegitimize critics of US foreign policy and deny migrant agency. As mentioned in chapter 4, the Border Patrol Tactical Unit's assault on hunger strikers as they linked

Detention as Counterinsurgency

their arms together in solidarity further evidences how counterinsurgent, militarized forms of retaliation in enforcement operations were already being enacted.

In sum, despite the stated intent of operational procedures, transfers, segregation, isolation, and other counterinsurgent security measures used in jail keeping, such as counts and shakedowns, ultimately served the dual purpose of retaliating against migrants and silencing them in the system. Today, these practices are ubiquitous features of "civil" detention operations.

Beyond routine operational INS tactics intended to quell unrest in detention, a pattern of physical and sexual abuse perpetrated by INS officers grew, long entrenched in a patriarchal culture of secrecy. Although such abuse has been found to be widespread and systemic throughout immigration detention's history, the 1980 INS "Standards for Detention" forbade corporal punishment: "Personal abuse and conditions and practices injurious to the well-being of detainees violate the legal protections available under the U.S. Constitution." Yet, migrants were routinely threatened physically and denied such rights by INS officers. The INS *Immigration Detention Officer Handbook* opens with the officer's central mission: "The fair and humane treatment and transportation of detained aliens." The handbook also forewarns, "Many of our detention officers, by the nature of their work, are rendered highly visible and vulnerable to public scrutiny and possible criticism. It is therefore essential that the highest standards of personal conduct be maintained to ensure fair and decent treatment of all aliens in Service custody." With an emphasis on attitude, dignity, and self-control, the handbook expressly forbids detention officers from accepting gratuities or bribes, transacting business with detained migrants, or having intimate contact with anyone of the opposite sex.[101]

The broader punitive turn of Reagan's revanchist politics and new detention policies served only to further embolden the INS's abusive practices. From 1980 to 1981, complaints of INS corruption and criminal civil rights violations increased by 79 percent. These complaints included allegations of officers taking bribes, the unlawful use of force, and "serious supervisory misconduct."[102] However, retaliation against whistleblowing among guards was also part of INS culture. In a memoir about his experiences as a guard at the Port Isabel detention center in Texas in the early 1980s, Tony Hefner documents the shocking number of incidents of abuse and corruption that took years to come to light. Reflecting on the culture of secrecy at the detention center, Hefner claims, "If guards witness or are victims of wrongdoing on government property, they can and do lose their livelihoods by reporting it." He recalled Assistant District Director Cecilio L. Ruiz Jr. addressing the new guards on Hefner's first day: "Women are my passion. I am not homosexual. It is not allowed. No homosexuals will be running my camp. . . . If you girls have any trouble at all . . . come to my office. . . . I will personally take care of you. . . . But if one of you men darkens my doorstep asking for any help, I will fire you. Do you understand?"[103] Ruiz's sexist and homophobic comments alluded to the impunity male guards could enjoy.

Hefner also describes INS officers at Port Isabel stealing belongings and money from migrants, destroying property, and buying and selling drugs; pregnant women who alleged rape being deported before delivering their babies; and threats and assaults made on female guards, assaults on minors, and male officers paying male and female minors for sex. After witnessing these abuses, Hefner, along with people who had been detained and several other guards, reported them on radio and television news programs and prompted government investigations that did not bear fruit until the Clinton administration.[104] According to Hefner, it took so many years for the abuses he described to come to light because of the reluctance of well-paid guards in an impoverished area to step forward and risk losing their jobs, aided by higher-up officials wishing to keep allegations of such abuses quiet. Even then, civil detention standards remained uncodified in law, effectively unenforceable, and such abuses continue—now systemic and routine. Similar to reform efforts that have failed to improve conditions inside jails and prisons over the years, the INS's culture of impunity reveals the futility of ongoing reform efforts to improve detention conditions.

Total War

The Immigration and Naturalization Service has become
therefore, the domestic extension of the Total War
waged against the people of Central America.

Sanctuary: A Justice Ministry, 1986 booklet

In October 1981, Border Patrol agents pulled over a car carrying four adults— two US citizens and two Salvadorans—at a traffic checkpoint in Miami, Oklahoma. The four were traveling to participate in a speaking tour of colleges and universities across the Northeast organized by CISPES and the Revolutionary Communist Youth Brigade. Even though the Salvadorans had filed for political asylum upon their arrival in the United States and their cases were pending, the Border Patrol arrested the four. The federal government charged

Detention as Counterinsurgency

the two Salvadoran men for being in the country illegally while charging the two US citizens, Carol Jeane Tsuji and Manuel Compos-Sevilla, with "felony transport of illegal aliens" and a possible five-year prison sentence. All charges were eventually dropped after a trial that drew "nuns, lawyers, Black revolutionary nationalists, youth and others" together in solidarity, which received nationwide media coverage. During the trial, letters, telegrams, and phone calls protesting the charges flooded the US prosecutor's office. The Youth International Party newspaper *Overthrow* reported, "The U.S. government is determined to decisively deliver a clear-cut and forceful blow to revolutionary immigrants and anyone who aids or associates with them," while Tsuji's attorneys argued that the arrests were a "conspiracy by the federal government to silence the tour."[105]

Shortly after attorney Robert Kahn began working at Proyecto Libertad in Texas in 1982, he remembers the phone ringing every morning at six o'clock and then, upon answering, hearing a click and a hang-up. He filed a Freedom of Information request to obtain the FBI's file on its investigation of Proyecto, part of its larger investigation of migrant legal aid groups between 1982 and 1985. Kahn found that the FBI's monitoring of his activities directly violated a 1981 consent decree in which the FBI agreed to cease illegal spying on activities protected by the First Amendment.[106] The FBI was "gearing up for a major investigation of Salvadoran terrorism" during these years, alleging that a massive influx of Salvadoran refugees in the United States, "either on their own or with the help of members of the newly emerging Sanctuary movement— could, indeed, be a channel by which Salvadoran left-wing terrorists could be infiltrating the United States to plan a campaign of covert violence."[107] The FBI investigation did not find any evidence that Proyecto had any terrorist connections, but the US government's labeling of Salvadoran migrants and their allies as "terrorists" reveals its attempts to justify escalating retaliation against its critics. Agents of the Reagan administration's immigration and foreign policies used covert tactics—paid informants, private investigations, fear and intimidation—to wage total war against their opponents.

As president, Reagan embraced a return to the use of covert operations in domestic law enforcement. Within months of entering office, Reagan signaled this by pardoning W. Mark Felt and Edward Miller, the only FBI officials convicted of crimes in the wake of revelations of COINTELPRO operations against Black nationalist movements. In December 1981, Reagan issued Executive Order 12333, legalizing infiltration tactics in US domestic security and terrorism investigations for the first time in US history. In addition to extending this privilege to the FBI and anyone working on its behalf as a private contractor, the directive also authorized CIA "special activities" to operate anywhere "in support of national foreign policy objectives abroad."[108] In sum, the executive order effectively legalized interagency cooperation and use of military equipment and personnel in domestic counterintelligence activities. Under the leadership of Oliver North, the National Security Council would also soon orchestrate a series of break-ins and "dirty tricks" to deter opponents of Reagan's Central American policies. As Brian Glick concluded in a 1989 pamphlet for activists titled *The War at Home*, "Official secrecy has been restored."[109]

Although Alan Nelson publicly denied that an active investigation of the Sanctuary movement was underway, INS, Border Patrol, and FBI agents had been monitoring the movement closely all along. On the day of Sanctuary's unveiling in Tucson in March of 1982, John Fife recognized a man in plain clothes taking photographs outside his church as a Border Patrol agent. Fife joked to reporters about it, wondering why INS agents felt the need to attend the event in an undercover capacity.[110] That night, a second intelligence agent attended the march and ecumenical church service and reported to his superiors, "Aside from the old people, most of them looked like the anti-Vietnam war protestors of the early 1970s. In other words, political misfits." He reported that the "Frito Bandito"—the "alleged El Salvadorian wearing a black mask"—was trotted out purposefully for the cameras and concluded, "It seems that this movement is more political than religious but that a ploy is going to be Border Patrol 'baiting' . . . in order to demonstrate to the public that the U.S. government via its jack-booted gestapo Border Patrol agents think nothing of breaking down the doors of their churches to drag Jesus Christ out to be tortured and murdered. I believe that all political implications should be considered before any further action is taken toward this group."[111] Reflecting its bias, the FBI also discredited the movement by defining it as political rather than religious in its counterinsurgent harassment campaign against Sanctuary activists.

In the summer of 1982, FBI agent Frank Varelli created a "Terrorist Photo Album" as part of an investigation called Operation Pipil. The Indigenous Pipil people of El Salvador are a campesino class who were subjected to state-sponsored ethnocide in the 1930s in response to their protests against growing inequality—an irony likely not lost on the FBI. Varelli compiled around 700 entries, ranging from people with known ties to Soviet bloc agents to political and religious activists, members of US Congress, Mexican president José López Portillo, and former US ambassador to El Salvador Robert White for having "terrorist tendencies." Varelli admitted to Congress in 1987 that the

FBI had been working to infiltrate CISPES since 1980. He testified, "In reality, the album frequently contained the names of people who simply opposed the Central America policies of President Reagan." One album entry was for Sister Peggy Healy, a major Sanctuary figure convicted in 1986 of violating immigration laws by sheltering undocumented Salvadoran migrants. Varelli's notes read, "She is a nun with the Maryknoll Order. . . . It is a community of priests, brothers, sisters and lay people that are supposed to be spreading the gospel all over the world. Instead they are front runners in preaching the Marxist-Leninist 'Liberation Theology.' . . . Operating under the banner of 'human rights violations,' they are operating against the U.S. government."[112] The Reagan administration's preoccupation with El Salvador as a site of political subversion fit into its larger imagining of a broader threat of Latin American migration.

Over time, the INS shifted its view on making Sanctuary-related arrests. By 1984, Alan Nelson asserted, "Religious affiliation or motives cannot insulate anyone from the consequences which flow from a violation of other criminal or civil laws. . . . No special exemption from prosecution can be tolerated." And so, in 1984 the INS began arresting Sanctuary refugees and those assisting them; the first were Stacy Merkt and Jack Elder, Sanctuary workers in Texas. In 1985, the INS launched Operation Sojourner, sending paid informants into Sanctuary communities.[113] Two informants, going by the names Jesús Cruz and Salomón Delgado, attended Tucson strategy meetings and Bible study classes, surreptitiously taping hours of Sanctuary movement discussions. The *Nation* revealed that Cruz and Delgado, whose real name was Graham, had worked as paid informants for the INS after being arrested for organizing a smuggling ring. Graham had long been involved in the Arizona farmworkers' movement and had a reputation for offering prostitutes to farmworkers. As Graham and Cruz infiltrated Sanctuary, they promised migrants social security cards and coached them to reveal details about their movements to INS officials in their asylum cases. The INS denied any knowledge of this.[114]

In 1986, the US government brought a seventy-one-count criminal indictment against sixteen leaders of the Sanctuary movement from Arizona and Mexico, including Jim Corbett, John Fife, Mary K. Espinoza, and Franciscan sister Darlene Nicgorski, culminating in a high-profile series of trials in Arizona. The government's evidence hinged upon informant tapes; prosecutor Donald Reno argued that because they discussed "criminal activity" rather than religion, their content was not protected under the First Amendment. However, most of the tapes' content was not incriminating. For example, Cruz almost taped Corbett discussing bringing Pilar Martinez's sister-in-law Elba

SANCTUARY BREAK-INS

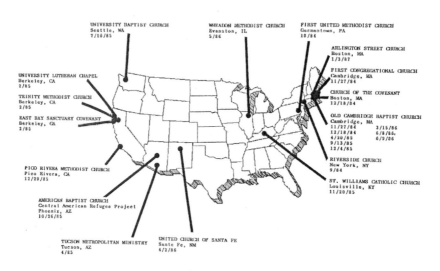

A map showing the locations of twenty-three break-ins occurring at sixteen sanctu-ary-participating church locations across the United States between 1984 and 1987. University of Washington Libraries Special Collections, University Baptist Church Sanctuary Movement Records, 5346–001, B2 F4.

over the border from Mexico, but his tape ran out before he could capture the details.[115] During the trial there was an escalating series of break-ins and harassments at Sanctuary churches and at the defendants' and other organiz-ers' homes. Between 1984 and 1986, churches were broken into twenty-three times in twelve cities across the country. Garrett Brown of Old Cambridge Baptist Church in Massachusetts, which had the highest number of break-ins, said, "Who has done this sort of thing before, and who benefits from it? The answer to those questions is the same. The government." In 1986, intruders broke into Mary K. Espinoza's home three times, only removing files. But in one instance, they set a house fire and poisoned her dog. Witnesses said they wore the khaki and camouflage-cap uniform of a mercenary group working with Nicaraguan Contras and the Border Patrol.[116] Ultimately, eight leaders were charged with alien smuggling, while the rest were acquitted or given brief house arrest.

The Reagan administration's total war on Sanctuary also included a shift in INS approaches to the media and managing its public relations. The INS closely monitored its image in the press, keeping the attorney general apprised

Detention as Counterinsurgency

of controversies and potentially negative publicity. The INS also monitored and restricted the media and public's view into detention. INS's *Deportation Officer Handbook* from the early 1980s mandated that news representatives who wished to visit any facility must first make an appointment in advance and then obtain approval in writing from the district director. Before any interview would be approved, the handbook required, "detainees must authorize the INS to respond to comments made in the interview and to release information to the news media relative to the detainees['] comments."[117] In other words, the INS had the final word coming out of the detention center.

The growing visibility of dissent remained a central concern of administration officials. However, the INS worked to maintain public support, banking on the widespread appeal of immigration restriction. In May 1985, a year before the Sanctuary trial, the INS held a Public Affairs Conference in Glynco, Georgia. It issued a thick *Media Relations Policy Guidance* booklet for district directors and all attendees. An effort to streamline INS messaging, the booklet provided press guidance for media inquiries about Sanctuary, arguments in favor of contract detention facilities, and rules for media visits to detention centers meant to prevent "in-depth interviews" or "long conversations with any detainee." A presentation by Seattle district director James B. Turnage titled "El Salvadorans in Seattle—and Telling Our Story" reveals a unique view into INS culture and its turn toward public relations. Acknowledging that secrecy had long worked in the INS's favor, Turnage began, "Throughout most of our history, this Service has shied away from public exposure. Our tendency was to keep our good deeds, as well as bad, within the confines of this agency. In short, we were a secret. But . . . public exposure—getting *our* point across to the masses by letting them see the incoming tide of illegal aliens—could aid our cause." He detailed his recent media work, giving interviews and debating University Baptist Church pastor Donovan Cook on *Newsline*. He recalled, "The opposition knew how to turn a phrase, was photogenic, and instead of giving the appearance of a quiche eater, turned out to be a former Stanford quarterback!" Throughout, he emphasized the belief that the majority of Americans supported the INS's mission, the "side of truth and reason," and cited information provided by the restrictionist, white nationalist Federation for American Immigration Reform. Turnage concluded, "We have to sell ourselves and our program or face drastic, unpalatable changes—even extinction through reorganization or consolidation. . . . In summary, our story will be told. If we don't do it, our adversaries will."[118]

In 1987, Donald Reno, the US attorney prosecuting the Sanctuary case, moved to Seattle. He did not reveal details of his new assignment to the press, only saying he worked for top INS officials. He would be the first named special assistant federal prosecutor in the United States, a position created in 1984. Thirty Sanctuary activists staged a party outside of his office to greet his arrival with balloons, a replica key to a local church, a cake reading "Welcome Donald M. Reno," and questions. One activist asked, "Why is he here? What will he be doing? Who sent him? Is he here to intimidate us or start a grand jury?" Reno would not meet with them, telling a reporter instead, "Sanctuary is over. Sanctuary is history. In my opinion the movement is virtually dead."[119] However, movement activity continued into the 1990s, when the civil wars in El Salvador and Guatemala came to an end. Renny Golden reflects, "Some would say it plateaued; some would say it ended. We were all supposed to be really scared. It wasn't over for us."[120]

Unfinished Revolutions

Those mothers of the disappeared walked
through fire. I don't know what else I believed then
but I believed in them.

"Gamblers," Renny Golden, 2017

This chapter has explored inside-outside resistance to immigration detention—positing detention itself as a counterinsurgent set of practices and narratives of erasure and denial. As abuses in detention continued—embedded in detention's very design—dehumanizing conditions served to justify detention's expansion, adding new layers to the carceral palimpsest. Systemic violence and the suppression of truth in detention spaces have also reverberated beyond prison walls to target and label allies as enemies of the state.

On his participation in the peace movement during the early years of the Reagan administration, Van Gosse wrote, "Many people remember that period ruefully, as one of 'triumphalism,' the unquestioned conviction that Washington was incapable of framing an effective counter-insurgency strategy."[121] In the face of mounting contestations inside and outside of detention, Reagan era revanchism was marked by an increasing reliance on secrecy, denial, and covert tactics in pursuit of foreign and domestic policy aims. Even so, there were alternatives. Revolutionary factions of the Central American peace and Sanctuary movements, as well as Jesse Jackson's 1984 presidential campaign, rallied opposition under a banner of broader resistance to US imperialism. Indeed, Jackson's Rainbow Coalition enunciated an "emancipatory internationalism" never before seen in mainstream US politics. At the time, Cornel West commented that Jackson's presidential campaign presented the "most important challenge to the American left since the emergence of the civil rights movement."[122]

Gosse identified another problem that plagued solidarity: "The refusal to listen to the representatives of the people doing the struggling." Even if well-intentioned, expressions of white saviorism can result in disproportionate state retaliation against communities of color and the reproduction of social hierarchies and inequality. Questions of whose stories get to be told and how, what forms resistance should take, and what it means to be in solidarity plagued movement organizers, and still remain. Acknowledging the persistence of "chauvinist sentimentality" or "illusions of altruism" among US participants in the solidarity movement, Van Gosse reflected on what solidarity meant to him: "This is where solidarity begins, in accepting and sharing responsibility, in beginning to learn instead of to instruct, in staking out one's own agency as an imperial citizen while imagining unbounded Americas."[123]

Ultimately, migrants were final, even if conflicted, arbiters of their stories and visage. Truth remained a prevailing theme in migrant testimonies, called upon as a shared value across Sanctuary spaces. As Juan, a Salvadoran addressing churchgoers in San Francisco, related, "I still have plenty of fear. But I am more afraid to remain silent. My fear here is nothing compared to that of my friends and family back home.... You have beautiful concepts here. You believe in truth. The people react when they hear the truth."[124] During Pilar's media tour after her and Elba's detention, she continued to cover her face with a bandanna and never allowed photographs of her or her family that could be identifying. Speaking of her arrest, she observed that the United States was not as free as she initially thought because of retaliation against protesters. "I've been treated well by the people but not by the government," she said. "The soldiers [INS] looked for weapons in my apartment. The only weapon we have is the truth." Although Elba and Pilar refused to testify in the Sanctuary trial and were ordered deported, they both eventually won their asylum cases.[125]

When asked for recommendations for US citizen allies of the Sanctuary movement, a member of the Hernandez family living in sanctuary in Olympia, Washington, stated it simply: "If I am more free, the American people will know more of the truth."[126]

Somos los Abandonados

Prison Uprisings and the Architectures of Erasure

Dear Citizens of the United States, Thank You for your
Hopes and Prayers. We do not want to blow it!

Banner at Oakdale detention center placed by Mariel Cubans, 1987

A few minutes after Tom Brokaw announced on *NBC Nightly News* on November 20, 1987, that the United States and Cuba had signed an agreement for Mariel Cubans in Bureau of Prisons custody to be repatriated to Cuba, a Cuban man detained at a federal detention center in Oakdale, Louisiana, walked into the cafeteria and hurled an empty food tray at a service worker's head. He proclaimed it an act of protest, a cue prompting other Cubans in the dining hall to throw food, trays, and silverware against the walls. Guards subdued the disturbance. That night, while all was quiet, Cubans planned their rebellion. The next day, rumors circulated that they were planning an escape. The BOP moved all female staff out of the facility, fearing they would be raped, and called in the El Paso Border Patrol Tactical Team for assistance. After dinner, 250 Cubans gathered in the yard, brandishing homemade clubs and knives. They began chanting, "Somos los abandonados [We are the abandoned ones]!" Over the next several hours, they clashed with guards, the Border Patrol Tactical Team, and FBI snipers; set fire to the library and administrative buildings; and took twenty-eight hostages. By 9:00 p.m. they had total control over the prison.

Two days later, a small group of Cubans held at the Atlanta federal penitentiary set fires and began taking hostages, and eventually took over the entire prison, in a similar pattern. One Cuban was shot and killed by a guard in the only fatality during what would become the longest dual-prison takeover in US history, lasting until negotiations came to an end in Atlanta on December 3. During the siege, family members of detained Cubans appealed to the government and the public for compassion. One wife told the Associated Press, "I talked with my husband yesterday, and he said he'd rather die than go back to Cuba for no reason. I know many men in that prison. I came over with them in 1980 and this was bound to happen sooner or later." Another family member said, "That place is nothing more than a concentration camp. . . . They just picked these people up off the streets and brought them here." Ray Bourgeois, recently released after serving a six-month sentence at Oakdale for protesting US policy in Central America, told the *Washington Post* of recent Cuban suicide attempts there. "You could feel the tension building. Most of the Cubans had been detained indefinitely in this place that they thought was a strange jungle." Meanwhile, federal officials told the media that attempts to escape from immigration detention were rare and "the rebellion of the sort that erupted here this weekend is even rarer."[1]

The US government's assertion that rebellions in detention were rare was a lie. The Oakdale and Atlanta uprisings of 1987 marked only the most explosive flashpoint in the tragic saga of Mariel Cubans who were subjected to indefinite detention throughout the decade. Although immediately sparked by the news of impending deportations, the uprisings were a culminating response to the exceptional forms of violence—legal, physical, and psychic—inflicted upon Mariel Cubans by the US government since their arrival in the United States. No mere act of anarchy, the prison takeovers were instead a highly organized public plea. During negotiations, Cubans in control of both prisons ran them in a coordinated, theatrical manner, staging threats of violence to gain media access and address the US public directly. Newly available Department of Justice (DOJ) records detailing the negotiations process reveal how the US government's continued racial profiling, antipathy, and disregard of Mariel Cuban life exacerbated the crisis. Although the standoff ended peacefully with a promise to halt deportations and provide individual case review, the

INS would largely renege on this promise. Mariel Cubans were, once again, dispersed across the US prison landscape and forgotten.

The uprisings were also a catalyzing event, leading to a reinscription of state retaliation in detention architectures as exemplified in Oakdale's resurrection as a facility for "criminal aliens" and a centralized deportation hub, buttressed by new laws affirming crimmigration by decade's end. This final chapter traces the interweaving trajectories of the US government's indefinite detention of Mariel Cubans leading up to the uprisings of 1987 and the Reagan administration's attempts to establish long-term and contingency detention sites in fulfillment of its Mass Immigration Emergency Plan. These included the construction of Oakdale as a model "mixed-use" INS and BOP facility and the adoption of private prison contracting. The extraordinary forms of violence inflicted upon Mariel Cubans and the afterlives of resistance and retaliation became embedded in these new iterations of incarceration, revealing the lasting legacies of Reagan's Cold War on immigrants.

The story of Oakdale, told most dramatically in its literal destruction and rebuilding after the Mariel Cuban uprisings, exemplifies the coalescence of Reagan's carceral palimpsest. First, Oakdale's establishment as a model facility provided the INS with a new raison d'être, boosting agency funding, pride, and purpose. Second, the administration touted community support for the facility and Oakdale's remote location as an ideal resolution to the dual crises of prison overcrowding and the indefinite detention of Mariel Cubans. Finally, the facility's rapid evolution from its stated intent as a "processing center" for undocumented migrants, to its role of solely housing Mariel Cubans, and then, after the uprisings and facility's near-destruction, to its repurposing as a facility for "criminal aliens" evidences the dissolution of a refugee/criminal distinction and the normalization and entrenchment of routine violence in ongoing, overlapping processes of erasure.

This story also charts a rhetorical transformation accompanying new architectures of detention as neoliberal language obscured processes of retaliation and erasure required to construct new detention sites. As the Justice Department worked to convince the public that prisons were self-sufficient operations that would boost local economies, and as DOJ officials debated the crisis of prison overcrowding in terms of budgets and "bed space," "beds" became a proxy for "bodies," masking the human cost. Recast in humanitarian, neoliberal terms of the post–civil rights era, white-washed prison boosterism and private contracting were sold as a "modern," "clean," and "recession-proof" industry to emerging Sunbelt economies. These moves also ushered in a shift in INS rhetoric and purpose.

Budgets and Bed Space

Reagan's commitment to criminalizing migration, coupled with the US government's indefinite detention of Mariel Cubans, exacerbated a growing "crisis" of prison overcrowding, creating a feedback loop justifying the carceral system's expansion more broadly. The Mass Immigration Emergency Plan, the attorney general's mandate for expanding contingency detention space, also called for new structures of mass detention. Yet it left open the question of who should be responsible for migrant detention—the INS, the Bureau of Prisons, local and county jails, or a private entity. These pressures, as well as resistance to detention construction from across the political spectrum, facilitated hasty solutions and invisibility as the administration utilized prison space where it already existed while carving out new spaces for detention where it could. This resulted in a haphazard network of all of the above facility types—a carceral palimpsest, still in existence, of new detention practices layered atop and alongside existing ones.

Resistance to the administration's efforts to expand the detention system came not only from pro-migrant sectors on the left, the Central American peace movement, or the Sanctuary movement. The battle over siting a long-term detention facility reveals a different kind of resistance—this time from xenophobic US communities. As the INS and the BOP sought an ideal location for their new detention site, they also sought short-term solutions in temporary tent and private contract "turnkey" facilities. Contestations leading to the selection of Oakdale in 1983, the same year the administration also embraced private prison contracting, illustrate how these roads converged. Private contract facilities emerged out of these crisis conditions, yet implementation did not occur smoothly, exposing the precarity of Reagan's detention plans.[2] Assessing the administration's search for emergency solutions also reveals pushback and incongruencies within the state—cracks and fissures in the architecture—creating new possibilities for resistance.

Contingency planning became one rationale for ballooning INS budgets in the early 1980s. At the advent of the Mariel boatlift, many veteran INS officials actually resigned in frustration, expressing concern that prolonged migrant processing and detention would spell the death of the agency by drawing resources away from its bread-and-butter central mission of cracking down on undocumented workers. Instead, the Reagan administration's renewed commitment to detention breathed new life into the agency. The INS effectively leveraged the issue of bed space during congressional budget hearings to secure increasing funding in the years after Mariel. Between 1975 and 1985, detention funds increased almost fifteen-fold, from $2.5 to $36.5 million. In 1983, the INS's overall budget broke $1 billion; in 1986, the agency requested an increase to $1.6 billion with the construction of the Oakdale facility as a main justification.[3] By 1988, detention capacity across all INS and private contract facilities was 4,200 under "normal" conditions and 9,200 under "emergency" conditions, thus making detention during the Reagan era a growth industry for the INS overall.[4]

Mariel continued to serve as another rationale for INS budgeting, especially as the OMB continued to question Reagan's new detention policies. When the Office of Management and Budget recommended INS budget cuts in 1985, INS commissioner Alan Nelson appealed to Reagan's new attorney general, Edwin Meese. Nelson acknowledged that budget cuts were a reality across the DOJ but asked that they not be applied to the agency's detention plans, especially for the construction of Oakdale. "I do not believe we should turn back the clock on the progress this agency has made," he argued, listing the INS's contributions to national defense, detention and deportation, public health, the War on Drugs, and litigation. He concluded that funding for Oakdale in particular "must be restored," citing the collapse of US-Cuba repatriation agreements and the continued need to detain Mariel Cuban "criminals."[5]

Mariel Cuban repatriation took center stage in debates over prison budgets and bed space in the early 1980s. US-Cuba prisoner exchange negotiations during these years also paralleled recurrent Mariel Cuban unrest in detention. The attorney general routinely updated Congress on efforts to negotiate a repatriation agreement with Cuba as "the only long-term solution for about 6,000, or more," Mariel Cubans, "many of whom are in custodial institutions, and who *exacerbate the prison problem* [emphasis added]."[6] In 1987, when the Oakdale and Atlanta uprisings began, 3,800 Cubans were in federal custody, with 1,050 at Oakdale, over 1,000 at Atlanta, and others in smaller numbers at sixty other jails and prisons across the country. In the seven years since the boatlift, around 2,500 had been detained indefinitely in federal custody. In addition, around 3,000 more had been arrested and re-incarcerated after resettlement, a result of heightened policing and surveillance of this migrant group nationwide. This trend affected men like Hector, described by one legal advocate as "friendless, black, and very much alone." Hector was paroled after the boatlift but then diagnosed with paranoid schizophrenia and accused of trying to stab a police officer. He told the legal advocate he was sleeping on the street, with a knife in his pocket, when police officers accosted him. In a hearing after the uprisings, Hector told the Border Patrol agent serving as a

Prison Uprisings and the Architectures of Erasure

judge, "I don't know why I'm here." When the agent told him that he tried to stab a police officer, Hector whispered, "God knows I didn't."[7]

The United States had been attempting to deport its list of those detained indefinitely and deemed "hard-core" and "undesirable" since the end of the Mariel boatlift in 1980. Negotiations to exchange Mariel Cubans with US citizens imprisoned in Cuba on political grounds had been ongoing yet eventually failed due to diplomatic breakdowns. The Carter administration nearly reached an agreement to return Mariel Cubans in US federal custody to Cuba by January 1981, but once Reagan took office all communications with Cuba halted. A stalemate continued as the US government refused to accept former Cuban political prisoners unless Cuba would accept Mariel Cubans in return.[8] Talks resumed in 1982, until US forces captured and detained nearly 800 Cuban nationals in the invasion of Grenada in 1983. Members of US Congress saw this as an opportunity to return imprisoned Mariel Cubans. Florida representative Bill McCollum wrote to Reagan two days after the invasion: "The circumstances of the Cubans in Grenada present an ideal opportunity to return to Cuba at least the 1,000 or so Marielito criminals in the Atlanta penitentiary." He issued a press release and obtained signatures of over 100 House members in support within two hours. Florida senator Lawton Chiles led a similar effort, writing in a telegram, "We now have the leverage to force the Castro regime to receive those Cuban criminals" and to "rid ourselves of this problem." As a result, the Senate tacked on an amendment to a public debt increase bill requiring Reagan to prioritize repatriating Mariel Cubans in negotiations with Cuba after Grenada.[9] Attempts at negotiations continued. Meanwhile, the indefinite detention of Cubans in US prisons became increasingly explosive.

Although the Reagan administration would not admit it, Jesse Jackson's visit to Cuba during his 1984 presidential campaign opened the way for the resumption of talks resulting in a US-Cuba "Repatriation List" agreement later that year. Although Jackson was a critic of Reagan's hard-line foreign policy and a champion for detained Haitians and Central Americans, he supported the deportation of Mariel Cubans in his negotiations for the release of US political prisoners in Cuba and normalizing US-Cuba relations overall. In a telegram to Reagan sent after his trip, Jackson relayed that Castro was ready to discuss a "Mariel prisoner exchange immediately" and that Castro was open to negotiations "because of my trip to Cuba."[10] This is but one example of how thorny politics surrounding Mariel Cubans often excluded them from leftist advocacy on behalf of detained migrants. Reagan rebuffed Jackson, publicly calling Jackson's trip a "scandalous" and "disruptive" violation of the

Logan Act, which forbids US citizens from engaging in diplomatic relations abroad. Privately, the State Department acknowledged Jackson's trip was the "catalyst" for a repatriation agreement. US-Cuba talks resumed once again, and in December 1984, Cuba agreed to accept 2,746 Mariel Cubans and release US political prisoners. In return, the United States would raise its annual cap of Cuban immigration to 20,000 to allow for family reunification. As US negotiators dictated their list of Cubans to deport late into the night in a smoke-filled room in Manhattan, the Cubans in the room erupted in laughter when the name "Nome Hodes" was read—*no me jodes* is Spanish for "don't fuck with me." The name was clearly recorded by an unwitting INS agent screening Mariel Cuban arrivals in 1980—a humorous act of defiance, yet one that reveals the US government's lack of knowledge, care, and accurate record-keeping of Mariel Cuban identities and histories.[11]

Indeed, the exceptional legal exclusion and violent conditions inflicted upon Mariel Cubans prompted waves of resistance inside detention that ultimately led to the 1987 uprisings. Cubans were also not without advocates on the outside as their situation drew support from religious and civil rights organizations as time went on. Still considered "entrants" not technically admitted to the United States, Mariel Cubans who were deemed excludable and detained indefinitely had even fewer due process rights within the already restrictive world of civil immigration detention.

Cuban attempts to challenge their indefinite detention in US courts also came up short. Some district judges, including Marvin Shoob in Atlanta, sided with Cubans to rule indefinite detention unconstitutional in the early 1980s. However, instead of releasing them, Shoob ordered the attorney general to institute a review process. Not surprisingly, the INS's review process was highly flawed and its paperwork often inaccurate. The INS also successfully appealed Shoob's ruling in the Eleventh Circuit in 1986, reaffirming the legality of indefinite detention. The Supreme Court refused to take up the question of equal protection rights for Mariel Cubans, marking an end of the road for legal appeals and leaving the status of Mariel Cubans unresolved for another two decades. Throughout the 1980s, many Cubans determined eligible for release by the INS remained imprisoned, resulting in what Cubans called "pocket freedom"—freedom on paper but not in practice.[12] Other reasons Cubans were not released included a lack of sponsors on the outside and a lack of space in halfway houses, exacerbated by Reagan-era public funding cuts. This fueled an ongoing sense of betrayal and rage, directed especially at the INS.

New laws criminalizing migration passed during Reagan's second term reinforced Reagan's new detention trends. The 1986 Immigration Reform and Control Act (IRCA), most known for its granting of so-called amnesty to those currently residing in the United States since 1982 without documentation, ultimately legalized the status of 2.7 million people. However, "amnesty" is also a misnomer. As its name implies, IRCA also contained less-publicized provisions expanding immigration enforcement—wedding reform with "control" as a requisite logic guiding future immigration legislation. Migrants had to demonstrate they had earned the right to legalize their status through onerous residency, work, and English requirements. The law provided for a 50 percent increase in the Border Patrol's budget, and workplace raids spiked after IRCA's passage, all inflicting fear and trauma on migrant communities. Meanwhile, the law's employer sanction provisions went largely unenforced.[13]

An INS internal procedures handbook interpreting the intent of IRCA's enforcement provisions connected immigration control to the issue of prison overcrowding: "An item of concern for years is the lack of detention bed space and funding for the INS Detention and Deportation Program. It is *advantageous for the INS* and an efficient use of tax dollars to commence the lengthy deportation and exclusion process against criminal aliens who are serving sentences" (emphasis added). It concluded, "It appears to be the intent of Congress . . . to take steps to alleviate the nationwide problem of prison overcrowding by addressing expeditiously the large illegal alien population encountered in corrections systems in many states." This reveals how expanding migrant detention through criminalization was a recognized boon to the agency.[14]

"A Modern Facility for Aliens"

Mass immigration by Cuban and Haitian citizens to the
United States in the 1980s presented the Immigration and
Naturalization Service with detention responsibilities
that were new and unique to the agency.

US Department of Justice, 1982

When the Reagan administration closed Fort Chaffee in February 1982 and transferred remaining Cubans to federal penitentiaries, the *New York Times* reported that the fort's closure left the adjacent small town of Fort Smith, Arkansas, "with a touch of xenophobia." The town had rejected an offer from the government to make Fort Chaffee a permanent site for migrant detention, despite official projections that passing up the offer would ultimately cost the town $50 million a year. Community leaders apparently resented Fort Chaffee's feast-or-famine impact on the local economy, the camp's poor administration and security measures, and the notoriety Mariel Cuban detention brought Fort Smith. On the decision, Mayor Jack Freeze said, "Our people are unique in that they don't want to get involved in anything other than being happy.... Quality of life is more important to our people than making a dollar."[15]

The indefinite detention of Mariel Cubans in US prisons—the Reagan administration's "interim" solution to demands to close Fort Chaffee—remained at the center of immigration and prison policy making in coming years. As the administration stayed committed to expanding the number of people subjected to criminalization and to detaining asylum-seekers, the INS sought more detention bed space. Prison overcrowding also stymied the Justice Department's directive to locate permanent sites for long-term detention in fulfillment of the Mass Immigration Emergency Plan. Not only did Mariel contribute to the larger issue of prison overcrowding, but communities directly referenced Mariel Cubans as they rejected government proposals to build new detention sites. In its search for an ideal site, the DOJ emphasized cost, flexibility, and contingency. However, community resistance rooted primarily in xenophobia led the administration to abandon its preferred sites in favor of the more remote choice of Oakdale, Louisiana.[16] Internal communications and community contestations reveal the administration's priorities and detention's punitive turn during this time, as broad community support for immigration control conjoined with economic perceptions to drive prison expansion in the US Sunbelt.

Similar to the resistance it had encountered when trying to relocate Mariel Cubans, as discussed in chapter 2, the DOJ faced multiple hurdles in siting a new facility. As communities from Texas to Virginia debated, and ultimately rejected, a permanent detention site, their arguments for and against detention reveal two sides of a coin. While rarely challenging the logic and purpose of detention, opposition was most often articulated in "not in my backyard" terms of proximity to undesirable migrant populations. Economically depressed rural communities like Oakdale, however, embraced prison-building as a "clean," recession-resilient industry, even adopting a humanitarian rationale that contradicted the unfolding realities of detention's increasingly punitive conditions and crimmigration trends. Arguments for detention also reflected the malleability of migrant detention's ambivalent status as the DOJ's model detention site was simultaneously pitched as a prison and not a prison and simultaneously humane and tough on crime. Ultimately, the Justice Department upheld its prototype, mixed-use facility as a point of pride as long-term detention infused the INS with new purpose.

When considering alternatives to Fort Chaffee, Attorney General William French Smith outlined three options: continue using Fort Chaffee, which would exacerbate existing political dissent but reduce "local citizen concerns in other areas"; locate an existing military site similar to Fort Chaffee, which the secretary of defense opposed; or acquire new types of facilities, such as a contract facility being offered by Valley Industrial Park near Glasgow, Montana. Smith admitted, "Even if the facilities and funds were available, the operational difficulties caused by decentralized facilities would preclude an effective and cost efficient program."[17] Transportation and building costs, efficiency, and proximity to existing BOP facilities and to the border were the DOJ's priorities for choosing a detention site. Associate Attorney General Rudy Giuliani also argued that local communities would be more likely to support detention centers adjacent to existing prison facilities. Indicating growing interagency cooperation as well as detention's new punitive intent, Smith directed the INS and the BOP to work together to select a site in the spring of 1982.[18]

If local communities were opposed, entrepreneurs in the transitional program and security industries seemed eager to capitalize on detention expansion. In December 1981, a private consortium pitched the "modern facilities" of Valley Industrial Park (VIP), a former air force base in Montana, to the Reagan administration. VIP's pitch listed why Glasgow would be the "most logical location for an Alien Processing Center," including the polled approval of local officials and the public, a lease agreement ready to be signed with the INS, and "turnkey" facilities ready to hold over 2,500 people that were superior in quality to Krome, Fort Chaffee, or Fort Allen, Puerto Rico. The pitch countered the Carter administration's prior rejection of Glasgow as a permanent site the year before as a "totally inappropriate place to house people from the Caribbean." Instead, VIP claimed, "During the time the base was operational, minorities were present in significant numbers and found no problem with the climate." Additionally, "isolation of the facility has one definite advantage, in that it tends to make the facility secure. If an escape is attempted, the open prairie, good visibility, and large distances make apprehension most certain." An isolated geographic location was more secure, they argued—and less visible to the public.[19]

The administration took VIP's proposal under serious consideration, compelled by the idea of a contract facility's flexibility—including in detaining shifting populations. The INS planned for Glasgow to hold three populations: Cubans needing rehabilitation and "antisocial" Cubans from Fort Chaffee, together about 550, with the remaining capacity of 1,150 to be filled by Haitians or other nationalities for whom space could not be found elsewhere.[20] VIP's proposal was attractive to DOJ officials as it offered "a total turnkey package provided by a private sector consortium" and "a primary objective of removing the entrants from government dependence."[21] However, like legal battles in Florida and Puerto Rico over Haitian detention, litigation threatened these efforts—this time by Native Americans of the adjacent Fort Peck Reservation claiming the INS had not filed an environmental impact statement. The INS tried to avoid a lawsuit by meeting with local Assiniboine and Sioux leaders. In the event that "educational efforts" did not succeed, INS's Land and Natural Resources division planned to sidestep environmental laws through an exemption for detaining Cuban/Haitian entrants written into the 1980 Refugee Education Assistance Act. INS litigation counsel reasoned, "If, at a later date, INS wants to introduce other nationalities into the facility, it would be relatively easy to argue that the environmental impact of substituting, say, a Nicaraguan for a Haitian is zero, and thus no EIS [environmental impact statement] would be required for a change in nationalities once the facility is operational."[22] Although the administration ultimately passed on VIP's proposal, the INS would continue evoking this exemption in detention efforts. Giuliani's appreciation for the bid expressed the administration's desire to "develop a modern facility for aliens" and the attractiveness of a "quick start-up time," but colocation with a BOP facility was more of a priority.[23]

After Fort Chaffee closed, the INS and the BOP narrowed their list of locations under consideration for a permanent detention site to McAlester and El Reno, both in Oklahoma; Petersburg, Virginia; and Oakdale, Louisiana. The INS had rejected its first choice, La Tuna, Texas, due to "historical difficulties with Texas"—referring to prior outrage expressed after Cubans and Haitians were transferred to the state. In short time, however, migrant detention would proliferate in Texas despite xenophobia expressed by Reagan's political allies. While the BOP preferred El Reno and Petersburg because BOP facilities already operated there, the INS favored Oakdale because of "extremely strong congressional and community support" and because it was "geographically well-situated for its purposes."[24]

Although early discussions were favorable, public opposition struck McAlester and Petersburg from the list—revealing Fort Chaffee's continuing fallout. Reflecting high levels of racism and xenophobia, representatives from each city expressed their constituents' concerns, including crime, disease, civil unrest, and strains on social services and public education. In both locales, city leaders included specific references to Cuban detention at Fort Chaffee in their general concerns about the impact of the presence of migrants in their communities. A resolution from Petersburg and surrounding cities stated, "Based upon the real experience of other detention centers, it appears that many illegal aliens have been detained for durations extending from months to years. Usually, relatives or friends of the detainees move to close proximity of the center so they can be near them. Often this creates an additional financial and social burden to the community."[25] Attorney General Smith tried to assuage xenophobia by touting the economic benefits of detention. He assured leaders that a detention center would have little impact on the local community and school system, would have "ample security," and would bring an estimated 500 local hires, or even more in emergency circumstances. "In virtually all respects the processing center would be a self-sufficient operation, though relying to a significant degree upon private contractors to deliver goods and services on the premises."[26] Notable here is Smith's nod to neoliberal notions of "self-sufficiency" and characterization of migrant "processing" as an economic boon.

These themes echoed again in El Reno, Oklahoma. However, arguments in opposition and in favor both affirmed the need to contain and expel migrants. At a congressional hearing in the summer of 1982, El Reno citizens and public leaders debated the pros and cons of building a detention center, revealing an overall neglect of migrant welfare in favor of economic concerns on all sides. Wade B. Houk of the Bureau of Prisons spoke first, reasoning that detained immigrants were not "criminals"; they just did not have papers. "You have probably read about the violence associated with some alien detainee groups," he said, "possibly some of the Cubans currently in detention at the U.S. Penitentiary in Atlanta, Georgia. It is clear that these detainees who have been deemed nonreleasable by the Attorney General would not be held in the type of detention facility proposed for El Reno." As Oakdale's future would show, Houk's statement was inaccurate. He also claimed that comparisons to Fort Chaffee were not valid, as Fort Chaffee was a "temporary processing camp run by the State Department, not a permanent detention center" run by the BOP and the INS.[27]

Of twelve citizens who testified, four women who opposed the facility were unconvinced. Dolores Sanders expressed sympathy for Mexicans who were "always deported," but this did not extend to other migrant groups. She asked, "Why is it that the Cubans, the Haitians are all brought into this country and considered legal, aided, given aid eventually. The Mexican comes in here the best way he can.... I cannot understand why we have to hunt him down like an animal, why he has to go back into the conditions that he comes from when we bring other people into this country to live here in a great land and we give them everything." Reflecting a misperception of public benefits and resentment toward migrant groups perceived as unworthy, Sanders's comments revealed a racial animus underlying economic concerns. Similarly, Sylvia Robbins said, "We need our policemen to get out there and make it better and get these illegals and delinquents, straighten what we've got right here instead of bringing more in and putting a greater burden on our community."[28] This contradictory logic, simultaneously supporting more and less policing resources, reflects a desire for migrant bodies to merely disappear.

Eight men in favor of the facility emphasized perceived economic benefits, as well as a faith in the "law and order" a facility would signify. First, they paraphrased fears expressed by a circulating petition against the facility: "We're going to get Fort Chaffee moved over here next week. The whole town is going to be running with dope peddlers and things like that and people are going to have to take special precautions because of the undesirable element that is going to be brought in here." Sixty-seven-year-old Del Derigo then countered these fears by appealing to El Reno's history as an already militarized detention site: "We had a center during World War II for the Italian prisoners in El Reno, for the German prisoners in El Reno; no problem.... When you've got the proper personnel controlling something, you're not going to have your problems." Faith in prisons and policing remained a common thread unifying statements both for and against the detention facility, despite accounts of INS abuse and corruption. Those in favor also appealed to visions of incarceration as a "clean" new industry. Derigo continued, "We know that this oil thing that we have here is very shortly going to depreciate.... We have got to look in the future because El Reno has to grow." Bill Copeland was so supportive of Reagan's detention policy that he called it "30 to 50 years behind time" and echoed the administration's intention of deterrence: "Somehow they will develop a philosophy to convince these people that if they want to become United States of America citizens, they must do it correctly and not by whatever means.... If we do not undertake to do something about the alien problem, there will be others who—just like Cuba, just by inundation, dumped many of their people on us."[29] Copeland's comments were met with applause. Senator Don Nickles of Oklahoma also wrote to Smith in support, concluding, "You have my full support for the Alien Detention Center because of my desire to see measures enacted which will discourage illegal immigration in our country."[30] Indeed, not all local communities protested the building of detention centers; some such as El Reno and Oakdale wholly welcomed the prospect of prison-building.

In Oakdale, a small town of 7,000 in south-central Louisiana, public support for a detention center was overwhelming. When the Justice Department indicated in April 1982 it was leaning toward El Reno, 150 telegrams from Oakdale residents flooded the attorney general's office along with congressional pleas that jobs were "desperately needed in this area."[31] Unemployment rates were at their highest since the Great Depression across the country, with Louisiana particularly hard hit. After a paper mill closed in the nearby town of Elizabeth, Oakdale's unemployment rate hovered around 25–30 percent between 1981 and 1983.[32] In Oakdale, public perceptions that a new prison would boost area employment overrode xenophobia.

Attorney General Smith's selection of Oakdale in February 1983 depended on two factors: public support and the condition that Oakdale be used as a contingency facility in fulfillment of the Mass Immigration Emergency Plan. Likely referencing Krome and Fort Chaffee, Giuliani commented, "The overwhelming community support at Oakdale means it is highly unlikely that lawsuits would be brought in an attempt to block our efforts."[33] The attorney general claimed it was a "close call" but acted on the INS's recommendation that location choice "be *tied* to an agreement that would provide for a suitable contingency site that would accommodate 2,000 to 5,000 aliens in temporary quarters."[34] When the BOP met with Oakdale officials in February 1983 to discuss details, it aimed to ensure that Oakdale would be flexible in using the site for other capacities beyond an INS processing center like Krome or El Centro—namely, as a contingency site or as a federal correctional facility. Public officials unanimously agreed to these two options in a letter of understanding: "In the event that there is a mass influx of Alien Detainees, a temporary facility may be activated at the Oakdale ADC [Alien Detention Center] within a fenced perimeter. . . . In the event there is not a sufficient population of Alien Detainees to permit utilization of the ADC, the ADC may be partially or wholly converted into a Federal correctional facility."[35] The DOJ predicted that a "tent city" erected in an emergency situation would meet opposition in El Reno but not in Oakdale, noting that Oakdale's geographic location and terrain would make it a "low-profile facility, not readily visible to area traffic."[36]

Upon Smith's announcement, the *Oakdale Journal* ran a five-inch headline in red: "WE GOT IT!!" Mayor George Mowad said, "The mood of this town changed from depression to euphoria." Mowad also distinguished detention from prison, saying migrants were "only poor people who came to this country to earn a living. They aren't criminals. The only crime they're guilty of is being born into abject poverty." Such humanitarian gesturing perhaps served to head off public xenophobia; however, the promise of jobs trumped all other rationales. In a statement to the Lower Mississippi Delta Development Commission, Mowad explained, "Rather than saying, 'Hey, we don't want it,' as most places had done . . . the more we looked into it, the more obvious the economic advantages. It is a recession-proof industry, unlike the timber industry which we have been faced with." In addition to the hundreds of public pleas sent to Reagan officials, 800 local residents attended a public town hall with the INS in the spring of 1982. Reverend Charles Soileau of Sacred Heart Church also held an all-night prayer vigil in support of the detention center. Resident John Trahan said, "Man, I tell you, it's like a blessing. Hundreds of prayers have been answered. Now I pray I can get a job there." The chairman of the Elizabeth-Oakdale Industrial Development Board also echoed Mowad: "It took 13 months of hard work and a lot of faith but now we've got a recession-proof industry."[37]

Oakdale was not without critics; a class action lawsuit in 1984 led by the ACLU and the Lawyers Committee for International Human Rights tried to block Oakdale's construction on the grounds that its remote location would limit access to legal counsel. Plaintiffs included "current and future detainees" from Afghanistan, Iran, El Salvador, Guatemala, Cuba, Honduras, and Haiti and attorneys from twelve legal aid groups. The case was dismissed as premature. Lawyer Arthur C. Helton predicted that a "vast majority" of those detained at Oakdale would be refugees from Central America and the Caribbean.[38] Reverend Ted Keating, a lawyer with Ecumenical Immigration Services who planned to establish a legal aid center for people at Oakdale, protested, "These people are utterly abandoned, innocent people ripped off the streets and put into a prison in the middle of Louisiana. This will create tremendous social needs. These people are not criminals. It's called a detention center, but it is a United States prison."[39] Interestingly, both proponents and opponents of Oakdale argued that migrants were not "criminals." However, this refrain has more often served to divide communities criminalized by the state while justifying carceral expansion overall.

Three years after the site's selection, construction at Oakdale, Louisiana, was complete. At an opening ceremony for the federal detention center on March 21, 1986, Warden Steve Schwalb addressed a crowd of 500: "Oakdale is a real proud day for a lot of people. Never before have I seen such an esprit de corps and a sense of purpose among a group of employees." After the

Prison Uprisings and the Architectures of Erasure

invocation, the presentation of the colors, music performed by the US Army band, the warden's speech, and the benediction, the dedication ceremony concluded with the band playing "God Bless America." The credits at the end of an INS video recording of the dedication ceremony read, "A Premier Mission, A New Location, A Community Asset, A Safe Humane Environment, An Opportunity for Due Process, A Self-Supporting Entity, A Career Opportunity, A Source of Pride: The Federal Detention Center, Oakdale, Louisiana."[40] This list of attributes, ostensibly coming together in the detention center for the benefit of the community and detained migrants, was instead a layering of lies.

In a sense, BOP reassurances that a new detention facility would not compare to refugee camps such as Fort Chaffee were correct; Oakdale was markedly more punitive. The first forty-six migrants detained at Oakdale arrived from El Centro on April 7, 1986: thirty men and sixteen women from Mexico and Central and South America, with twenty from El Salvador. Assistant Warden Ray Rowe relayed that the new prison was "a rather unique institution" with a mix of uses—including a "regular" capacity of 1,000 migrants, a maximum-security wing for 300 migrants with criminal records still under construction, and contingency space for tent facilities to detain over 5,000 migrants in the event of an emergency—a total capacity higher than all existing sites. The *New York Times* reported that upon arrival, migrants were "led into the handsome new prison, fingerprinted, told to shower, given new prison garb and taken to their quarters, doorless cubicles with bars on the windows. Outside the fence, two armed vehicles patrolled." Rowe said migrants would be given a recreational program, prison work for eleven to thirty-eight cents an hour, and Spanish lessons. However, in a move reflecting detention's increasingly punitive shift in the Reagan era, "we will not give them lessons in English. That only equips them to be better aliens."[41] Fort Chaffee, by contrast, provided English lessons to Cubans. A DOJ draft press release from the date of Oakdale's selection, February 11, 1983, originally stated that the new facility was part of the administration's "program to detain excludable aliens and to ensure their ultimate deportation." Before final release, the words "their ultimate deportation" were replaced with "adequate enforcement of our immigration laws."[42] Although whitewashed, the underlying intention remained.

"The Ultimate Franchise": Private
Prisons in the Carceral Palimpsest

America Rodriguez [NPR]: He put in wire-reinforced windows,
   a ten-foot fence, bolted the doors, and opened for business.
Man [translated]: You can bathe here. Over there in
   El Centro they keep us filthy, like animals.
Woman [translated]: We've heard Mexicans talking about
   the immigration prisons here and how they've been
   treated. But here it's all right. This is like a hotel.
Frank Okrand [ACLU]: It just seems to me it's quite distasteful
   philosophically. It's almost like slavery, the idea that you're
   giving control over another person's life to a private person.
Ted Nissen [Behavioral Systems Southwest]: He's got a
   mentality of the 1930s. Hospitals, mental institutions,
   dental institutions. Why is corrections left out?

"Prisons for Profit," NPR, January 31, 1984

In 1981, customs inspectors discovered twenty-six Colombian stowaways on
board the *Cartagena de Indios*, docked in the port of Houston. The INS sent
ten to the Galena Park jail and the remaining sixteen to a warehouse at 1201
Kellogg Street, home of Danner, a maritime and industrial security firm the
INS had a contract with. After the sixteen had been detained together for
two days in one small room, one of the Colombians, a twenty-four-year-old
named Ramon Garcia, tried to escape. A contract guard named William Hall
Robertson shot Ramon in the head, killing him. Robertson claimed it was
an accident, and a Harris County grand jury brought no charges. A federal
magistrate removed the Colombians from Danner's custody, and they were
all deported. The Houston chapter of the ACLU then filed a lawsuit against
the INS, Danner, and parent company E. S. Binnings on behalf of two of the
Colombians, Jesus A. Medina and Alvaro Montano, who had family in Los
Angeles. In May 1984, just one week after the first federally contracted private
prison in the world opened its doors in a Houston suburb office park, federal
judge John V. Singleton ruled in favor of Medina and Montano. Singleton declared, "Detention is a power reserved to the government and is an exclusive
prerogative of the state."[43]

That same week, another lawsuit was filed against the brand-new INS
Houston processing center on Export Plaza Drive, this time by its next-door

neighbor Imperial Interplaza II. Imperial's lawyer Joe Roady said, "The U.S. does not have the right to delegate to private persons the power to imprison people." Imperial's main concern was not migrant welfare but that the facility would bring down property values. The INS brushed off the lawsuit, claiming the new facility was not a prison but a short-term detention center where the average stay would be only three to four days. Deportation officer Clarence Putnam, who worked there, said it had dormitories rather than cells and was "much more relaxed than a prison." Roady laughed at Putnam's statement, "You'll get a good bit of argument from the aliens if you say it's not a prison." INS district director Paul O'Neill also scoffed at the lawsuit, saying, "Have you been out to look at the place? None of the buildings in the office park are as nice as ours. The facility is very attractive and low-key." Putnam added, "The first few weeks have gone remarkably smoothly."[44]

In its first year of operation, the Houston facility of the Corrections Corporation of America (CCA) was already under fire in the media after reports that a detained Salvadoran woman had been in a "catatonic trance" and in dire need of psychiatric care but was ignored for six weeks before being removed from the facility.[45] Such reporting, coupled with Judge Singleton's decision and news of Imperial's lawsuit, appeared to serve a death blow to the burgeoning private prison industry, at least according to media interpretations that believed Judge Singleton's ruling rendered private prisons illegal. In a media advisory, the INS's Office of Public Affairs reassured its employees this was not the case, explaining that Singleton had left open the question of whether the government could contract out prison functions to begin with, instead merely ruling that contract facilities had to abide by government "standards." The INS successfully appealed the decision and maintained the right to use private contracts.[46] The talking points for the agency in defense of private contract facilities listed that they were flexible, could be opened and closed quickly, and could be designed specifically for "special" groups such as asylum-seekers, minors, and females or as halfway houses for paroled Mariel Cubans. The INS also argued that private prisons were meant only for short-term detention, thereby making them more "humane."[47]

The Reagan administration's ad hoc, emergency adoption of private prison contracting in 1983 would have grave implications for the character and growth of the detention system. Appealing to efficiency, innovation, and a get-tough mentality, the early private prison industry aligned itself with dominant cultural values of the Reagan era.[48] Scholars have characterized prison boosters' imagining of the Sunbelt as a "frontier-for-the-taking" and a "blank slate upon which a prosperous future could be built."[49] Indeed, the country's first prison profiteers emerged from Reagan's Sunbelt political coalition. In 1984, the same year that the CCA (rebranded as CoreCivic since 2017) and the Wackenhut Corporation each received INS contracts to build detention centers in Houston, Texas, and Aurora, Colorado, respectively, Ted Nissen of the for-profit detention operator Behavioral Systems Southwest defended private prisons in an interview on NPR. He appealed to US history and a return to the frontier. "The first American prisons were private," he pointed out, and it was time "for private enterprise to again take over the penal system."[50] The rise of private contracting in incarceration during the Reagan era was not solely confined to migrant detention, nor has it been the prime driver of incarceration rates, but this iteration of Reagan's carceral palimpsest has produced some of the system's most violent forms of erasure—and its more invisible, but enduring, scars.

How did prison privatization gain traction during this time? The manufactured crises of crime, immigration, and prison overcrowding in the late 1970s and early 1980s—which Mariel Cubans were a central part of—supported arguments for privatization. The detention of groups labeled problematic, or nontraditional, by the state in particular also supported these arguments. As the Reagan administration favored privatization of government services more broadly, in fact encouraging experimentation with it in low-stakes settings, the INS also embraced it in this moment of crisis as a quick, if not preferable, solution.

The United States has a long history of private contracting in prison functions and an even longer history of incarceration for profit, intertwined with legacies of slavery and the convict leasing system.[51] These histories bear a significant relationship to migrant detention, which in turn provides crucial links for understanding the spread of private contracting in prisons from a local to a federal scale and from the use of contracting for discrete services to the building and running of entire facilities. The first of these links has a much longer yet more invisible history—as Elliott Young points out, migrants have been disproportionately incarcerated in halfway houses and mental, juvenile, and penal institutions throughout US history.[52] Second, a confluence of factors converging in the Reagan era served to justify contract detention facilities, with marginalized and vulnerable migrants serving as test populations for such experimentation.

Critics of privatization point to the nondelegation clause of the US Constitution in questioning the legality of delegating responsibility for restricting liberties; however, that did not deter the private prison industry's eventual expansion.[53] The economic recession of the late 1970s prompted burgeoning

Prison Uprisings and the Architectures of Erasure

conservative think tanks like the Heritage Foundation and the Reason Foundation to support austerity through privatizing government services. They claimed privatization would ameliorate prison overcrowding because facilities could be built at a faster rate with more innovation, would be more flexible in addressing correctional needs, and would attract higher quality workers, all at less cost.[54] A 1981 op-ed by California's RAND Corporation claimed the government had failed to fix prison overcrowding and violence, suggesting that one prison be run on an "experimental basis" for a limited time to test privatization's effectiveness. Reflecting a faith in the free market, it concluded that private prisons would be free to innovate and "use the latest technology and management techniques as in any profit-motivated service industry."[55] This line of reasoning went hand in hand with the growing disdain for government waste and bureaucracy articulated by the Reagan campaign.

Juvenile and mental health facilities and migrant detention—minimum security forms of incarceration—facilitated the rise of the private sector in the late 1970s while attracting little public scrutiny. By this time, most states employed contracts for various services in prisons.[56] By the late 1970s, 70 percent of federal contracts to place incarcerated persons in community treatment centers were with private providers. State and federal measures were also enacted to lift restrictions on private sector use of prison labor. The Department of Justice's Law Enforcement Assistance Administration, a program established by the Johnson administration, adopted a free venture model that encouraged private sector experimentation in the organization of prison labor. In 1979, Congress established a wage for labor in immigration detention of a dollar a day—often less, as seen at Oakdale—which has not been raised since.[57] Since the 1980s, the majority of private companies in the prison-industrial complex have been vendors and service providers. Food, medical, and security contracts were commonplace in Mariel Cuban detention on US military bases and in INS facilities. A few small facilities for juveniles and community-based programs such as halfway houses and drug rehabilitation centers began to operate on a for-profit basis in the late 1970s, but the use of private prisons to incarcerate adults, "total institutions" built from the ground up, was not attempted until after the Reagan administration launched its broad privatization initiative.[58]

Once in office, Reagan launched the President's Private Sector Survey on Cost Control, better known as the Grace Commission. Penned by 161 executives from the private sector, the commission's 23,000-page report on government waste and inefficiency released in 1986 determined that privatization could save the government $424 billion over the next three years.[59]

The Grace Commission's findings marked an important turn in affirming the president and the public's support for privatization. The report included a chapter that recommended prison privatization as a more flexible solution to the issue of overcrowding. Tellingly, it singled out the INS as an agency that should be especially "encouraged to continue to *experiment* and to evaluate the cost and effectiveness of contracting its detention facilities" (emphasis added).[60] It did not state why, but a broader societal devaluation of migrant life may have contributed to this view of migrant detention as a low-stakes environment for experimentation.

The INS began contracting with private firms in 1979 to hold migrants pretrial, including in local hotels and motels. In 1980 the INS granted the first facility-management contract via competitive bidding to Ted Nissen's California-based company, Behavioral Systems Southwest. Nissen, a former guard at San Quentin State Prison, ran a nonprofit drug treatment center in California in the mid-seventies. The *Los Angeles Times* described Nissen's Pasadena facility, a converted convalescent home, as an "experimental sort of cozy custody . . . the first of its kind." It opened in December 1980 as a "money-saving effort," according to an INS representative, and housed a dozen Cubans from Fort Chaffee along with migrants fleeing war-torn Nicaragua and Honduras waiting on asylum hearings. Residents expressed appreciation for the family unity and hostel-like living conditions allowed, while the INS told the *Times* that centers like it could save money and provide a "far less threatening" kind of security. "We've tried to keep it as un-penal as possible."[61]

As detention became increasingly punitive under the Reagan administration, these distinctions began to fade. By 1984, Behavioral Systems Southwest was the largest for-profit operator in corrections, netting $4 million in profits a year. In an NPR interview where participants debated the pros and cons of privatizing corrections, Nissen admitted, "I have to say first I'm in it to make money." But, if he failed to provide "good service," he added, "then I have a right to be pulled out. Some people may say, 'My God, you're opportunistic.' And I have to say, 'Yes, I am.' You know I don't think that's bad in the business sense."[62] Nissen's personal shift reflected a larger cultural one as a bipartisan consensus confirming the Reagan administration's neoliberal turn emerged.

Debates over privatization within the administration revealed that private contracting was not necessarily ideal but was adopted as a quick fix. Administrators deemed service contracts used in Mariel Cuban and Haitian detention highly effective. At Fort Allen, the INS claimed contracts were necessary for activating the site "in the most expeditious manner" and in an "emergency situation."[63] After a BOP staff visit to Fort Allen in November 1981, a warden from Miami praised Fort Allen's management, calling its successful use of contract services the "best I have ever seen." He claimed contract guards related well with Haitians and showed professionalism and compassion. As a "necessary force," he wrote, the guards' drilling in view of the enclaves served as a "deterrent to Haitians who would be inclined toward being rebellious" and concluded, "There is a prevailing sense of pride at Fort Allen and I believe it is a result of capable leadership. . . . The professionalism and performance of all the staff at Fort Allen is an example for all other similar centers to emulate."[64] Such a described culture of "service" and pride contrasts sharply with Haitian testimonies of medical and mental health crisis at Fort Allen, or of the abuses and corruption of contract guards at Port Isabel, Texas, detailed earlier—evidencing the growing gap between rhetoric and reality, or rather, whose version of the truth won out.

The attorney general's office was not entirely convinced of the effectiveness of private contracting. In considering transferring responsibility for migrant detention from the INS to the BOP in the spring of 1982, the office weighed pros and cons, concluding, "INS contract guards have not performed well, however, and not using contract guards is an advantage from a management perspective."[65] In the spring of 1983, the administration still sought to address overcrowding. A proposal for the INS to acquire a BOP facility in Florence, Arizona, justified the transfer due to a "significant increase in alien apprehensions" and as a better alternative to "INS dependence on scarce and expensive contract facilities."[66] The BOP and the INS did not seem to favor contract facilities for their cost and questionable quality, yet in only a few months' time the Corrections Corporation of America landed its first INS contract to build a facility in Houston. What explains this decision?

The selection of Oakdale for a permanent detention site marked a step toward fulfilling the administration's long-term enforcement plans, but the INS still aimed to locate interim detention space. When the attorney general issued a directive to establish emergency "temporary tent facilities" near the southern border, the INS and the BOP responded, "The need for a dual approach to acquiring additional detention space is evident. This will require the use of both contract 'turnkey' facilities and preparation of sites suitable for activation as temporary tent enclaves. . . . Further, BOP/INS are exploring the feasibility of a joint venture of acquiring new contract detention space in Texas to be shared by the two agencies."[67] A contract facility could suffice in the interim while Oakdale was under construction. For short-term detention solutions, the Reagan administration turned to "tents" and "turnkeys"—a hasty decision with lasting ramifications.

The private prison industry's rise also mapped onto geographies of border control in the Reagan imaginary, emerging out of a new Republican political coalition across the US Sunbelt. Perhaps it is no coincidence that the first two companies given federal prison contracts were Tennessee's Corrections Corporation of America and Florida's Wackenhut Corporation, charged with building immigration detention facilities in Texas and Colorado, respectively.[68] A closer look at the CCA's founding reveals the socioeconomic, cultural, and political conditions giving rise to today's "immigration-industrial complex," exemplifying the coalescence of Reagan's new security state.[69]

Nashville businessmen, Vietnam veterans, and former West Point roommates Thomas Beasley and Doctor ("Doc") Crants say the idea of prison privatization came to them at a Republican presidential fundraiser early in 1983 during a conversation with an executive who said "he thought it would be a heck of a venture for a young man: To solve the prison problem and make a lot of money at the same time." Crants also remembered Beasley excitedly saying that privatizing a jail would be "the ultimate franchise."[70] Beasley was chairman of the Tennessee Republican Party and had served on a committee in the late 1970s researching state corrections. He believed that "the application of a few simple business practices" could address problems of tight budgets and prison overcrowding and recalled, "We knew the era of big government was over. We could sell privatization as a solution, you sell it just like you were selling cars, or real estate, or hamburgers."[71]

Beasley and Crants incorporated the CCA in January 1983 with the stated purpose "to provide an innovative alternative to the problems of corrections and detention facility planning, financing design, construction and management."[72] Having no prior experience with prisons, Crants and Beasley recruited American Corrections Association president T. Don Hutto as a cofounder. While the CCA championed Hutto as a reformer, his credibility was questionable. A 1978 Supreme Court decision in *Hutto v. Finney* found that during Hutto's tenure as Arkansas's director of corrections in the 1970s, prison conditions constituted cruel and unusual punishment. The case details rape, torture, and ten-hour workdays, prompting the court's comment that "the administrators of Arkansas' prison system evidently tried to operate their prisons at a profit." The court also noted Hutto's failure to hire an adequate number of African Americans during his tenure.[73] Digging deeper into Hutto's history, Shane Bauer argues, "For Hutto, the idea of making money from prisoners was as old as the idea of forcing black men to pick cotton." In 1967, Hutto became warden of the Ramsey prison plantation in Texas, a place where the spirit of convict leasing and slavery never ended. Hutto lived on

Prison Uprisings and the Architectures of Erasure

the Ramsey plantation with his family, where per tradition a "houseboy," or an incarcerated servant, cooked and cleaned for the family.[74] Hutto's own life, it seems, created a historical through-line linking convict leasing to migrant detention.

Together, Crants, Beasley, and Hutto pitched their private prison concept to venture capitalist Jack Massey in February 1983. Massey's investment group had also funded Kentucky Fried Chicken, the Hospital Corporation of America, Mrs. Winner's Chicken and Biscuits, and a major franchisee of Wendy's.[75] After a fifteen-minute presentation, Massey committed half a million dollars to the CCA. Within six months the CCA won its first contract of $8.2 million to build a 350-bed INS detention facility in Houston, Texas. Two years later, Beasley told *Financial World* magazine, "We're on the ground floor of a multibillion-dollar industry." In 1988, Crants admitted that the company's profit-making formula was "so simple, it's shocking."[76]

In a video interview set to upbeat big band music that has since been removed from CoreCivic's website, Beasley recalls that the CCA promised to design and build the INS facility in ninety days. As the deadline neared, Hutto and Beasley flew to Houston on New Year's Eve to find a site. By 1:00 a.m., "we were both getting pretty weary. . . . And we saw this big ol' sign, 'The Olympic Motel.' Made an offer to lease the hotel for four months and . . . we finally signed the deal." The motel-turned-detention-center, with a twelve-foot-high cyclone fence erected around its perimeter and bars put over its windows, opened in 1984 on Super Bowl Sunday. The first migrants arrived at ten o'clock that night. Beasley chuckles at the memory as Hutto recalls, "I actually took their picture and fingerprinted them . . . and several other people walked them to their 'rooms,' if you will, and we got our first day's pay for 87 undocumented aliens."[77]

Lying on the edge of a residential neighborhood, the motel was a temporary arrangement while the CCA constructed its larger facility south of the Houston airport. Soon after migrants arrived, seven of them escaped by pushing the air conditioning units out of their room windows, crawling through the holes, and climbing over the fence.[78] Hired guard Joe Beezley said, "It's not bad for a jail . . . but still, I think if I were here I'd try to climb that fence." The *New York Times* reported that the escapes did "nothing to calm the fears of some area residents who were already jittery about having the detention facility in the neighborhood."[79] In addition to furthering migrant criminality in the public mind, the escapes also raised questions of the legality of contracting out detention functions, as guards were powerless to chase and apprehend noncitizens. But detaining immigrants enabled the CCA to experiment in a minimum security setting while attracting relatively little attention, despite local public concerns. As Beasley told the American Bar Association, "We plan to do minimum security facilities first, develop a track record, then go into other possibilities. . . . We're on the cutting edge of a new industry."[80]

Some early reviews of the CCA's Houston facility were positive. American Corrections Association director Anthony Travisono told *U.S. News and World Report*, "Many public officials hate running jails and find it attractive to get the problem off their backs while saving tax money."[81] Houston INS director Paul O'Neill called the facility "a perfect installation" and related, "It's been an absolutely outstanding relationship. They know just exactly what they are doing."[82] Former INS director Leo Castillo also said, "Physically, by INS standards, this facility is one of our best."[83] Reverend Thomas Sheehy of the Roman Catholic Archdiocese of Galveston-Houston in charge of liaison with the detention center said, "If I had a choice . . . I would take this private organization. They're much more humane. The guards haven't been in the business that long, so they're not calloused."[84]

Reflecting Reagan's anti-labor politics, the *Wall Street Journal* argued that by bypassing civil service and union restrictions, privatization enabled efficiency and lower costs.[85] The CCA acknowledged that construction in suburban Sunbelt regions had the benefit of avoiding heavily unionized areas while also tapping into a growing immigration and border enforcement network.[86] After the CCA secured its first contract, it won a second to build an INS facility in Laredo, Texas, followed by a workhouse-penal farm in Hamilton County, Tennessee, as well as jails in Florida, Nevada, New Mexico, and West Virginia. The Wackenhut Corporation (which would later become the GEO Group), headquartered in Palm Beach Gardens, Florida, and already the largest independent private security firm in the United States, won an INS contract to build a detention facility in Aurora, Colorado, shortly after the CCA's first. Its future contracts would include two INS facilities in Texas and a 1,300-bed medium security facility in Florida. By 1989, the CCA was operating sixteen facilities in five states, with a capacity of 4,238 beds.[87]

Adopted as interim solutions that soon became permanent, the INS's detention of migrants in mixed-use prisons and contract facilities, including converted homes, halfway houses, and hotels, became embedded into the patchwork of Reagan's carceral palimpsest. Mayra, who left El Salvador at age thirteen with her family and spent two months detained in Behavioral Systems Southwest's contract facility in Pasadena in 1983, says she was treated nicely by staff, but "there were still bars." Another memory haunts her, of walking to Hollywood High School in California a few years later. Every morning, she

Prison Uprisings and the Architectures of Erasure

passed by a hotel turned INS detention center on the corner of Las Palmas and Delompre Avenues, where she saw migrants looking out the windows through bars. "I would see people standing there. They were prisoners, you know, they were waving out the window and saying, 'Get me out of here!' It still gives me sad thoughts."[88] She also remembers seeing occasional protests by community members outside the hotel.

Although private prisons have spurred highly charged policy debates as human rights organizations have labeled them as more abusive, successive administrations have continued to uphold them as efficient and cost-effective. Ostensibly leaving the historical stigmas of prisons—and their populations— behind, Reagan-era administrators touted private and mixed-use facilities as humane alternatives. The pride and excitement surrounding the Oakdale facility and private prison contracting evidenced a growing trend. As Judith Greene explains, "Prison boosterism has come to pervade the thinking of many small-town mayors and county legislators, for whom prisons represent a 'clean industry' more than a penal institution."[89] Although a widespread belief in the economic benefits of prison-building still remains, especially in the rural Sunbelt, studies reveal that prison-building does not benefit local economies.[90] Volker Janssen argues that as suburban landscapes fostered a new political approach to crime and social control, privatization "became the Sunbelt's way of dissolving the contradictions between its ideological blend of individualism and pick-and-choose libertarianism on the one hand and its deep debt to postwar growth liberalism on the other."[91] In other words, privatization has served as a salve, papering over the inherent contradictions of Reagan's social divestments paired with soaring military and prison budgets. A year and a half after the Oakdale federal detention center's opening, the town of Oakdale remained steeped in recession—and its new point of pride was engulfed in flames.

The 1987 Mariel Cuban Prison Uprisings

In a contrasting setting from the CCA's facility in the warehouse-district out-skirts of Houston, on November 6, 1987, the migrant rights organization La Resistencia held a demonstration in the heart of downtown to protest the one-year anniversary of the passage of the Immigration Reform and Control Act. A bilingual flyer advertising the protest testified to IRCA's harmful impacts. A solidarity statement of "We are all Illegals!" headed the flyer, followed by "No registration for deportation and death camps!" and "Some anniversary! What's to celebrate?" The flyer's text described IRCA as a yet another assault against migrants in the Reagan era, furthering unemployment and driving migrants "into the nets of La Migra for deportation." Wary of government surveillance and the gathering of "extensive family data" as a requirement for amnesty, the flyer also mentioned the recent revelation of Reagan's secret "Rex84" program: "Amid the lies and coverups of the Irangate hearings, this much did come out: the government has contingency plans for martial law and plans and facilities for mass roundups of immigrants." Connecting IRCA to a broader landscape of enforcement, it read, "Meanwhile the border is further militarized to 'protect America' from alleged 'drugs, crime, and terrorism'" and decried US-fueled death squad violence in Central America, medical abuse of Haitian migrants at Krome, and US courts that had found the government "not responsible." It concluded with a call: "Those who know the truth and care must ACT."[92]

Just two weeks later, the Oakdale detention facility in Louisiana and the Atlanta federal prison erupted in protest. Media coverage and public debate surrounding the uprisings were shifting and divisive; while elevating detained Cubans' status to national attention, narratives both affirmed Mariel Cuban criminality and elicited public sympathy. Mariel Cuban resistance to detention took forms similar to that of Haitians and Central Americans, yet Cubans and their allies positioned themselves somewhat differently. Resulting from a FOIA request I filed in 2018, newly available documents from the Department of Justice regarding the uprisings shed light on the tense negotiation process and reveal the tenor of the DOJ and Attorney General Edwin Meese's retaliation efforts as they closely monitored and refuted sympathetic media coverage of the standoff. At the same time, Cubans carefully staged negotiations, leveraging hostages, inside-outside relationships, and religious and pro-US messaging to access the media and appeal directly to the US public, raising awareness of the injustice of their prolonged detention in the process.

With a stigma of criminality and deviance preceding them, Mariel Cubans faced extreme prejudice and violent conditions at the Atlanta penitentiary, Oakdale, and over sixty other prison sites across the country in the years leading up to the 1987 uprisings. In 1983, Mariel Cubans were some of the first arrivals at the facility in Florence, Arizona, which the INS acquired from the Bureau of Prisons—another "mixed-use" site of overlapping martial and carceral histories in the emergent Sunbelt carceral landscape. Before their arrival, the Florence chief of police admitted to the press he had "never even seen a Cuban" but had learned of their criminality from interactions with Los Angeles and Las Vegas police agencies. He continued, "Knowing what I know of them, I approach them in the same way I would a rabid dog."[93]

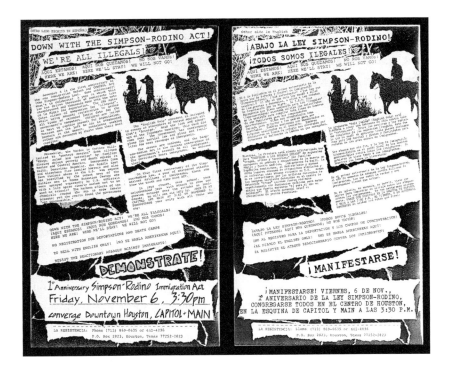

A bilingual La Resistencia flyer advertising a demonstration against the passage of the Immigration Reform and Control Act in Houston, Texas, on November 6, 1987. A solidarity statement of "We're all illegals!" heads the flyer, followed by "Here we are! Here we'll stay! We will not go!" and "No registration for deportation and death camps!" Presbyterian Historical Society, Philadelphia, PA.

In October 1984, tensions escalated at the Atlanta penitentiary after guards tried to put down a demonstration during which Cubans wielded banners made of bedsheets reading "Liberty or Death," resulting in a fire and a group of Cubans seizing a cellblock for several hours. In retaliation, Mariel Cubans at Atlanta were placed on lockdown for two years. Patrick O'Neill, who was serving time in the adjacent minimum security facility for antinuclear activism, relayed to the media that the prison had also confiscated and burned Cuban belongings in the yard. After his release, O'Neill, along with friends Carla Dudeck and Sally Sandidge, formed the Coalition to Support Cuban Detainees. They began holding monthly vigils outside the prison on behalf of Cubans, attracting national media attention.[94] As Elliott Young concludes, the 1984 rebellion "demonstrated what Cubans could accomplish if even a small group of them acted in concert." It also mobilized support for Cubans on the outside. The US government brought two Cuban leaders of the rebellion to criminal trial, including Geraldo Mesa-Rodriguez, who would also play a leading role in the 1987 uprisings; a sympathetic jury found them not guilty.[95]

After reaching its repatriation agreement with Cuba in late 1984, the United States deported 201 Cubans in early 1985, but Cuba soon canceled the agreement when propagandistic US broadcasts of Radio Martí went on the air in May, angering Fidel Castro to the point of calling Reagan the "worst terrorist in the history of mankind." Preventing Radio Martí from airing was a central concern of the Cuban government in its negotiations with the United States, but the program was a top priority for the pro-Reagan Cuban American National Foundation and its founder, Jorge Mas Canosa.[96] That summer, Cubans in detention organized a wave of hunger strikes across multiple sites that were met with retaliation and violence. At Florence, a hunger strike escalated to unrest and the destruction of a cellblock. News of these incidents confirmed Cuban criminality to many audiences, but it also raised public awareness. At Atlanta, hundreds of Cubans participated in a hunger strike that lasted for fifty-five days. To contradict authorities who claimed the strike was over, Cubans smuggled a letter to the *Atlanta Constitution* stating the strike would continue "until the end of our lives." The letter described the use of solitary confinement to silence dissent, INS collaboration in force-feeding 50–120 Cubans a day, and the prison's medical doctor threatening Cubans with medication that would make them "crazy." Ernesto Crespo explained why he was on hunger strike: "I thought it was the only way the government would pay attention to our request."[97] At Krome in 1986, Cubans set fire to their mattresses in protest and were subsequently transferred to other facilities, including Atlanta and Oakdale.[98] Aware of Atlanta's reputation as one of the most violent prisons in the country, fifty-five Cubans began rocking a bus taking them from Krome to Atlanta, causing it to pull over; forty police officers searched them before resuming the trip. Jenna Loyd and Alison Mountz count at least twenty-five other instances of unrest across the detention system between 1985 and 1989.[99] Scattered across the country, Mariel Cubans led or played a part in many of these.

At the same time, Mariel Cubans gained support outside of detention, including from the ACLU, the National Council of Churches, the Presbyterian Criminal Justice Program, La Resistencia, and the Coalition to Support Cuban Detainees in Atlanta. The Presbyterian Criminal Justice Program passed a resolution in support of Cubans at the Atlanta penitentiary as part of a broader international campaign to persuade the Reagan administration to investigate US prison conditions. BOP director Norm Carlson responded, blaming Mariel Cubans for their condition: "As a group they have been violent,

Prison Uprisings and the Architectures of Erasure

A 1986 vigil in solidarity with Mariel Cubans imprisoned indefinitely at the Atlanta federal penitentiary attended by lawyers, church people, and human rights advocates. The Coalition to Support Cuban Detainees sent this photograph to Cubans on the inside with a holiday greeting. Presbyterian Historical Society, Philadelphia, PA.

hostile, and extremely difficult to manage."[100] A congressional inquiry into conditions at Atlanta in 1986 revealed horrific and abusive conditions, finding Mariel Cuban imprisonment akin to being kept "like animals in cages" and concluding, "These detainees—who are virtually without legal rights—are worse off than virtually all other Federal sentenced inmates."[101]

Violent conditions at Atlanta and Oakdale continued to escalate. The Atlanta penitentiary, along with Leavenworth, Kansas, had the highest rate of violent assaults by guards of any prison in the country. The Minnesota Lawyers International Human Rights Committee also documented cruel conditions at Atlanta that year. In April, a guard choked a Cuban named Santiago Peralta-Ocana to death in front of six detained men and seventeen guards after making a racist comment to Peralta that elicited an altercation. The prison warden attempted to bury the autopsy, and although the truth came out, there were no indictments.[102] At Oakdale, a minimum security facility, the assault rate was twice as high as Atlanta. Before Oakdale's opening, the DOJ assured Mayor Mowad that it would be used to detain "ninety-five percent Mexicans" and that uprisings and escapes were rare. Within months of the facility's opening, however, Attorney General Meese announced a shift in plans—Oakdale would now be used to detain Mariel Cubans transferred from Atlanta, Krome, and elsewhere, ostensibly to facilitate their release into halfway houses. Meese claimed this decision was made to relieve overcrowding across BOP facilities, reported to be at 156 percent capacity across the system. Advocates called this decision an attempt to obstruct legal aid as Cuban protest continued.[103] Claiming there were only three lawyers in all of Oakdale willing to represent migrants at the largest detention center in the country, a lawyer with the ACLU concluded, "The government has rendered the refugees' right to legal counsel meaningless."[104]

Narratives of Cuban criminality continued. A few months before the uprisings in the summer of 1987, INS district director Louis Richard described those still imprisoned: "We've got everything from skyjackers, arsonists, rapists, murderers, aggravated assaults, crimes of virtually every type you can think of. A couple hundred are hard-core deviates that do strange things. They are psycho cases. I would be for keeping these people in jail for the rest of their lives before I would take a chance on letting one harm your child."[105] Reflecting homophobia and ableism, these comments show how Mariel Cubans were simultaneously criminalized and pathologized. Richard's description was also grossly overblown—when the INS appealed Judge Shoob's decision in the Eleventh Circuit, the agency submitted a list of "serious crimes" committed by Mariel Cubans, the total of which numbered less than 1,200, most of which were low-level property and drug charges. There were only 5 cases of murder, 11 of rape, and 150 of assault.[106] Regardless, all Mariel Cubans in INS custody had finished serving time for their crimes and were in civil detention awaiting deportation. Cuban testimonies shared with advocacy groups, lawyers, and the media detailing police brutality, INS lies, and abusive prison conditions contrasted sharply with the official story.

Although the Eleventh Circuit ruling in 1986 upheld indefinite detention, several months before the uprisings the INS promised to provide Mariel Cubans still in custody with individual case reviews. Human rights lawyer Arthur C. Helton explained to the New York Times that this raised Cuban hopes once again—but their "soaring expectations" were dashed by the "crushing reality" of the news of the renewed US-Cuba repatriation agreement on November 19, 1987.[107] While the uprisings were immediately sparked by news of impending deportation, they took place against the broader backdrop of abusive prison conditions and INS betrayals. Political and religious overtures made by Cubans during the rebellion reveal their pro-US, but anti-INS, stance. Main supporters on the outside included the Coalition to Support Cuban Detainees, Atlanta Legal Aid lawyer Gary Leshaw, the ACLU, civil rights

Prison Uprisings and the Architectures of Erasure

leaders Joseph Lowery and Hosea Williams, and House representatives Robert Kastenmeier and John Lewis. Cuban American bishop Agustín Román from Miami served as a mediary during negotiations; detained Cubans also saw him as a spiritual guide.

Meese's chief of staff Mark Levin, today a conservative talk show radio host, carefully documented each day of the siege, including meetings between lead negotiators Meese and BOP director Michael Quinlan and interagency coordinators. On November 23, Levin noted that "there had been no sign of uprising (no early signs). Was spontaneous." Meese ordered for all Cubans in other facilities to be "properly watched."[108] Two days later, *USA Today* reported that prisons across the country were isolating Cubans, listing segregation, escapes and attempted escapes, and small-scale acts of rebellion in Texas, Florida, California, West Virginia, Mississippi, Illinois, and Missouri. This belied the official line that rebellions and escapes were rare in detention.[109]

The Oakdale and Atlanta uprisings were both similar to and distinct from other US prison rebellions, such as the infamous Attica uprising of 1971 during which 1,000 incarcerated men took 40 hostages, resulting in the death of 43 people, including 10 guards, when New York state troopers raided the facility to end the siege. The Mariel Cuban uprisings of 1987 were distinct in their transnational anti-deportation politics, yet similar in being an organized and deliberate attempt to take control of the prison in pursuit of a goal. The only death occurred within the first ten minutes of the Atlanta takeover as a guard shot one Cuban, José Peña-Perez, who wielded a homemade knife. Cubans also acted compassionately toward hostages. As lawyer Mark Hamm, who represented Cubans in subsequent case review hearings, argues, "The outstanding feature was respect for life and human dignity." Initially, Cubans gave many prison staff the opportunity to leave the prison. Then, they kept the 28 hostages taken at Oakdale and 102 at Atlanta aware of their plans, including reassuring them they would not be harmed. One injury, however, was inflicted on a hostage at Oakdale, while many were released during negotiations due to medical needs. After the incident, most released hostages reported they were treated well and had been given access to showers, exercise, medicine, and plenty of food.[110] But dramatic hostage survivor stories in the media also confirmed public notions of Cuban criminality.

Despite official narratives to the contrary, the Cuban takeover of Oakdale and Atlanta operated with order and ceremony. Organizing horizontally, no one individual leader emerged. Cubans demonstrated a high level of cooperation, assigning each other to be cooks, guards, unit managers, lieutenants, and drill sergeants. They created a meal schedule and rationing program;

Cubans wave from the roof of the Atlanta federal penitentiary during their two-week takeover of the prison in November 1987. They wrote a message to the US public on the wall: "We do appreciate very much citizen support." Atlanta History Center.

often, meals were elaborate and celebratory occasions. They also used the radio PA systems at the prisons in negotiations and to broadcast their own commentaries on the takeover, which they called "Radio Mariel." Levin told a different story in his notes. On November 24 he wrote, "No real leadership we can deal with in facilities," but on the next day he noted, "Homosexual prisoners are emerging as the strongest negotiators." This point of view dismissed the horizontal and inside-outside organizing that had built communication networks via phone and written correspondence across detention sites in the years leading up to the coordinated dual-prison takeover. Levin's notes also indicated that the security team outside had cut off gas and water to the facilities, leading to the US government's belief that both sites were low on food and water, which was untrue.

Cubans staged a series of theatrics to successfully negotiate for gas, water, and electricity to remain on, for FBI and National Guard helicopters to stop circling overhead, and to gain access to the media to speak directly to the US public. Using Polaroid cameras, radio broadcasts, and television news, they performed convincing threats of violence to hostages through fake stabbings and immolations. One hostage relayed over the radio, "They have us handcuffed and have machetes at our throats and would behead us if you try to come in with force."[111] On November 21, Levin noted an early concession that no one would be forced to return to Cuba and "they may kill a hostage—this was picked up by BOP intel sources." In the early morning of November 24, Cubans constructed a platform in the yard at Oakdale and placed a hostage

Prison Uprisings and the Architectures of Erasure

time. We have no intention of hurting anyone, unless forced to do so. That force depends the force excerted by the Police, etc who attempt to overtake us. With meeting our negiations. We want the People, the Staff, the Government to Understand that all we are asking for is our freedom in which we are rightly due.

in an electric chair, threatening to set him on fire, and the helicopters abated. Regardless, the US government responded to the uprisings with a massive show of force and "endless patience," in the words of Michael Quinlan. The US Air Force, the Coast Guard, the BOP, SWAT, the FBI, the National Guard, US Marshals, the Border Patrol, the Public Health Service, the INS, the Georgia Bureau of Investigation, local police and fire departments, and the Salvation Army and Red Cross were all at the scene. Despite their theatrics, Cubans grew frustrated at media reporting depicting them as violent. On November 26, they displayed a hand-painted sign in red letters at Oakdale that read, "Mr. Reagan, if you deny our freedom, you kill us!" And on November 27, CNN showed footage of them unfurling two banners on the roof of the dining hall with pleas, "Dear Citizens of the United States, Thank You For Your Hopes and Prayers, We Do Not Want To Blow It!" and "We Want to Talk To Someone We Can Trust!"[112]

Religious faith, particularly Santería and Catholic beliefs, played a central role in guiding Cubans' actions during the takeover. Presbyterian reverend Russ Mabry, who was moved to work in prison ministry after losing his own son to suicide after incarceration, was at Atlanta with one other chaplain during the takeover. He recalled respectful treatment of hostages, who were given three meals a day, medical attention, and adequate bedding. Medical personnel were confined to the medical bay, but Mabry and the other chaplain could move about freely. Cubans held prayer meetings and a Thanksgiving mass and built two shrines on opposite sides of the prison to which they added candles, paintings, and hundreds of dollars and coins from vending machines. Mabry related, "At that point, the priest said to me, 'We are safe.'" Mabry also testified to the ongoing mental health needs of Mariel Cubans and their commitment to remaining in the United States. "I heard some of the greatest patriotic speeches from the Cubans," he recalled.[113] The main target of Cuban ire, however, was the INS.

On November 24, Cubans submitted a handwritten list of demands to negotiators at Oakdale, for INS eyes only: "We the Cuban detainees here at FDC Oakdale have been incarcerated in an average of 8 years. . . . Because we know how the system is run, we feel that we should be treated likewise. . . . In 1984 during the Atlanta Uprising, INS promised to release all Cuban Detainees, within a reasonable period of time. It has been 3 years and the majority of us are still incarcerated. Therefore, we feel the INS has not lived up to its promise. We have lost faith in the INS." They cited the "undue stress and emotional turmoil" placed on themselves and their families in the United States caused by their indefinite incarceration and by "not being treated as human but more as animals being caged to see what our behavior will be." They stated they had "no intention of hurting anyone, unless forced to do so. That force depends on the force exerted by the police." Their statement demanded that all negotiations take place before the media with Senator John Breaux and a top INS official present at all times, followed by the release of Cubans to families, sponsors, halfway houses, medical facilities, or, in last resort, to a third country other than Cuba, and the promise that they would not be held liable for any damages. Importantly, Cubans laid blame solely on the INS, making clear that the BOP, other incarcerated citizens, and prison staff did not have "any part in this situation. They were unfortunate to be here with us when we had gotten enough of injustice. . . . Therefore, the American[s] . . . are here . . . in evidence of our injustice by INS."[114]

Meese's refusal to include trusted Cuban advocates stalled negotiations, which only furthered Cuban fear of retaliation and continued mistrust of Meese and the INS. As several Cubans told Hamm after the uprisings, "We didn't want to give in—we thought we would be killed if we did," and "One man can't fight against a whole troop!" The government brought in a host of "impartial" mediators, mostly from the Cuban American exile community in Miami, including CANF leader Jorge Mas Canosa and former Cuban political prisoner Armando Valladares, whose presence Cubans booed. In his memoir, imprisoned Mariel Cuban Enrique González Sarasa explained their mistrust of the Cuban American representatives: "We did not accept them and we told them to go to hell." Cubans demanded instead that lawyer Gary

Prison Uprisings and the Architectures of Erasure

Leshaw and Bishop Agustín Román of Miami be included in negotiations. At Atlanta, Cubans wrote Leshaw's name on signs and in graffiti on the prison walls. On November 28, Cubans held a bedsheet in front of television cameras that read, "America, do not be deceived. The BOP is delaying release by denying Archbishop San Roman from attesting to the agreement. Why?" Meese repeatedly rejected this option due to Román's liberal politics, while the Coalition to Support Cuban Detainees in Atlanta told the *Washington Post* that the warden at Atlanta invited Román, but Quinlan told him not to come because it would be too "disruptive." The standoff continued.[115]

Even though leading negotiators included queer Cubans and single men without community ties, media depictions of the uprisings augmented the "family man" identity of Cubans leading the prison siege, centering the voices of wives and children on the outside. Bishop Román echoed this sentiment, arguing that deportation was inhumane due to Cubans' establishing families in the United States.[116] Media coverage sympathetic to the Cubans' situation increased toward the end of the standoff and after. On November 26, Thanksgiving, often a day used to narrate the United States as an immigrant nation owing thanks to Native Americans, the conservative-leaning *Washington Times* reflected, "It may seem odd that Cuban felons have decided to become a perverse form of freedom fighter, but their fight casts into bold relief the blessing of America's liberal democracy." A *Washington Post* editorial asked, "Since when does the United States lump together criminals and mental patients?" On December 1 at Atlanta, Cubans staged a celebration, sang "Happy Birthday" to Carla Dudeck, cofounder of the Coalition to Support Cuban Detainees, and released one hostage. This heightened media interest. After negotiations ended and all hostages were released by December 3, many expressed empathy toward their captors. Prison staff and the media also levied critiques at the government's handling of negotiations, withholding of information, and continued lack of media access to detention sites.[117]

A New Orleans *Gambit* magazine piece by Pierre DeGruy reflecting on the media's experiences at Oakdale titled "The Press Held Hostage" conveyed journalists' frustrations as they tried to gain access to negotiations and their growing empathy for Cubans. DeGruy asked, "What happens when the government's obligation to protect collides with the public's right to know?" As the DOJ stonewalled the press, reporters instead spoke to local citizens, many of whom had come to resent the detention center. When Mayor George Mowad announced at a news conference during the siege his plans to rebuild the facility, he elicited an angry response. As DeGruy described, "A couple of the crusty tobacco-chewing redbones of Oakdale swore they'd turn ole

George into a mannequin for display at the local Wal-Mart store." Over time, DOJ spokesperson Mark Sheehan warmed up to some journalists, telling them jokes and stating his belief that the SWAT team should end the standoff by going in and shooting Cubans. Other journalists shared their reflections. One noted, "The Cubans got around [stalled negotiations] with the signs which was ingenious," while a photographer acknowledged, "I had more sympathy for the prisoners after I saw them and the stand-off."[118]

At Oakdale, negotiations came to an end on November 29, after Meese allowed Bishop Román to fly in. When all was quiet, the INS allowed the press only limited access to Oakdale through one-hour tours led by a gruff Border Patrol agent. No one was allowed near Cubans or into any buildings. Meanwhile in Atlanta, Cubans remained distrustful as the US government escalated its police and military presence. The standoff finally ended after a long day of back-and-forth negotiations on December 3 aided by an audio recording by Román encouraging Cubans to give in and by an impassioned speech by FBI agent Pedro Toledo, who told Cubans in Spanish, "You cannot and you will not bring the United States to its knees."[119] Finally, after midnight, a commission of eight Cuban leaders signed the agreement; 1,100 detained Cubans had voted in favor, with 270 voting against. There was a final tense moment during which Cubans retreated into a building once again to deliberate, it seemed, for twenty minutes more. It turned out they were preparing for the occasion. Of the group who emerged to sign the agreement, one Cuban wore a suit and carried a briefcase with a Bible inside it; another had an American flag draped over one shoulder and a Cuban flag over the other.[120] In the end, Cubans believed they had obtained promises not to be deported, not to be charged with any facility damages, and to receive individual case reviews.

As Cubans left the Atlanta prison on the symbolic date of December 4—a feast day for Catholic patron saint Barbara and Santería warrior deity Changó—it was a joyous moment. They played salsa music over a loudspeaker while briefly allowed to embrace family members outside.[121] Once the DOJ regained control of the prison, the press reported the government's "astonishment" that Cubans had "set up their own bureaucracy" complete with stationery, interoffice memos among command posts, and a chit system that allowed commissary purchases by those sympathetic to the takeover. Prison administrators found that drugs in the medical bay remained untouched, but Cubans had made an alcoholic mash from raisins, peanuts, and coconuts. Finally, the most surprising find was "a ceremonial sword manufactured in a prison workshop for the rebel commander."[122]

Throughout the uprisings and afterward, the DOJ continued exaggerating Cuban criminality to the public while racially profiling Cubans internally. Contrary to the INS's public assertions affiliating Mariel Cubans with violent crimes, data from the National Crime Information Center in DOJ files on the uprisings reveal that among detained Mariel Cubans, the number one offense at Oakdale was "Halfway House/INS parole violations" and at Atlanta, "dangerous drugs."[123] The files also acknowledge that of the thousand Cubans at Oakdale, over half had already been granted parole by the INS. The criminalization of migrants, especially of Mariel Cubans, was well underway by this time, but this reflects the long-standing practice of the INS (and today, ICE) to misrepresent migrants' criminal records to stoke public fears.

Further, a November 29 memo to FBI director William Sessions regarding Oakdale and Atlanta (referred to as Major Cases #15 and #16) and seeking the president's approval for the use of military force to quell the "insurrections" included the FBI's psychological profile of Mariel Cubans. The "Population Profile" revealed the US government's imperial gaze, as well as its raced, gendered, and ableist characterizations of the migrant group. Under "typical psychological characteristics" of the "Cuban majority," it listed these:

1. Low tolerance for frustration

2. Impulsive; seek immediate gratification wishes

3. Concrete thinking; low average intelligence

4. Willing to take risks without considering consequences

5. Psychologically naive; able to be influenced by more sophisticated manipulators

6. Criminal mind-set due to time served in U.S. and Cuban prisons

7. Exaggerated pride in masculinity and bravado

8. Emotionally labile; quickly shift emotions (sometimes in a matter of minutes) from one extreme to another

9. Minimal social skills; unable to function in a complex society

10. Unrealistic hopes and aspirations about life/freedom in U.S.

11. Positive feelings for U.S. but negative feelings toward U.S. government

The memo continued by summarizing the "model Cuban prisoner" as someone who was "both culturally disadvantaged and developmentally retarded." While able to distinguish right from wrong, he was "primitive" but had "street sense" and was "willing to lie and take advantage of situations." He had "come to the United States with the unrealistic perception that most of his physical needs can be easily met, but when faced with the reality he is only capable of holding the lowest paying jobs." Finally, he had "neither the self discipline nor the patience required to better himself through more acceptable social ways."[124]

This declassified file speaks volumes—revealing the US government and the INS's conflation of criminality with assumptions about Blackness, gender-queerness, disability, and a backward, feminized communist Cuba more broadly. However, it also notes prison's ill effects—conceding that prison itself creates criminality. Seven years after Mariel, it was apparent that the highest levels of the US government had written off the humanity of "undesirable" Mariel Cubans still in custody. This much was clear in the retaliation meted out to those involved in the uprisings.

"Freedom or Death!"

Two weeks after the end of the siege, Edwin Meese and Michael Quinlan spoke at a ceremony outside of Oakdale honoring hostages and prison staff. "Those people who committed acts—ringleaders, hostage-takers, and so on, will all be sifted out and appropriate penalties will be made," Meese assured. "Nobody is going to be treated leniently. Nobody is going to be in a better situation than they were in before the uprising." Indeed, Mark Levin had noted during negotiations that the DOJ already had "an extensive plan to move prisoners when this is over."[125] Mariel Cubans from Oakdale and Atlanta were immediately transferred to prisons across the country. Although the BOP adopted a new policy of dispersal that no more than thirty Mariel Cubans would be held in any one facility, 719 were sent to Leavenworth, Kansas, exceeding the prison's capacity of 827 to 1,900. There, Cubans experienced extreme overcrowding, inadequate meals, communication cutoffs, punitive lockdowns, and abuse such as being chained naked to their bunks and left alone for hours. In a letter to the Coalition to Support Cuban Detainees, Arnaldo Rivas wrote, "It is a general feeling that we are not only being mistreated but also treated worse than animals."[126] Ultimately, the INS failed to fulfill Meese's promise to review individual cases in a fair and timely manner. In the meantime, Oakdale was rebuilt and reopened in 1989 as a federal detention center for "criminal aliens," marking a full shift toward crimmigration by decade's end.

Hunger strikes and inside-outside organizing continued as Mariel Cubans' communications with advocates revealed the extent of US government retaliation and betrayal. Six Cubans who were transferred to the Metropolitan Correctional Center in Chicago wrote to coalition advocate Steve Donziger in Atlanta, who relayed their messages of "mental torment" and "repression" to the press. Leonardo Jimenez, formerly at Oakdale, said Cubans were planning to go on hunger strike if they did not receive news on their cases by December 30. "The hunger strike will be the only way to make them give our freedom," he wrote, continuing, "Freedom or Death! We have a few old men with us, they are ready to die for their freedom, too." Carla Dudeck of the coalition relayed to the media that 101 Cubans at a prison in Lompoc, California, were also planning a hunger strike. "They're pretty consistent," she said of the conditions described in Cubans' letters. "It's the same treatment—lockdown, handcuffs when they leave the cell, no access to news or information regarding their status."[127]

The spectacle of the siege drew public attention to what would happen next. In the month after the uprisings, sympathetic media coverage surrounding Mariel Cubans spiked but then subsided. Criticism of the US government's handling of events abounded, ranging from anger over lax security levels to outrage at the mistreatment of Cubans. Throughout December 1987, national headlines read "Transferred Detainees Detail Abuse," "Rights Sought for Cuban Inmates," "Guards Beat Us, Krome Inmates Say," and "Cuban Inmates Complain of Isolation, Abuse." Advocates for Mariel Cubans finally had a moment in the spotlight. As the *Christian Science Monitor* reported, "The handful of lawyers, politicians, and conscientious activists who, along with one federal judge [Shoob], have been sounding the plight of the Cuban detainees for years without significant effect, now have the clout that comes with access to the news media." However, public attention and vocal support from politicians went only so far, and transfers distanced Cubans from the tenuous support they already had. The Coalition to Support Cuban Detainees told the *Miami Herald* it could not afford to send 110 law students and volunteers trained in Atlanta and Oakdale to support Cubans in case review hearings at new prison sites. The coalition also expressed disappointment at a lack of support from the Cuban American community; the newspaper mused that perhaps the coalition needed to "overcome a sort of leftist image."[128]

At first, the DOJ moved slowly in fulfilling its promise to review all cases, but the process sped up in the spring of 1988. However, as legal advocates and Judge Shoob charged, the INS review process was ambiguous, arbitrary, and outright unfair. Even the BOP was aware of this bait and switch, as admitted in an after-action report describing how many Cubans "had attempted to work within the framework of a release program only to see that program end and a new one, with new rules and regulations, initiated. . . . Many detainees appeared to believe that they had been unfairly treated, that INS had made them many promises which had not been kept." Shifting blame away from the BOP, the report also noted that Cubans "repeatedly told hostages that Immigration and Naturalization Service, not the Bureau of Prisons, was the target of their anger and frustration."[129] A report from the acting associate attorney general to Louisiana representative Robert Kastenmeier revealed the government's view that the "underlying reason" for the uprisings was "the completely unique population" imprisoned.[130] In other words, the government laid blame squarely upon Mariel Cubans, who continued to languish in prison while the US public turned its attention away once again.

In a House hearing on the uprisings in February 1988, Atlanta representative and civil rights leader John Lewis blasted the Reagan administration. "It should be less than surprising when they revolt against this system," he said, which he called a "mockery" in "a country that has prided itself in welcoming oppressed people yearning for freedom. The last seven years have been wasted years for these Cuban detainees. We have wasted a significant portion of their lives."[131] Judge Shoob, who had reviewed hundreds of Mariel Cuban cases in Atlanta, also testified, arguing that many Cubans should never have been detained in the first place. He gave one example of three teenagers who were sent to Atlanta after their halfway house closed due to budget cuts. The INS responded to such examples by admitting that some Cubans "slipped through the crack."[132] By then, despite the spike in public sympathy, only 280 out of 1,300 Mariel Cubans approved by the INS for release actually were released, with lack of sponsors or space in halfway houses as alleged reasons. However, advocates accompanying Cubans during INS hearings in the coming months found that some Cubans with willing sponsors, like Antonio, who was arrested in New York for jumping a subway turnstile and whose sister in Miami said she would do anything to support his release, were being held indefinitely for no apparent reason—other than being HIV positive.[133] Ultimately, 1,400 Mariel Cubans were paroled after the uprisings. By the end of 1988, 15 Cubans determined to be "incorrigibly violent criminals" by the Justice Department's new review process were ordered deported and sent to the Talladega prison in Alabama, where they were put on "lockdown" to prevent further unrest. By 1990, only half of Mariel Cubans whose cases had been reviewed had been released.[134] Lawyers working on behalf of Cubans, including Rafael Peñalver,

Prison Uprisings and the Architectures of Erasure

a Cuban American who helped Bishop Román broker negotiations, promised to continue supporting Mariel Cubans and protesting deportations.[135]

One ACLU lawyer from Atlanta traveled to various prison sites to represent Mariel Cubans in their INS hearings in the spring and summer of 1988, while the Coalition to Support Cuban Detainees helped recruit teams of local volunteers to accompany them in court. In Springfield, Missouri, an anthropology graduate student named Kenneth Batsalel volunteered to assist the lawyer, later publishing his journal reflecting on INS hearings that he could describe only as "Kafkaesque." Unable to find local lawyers willing to help because "there is no money in immigration law," Batsalel held a workshop in his home for the lawyer to train a handful of volunteers who had little in common other than "their sense of commitment to issues outside themselves." On Batsalel's first visit to the prison, they met a Cuban who had been on hunger strike for several weeks and was being fed intravenously. He said he was "determined to die rather than be deported." Batsalel asked himself, "How can I help? How can I live a more meaningful life? These are the questions that are important. These are the stories I need to tell."[136]

He recorded several Cubans' stories, revealing a systematically unjust review process in a brutal and uncaring system. As a visitor to the prison, Batsalel felt "the walls closing in, a sense of panic," but was aware that he could retreat to a courtyard with flowers while Cubans could not—they were confined to a medical facility and locked down for twenty-three hours a day. During the hearings, no one could ask questions or bring or cross-examine any witnesses. The "judge" was often a Border Patrol officer. The file of one Cuban named Ramon indicated he was charged with rape, attempted murder, and auto theft. "From our perspective, things did not look good," Batsalel admitted. "Then we talked to Ramon." They learned Ramon's original charges were reduced to assault, with time served, but he was re-detained after the highway patrol pulled him over for not yet registering a car he recently bought, handing him over to the INS. Jose, an Afro-Cuban and former cane worker, had no criminal record or incarceration history, but his file read that he had "diminished mental capacity." He was turned over to the INS after an argument with his landlord led to a police call. A young man named Alfredo was imprisoned for stealing things out of parked cars, hungry, at his job in Miami. When asked why he wanted to remain in the United States, he broke into a smile: "Freedom lives here!" Miguel's file, according to the INS, had been burned in Atlanta. He had a US-citizen wife and child and was charged with selling drugs. The file the INS gave Batsalel to review was filled with redactions.[137]

During the hearings, one Cuban took his life into his own hands, ending it by suffocating himself in his prison cell. As the ACLU lawyer moved on, Batsalel could not continue. Struggling with guilt, he wondered if his accompaniment was even helpful or if instead "our handling of the detainees' cases simply legitimated the system" by allowing the INS to claim Cubans were being provided due process. Reaching "the limits of commitment," Batsalel concluded with resignation, "Perhaps it is a question of courage but I am unable to go out to the prison again."[138]

The fifteen Mariel Cubans in Alabama who were ordered deported appealed to a federal court in Birmingham but lost. Deportations in small groups began, and resistance continued. In August 1991, 121 Cubans rebelled at the Talladega prison, taking over a cellblock and ten hostages. Bishop Román once again served as an intermediary, but after ten days a special operations team of 200 BOP and FBI agents raided the prison, effectively putting down the rebellion. By this time, patterns of resistance and retaliation in detention were firmly in place.

Lawyer Mark Hamm and his students represented over 200 Cubans in their parole hearings after the uprisings. He published a book detailing the uprisings and their aftermath, recording the stories of Cubans forgotten in the system, such as the "tragic case of Alberto Herrera" who was forty years old and still imprisoned in 1991. Herrera had spent seven years before the boatlift imprisoned in Cuba for a failed attempt to steal food for his family. When the boatlift began, a guard instructed him to leave the jail and get on a boat. Confused, Herrera felt hopeful hearing conversations with people on board planning to reunify with family members in the United States. But the INS sent him from the boat to the prison upon arrival, stigmatized by his prison past and tattoos of Catholic saints covering his body. Throughout his imprisonment at the Atlanta penitentiary, Herrera never learned English and never had a sponsor. He attempted suicide six times by hanging, drinking gasoline, and self-mutilation. Two days after the uprisings concluded, the BOP transferred him to another prison. Hamm's team failed to secure his release because they could not find him a sponsor. Although he lost contact with Herrera, Hamm gives him a final word in his book: "Life was not good in Cuba. Life was difficult for a laborer. I came to the United States looking for liberty. I found prison."[139]

Prison Uprisings and the Architectures of Erasure

Architectures of Erasure

A few years from now, when this country looks back at the 1980s, we are going to ask ourselves as a nation, "How could this have happened in the US? How could we have kept thousands of individuals locked up in indefinite detention year after year, warehousing them without any kind of civil rights?" . . . That has to be one of the darkest pages in the history of American justice.

Rafael Peñalver, Cuban American lawyer, 1986

Tracing the long crisis of Mariel and the extraordinary exclusion of Mariel Cubans exposes gaps—between immigration and criminal legal systems, law and discretion, and left and right politics—that swallowed the lives of those subjected to indefinite detention. At the center of public hysteria over race, gender, immigration, and crime, Mariel Cuban experiences also reveal crucial connections, showing how foreign and domestic policies converged in the Reagan imaginary to forge new incarceration trends. The criminalization of Mariel Cubans also uncovers the parallel histories and futures of mixed-use facilities like Oakdale and private prisons. As crimmigration bolstered an emergent border-industrial complex—a merging of border enforcement state and private interests—in subsequent decades, detention uprisings continued to flash in and out of public view. The new architectures and rhetorics of state power that Reagan cemented into place would continue to render the undercurrents of state violence invisible.

After the uprisings, the administration moved quickly to rebuild Oakdale. In all, they cost the US government $110 million, including law enforcement attempts to quell the rebellion, property damage, and rebuilding costs.[140] However, these events did not tarnish Oakdale's reputation as a model facility or stymie the US government's commitment to merging criminal and immigration enforcement. Instead, the uprisings only seemed to boost consolidation efforts through the reinscription of state retaliation on the blank slate of Oakdale's ruins.

Louisiana senator L. Bennett Johnston supported rebuilding—as long as Cubans would no longer be detained there. "We moved heaven and earth to get it," he recalled, citing the city's high unemployment rate as the impetus for building the prison. "We got it and it was successful, up until the time they put the Cubans there," he explained, because the detention center was originally meant to house undocumented immigrants who were "not dangerous." He added, "The Cuban situation is a transient, fading phenomenon, hopefully quickly fading. They should not come back to Oakdale by any means."[141] Mayor Mowad also saw the uprisings as an opportunity to secure funding for the prison's rebuilding and expansion. He wrote to Louisiana's other senator, John Breaux: "It is important that we push to expand now since the memories of the riot is so front in everybodys mind [sic]."[142]

In January 1989, Oakdale I reopened as a "criminal alien" facility for non-citizens convicted of federal offenses. Oakdale II, an adjacent site with plans in place before the uprisings, opened in March 1990 as a federal immigration detention facility and deportation hub, complete with an airstrip and 80,000-square-foot administration building to streamline on-site Executive Office of Immigration Review court proceedings. Buttressed by new laws, this resurrection of a mixed-use "criminal alien" facility further dissolved divisions between refugee and criminal, normalizing and sterilizing routine violence and the rise of crimmigration in the process.

Although the construction of facilities in rural places such as Oakdale seemed to have little to do with border geographies, remote locations resolved political tensions and facilitated the system's ongoing invisibility. Oakdale became a "long-lasting node" in the carceral palimpsest, as the agglomeration of transportation and legal infrastructures simultaneously facilitated, and obscured, the expansion of the border-industrial complex.[143] While no one site fully exemplifies the emerging carceral palimpsest, nor for any one reason, Louisiana was also centrally located between Texas and Florida, gateways to the Caribbean and Central America—the United States' "third border" in the Reagan imaginary.

A tragic irony remained: the Mariel migration of 1980 inspired new detention structures and laws that then served to further exclude Cubans after the uprisings. This reflected both the ongoing public and political backlash against Mariel Cubans in particular and, more broadly, the fruits of Reagan's Criminal Alien Program. The passage of IRCA in 1986 introduced the idea of instituting a program to target noncitizens with criminal convictions for deportation in response to prison overcrowding, further buttressed by the 1986 and 1988 Anti-Drug Abuse Acts—capstones of Reagan's War on Drugs. The 1986 act established the basis for immigration detainers, which are INS requests for local law enforcement to "hold" someone in order for the federal government to initiate a deportation case. The 1988 act further expanded criminal penalties for drug offenses, established mandatory minimum sentences, and provided for the deportation of noncitizens convicted of "aggravated felonies"—namely, murder, drug trafficking, and illicit firearms trading. This

Prison Uprisings and the Architectures of Erasure

category would broaden through subsequent reforms over the next decade, creating a widening net targeting migrants for deportation that today includes driving under the influence, shoplifting, and other crimes of "moral turpitude."[144]

The Reagan administration officially launched the Criminal Alien Program in 1988 with plans to "purge" noncitizens from the criminal legal system by enlisting local law enforcement to assist the federal government in identifying noncitizens serving time in US prisons and jails to target for deportation. The US government's indefinite detention of Mariel Cubans, perceived as exacerbating prison overcrowding, drove the Criminal Alien Program's intent to filter migrants through the criminal legal system and ultimately out of the country. This created a feedback loop that both was fueled by and further contributed to the hyper-incarceration of Black and Brown youth.[145] Together, Oakdale and the Criminal Alien Program exemplify the tandem rise of migrant detention and mass incarceration. In subsequent decades, the Criminal Alien Program would further boost the emerging private prison industry and the coalescence of Reagan's neoliberal security state. Immigration attorney Andrew Free estimates that in recent years, up to 90 percent of migrants in today's detention system have been detained in for-profit facilities, especially those serving as the nation's largest deportation hubs in the US South.[146]

Postscript

Writing about the Abuses against Us

Detention Stories and Abolitionist Imaginaries

Caribbean and Central American migrations shaped new immigration enforcement measures enacted in the early 1980s that constituted Reagan's Cold War on immigrants: the weaponization of detention to deter undocumented migrants and asylum-seekers, interdiction on the high seas, the militarization of border enforcement in the War on Drugs, and private prison contracting. Containing the specter of mass migration became a top priority at the highest levels of government, driving many of the themes Reagan has been identified with: the resurgence of Cold War nationalism; a politics of fear surrounding crime, drugs, and people of color; and neoliberal economics. As the US government's "prose of counter-insurgency" cast migrants and their allies as enemies of the state, a bipartisan consensus emerged embracing enforcement as deterrence.[1] The Reagan administration thus laid new foundations of the carceral palimpsest, and the subsequent growth and character of the US immigration detention system has borne the imprint of this era.

Revisiting the rise of immigration restrictions during the Reagan era is especially instructive, not only for its sharp punitive turn but for the resistance it prompted. This book has explored the mechanics of detention, defining it as a counterinsurgent set of practices and narratives of erasure and denial and a place where the violent ends of US empire are simultaneously reified and rendered invisible. Mass mobilizations against mounting enforcement in the 1980s—orchestrated from within detention, through inside-outside coalition building, and in the broad civil disobedience of the Sanctuary movement—also set the stage for future contestations. The criminalization of migration has since become normalized. Yet, alternate visions also sustained mass support in the 1980s and beyond. Migrants in detention have long wielded their voices to map abolitionist imaginaries, blueprints for building a world free from state violence.

In the years 1993–96, the Clinton administration enacted a set of laws and enforcement measures that built upon the foundations laid by Reagan's Cold War on immigrants. In 1993–94, Clinton signed the North American Free Trade Agreement, while the Supreme Court upheld Reagan's Haitian interdiction program. The INS also launched Operation Distant Shore, an updated version of Reagan's Mass Immigration Emergency Plan, and Operation Gatekeeper, a Border Patrol "prevention through deterrence" initiative mandating new US-Mexico border wall construction. In 1994, Congress passed the Violent Crime Control and Law Enforcement Act, authorizing an $8 billion increase in state construction grants for prisons and boot camps, including two new facilities for "criminal aliens." These years also ushered in a new wave of prison revolts.[2]

In 1995, a migrant uprising at the Elizabeth Detention Center in New Jersey, run by Esmor Correctional Services, prompted an INS investigation. Almost 100 migrants, mostly asylum-seekers from Africa, participated in the uprising at the detention center, which the *New York Times* reported "sits on a dead-end street among a group of beige brick warehouses that constantly shake beneath the roar of jets landing at nearby Newark International Airport. . . . There is nothing from the street to indicate that, instead of boxes and crates, this warehouse stores human beings." A Cuban man named Akenis Montane Santos said unrest was triggered by detained migrants being forced to wear used underwear and drink spoiled milk. Migrants also reported a lack of privacy in filthy bathrooms, lights left on twenty-four hours a day, freezing temperatures at night, no outdoor recreation, and routine harassment by guards, especially for practicing Islam. When lawyers and loved ones visited, migrants were shackled to the table and by their feet.[3] Within a year of the facility's opening, there was a hunger strike and a small-scale disturbance led by Cubans. After Esmor continued ignoring their complaints, migrants took out their frustrations on a larger scale in June. During the rebellion, they briefly took two guards hostage, but they mainly targeted the architecture of detention itself—breaking windows, destroying furniture, and tearing tables and chairs from the concrete visitation booths. As historian Mary Rizzo surmises, these acts reflected resentment toward Esmor and the INS's systematic violation of migrants' material rights.[4]

After the uprising, the INS transferred migrants to facilities across the country, and lawyers and families struggled to locate them. When twenty-five men were sent to the Union City Jail in New Jersey, guards assaulted them upon arrival.[5] Although citizens of Elizabeth, New Jersey, protested the further use of private jail facilities, and although the INS's follow-up report concluded that "no real control was exercised over Esmor guards by their mid-level supervisors," the Corrections Corporation of America would soon take over the contract, reopening the facility with the mayor of Elizabeth's support.[6]

Despite the continuation of the facility's for-profit management, the Esmor uprising did lead to the first court case in which detained migrants gained the right to sue a private prison contractor. In 1997, nineteen plaintiffs who were detained at Elizabeth sued Esmor under the Alien Tort Claims Act of 1789, a law allowing federal courts to hear civil lawsuits by non-US citizens claiming violations of international law—in this case, human rights violations. They also sued under the Religious Freedom Restoration Act of 1993, claiming the US government had unlawfully "burden[ed] a person's exercise of religion." In *Jama v. Esmor Correctional Services, Inc.*, lead plaintiff Hawa Jama, a female asylum-seeker from Somalia, testified in a deposition, "I complained personally to every INS person, every Esmor official. . . . I come to this country to save my life, to seek asylum. And they put me in jail, hell. I can describe hell . . . Esmor was hell." When the case went to trial in 2004, only nine plaintiffs remained due to deportations, settlements, and withdrawals. Ultimately, the court awarded Jama $100,001 in compensatory damages for violating her rights under the Religious Freedom Restoration Act, marking the first time a non-US citizen successfully sued a private company for violating human rights in detention.[7]

This case set an important precedent for a new series of six class action lawsuits by detained migrants against for-profit prison operators CoreCivic (formerly the CCA) and GEO Group in the late 2010s, challenging dollar-a-day detention wages and conditions of forced labor under the Trafficking Victims Protection Act of 2000 and state laws.[8] One of the lead complainants was Sylvester Owino, an asylum-seeker from Kenya who spent almost an entire decade in detention.

Protests, lawsuits, and negative media coverage did not deter the Clinton administration from passing legislation known as "the 1996 laws," which have spurred the growth of migrant detention most dramatically into the twenty-first century. The 1996 Illegal Immigration Reform and Immigrant Responsibility Act and the Antiterrorism and Effective Death Penalty Act broadened the mandate for immigration detention by expanding the list of crimes constituting "aggravated felonies," requiring mandatory detention and deportation. Together, the Clinton administration's 1994 crime legislation and the 1996 laws also gave boosts to the private prison industry. Due to these laws, the average daily INS detention population tripled between 1994 and 2001.[9]

Migrant detention in the United States accelerated further after the terrorist attacks of September 11, 2001, and subsequent passage of the 2001 USA PATRIOT Act and the 2002 Homeland Security Act that created the Department of Homeland Security, with two new enforcement branches, Immigration and Customs Enforcement and Customs and Border Protection, replacing the INS and the Border Patrol. The act granted the attorney general exceptional powers to detain immigrants, further concretizing interagency cooperation, surveillance, and secrecy inherited from Reagan era enforcement trends. In 2004, the Intelligence Reform and Terrorism Prevention Act directed the Department of Homeland Security to increase detention capacity by at least 8,000 beds each year between 2006 and 2010. In 2009, Senator Robert Byrd added an amendment to the Appropriations Act of 2010, lobbied for by the private prison industry, introducing what is now a minimum daily detention bed quota of 34,000.[10]

Twelve years after the Esmor uprising, I walked into the CCA's Elizabeth detention facility for the first time. I did not know of the events that occurred there; I didn't even know that for-profit prisons existed. The shackles during visitation were gone, but everything else remained the same—the windowless warehouse on a dead-end street, horrific conditions inside. A 9/11 commemorative mural depicting the Twin Towers with the words "Never Forget" beneath them covered the entrance hall to the visitation area. A guard boasted to me that detained migrants "volunteered" to paint it. I also noticed a boat crafted out of paper and food wrappers in a glass display case in the visitation room—an artifact of stolen time. I wondered, what do these displays mean to say?

As I researched this book, I began working with communities to document, archive, and mobilize detention stories that defy prisons and borders—and the prose of counterinsurgency that sustains them.[11] At Freedom for Immigrants' annual retreat in September 2015, Spanish professor and former Argentinian political prisoner Alicia Partnoy led visitor volunteers, people formerly detained including Sylvester Owino, and affected family members like myself in a "Transformative Storytelling" workshop.[12] We struggled with the prompt given to us: write five lines about our first time entering a detention center. "I'm not a writer," I heard someone whisper to nods of agreement. But soon, words began to flow and the message became clear. We all had a story, and those who had suffered or witnessed life inside detention were longing to tell it. As we adjourned, we agreed upon the sensitive nature of the information shared among us. But Carlos Hidalgo, who had been detained twice at the Adelanto Detention Facility in California, stood up in dissent. "There is nothing to be ashamed about here. I'm an undocumented immigrant—so what?" As for his story, he said, "Pass it out!"

Below are three sketches tracing the afterlives of the Mariel Cuban, Haitian, and Central American detention histories traced in this book, illustrating how voices from detention continue to call out for justice. To paraphrase the Greek poet Dinos Christianopoulos, whose words have long inspired freedom struggles, "They tried to bury us, they did not know we were seeds."[13]

> My loving heart seems to be struck with such bad luck
> I find myself fighting in the dark.
> The absence of the light have [sic] turned me blind
> By feel and touch in such darkness I have survived and still
> looking for hope to come to me.

> *"Lene Stranded from Cuba," New Lisbon Correctional Institution, 2014*

About a year ago, I learned of a Mariel Cuban named Lenin who has been imprisoned in the United States for forty years. Lenin arrived with the Mariel boatlift "terribly confused and fearful" in the summer of 1980 at age sixteen. Traveling alone and with no ability to speak English, he says elders advised him to change his name and his birth date so that he could fit in with US society and be old enough to find work. INS agents in Key West sent "Lene" to the Orange Bowl in Miami and then to Fort McCoy, Wisconsin, to await a sponsor and release.

In a few short weeks, Lenin's sponsor, Berniece Taylor, fifty-seven, was murdered in her home. According to Lenin, he had gone out for the night to see his girlfriend and English interpreter and was not present when the murder took place. But fearful of implicating his friends, he withheld this alibi from the police. Having just turned seventeen, Lene was tried as an adult and given a life sentence in prison in September 1980, with the judge's understanding that under Wisconsin law he would be eligible for parole after thirteen years. But due to immigration reforms in the 1980s and 1990s mandating detention and deportation for those convicted of aggravated felonies, Lene was never granted parole. In an appeal for a retrial in the spring of 1981, his lawyer argued that the "melee of confusion" at Fort McCoy gave Lene "no opportunity for him to in any way comprehend the involvements that he ultimately became entangled with." Basing the appeal on an overall lack of evidence, the lawyer also claimed that discriminatory treatment by the police and prosecutor during the investigation and trial played into "the latent prejudices that people in this area and this state and perhaps in the United States may have." Lenin remains in prison in Wisconsin to this day, where he maintains his innocence and has asked the US government to deport him.[14]

Forty years on, Lenin's story points to the Mariel migration's most tragic legacies: its impact on the expansion of the US carceral state and the harms of indefinite detention on individuals. This book has shown how the extraordinary exclusion of this migrant group in the Reagan era prompted new architectures of incarceration and erasure, which have broadened a net of enforcement targeting other migrant groups. My intention here is not to linger on the official narratives of criminalization surrounding the Mariel migration, themselves fueled by anti-Blackness, queerphobia, and ableism. Nor is it to idealize or exceptionalize individuals like Lene. Rather, I point to his story for how it survives, endures, and calls out.

In a prison blog last updated in 2014, Lene posted a letter to the public "to introduce myself and let you know who I am." He wrote of his experiences during the Mariel boatlift, his version of events in the murder case of Berniece Taylor, and the injustices of his continued incarceration. He also shared poetry and artwork from inside depicting a heart still in Cuba, the view from his grandmother's house there that he remembers, and life in prison—the only worlds he has known. To this day, the scars of the Mariel migration and incarceration remain. Many Mariel Cubans remain silent, while others express fears of retribution for speaking out about their experiences.[15] Despite such fears, a growing number of voices have gained strength in the past decade, supported by community-based memory and storytelling projects.

In 1994, 34,000 Cubans left Cuba for the United States on rafts in what is known as the Balseros crisis. The Clinton administration detained Cuban asylum-seekers at Guantánamo Bay, where President Bush Sr. had been detaining Haitian migrants since 1991. Mariel historian Alexander Stephens argues that one of President Clinton's primary goals in devising the "wet foot, dry foot" policy in response to Balseros was to avoid "another Mariel."[16] It seems Clinton had learned early in his political career that xenophobia was a winning strategy. While this new administrative rule expanded arriving Cubans' pathways to residency through the 1966 Cuban Adjustment Act, it simultaneously subjected Cuban migrants at sea to exclusion.

In 2004, journalist Mark Dow asserted that Mariel Cubans were "probably the most lasting victims of U.S. immigration detention."[17] Their status was allegedly resolved in 2005, when the US Supreme Court ruled that the indefinite detention of Cubans who had arrived in the boatlift and were deemed deportable in the repatriation list agreed upon between Cuba and the United States in 1984 was unconstitutional. During oral arguments, the Bush Jr. administration said it was no longer involved in such negotiations with Cuba, admitting, "No one is looking for excludables to send back, but if one of the 2,746 gets into trouble," that person would be deported. For twenty-five years the United States had reserved the right to keep Mariel Cubans imprisoned, even after they had served their sentences for crimes. This ruling freed around 750 Cubans still being detained, but some remained imprisoned, and by 2008 Mariel Cuban deportations were still occurring at a rate of 1–2 every couple of weeks.[18] Despite the court's ruling and heightening collaboration between ICE and criminal legal systems, there are no systematic screenings to locate Mariel Cubans still in custody—like Lenin—who have fallen through the gaps.

The Obama administration officially ended the "wet foot, dry foot" policy in 2017 as part of normalizing US-Cuba relations, but one side effect has been the facilitation of Cuban deportations. Under the Trump administration, Mariel Cubans with criminal pasts were targeted for deportation once again, with ICE's list of those deemed deportable growing into the thousands. Meanwhile, newly arriving asylum-seekers from Cuba have been detained in increasing numbers, often in private contract facilities. Jose Antonio Hernandez Viera, speaking from the Pine Prairie facility in Louisiana in 2018, said, "They send Cubans back to Cuba. There's something happening, and I'm sure—I'm convinced—that they don't want us here."[19]

Speaking out from and against spaces of incarceration and marginalization, Mariel Cuban memory projects have grown in number over the past decade, serving to connect past to present, counter public misperceptions about Mariel, heal personal trauma, and disrupt "deserving" versus "undeserving" immigrant narratives that have normalized criminalization. Some have been led by Cuban scholars, others by community organizations, and some by imprisoned Mariel Cubans themselves, like Lenin, who tell their stories on their own terms.[20]

As COVID-19 has torn through prisons and detention sites across the United States over the past two years, a new series of hunger strikes, unrest, and calls for abolition have once again laid bare the abusive inner workings of detention. In early 2021 detention numbers reached their lowest in two decades due to the pandemic, but under the Biden administration they are again rising.[21] A letter written by Cuban asylum-seeker Reineris Perez Gonzalez and signed by dozens of others detained in Eloy, Arizona, in the fall of 2020 and published online in *IMM Print* speaks to experiences of timelessness, racial discrimination, vulnerability to COVID-19, lack of safety protocols, and threats made by guards. "This affects us psychologically, being locked up," Gonzalez wrote. "In addition, there's a lot of COVID-19 infections here, but it's impossible to maintain social distancing. We get to see daylight maybe one hour a day. We fled Cuba so we wouldn't be put in prison and here we are, in prison. . . . We're treated like commodities."[22]

In one of Lenin's poems posted to his blog, *Lene Stranded from Cuba*, he says he is "trying hard to survive" and "to find freedom in all things as I was promised as I entered this country." In another, he writes, "Everything that has a beginning must always have an end."[23]

Beyond the 1980s, Cuban and Haitian migration experiences would continue to overlap, despite their different fates in the immigration system, through the disproportionate impact of the HIV/AIDS crisis on both migrant groups and as the 1990s brought new displacements of Cuban and Haitian "boat people." These new migrations would prompt the Bush Sr. and Clinton administrations to strengthen the offshore deterrents to Caribbean migration put in place by the Reagan administration, including concentrating detention efforts at Guantánamo Bay, Cuba. Haitians, however, would continue to experience exceptional discrimination through the continuation of the interdiction program and prolonged detention in a Haitian HIV-quarantine camp at Guantánamo.

The entanglements of "xenophobia, racism, nationalism, and fears of HIV/AIDS" in the late 1980s and early 1990s led to coalition organizing that brought queer and migrant rights groups together in common cause.[24] In its lesser-known history, the AIDS Coalition to Unleash Power (ACT UP), a direct action organization responding to the HIV/AIDS crisis, began building coalitions with immigrant rights groups and organized actions on behalf of detained migrants in Los Angeles and New York. ACT UP members also played a central role in the fight to close the Haitian refugee HIV-quarantine area that was established at Camp Bulkeley at Guantánamo Bay by the Bush Sr. administration in the early 1990s.

Two sites of ACT UP actions, outside of a hotel the INS used to detain migrants in Los Angeles in 1988 and at the Varick Street detention center in New York in 1991, featured a range of storytelling tactics and mobilized a "coalition of voices."[25] In New York, a series of ACT UP actions protesting the detention of HIV-positive Haitians at the Varick Street jail and in the quarantine camp at Guantánamo Bay were recorded and produced as a series of episodes of DIVA (Damned Interfering Video Activists) TV. In these productions, formerly detained migrants shared their stories while advocates read letters and testimonies from those still detained. ACT UP members were also fundamental in locating housing for Haitians released from Guantánamo and paroled into the United States. Karma Chávez asserts the importance of remembering and uncovering these histories. As "imperialism, poverty, homophobia, sexism, and racism promulgate what continues to be, for many, a deadly disease," "queer archive activism" such as DIVA TV and conducting oral histories provide a "model for queer coalition building and AIDS activism that accounts for the complexities of oppression, repression, and illness."[26]

A. Naomi Paik argues that the United States' humanitarian and "benevolent" premise of establishing the HIV-quarantine camp veiled its extraordinary forms of violence. Ultimately, litigation and inside-outside activism led to the closure of Camp Bulkeley. As lawyer Michael Ratner recounts, a hunger strike organized and led by Haitians sequestered at the camp for having or being suspected of having HIV, and joined by university students across the United States, galvanized a campaign that resulted in the camp's closure in 1993. Creole interpreter Ronald Aubourg recalls that Haitians had developed their political consciousness in fighting repression in Haiti and "brought that skill with them in organizing the camp."[27] Haitians resisted their detention at Bulkeley by forming the Association des Refugies Politiques Haitians, modeling representative democracy to uplift testimonies from detention and organize the hunger strike as a collective way to "expose their living death," in Paik's words.[28] Haitians' intersectional positionality brought together a wide array of constituencies. AIDS activists, Haitians, African Americans and civil rights leaders including Jesse Jackson, Sanctuary and human rights organizations, religious leaders, students, Hollywood and public figures, anti-imperialists, and Haitian democracy advocates all contributed to the campaign. Ratner argues that coalition building and following the leadership of those in detention led to the campaign's success.[29]

In the spring of 2017, my work with Freedom for Immigrants took me to the border in Tijuana, Mexico, where I met deep need and radical hope. I learned about the work of the Border Angels; the Deported Veterans and Veterans for Peace; the legal aid organization Al Otro Lado and its fearless attorney Nicole Ramos, who represented the Adelanto 9 and who continues to challenge Customs and Border Protection's repeat violations of US asylum and international law in court; and the churches and migrant shelters accommodating growing numbers of Haitian, Latin American, African, South Asian, and other deported migrants and asylum-seekers in transit through networks of mutual aid.[30] Tijuana has become host to a vibrant Haitian community; many plan to stay, while others await asylum appointments with Customs and Border Protection—many of which never come.[31] Others who could not wait have crossed over alone or in groups.

I befriended Guerline Jozef of the Haitian Bridge Alliance, a Haitian immigrant herself who conducts cross-border advocacy to support Haitians and other Black migrants in US detention. Echoing the reporting of the solidarity publications *Off Our Backs* and *No More Cages* in the 1980s, she told me of an alarming escalation of reproductive violence experienced by Haitian, African, and Latinx women in detention in the US South under the Trump administration. When a whistleblower soon revealed that a Dr. Amin was performing nonconsensual hysterectomies and other procedures on women at the for-profit Irwin detention facility in Georgia in 2020, ICE threatened to deport three women at the facility to Cameroon using false documents.[32] Activism surrounding revelations of abuse and retaliation at Irwin have contributed to the facility's recent closure.

As I write this in late 2021, the Biden administration is conducting one of the largest-scale instances of mass expulsion of thousands of Haitian asylum-seekers at the border in decades, if not ever. Despite the administration's admission that Haiti is unsafe—due to a confluence of political, economic, and ecological crises—through its recent granting of Temporary Protected Status to a limited number of Haitians already here, the Department of Homeland Security is once again meting out exceptional violence and discrimination against Haitians. Images of mounted Border Patrol agents wielding whips against Haitian migrants at the border in Del Rio, Texas, flooded media and social media networks on a Sunday in September as six deportation flights to Haiti took off, with six scheduled the next day. Reflecting the agency's long-standing racism and misogyny, one agent yelled, "This is why your country's shit, because you use your women for this!" at several Haitian women carrying food and personal belongings.[33] Networks of resistance and mutual aid are again strengthening in response to a Department of Homeland Security announcement of its plans to renew a 2002 contract to "process" migrants at Guantánamo Bay. In a scene reminiscent of Cuban and Haitian resistance at Krome, Haitians being removed from the Texas border region rebelled by overtaking a bus transporting them. Several escaped but were quickly re-detained.[34]

Many identify environmental conditions and climate change as key contributors driving Haitian migration, layered atop the histories of US imperialism and militarism explored in this book—themselves extending from slavery, the Haitian revolution, US occupation, and ongoing freedom struggles. Climate change poses the biggest challenge to the United States' globalized migration deterrence apparatus yet. Journalist Todd Miller reveals that the United States has long been forming a militarized response to climate migration. The Department of Homeland Security's 2014 Strategic Sustainability Performance Plan states that "a mass migration plan has been developed" for climate displacement and "increased operations planning of mass migration is under development."[35] During a recent conversation about the increasing role of climate change in Caribbean and Central American displacements, Guerline Jozef told me, "Climate change isn't coming tomorrow. It's now. It's something we should have prepared for thirty years ago, but now that it's here, how do we protect people?" The most important lesson from history, she said, is understanding "how the fear of the other was used to create the system that we have today. The notion of open borders is not an alien concept; open borders are available right now for people who are in power. The concept of a closed border is being put on people to oppress them."

In June 1989, the Bush Sr. administration launched a monthlong pilot program of "expedited adjudication" called Operation Hold the Line in Texas's Rio Grande Valley that marked both another targeting of asylum-seekers and a harbinger of subsequent efforts to consolidate and streamline exclusion. When INS commissioner Alan Nelson traveled to Brownsville to announce the project's launch, he called Central American asylum applicants "frivolous" and "manipulators of America's generosity." The program was a retaliatory response to a crisis of the INS's own making—a decision earlier that year that asylum applicants could no longer leave the Harlingen district near Port Isabel. In effect, thousands of asylum-seekers became stranded in an "open-air prison," living on the streets and in makeshift encampments, overwhelming the Red Cross and legal aid organizations like Proyecto Libertad. Meanwhile, the INS moved its offices to the Port Isabel detention center and brought in 500 additional INS and Border Patrol personnel. The plan also called for the "soft" detention of families through contracts with the Red Cross and other charity organizations. Some Central Americans were forced to walk up to thirty miles for fifteen-minute asylum interviews; others reported Border Patrol officers ripping up their asylum applications.[36] A few weeks into the program, 100 percent of Salvadoran, Guatemalan, and Honduran asylum applications were denied, further boosting detention numbers.

The INS also erected a temporary "tent city" at Port Isabel that year for holding up to 10,000 migrants—the same number of migrants that human rights groups estimate have been killed by the border wall since its construction in the 1990s. The tents never came down. Today, tent cities, military bases, and private contract facilities detain 13,000 migrant children across the Sunbelt; most unaccompanied youth arrive from Central America.[37] In 2006, the Bush Jr. administration resurrected the practice of detaining families in for-profit prisons. After years of litigation and agitation against it, the CCA's T. Don Hutto Residential Center in Taylor, Texas, stopped detaining migrant families in 2009. Another planned family immigration detention center in Texas was defeated by public dissent in 2012.[38]

In 2014, however, the United States appeared to be in the midst of another immigration "crisis." Fleeing poverty and violence, tens of thousands of minors without parents were apprehended in the southern Texas and California borderlands, most of them from El Salvador, Guatemala, and Honduras. Children like Alejandro, an eight-year-old from Honduras, traveled alone with nothing but a birth certificate, hoping to reunite with US family members upon arrival.[39] The Obama administration used the militaristic term "surge" to describe the mass migration, while migrant rights groups called it a humanitarian crisis born out of the same foreign policy failures that characterized the 1980s. Facilities used to hold the children, mostly military bases, quickly became overcrowded in a pattern that would repeat on an unprecedented scale under Trump. Even more appalling, the organization Earthjustice reports military sites used for detaining migrant children frequently contain hazardous levels of toxic chemicals and waste.[40]

On June 20, 2014, World Refugee Day, Obama announced the administration's plans to expand the practice of family detention in response to the current crisis and requested emergency funding from Congress and the granting of broader powers to immigration officials in order to speed up deportations. Obama appeared on ABC's *Good Morning America* with a message to the people of Central America: "Don't send your children unaccompanied on trains or through a bunch of smugglers. That is our direct message to families in Central America. Do not send your children to the borders. If they do make it, they'll get sent back. More importantly, they may not make it."[41] Obama's warning to Central American families echoed the Reagan administration's stated new intentions for immigration detention in 1981, namely, the use of detention and deportation to deter would-be migrants abroad. Since the 1980s, the United States has also pressed Mexico into increased cooperation in restricting Central American migration across its southern border through militarized cross-training and "trade and aid" initiatives. US funding has flowed into the building of the Siglo XXI detention center in Tapachula, Chiapas—the largest in Latin America—and Mexican immigration enforcement trainings that have contributed to recent brutal repressions of migrant caravans attempting to travel into Mexico and on to the United States.[42]

In response to escalating immigration enforcement in the twenty-first century, a new Sanctuary movement has also reemerged. An increasing emphasis on the importance of youth-led and migrant-led organizing has breathed new life into the movement to end immigration detention, and a dialectic of migration, resistance, and state retaliation continues.

Carlos Hidalgo fled El Salvador's civil war with his family in the early 1980s, arriving in the United States at age eleven. After receiving several criminal convictions as an adult, he was arrested by ICE and detained twice at the Adelanto Detention Facility in 2013–15. Describing the facility's dehumanizing and unsafe conditions, including maggots in spoiled meat served to the men, he wrote, "There was only so much we could do, so we focused our time on fighting our cases ourselves. All we had were each other, in solidarity." Many of the men, like Carlos, were detained due to having prior, but resolved, criminal convictions, which he claimed "seems like double jeopardy."[43] Carlos won his release on bond but was soon re-detained at the Theo Lacy jail in Orange County and then returned to Adelanto, where he helped organize a multi-week, 400-person hunger strike. For that, he spent six days in solitary confinement.[44] Free again, Carlos is now an outspoken migrant rights advocate, often speaking publicly against detention, including outside Adelanto on multiple occasions. Recording his story in a Freedom for Immigrants digital history project, he asked, "Taking the dignity and pride is one thing, but taking away your dreams . . . what's after that?" Reflecting on helping other men during his time inside, Carlos said, "I didn't realize how much I impacted people." He continued as his voice broke, "I didn't feel myself being a leader. But I felt I was someone who could make an impact. But those that don't know what I know, you know, speak like I do, who's going to speak for them?"[45]

Hidalgo and Sylvester Owino both contributed poems they wrote during Alicia Partnoy's writing workshop to an anthology self-published by Freedom for Immigrants. We titled it *Call Me Libertad*, after the pseudonym Carlos used during his time in detention to organize and communicate with the outside world. His poem ends with the statement, "We don't ask for much. Just for liberty and justice for all." Sylvester, who was detained at the El Centro and Otay Mesa facilities in San Diego and at the Etowah County detention center in Alabama, said he always kept a journal during his near-decade of detention. "Writing about the abuses against us was the only way to let it out, slowly, so slowly. It is still coming out. I wonder if it will ever end."[46] Today, he runs a popular Kenyan food stand, Rafikiz, in San Diego, always with a smile. Sylvester is safe from deportation and awaits the outcome of the pending class action lawsuit *Owino v. CoreCivic, Inc.*

I did not meet Isaac of the #Adelanto9 in person until the fall of 2017, after he and the others were released. He visited community meetings, sharing his story. Isaac, Omar, and others filed a lawsuit against the US government for their mistreatment, which resulted in a rare victory—a settlement from GEO Group in February 2020 and the release of video footage confirming the assault.[47] They are still pursuing their asylum cases. Also in 2020, I provided an affidavit in a lawsuit led by Citizens for Responsibility and Ethics in Washington, which was suing the National Archives and Records Administration for approving ICE's petition to destroy records of sexual abuse and assault, death reviews, and the use of solitary confinement in detention. We won.[48] These victories, small they may seem, feel significant.

"La luche sigue," Isaac says. The struggle continues.

Acknowledgments

As Mariame Kaba often says, "Nothing that we do that is worthwhile is done alone." The most important thing I have learned in writing this book is that I have never been alone. Many times, however, surfacing pain and trauma has led me to feel isolated, speechless. Other times, collective rage at injustice and the courage of others have helped me find my voice. All credit goes to those who have inspired and encouraged me; all errors are my own.

This project was born of love. Andis, for all you have given and taught me, thank you. My deepest gratitude also goes to Denada, Jolanda, and Kol.

There could not have been a more wonderful, brilliant, or important mentor for this project than Emily S. Rosenberg. The Wisconsin School's finest pupil and critic, she fearlessly challenged the past to forge her own path through a field crowded with men and into the cultural turn. Beyond the meticulous attention, vast breadth of knowledge, and excitement Emily poured into this project's shaping, her unwavering belief in my potential helped me grow as a person first and a scholar second, modeling everything a mentor should be. If I can contribute a fraction of what she has to the world, I will consider it a wild success.

I conducted research and wrote this book during my time at the University of California, Irvine; the University of Southern California; Harvard; and the University of North Carolina at Charlotte. I am grateful to the intellectual communities that embraced me at each and for their financial support. It is my work to pay out the resources I have amassed at each of these institutions to students and the community, who have really been my greatest teachers. At UC Irvine, my cohort and friends kept me afloat during my hardest years after Andi's deportation. Shanon Fitzpatrick, Annessa Stagner, David Wight, Aubrey Adams, Nick Bravo, David Fouser, Ernesto Bassi, Nicole Rebec, Emily Sundstrom, Everardo Carvajal, Teishan Latner, Dan McClure, Mike Koncewicz, Cynthia Cardona, Allison Salazar, Young Hee Kim, Kate Marsden, Christine Eubank, Angela Hawk, and Natasha Synycia all lent their eyes and encouragement to my work in its crucial formative stages. Special thanks to UC Irvine faculty who encouraged me most, especially Jon Wiener, who taught me to always question the dominant narrative; Rubén Rumbaut, who has shown me that history provides a crucial bridge to all disciplines and must be actionable in the present; and David Igler, who pushed my work in new directions and always lent a friendly ear. Additional thanks are due to Laura Mitchell, Steve Topik, Alana Lebron, Carol Burke, Vinayak Chaturvedi, Anita Casavantes Bradford, Andrew Highsmith, Larisa Castillo, Susan Morse, and Shadee Malaklou. Special thanks go to Abby Reyes for her kind and collaborative spirit and to Saumaun, Bo, Angelica, Karina, Magaly, and Nichole. The UC-Cuba Academic Initiative and UC Critical Refugee Studies Collective helped fund my work and provided space for new engagements in Cuban and critical refugee studies, respectively. Thanks go to Raúl Fernández and Yến Lê Espiritu for leading these crucial initiatives.

My years pursuing scholarly work were interspersed with years of community work that enriched and informed my weaving together the many strands of this project. At the Detention Watch Network, Andrea Black became an exceptionally kind and generous mentor, introducing me to the beauty, messiness, and power of community organizing. I am indebted to the work and leadership of many activists, organizers, and formerly imprisoned friends working to end detention and to abolish prisons and borders in their entirety, especially Sylvester, Carlos, Gretta, Cesar, Kapi, Lalo, Jason, Roberto, Ruben, and Mayra. A special thank you is due Aly Wane, whose generosity in spirit, wisdom, and friendship has lifted me more than he knows, as well as Jamila Hammami, Vickie Mena, and Monica Curca. The Pro-Migrant Blog Squad schooled me on digital activism, narrative change, and never giving up: Kyle de Beausset, Prerna Lal, Roberto Lovato, Nezua, David Bennion, Mary Hopkins, Will Coley, Eric K. Ward, Tony Herrera, Tara Tidwell Cullen, Kety Esquivel, and the Dream Activists. I am also grateful to the Free Migration Project for providing a forum for me to share many of the ideas shaping this book.

The Open Society Foundations and Soros Justice Fellowship provided not only funding in support of my research and detention storytelling work but also a community. Special thanks go to Reyna Montoya, Olga Tomchin, Heather Ann Thompson, Angie Junck, Set Hernandez Rongkilyo (no, you're my mentor), Mariame Kaba, Alice Kim, Joey Mogul, Danny Murillo, Eliza Hersh, Teresa Hodge, Isaac Bailey, Ebony Underwood, Steven Czifra, Anne Parsons, Noran Sanford, Renee Feltz, Kandace Vallejo, Luis Angel Reyes-Savalza, Ola Osaze, Phal Sok, Chanravy Proeung, Eddy Zheng, Rose Elizando, James Kilgore, Linda Heng, Tung Nguyen, Anthony Robles, Erin

Acknowledgments

Siegal McIntyre, Seth Freed Wessler, Greg Constantine, Judy Greene, Adam Culbreath, and Chrissy Voight. They have all generously engaged with and challenged my work and ideas, helping me evolve as a scholar and abolitionist. I owe innumerable debts to Freedom for Immigrants. Christina Fialho and Christina Mansfield are a force; I thank them for everything. Jan Meslin's mentorship in enacting the kind of love that is world-transformative means everything to me. Special thanks also go to Rebecca Merton, Paula Kahn, Cynthia Galaz, Gene Lockett, Cindy Knoebel, Sofia Casini, Bud Conlin, Bob Libal, Katherine Weathers, Christine Ho, Elaine McCain, Liza Diniakos, Louis Watanabe, Sally Pillay, and the visitation network.

I am honored that several people in particular lent me their time and firsthand perspectives, trusting me with their stories shared here: Isaac of the Adelanto 9, Mayra, Carlos Hidalgo, Sylvester Owino, Guerline Jozef, Bruce Bowman, and Renny Golden.

Recalling Pete Seeger's parable of the "teaspoon brigades," I am humbled knowing this book will join a quickening stream of abolitionist scholarship speaking irrefutable truth to power. I am grateful to the many scholars who contributed their feedback and helped shape the intellectual life of this project. Tanya Golash-Boza convened an exceptional cohort of detention scholars who provided early feedback on my project, including Caitlin Patler, Leisy Abrego, Christine Wheatley, Roberto Lovato, Alfonso Gonzales, Katie Dingeman, Irene Vega, and Maria-Elena De Trinidad Young. At USC, Bill Deverell was a great ally and mentor; I appreciate his encouragement and the space he made for me to share my work. Harvard's Charles Warren Center provided me an exceptional home for shaping this project its final stages and space for developing abolitionist scholarship and praxis. Thanks go to Elizabeth Hinton, Walter Johnson, and Vincent Brown for their ongoing support. Unmeasurable love and thanks go to my writing squad—Christina Davidson, Hannah Waits, and Courtney Sato. Thanks are also due to Yareli Castro Sevilla, Tej Nagaraja, Juliet Nebolon, Jessica Wang, Saje Matthieu, Kevin Kim, Ken Osgood, Takeo Rivera, Nicole Guidotti-Hernández, Robert Diaz, Marisol LeBron, Angie Chavez-Bautista, Angel Rodriguez, Jon Booth, Roberto Gonzales, Jenny Allsoop, Laura Cuellar Cortazar, Monnikue McCall, Arthur Patton-Hock, Syed Zaman, Eleanor Craig, and UndocuAllies. I am very lucky to have such brilliant and encouraging colleagues at UNC Charlotte, especially Karen Cox, Jurgen Buchenau, Mark Wilson, Carol Higham, John Cox, Christine Haynes, Ritika Prasad, Dan Dupre, Gregory Mixon, and Peter Ferdinando, who provided helpful feedback on a chapter draft. I also thank Lisandro Pérez, Hannah Gurman, Tom Zeiler, Julio Moreno, Kyle Longley, Marilyn Young,

Laura Belmonte, Samuel Truett, Bill Lopez, Nicole Novack, Ana Minian, Mary Rizzo, Nigel Hatton, Ingrid Eagly, Tanaya Dutta Gupta, Maria Barbero, Carly Goodman, Mirian Martinez-Aranda, Lizbeth Santana, Marla Ramírez, James Stocker, James Campbell, and Juliet Hooker. I am especially indebted to detention scholars David Hernández, Jessica Ordaz, Elliott Young, Jennifer Cullison, Carl Lindskoog, and readers A. Naomi Paik, Jana K. Lipman, and Jenna Loyd for their time and immense generosity.

This project could not have been completed without the tremendous help of archivists, researchers, and editors. Special thanks go to Thaomi Michelle Dinh and Jodie Shull for their invaluable research assistance, Harvard Inter-library Loan and the Miami-Dade Public Library staff for helping me track down a hard-to-find source, and Harvard librarians Fred Burchsted and Josh Lupkin. Archivists at the National Archives in Maryland were especially help-ful in assisting me with a FOIA request and regaled me with stories of Reagan's attorney general Ed Meese asking for a quarter to pay for his parking in front of the NARA building in the 1980s—just when Reagan was attempting to cut NARA's budget. Special thanks go to Tricia Gesner at Associated Press, Annie Sollinger at UMass Special Collections, Jena Jones at the Atlanta History Center, Lisa Jacobson at the Presbyterian History Society, Emily at University of Washington Special Collections, Michael Carlebach, and Gary Monroe for their assistance in obtaining images for the book. Thanks to Julie Bush and Joseph Stuart for their impeccable copyediting and indexing. The research for this monograph has also been funded by the Society for Historians of American Foreign Relations, the Organization of American Historians, the Immigration and Ethnic History Society, and the Goizueta Foundation at the University of Miami's Cuban Heritage Collection. As a graduate fellow in residence, I found community, continued support, and opportunities for collaboration.

It has been a joy to work with the University of North Carolina Press and the Justice, Power, and Politics series. I am ever grateful for Heather Ann Thompson's mentorship and for her and Rhonda Y. Williams's support of my work. Brandon Proia has been engaged with this project since the beginning; I thank him for believing in it from the start and for his exceptional insight, conversations, patience, and expert shepherding of the manuscript into its final stages. Special thanks go to Michelle Angela Ortiz for her artivism and for generously sharing her artwork, *Growth* (2020), for the book's cover.

I owe so much to my family and friends. A special shout-out goes to the GBallers: Marie, Vanitha, Brianne, Kim, Janice, Sakura, Melinda, and my NYC community who supported me the most during Andi's detention and deportation. Amber, Gabby, Maria, Billy, Mary, Tara, Amanda, and Jacqui Lewis at Middle Collegiate Church always extended love and published my story. I thank Dani for always being there and believing in me. Last but not least: Dean, my lucky star. He lifted me up when I was at my lowest. He even color-coded and organized my files.

I am incredibly grateful for the constant support and friendship of my parents, Joseph and Jodie Shull. They taught me to be funny and kind and to write for what's right. I thank them for always believing that my meandering paths will have meaningful ends. My mother has also been an incisive and encouraging editor. My husband and best friend, Craig, has contributed more to this project behind the scenes than anyone else. Craig, Gigi, and Huey, you fill my heart with the greatest happiness.

Notes

ABBREVIATIONS

AFA Alina Fernandez Addendum, Special Collections, University of Arkansas Libraries, Fayetteville, AR

AFP Alina Fernandez Papers, Special Collections, University of Arkansas Libraries, Fayetteville, AR

CCEM Component Correspondence Files of the Attorney General; Edwin Meese, 1985–1988, Records of the Department of Justice, Record Group 60, National Archives and Records Administration at College Park, MD

CFRG Chronological Files of Associate Attorney General Rudolph W. Giuliani, Records of the Department of Justice, Record Group 60, National Archives and Records Administration at College Park, MD

CHTF Cuban-Haitian Task Force Files, Jimmy Carter Presidential Library and Museum, Atlanta, GA

CO Countries, White House Office Records Management Central Files (WHORM) Subject Files, Ronald Reagan Presidential Library and Museum, Simi Valley, CA

DNP Darlene Nicgorski Papers on the Sanctuary Movement, Honnold/Mudd Library, Claremont University Consortium, Claremont, CA

FCC Fort Chaffee Collection, Cuban Heritage Collection, University of Miami, Coral Gables, FL

FHF Francis S. M. (Frank) Hodsoll Files, Ronald Reagan Presidential Library and Museum, Simi Valley, CA

HRC Haitian Refugee Collection, Schomburg Center for Research in Black Culture, New York Public Library, New York, NY

IM Immigration/Naturalization, White House Office Records Management Central Files (WHORM) Subject Files, Ronald Reagan Presidential Library and Museum, Simi Valley, CA

JCF James Cicconi Files, Ronald Reagan Presidential Library and Museum, Simi Valley, CA

JMLF J. Michael Luttig Files, Ronald Reagan Presidential Library and Museum, Simi Valley, CA

OAPR   Records Relating to the Oakdale and Atlanta Prison Riots, 11/23/1987–12/4/19, FOIA Request #60856, Records of the Department of Justice, Record Group 60, National Archives and Records Administration at College Park, MD

SFRG   Subject Files of Rudolph W. Giuliani, 1981–1983, Records of the Department of Justice, Record Group 60, National Archives and Records Administration at College Park, MD

UBC   University Baptist Church Sanctuary Movement Records, Special Collections, University of Washington, Seattle, WA

USCIS   USCIS History Office and Library, Washington, DC

PREFACE

1. Martin Luther King Jr., "Beyond Vietnam—A Time to Break Silence." (speech, New York, April 4, 1967, American Rhetoric, https://www.americanrhetoric.com/speeches /mlkatimetobreaksilence.htm.

2. Some of the most extreme forms of abuse that routinely occur in detention are medical neglect and sexual assault, while formal complaints often go ignored. For example, a Freedom of Information Act request by Freedom for Immigrants revealed that out of 33,000 complaints of sexual and physical abuse in detention made to the Department of Homeland Security (DHS) between 2010 and 2016, less than 1 percent were investigated. See "Widespread Sexual Assault," Freedom for Immigrants, 2018, https://www .freedomforimmigrants.org/sexual-assault.

3. "Adelanto Hunger Strike Complaint to DHS Office of Civil Rights and Civil Liberties," June 22, 2017, https://www.documentcloud.org/documents/3887174-Adelanto -Hunger-Strike-Complaint-to-DHS-Office.html.

4. "Mistreatment of Detainees Participating in a Hunger Strike at Adelanto Detention Facility," American Civil Liberties Union of Southern California, June 30, 2017, https:// www.aclusocal.org/sites/default/files/field_documents/aclu_letter_re_adelanto_hunger _strike.pdf.

5. "Migrant Detainees at GEO Group's Adelanto Resume Hunger Strike," *Telesur*, June 22, 2017, https://www.telesurenglish.net/news/Migrant-Detainees-at-GEO-Groups -Adelanto-Resume-Hunger-Strike-20170622-0031.html.

6. Freedom for Immigrants, "#Adelanto9 Launch Hunger Strike in California," *Imm Print*, June 12, 2017, https://imm-print.com/adelanto9-launch-hunger-strike-in-california -e189bbcdc26b/.

7. Recounted from the author's witnessing and communications with people in detention.

8. "ICE and GEO Group Admit Assaulting Migrant Hunger Strikers at Adelanto Detention Compound," *TeleSur*, June 16, 2017.

9. That year, the California state budget limited the growth of private-contract detention in the state and appointed the state attorney general's office to oversee and report on conditions in detention facilities. When the office released its first report in February 2019, it detailed widespread continuing abuses across the system. Although the COVID-19 pandemic has reduced detention numbers, private prison companies are capitalizing on the crisis to expand. See Marie McIntosh, "California's Attorney General Reveals Abuses in Immigration Detention Conditions Report," Immigrant Legal Resource Center, February

                                                                       Notes to Pages xiii–xvii

26, 2019, https://www.ilrc.org/california%E2%80%99s-attorney-general-reveals-abuses
-immigration-detention-conditions-report.

10. Eunice Cho and Joanna Naples-Mitchell, "Abuse and Retaliation against Hunger
Strikers in Detention," *Just Security*, June 23, 2021.

11. While not a new practice, there was a new surge in family and child detention under
the Trump administration. The COVID-19 pandemic dramatically reduced detention
numbers in 2020–21, yet they are again increasing under the Biden administration. As
of August 2021, ICE is holding around 25,000 migrants in detention. See "Immigration
Detention Quick Facts," Immigration Detention Primer, Trac Immigration, 2021,
https://trac.syr.edu/immigration/quickfacts/.

12. Trouillot, *Silencing the Past*, 27; Guha, "Prose of Counter-Insurgency"; Paik, *Rightlessness*, 17.

13. Loyd and Mountz, *Boats, Borders, and Bases*, 52–53.

14. W. Lopez, *Separated*; Abrego, "On Silences."

15. Espiritu, *Body Counts*, 19–20.

16. Paik, *Rightlessness*, 3–4. Robin D. G. Kelley's concept of "hidden transcripts" of
everyday resistance builds upon the work of James Scott, George Lipsitz, Victor Rios,
and others, where oppressed people can "exercise power over, or create space within, the
institutions and social relationships that dominated their lives." Cited in Chase, *Caging
Borders*, 17.

17. "Critical Vocabularies," Critical Refugee Studies Collective, accessed December 21,
2021, https://criticalrefugeestudies.com/resources/critical-vocabularies.

INTRODUCTION

1. Migrant detention itself has yet to be theorized as an extension of US "low-intensity
conflict" doctrine characterizing the Cold War era and its relationships to border enforce-
ment and carceral buildups. In coming to define detention as a form of counterinsurgency,
I thank Jenna Loyd and build upon the work of Timothy J. Dunn, Stuart Schrader, Jordan
T. Camp, and Rachel Ida Buff. Historians who emphasize the intersections of war, foreign
policy, and immigration include Donna R. Gabaccia, Yến Lê Espiritu, Jana K. Lipman,
Ellen Wu, Carl bon Tempo, Meredith Oyen, María Cristina García, Elliott Young, and
Hideaki Kami. Scholars who focus on migrant detention in the Reagan era include Robert
S. Kahn, Jenna M. Loyd and Alison Mountz, David Manuel Hernández, Carl Lindskoog,
Ana Raquel Minian, Jessica Ordaz, Patrisia Macías-Rojas, Jeffrey S. Kahn, and César
Cuauhtémoc García Hernández.

2. For more on the "spectacular dynamics" of immigration enforcement in this era, see
Loyd and Mountz, *Boats, Borders, and Bases*, 2–3.

3. As E. Tendayi Achiume argues, "Insofar as certain forms of international migration today are responsive to political subordination rooted in colonial and neocolonial
structures, a different conceptualization of such migration is necessary: one that treats
economic migrants as political agents exercising equality rights when they engage in 'deco-
lonial' migration." See "Migration as Decolonization."

4. As of June 2020, the top five "most serious criminal convictions" that have served as
grounds for removal since 2003 have been: no conviction, illegal reentry, driving under the
influence, assault, and traffic offense, with no conviction comprising 70 percent of the total

of over 5 million removals. TRAC Immigration, Syracuse University, accessed December 21, 2021, https://trac.syr.edu/phptools/immigration/remove/.

5. Stumpf, "Crimmigration Crisis"; Greene, Carson, and Black, *Indefensible*.

6. Pueblo Sin Fronteras, "2018 Refugee Caravan: Viacrucis Migrantes en la Lucha," Prison Industry Divestment Movement, Freedom to Thrive, March 22, 2018, https:// prisondivest.com/2018/03/22/2018-refugee-caravan-viacrucis-migrantes-en-la-lucha/; Héctor Efrén Flores, "This Caravan Is Yours, Mr. Trump," Latino Rebels, April 10, 2018, https://www.latinorebels.com/2018/04/10/caravanisyours/.

7. Banham, "The Transportation Palimpsest," in *Los Angeles*. For the use of "palimpsest" in prison contexts, see Paik, "Guantánamo Bay"; The ACE Steering Committee, "Prison as Palimpsest: The Dialectics of the Cell in Everyday Life," in *The Prison Cell*, 143–63.

8. As David Manuel Hernández asserts, a "*confluence* of immigration and national security crises lead to future policy changes and further 'cast immigrants as the enemy within.'" "Undue Process," 60.

9. In using the term "total war" to describe the Reagan administration's offensive against migrants and their allies, I borrow from the language of the Sanctuary movement itself and also from Kenneth Osgood's work on the Eisenhower administration's global Cold War propaganda campaign. See Osgood, *Total Cold War*.

10. Dunn, *Militarization of the U.S.-Mexico Border*, 20. Originating in the Pentagon's division of the "spectrum of conflict" in military engagement, low-intensity conflict aims to avoid sustained deployment and casualties of US troops. CIA officer Theodore Shackley's 1981 book, *The Third Option*, served as a mass-market primer for many Reagan administration officials on the use of guerrilla warfare, counterinsurgency techniques, and covert actions, especially in Central America. (The first option was direct military engagement and the second was doing nothing.) Grandin, *Empire's Workshop*, 92–93.

11. See Zaretsky, *No Direction Home*; García, *Seeking Refuge*, 86; and Shull, "'Nobody Wants These People,'" 7–8. On "compassion fatigue" and Southeast Asian refugees, see Espiritu, *Body Counts*.

12. Grandin, *End of the Myth*, 225; Belew, *Bring the War Home*.

13. Rudolph W. Giuliani, "The Interdiction Program," *INS Reporter*, Summer 1982, 3–4.

14. FAIR would later be categorized as a hate group by the Southern Poverty Law Center. See Southern Poverty Law Center, "John Tanton's Legacy," July 18, 2019, https:// www.splcenter.org/hatewatch/2019/07/18/john-tantons-legacy; Carly Goodman, "The Shadowy Network Shaping Trump's Immigration Policies," *Washington Post*, September 27, 2018; and Denvir, *All-American Nativism*.

15. Bon Tempo, *Americans at the Gate*, 168–69. See also Lee, *America for Americans*.

16. Simon, *Governing through Crime*, 3–6, 173.

17. Shull, "'Nobody Wants These People'"; Edward Walsh, "Next Cuban Exodus May Not Get as Warm a Welcome as '80 Boatlift," *Washington Post*, April 28, 1981.

18. Memo, William French Smith to Ronald Reagan, June 26, 1981, box 15, FHF; Charles R. Babcock, "Immigration Plan Includes Amnesty, Tighter Controls," *Washington Post*, July 31, 1981.

19. "Draft Presidential Crime Speech," folder "Statements/Testimony, Others," box 16, SFRG.

20. See Dunn, *Militarization of the U.S.-Mexico Border* and *Blockading the Border*. Dunn asserts that the range of measures implemented by US government agencies during this time period amounted to a gradual "militarization" of the US-Mexico border region,

defining militarization as the "use of military rhetoric and ideology, as well as military tactics, strategy, technology, equipment, and forces." *Militarization of the U.S.-Mexico Border*, 3. See also Nevins, *Operation Gatekeeper*; Grandin, *Empire's Workshop*.

21. "New Approaches to Enforcement" and "Interagency Cooperation Produces Results," *INS Reporter*, Fall–Winter 1983–84, 9–14, 18–21; Dunn, *Militarization of the U.S.-Mexico Border*, 43–45. A buildup of equipment such as helicopters, spotlights, and loudspeakers was used for more than just detection and surveillance; it was also used to intimidate and deter migrants from crossing the border.

22. Dunn, *Militarization of the US-Mexico Border*, 35; Glick, *War at Home*, 30–31.

23. Robert Manning, "Reagan: Sights on a New Order," *South*, September 1983, 9.

24. Macías-Rojas, *From Deportation to Prison*, 1–11, 54–75.

25. Six reports issued by the DHS's Office of Inspector General since December 2020 detail findings of ICE detention conditions in violation of written standards. See "Immigration and Customs Enforcement," Office of Inspector General, Department of Homeland Security, accessed December 21, 2021, https://www.oig.dhs.gov/taxonomy/term/3.

26. Espiritu, "Toward a Critical Refugee Study"; Abrego, "On Silences."

27. Hinton, *America on Fire*; See also Kaba, *We Do This 'til We Free Us*.

28. "Alfredo at East Shore Unitarian Church," July 18, 1984, folder 3, box 3, UBC.

CHAPTER 1

1. Taparata, "'Refugees as You Call Them,'" 10; Lee, *America for Americans*, 36. As Lee shows, racialized exclusions were also embedded in American colonial law before the Revolution.

2. K. Hernández, *City of Inmates*, 9.

3. Agamben, *Homo Sacer*.

4. Written testimony by Simon, June 17, 1980, box 2, FCC.

5. Kanstroom, *Deportation Nation*, x. See also Zolberg, *Nation by Design*.

6. Camp, *Incarcerating the Crisis*, 17.

7. Kanstroom, *Deportation Nation*, 22, 33–60.

8. Hirota, *Expelling the Poor*; Law, "Lunatics, Idiots, Paupers, and Negro Seamen"; N. Shah, *Contagious Divides*, 183; D. Hernández, "Carceral Shadows," 70–71. For more on "medicalized nativism," see Molina, *Fit to be Citizens?*, 58; and Young, *Forever Prisoners*. Young sheds light on a larger but hidden form of detention in a network of poorhouses and mental asylums that, when combined with penal institutions, incarcerated 70,000 migrants a year by the early 1900s across the country. For more on scientific racism and eugenics, see Stern, *Eugenic Nation*.

9. Anti-Chinese, or Orientalist, sentiment was a global phenomenon circulating throughout the Americas, an "inheritance from the long colonial experience." S. Miller, *Unwelcome Immigrant*, 38; Lee, *At America's Gates* and "'Yellow Peril.'"

10. Du Bois, "Spawn of Slavery." On convict leasing as an extension of slavery, see LeFlouria, *Chained in Silence*; Haley, *No Mercy Here*; and Fierce, *Slavery Revisited*.

11. Shichor, *Punishment for Profit*, 42. In Texas, the remnants of convict leasing lasted through the 1960s, and the plantation-style labor practices at the Louisiana State Penitentiary, otherwise known as "Angola," demonstrates a through line to the present. See also Blackmon, *Slavery by Another Name*; Alexander, *New Jim Crow*; and Bauer, *American Prison*.

12. Lee, *At America's Gates*; Young, *Alien Nation*; Romero, *Chinese in Mexico*; Hsu, *Dreaming of Gold*.

13. K. Hernández, *City of Inmates*, 87.

14. In *Chae Chan Ping v. United States* (1889), the court invoked national sovereignty in upholding the government's right to exclude immigrants. In *Fong Yue Ting v. United States* (1893), the Supreme Court affirmed the Geary Act and the government's right to deport noncitizens as a matter of plenary (absolute) power unregulated by the Constitution and ruled that deportation and deportation hearings were "not punishment for a crime." *Wong Wing v. United States*, decided in 1896, the same year the Supreme Court upheld Jim Crow segregation in *Plessy v. Ferguson*, upheld the government's right to detain a noncitizen pending removal yet labeled it "not imprisonment in a legal sense." K. Hernández, *City of Inmates*, 88–89; D. Hernández, "Carceral Shadows," 66–67. Justice Brewer's dissent in *Fong Yue Ting* reads, "It needs no citation of authorities to support the proposition that deportation is punishment. Everyone knows that to be forcibly taken away from home and family and friends and business and property, and sent across the ocean to a distant land, is punishment, and that oftentimes most severe and cruel."

15. Ngai, *Impossible Subjects*. Kelly Lytle Hernández asserts the 1929 act "dramatically remade the story of imprisonment in the United States" by fueling federal imprisonment in the borderlands. K. Hernández, *City of Inmates*, 146.

16. For more about 1930s mass repatriations and their intergenerational legacies, see Balderrama, *Decade of Betrayal*; and Ramírez, "Making of Mexican Illegality."

17. Executive Order 9066, February 19, 1942, The US National Archives and Records Administration, https://www.archives.gov/historical-docs/todays-doc/?dod-date=219.

18. Hirabayashi, *Principled Stand*.

19. Chase, "Carceral Networks," in *Caging Borders*, 25–26; Nebolon, "'Life Given Straight from the Heart'"; Young, *Forever Prisoners*.

20. K. Hernández, *Migra!*, 41; D. Hernández, "Carceral Shadows," 68–75. See also Rosas, *Abrazando el Espíritu*; and Goodman, *Deportation Machine*.

21. Bon Tempo, *Americans at the Gate*.

22. United Nations General Assembly, *Convention and Protocol Relating to the Status of Refugees*.

23. Bon Tempo, *Americans at the Gate*, 5–9.

24. "Humanizing the Administration of the Immigration Law," address by Attorney General Herbert Brownell Jr., January 26, 1955, US Department of Justice, https://www.justice.gov/sites/default/files/ag/legacy/2011/09/12/01-26-1955.pdf; *Leng May Ma v. Barber*, 357 US 185 (1958).

25. Ordaz, *Shadow of El Centro*, 6. See also Cullison, "Valley of Caged Immigrants."

26. Schrader, *Badges without Borders*; Camp, *Incarcerating the Crisis*; Seigel, *Violence Work*.

27. Hinton, *From the War on Poverty to the War on Crime*, 11. See also Thompson, "Why Mass Incarceration Matters"; and Murukawa, *First Civil Right*.

28. Paul Kramer, "The Water Cure," *New Yorker*, February 17, 2008.

29. Seigel, *Violence Work*, 27; Schrader, *Badges without Borders*.

30. Camp, *Incarcerating the Crisis*, 4, 8–9.

31. Schrader, *Badges without Borders*, 2, 28–29; Seigel, *Violence Work*, 26.

32. Galeano, "Invisible Sources of Power," 134–72. See also LaFeber, *Inevitable Revolutions*; Rabe, *Killing Zone*; Grandin, *Empire's Workshop*; Lipman, *Guantánamo*.

33. Rosenberg, *Financial Missionaries*; Seigel, *Violence Work*, 27; Holmes, "Economic Roots of Reaganism."

34. Gill, *School of the Americas*, 8–9.

35. For more on white flight suburbanization, see Avila, *Popular Culture in the Age of White Flight*, 1–20.

36. Chase, "Carceral Networks," in *Caging Borders*, 13–15; Gilmore, *Golden Gulag*, 36; Volker Janssen, "Private Prisons," in Chase, *Caging Borders*, 279–83.

37. Latner, *Cuban Revolution in America*, 1–2.

38. Felber, *Those Who Know Don't Say*; Thompson, *Blood in the Water*. See also Latner, *Cuban Revolution in America*; and Gómez, "'Nuestras vidas corren casi paralelas.'"

39. Camp, *Incarcerating the Crisis*, 9–10.

40. California Governor's Commission on the Los Angeles Riots, *Reports of Consultants*.

41. Ronald Reagan, "Speech by Governor Ronald Reagan before the University of Southern California Law Day Luncheon, Los Angeles," April 29, 1967, Ronald Reagan Presidential Library, https://www.reaganlibrary.gov/archives/speech/april-29-1967 -speech-governor-ronald-reagan-university-southern-california-law-day.

42. Bardacke, "César Chávez," 209–24; Pawel, *Union of Their Dreams*; Holmes, "Economic Roots of Reaganism," 55–80, 63.

43. Gilmore, *Golden Gulag*, 37–44.

44. Buff, *Against the Deportation Terror*, 108–9.

45. Ordaz, *Shadow of El Centro*, 71.

46. Ordaz, 9.

47. Lipman, "Refugee Camp in America," 60.

48. Jana Lipman, "U.S. Military Bases Used to Welcome Foreign Refugees. Now, They Are Being Used to Scare Away Migrants," *Washington Post*, July 5, 2018.

49. Nguyen, *Gift of Freedom*; Espiritu, *Body Counts*; Lipman, *In Camps*.

50. Espiritu, *Body Counts*, 2.

51. The United States had used military bases to house refugees before, beginning with Hungarians fleeing communism in the 1950s. Lipman, "U.S. Military Bases Used to Welcome Foreign Refugees." See also Lipman, "Refugee Camp in America"; Lipman, "'Precedent Worth Setting'"; and Loyd and Mountz, *Boats, Borders, and Bases*, 36–42.

52. Lindskoog, *Detain and Punish*, 2; Buff, *Against the Deportation Terror*. See also Loza, *Defiant Braceros*; Izumi, "Prohibiting 'American Concentration Camps'"; and Coutin, *Legalizing Moves*.

53. Bon Tempo, *Americans at the Gate*, 10, 167–96.

54. Martin, *The Other Eighties*. See also the chapter "Abolishment of the INS/Border Patrol" in Patiño, *Raza Sí, Migra No*, 222–50.

55. Paik, *Rightlessness*, 30–53.

CHAPTER 2

1. Hamm, *Abandoned Ones*, 55; Llanes, *Cuban Americans*, 178.

2. "Cuban Refugees Riot at Fort Chaffee," *Washington Post*, June 2, 1980; "The Refugees: Rebels with a Cause," *Newsweek*, June 16, 1980.

3. Clinton, *My Life*, 275–77.

4. Karen De Witt, "New Cuban Influx at Fort Chaffee Arouses Hostility," *New York Times*, August 11, 1980.

5. "Freedom Flotilla: A Brave Skipper, a Grateful Family and Angry Florida Critics," *People*, May 26, 1980. A study of negative portrayals of the Mariel Cubans in national newspapers concluded that the number of those who had committed felonies or who were mental patients constituted less than 5 percent of the boatlift. However, "the attention focused on that small group eventually stigmatized the entire population." Hufker and Cavender, "From Freedom Flotilla to America's Burden," 322.

6. Rivera, *Decision and Structure*, 10.

7. "Gene Eidenberg unrehearsed conversation Sept 3 81," folder "Barbara Lawson: Cuban-Haitian Task Force Documents, 1980–1981," box 1, FCC.

8. Quoted in Llanes, *Cuban Americans*, 179–81.

9. For boatlift statistics, see Larzelere, *1980 Cuban Boatlift*.

10. Zaretsky, *No Direction Home*, 144–45. See also Hall et al., *Policing the Crisis*; Lee, *America for Americans*; and Cohen, *Folk Devils and Moral Panics*.

11. Engstrom, *Presidential Decision Making Adrift*, 28.

12. Some 14,000 unaccompanied Cuban children were also sent to the United States through Operation Pedro Pan in 1960–62, facilitated by the CIA and the US Catholic Church. See Casavantes Bradford, "Remembering Pedro Pan."

13. Jack Watson quoted in *Life* magazine, January 1981, reprinted in box 3, AFP. See also Kami, *Diplomacy Meets Migration*, 144–46; and Greenhill, *Weapons of Mass Migration*.

14. Edward K. Burns, "The Cuban Boatlift," *INS Reporter*, Winter 1981–82, 4. See also Engstrom, *Presidential Decision Making Adrift*, 63.

15. M. C. García, *Havana USA*, 68.

16. Hay, *"I've Been Black in Two Countries,"* 32; Peña, "'Obvious Gays,'" 496; Capó, "Queering Mariel," 89; M. C. García, *Havana USA*, 65. The term "undesirables" quickly increased in usage throughout media and government sources, appearing earliest in a White House policy memo dated May 13, 1980. See Engstrom, *Presidential Decision Making Adrift*, 105–6. In reporting that was largely discredited, the *Washington Post* claimed in July 1980 that 20,000 Mariel migrants in resettlement camps were "homosexuals." María Cristina García estimates that 1,000 were QTGNC, while Susana Peña says the US government, while not officially counting, estimated between 200 and 6,800.

17. M. C. García, *Havana USA*, 69–74. See also Aguirre, Sáenz, and James, "Marielitos Ten Years Later."

18. Steven R. Weisman, "President Says U.S. Offers 'Open Arms' to Cuban Refugees," *New York Times*, May 6, 1980, sec. A.

19. US Department of State, *Cuban Refugees*, 71.

20. M. C. García, *Havana USA*, 47–52.

21. In Marxist terminology, "lumpen" refers to "lumpenproletariat," or an underclass of people, including vagrants and "criminals," who lack revolutionary consciousness. Capó, "Queering Mariel," 83; Fidel Castro, "Speech by Cuban President Fidel Castro at International Workers' Day Rally Held at José Martí Revolution Square, Havana," May 1, 1980, full text in English at Marxists Internet Archive, https://www.marxists.org/history/cuba/archive/castro/1980/05/01.htm.

22. Capó, "Queering Mariel," 84. Castro quoted in Abel Sierra Madero, "Memorias del Mariel: Actos de repudio y violencia colectiva en Cuba," *El Nuevo Herald*, May 1, 2018. See also Fernández, *Mariel Exodus*, 23–41.

23. Testimony of Manuel Alvarez Machado, folder 2, box 2, FCC.

24. Antonio's story is recounted in M. Garcia, "Last Days in Cuba"; poster cited in Capó, "Queering Mariel," 87.

25. Carter's creation of this status was also, in part, a response to a 1980 ruling in *HRC v. Civiletti* requiring the INS to provide Haitian asylum-seekers due process.

26. "Refugees Stung by a Backlash," *U.S. News and World Report*, October 13, 1980, box 3, AFP. See also Guerrero, "Tenuous Welcome"; and Vong, "Compassion Politics."

27. Hinton, *America on Fire*, 207–11.

28. Portes and Stepick, *City on the Edge*, 46–50; "Miami Riot Continues," *Washington Post*, May 19, 1980; "South Florida Still Paying Boat Lift's Price," *Miami Herald*, April 19, 1981, box 3, AFA; Aja, *Miami's Forgotten Cubans*, 117. For an example of media coverage linking African Americans, Cubans, and Haitians to crime rates in Miami, see "Absolute War in Our Streets: Southern Florida: Riots, Refugees, and Now a Crime Wave," *Time*, November 24, 1980.

29. M. C. García, *Havana USA*, 69–73. Although "Marielito" is widely used and has been reclaimed by Mariel Cubans and scholars in subsequent years, I refrain from using it here.

30. Quoted in Llanes, *Cuban Americans*, 164–65.

31. Kami, *Diplomacy Meets Migration*, 165.

32. Larzelere, *1980 Cuban Boatlift*, 379, 434.

33. "Significant Activities, 18 May 80," folder "Gastón A. Fernández: Federal Control Center Documents, 1980 (1/2)," box 1, FCC.

34. "Federal Control Center Security Assessment (24 May 80)," folder "Gastón A. Fernández: Federal Control Center Documents, 1980 (2/2)," box 1, FCC.

35. Bob King, "Problems," folder "Gastón A. Fernández: Security Reports and Memoranda, 1980," box 2, FCC. See also Lipman, "'Precedent Worth Setting'" and "Refugee Camp in America."

36. Aguirre, Sáenz, and James, "Marielitos Ten Years Later"; Aguirre, "Cuban Mass Migration."

37. For an early example, see "Retarded People and Criminals Loaded on U.S. Boats in Cuba," *New York Times*, May 11, 1980, box 3, AFA. See also Aguirre, "Cuban Mass Migration."

38. Gosin, *Racial Politics of Division*, 66–80; Portes and Stepick, *City on the Edge*, 58.

39. Cesar E. Montejo, "Benefició a Castro éxodo del Mariel" [letter to the editor], *Miami Herald*, September 1, 1980, 4; Gosin, *Racial Politics of Division*, 76–78.

40. Haney and Vanderbush, "Role of Ethnic Interest Groups," 347; Bustamante, "Anti-Communist Anti-Imperialism?"

41. "El Centro De La Raza Statement," July 1980, folder "Immigration and Refugee Material: A.I.N.L.—Lutheran Immigration and Refugee Service," box 5, AFP.

42. William K. Stevens, "Arkansas Fort Receives First of Thousands of Cubans," *New York Times*, May 10, 1980.

43. Heidi Beirich, "The FAIR Files," Southern Poverty Law Center, July 23, 2010, https://www.splcenter.org/hatewatch/2010/07/23/fair-files-marielitos-are-'criminals -homosexuals-and-mentally-defective-persons'.

44. Gregory Jaynes, "Fort Smith Has a Bad Morning After," *New York Times*, February 12, 1982; Hufker and Cavender, "From Freedom Flotilla to America's Burden," 332.

45. William K. Stevens, "Pickets Add to Problems for Refugees in Arkansas," *New York Times*, May 11, 1980. The KKK also confronted Vietnamese refugees in the US South in the late 1970s. See Tang, *Asian Texans*. For a comparative analysis of the militarization of

Fort Chaffee between Vietnamese and Cuban detentions, see Lipman, "Refugee Camp in America"; and Loyd and Mountz, *Boats, Borders, and Bases*, 54–86.

46. Nathaniel Sheppard Jr., "Economic Standings Reflect Attitudes on Cuban Refugees," *New York Times*, June 30, 1980. See also Gilmore, *Golden Gulag*.

47. "Refugee VD Cases Reported," *Daily Oklahoman*, August 1, 1980; and "KKK Allegation Still Unconfirmed," *Southwest Times Record*, August 16, 1980, A7, both in folder "Other Newspapers," box 42, CHTF.

48. Letter, Frank White to Rich Williamson, April 20, 1981; and Peter Arnett, "Cubans Caught in 'Beauty, Tragedy' of System," *Arkansas Democrat*, April 19, 1981, both in folder "General Correspondence," box 9, FHF.

49. Loyd and Mountz, *Boats, Borders, and Bases*, 54–58.

50. Siro del Castillo, "One Day More or One Day Less," folder "Barbara Lawson: Cuban-Haitian Task Force Documents, 1980–1981," box 1, FCC.

51. Masud-Piloto, *From Welcomed Exiles to Illegal Immigrants*, 94. Histories of the US government's "assimilation" programs targeting Native Americans reveal the extent to which forced assimilation is a violent process. See Estes, *Our History Is the Future*; Hoxie, *Campaign to Assimilate the Indians*; and Ellinghaus, *Blood Will Tell*.

52. "Our Purpose," the Cuban-Haitian Task Force Public Affairs Office, December 15, 1980, folder "CHTF Office of Public Affairs," box 12, CHTF.

53. Eloy Gonzalez and Fernando Chang-Moy, LGBTQ Marielitos Oral History Project.

54. *La Libertad*, August 1, 1980, box 36, CHTF.

55. Fernando Chang-Moy, Ada Bello and Mark Cunningham, and Mark Segal, LGBTQ Marielitos Oral History Project; *Philadelphia Gay News*, August 21, 1980.

56. Rachel M. Schwartz and Peter D. Kramer, "Report on Status of Cuban Refugees at Fort McCoy, Wisconsin," August 1980, folder "Fort McCoy Wisconsin," box 21, CHTF.

57. "Refugee Site in Wisconsin a 'Keg of Dynamite,'" *Chicago Sun-Times*, August 30, 1980, folder "Fort McCoy," box 21, CHTF.

58. "Federal Control Center, Status of Commercial Contracts, 20–23 May," folder "Gastón A. Fernández: Federal Control Center Documents, 1980 (2/2)," box 1, FCC.

59. "Refugee Site in Wisconsin a 'Keg of Dynamite'"; John Simon, "The Cubans in Atlanta," *INS Reporter*, Fall–Winter 1982–83, 8–9.

60. Letter, Andrew Carmichael to Victor Palmieri, September 2, 1980, folder "INS [1]," box 36, CHTF.

61. "Refugees Stung by a Backlash"; Granados, "Cuban in the Tundra."

62. Undated letter from Jorge, folder 2, box 2, FCC.

63. Lipman, "Refugee Camp in America," 58–59.

64. "Half-Way House Gives Cubans a Second Chance to Adjust to New Life," *Arkansas Democrat*, September 30, 1980, box 3, AFP. Here, David Lewis of the US Catholic Conference also reported that some Cubans returned to Chaffee after being paid only one dollar an hour and that "we had a couple come back from a chicken farm. It was in a small town and the (Cuban) children were heckled in school." See also "U.S. to Probe Charges Refugees from Chaffee Worked without Pay," *Arkansas Gazette*, February 22, 1981, box 3, AFA.

65. Fernández, *Mariel Exodus*, 42–43.

66. Paul Heath Hoeffel, "Fort Chaffee's Unwanted Cubans," *New York Times*, December 21, 1980.

67. Peña, "'Obvious Gays,'" 499.

68. Hoeffel, "Fort Chaffee's Unwanted Cubans"; Peña, "'Obvious Gays,'" 503.

69. M. C. García, *Havana USA*, 71; "Meeting with Governor White on Fort Chaffee," February 20, 1981, folder "CHTF Office of Public Affairs," box 12, CHTF.

70. *La Vida Nueva* (Fort Chaffee), no. 152, December 13, 1980, Exile Journals, Cuban Heritage Collection, University of Miami. Translated from Spanish by author.

71. *La Vida Nueva*, no. 142, November 27, 1980, Exile Journals.

72. *La Vida Nueva*, no. 142, November 27, 1980, Exile Journals.

73. *La Vida Nueva*, no. 143, November 29, 1980, Exile Journals.

74. Sylvia Spencer, "Cuban Refugees at Fort Chaffee—Freedom in a Resettlement Camp?," *Arkansas Gazette*, March 1, 1981, box 3, AFA.

75. Hoeffel, "Fort Chaffee's Unwanted Cubans."

76. Perlstein, *Invisible Bridge*; I. López, *Dog Whistle Politics*, 56.

77. Ronald Reagan, "Inaugural Address 1981," January 20, 1981, Ronald Reagan Presidential Library, https://www.reaganlibrary.gov/archives/speech/inaugural-address-1981.

78. Heclo, "Ronald Reagan and the American Public Philosophy," 17–18. See also Lewis, "Telling America's Story."

79. Alexander, *New Jim Crow*, 47–48.

80. Memo, Kenneth Starr to William French Smith, November 13, 1981, folder "Attorney General's Office," box 1, SFRG.

81. Ronald Reagan, "Remarks Announcing Federal Initiatives against Drug Trafficking and Organized Crime," October 14, 1982, *Public Papers of President Ronald Reagan*.

82. "Politics Key to the Fate of Camp's Last Cubans," *New York Times*, January 4, 1982.

83. "Governor Outlines Strategy," *Arkansas Gazette*, February 22, 1981, box 3, AFA.

84. Memo, Lyn Nofziger and Richard Williamson to James Baker and Edwin Meese, June 11, 1981, folder "Detention Center and Chaffee Working Files (2)," box 8, FHF.

85. Latner, *Cuban Revolution in America*; Bach, "Immigration and U.S. Foreign Policy," 138; Nora Gámez Torres, "Cuba: How It Was Added to the List of Countries That Sponsor Terrorism," *Miami Herald*, April 18, 2015.

86. Robert Pear, "Plan Aims to Free Refugees in Jails for Crimes in Cuba," *New York Times*, January 30, 1981.

87. Memo, Frank Hodsoll and Kate Moore to Ed Meese, "Task Force on Immigration and Refugee Policy and White House/OMB Study on Related Management Issues," March 28, 1981, folder "Immigration and Refugee Matters (1)," box OA6518, Edwin Meese III Files, Ronald Reagan Presidential Library and Museum, Simi Valley, CA.

88. Reagan, "May 18, 1981," *Reagan Diaries*, 20.

89. "INS Detention Policy," undated, folder "Detention Center and Chaffee Working Files (6)," box 8, FHF.

90. Letter, James Baker III to Frank White, May 4, 1981; Letter, George Bush to Frank White, June 3, 1981, folder "Detention Center and Chaffee Working Files (2)," box 8, FHF.

91. Granados, "Cubans in the Tundra"; "Paradise Lost?," *Time*, November 23, 1981.

92. "Interagency Cooperation and Communication," June 24, 1981, folder "Conference Material 1981, 1983, 1984," box 5, AFP.

93. Memo, William French Smith to Ronald Reagan, June 26, 1981, folder "Report of the President's Task Force on Immigration and Refugee Policy," box 15, FHF.

94. Cited in Dunn, *Militarization of the U.S.-Mexico Border*, 39. On punitive conditions in immigration detention prior to 1980 that primarily targeted Mexican migrants, see Cullison, "Valley of Caged Immigrants"; and Ordaz, *Shadow of El Centro*.

95. Charles R. Babcock, "Immigration Plan Includes Amnesty, Tighter Controls," *Washington Post*, July 31, 1981; Dunn, *Militarization of the U.S.-Mexico Border*, 46.

96. Mary Thornton, "Reagan Wants Emergency Power: Bars to Immigration Sought," *Washington Post*, October 22, 1981, sec. A, folder "Immigration: Press and Clippings," box OA9445, Michael Ulman Files, Ronald Reagan Presidential Library and Museum, Simi Valley.

97. "Remarks by the Attorney General Houston Chamber of Commerce," August 3, 1981, folder "Attorney General's Office," box 1, SFRG.

98. Charles R. Babcock, "Resettling of Cuban Refugees Is Processing at a Slow Pace: Criminal Records, Homosexuality, Mental Illness Are Factors," *Washington Post*, February 10, 1981.

99. Jura Koncius, "Bainbridge Is Leading Refugee Site Choice," *Washington Post*, July 13, 1981.

100. "Cabinet Administration Staffing Memorandum" from William French Smith, July 6, 1981, folder "Detention Center and Chaffee Working Files (2)," box 8, FHF.

101. Robert Lindsey, "U.S. Is Finding That No One Wants to Accept Last Cuban Refugees," *New York Times*, August 9, 1981.

102. This idea first appeared in June 1980 as President Carter requested a report on possible ways to deport Mariel Cubans. Senator Daniel Inouye (D-Hawaii) suggested in Congress, "Take them to Guantanamo and open the gate and say go through there." Florida governor Bob Graham also recommended this to Frank Hodsoll in the Reagan administration's first year, saying, "I can't think of a better place to have a confrontation than our own military base." Don Irwin, "Study Outlining Possible Ways to Deport Criminal Refugees Ordered by Carter," *Los Angeles Times*, June 5, 1980, sec. B. For more on considerations of Guantánamo Bay under the Carter administration, see Engstrom, *Presidential Decision Making Adrift*, 136n121; and James Gerstenzang, "Graham Refugee Plan Goes to White House," *St. Petersburg Times* news clipping, folder "Florida," box 8, FHF.

103. "Using Guantanamo to Hold the Undesirables Who Arrived in the Mariel Boatlift," undated, folder "Detention Center and Chaffee Working Files (5)," box 8, FHF; "U.S. Officials Call Cuba Deal Story 'Absolutely False,'" *Washington Post*, July 5, 1981.

104. "Remarks in an Interview with Managing Editors on Domestic Issues December 3, 1981," *Public Papers of President Ronald Reagan*.

105. Memorandum, Edward C. Schmults to James A. Baker III, January 8, 1982, folder "RS/INS—Glasgow," box 52, SFRG.

106. "Politics Key to the Fate of Camp's Last Cubans," *New York Times*, January 4, 1982.

107. "Termination of Ft. Chaffee Operations," undated, folder "Immigration Policy: Cubans and Haitians," box 10, JCF.

108. "Cubans in Arkansas Will Be Transferred to 2 Federal Prisons," *New York Times*, January 23, 1982.

109. "Federal Prison and Alien Detention Policy" from Edward C. Schmults to James A. Baker III, Edwin L. Harper, Annelise Anderson, and James W. Cicconi, March 10, 1982, folder "Immigration Policy: Cubans and Haitians," box 10, JCF.

110. Hoeffel, "Fort Chaffee's Unwanted Cubans."

111. "#6: Side One: Lawson w/ Tulsa Trib 29 Jan 81," and "#5: RE Montana Transfer, B. Lawson," cassette tapes, January and August 1981, box 2, FCC.

112. Reagan, "February 26, 1982," *Reagan Diaries*, 71.

113. Note attached to memo, James A. Baker to Jim Cicconi, February 26, 1982, folder "Immigration Policy: Cubans and Haitians," box 10, JCF.

114. "March 1981 ABC/Post Public Opinion Poll," folder "Immigration and Refugee Matters [1]," box 21, Edwin Meese III Files.

115. The *Columbus Dispatch* article is cited in Guillermo Martínez, "Mariel Myths Feed Venom across Nation," *Miami Herald*, November 18, 1982, 31A, box 3, AFA.

116. "Remarks of Vice President George Bush at the Miami Citizens Against Crime Luncheon," February 16, 1982, folder "Task Force on South Florida (1)," box OA 11841, Edwin Meese III Files.

117. "Note to Richard" from Deni, August 27, 1983, folder "2–10," box 2, AFP; Quoted in Hamm, *Abandoned Ones*, 78. See also "Castro's 'Crime Bomb' inside U.S.," *U.S. News and World Report*, January 16, 1984; E. González, "Cuban Connection," 4–5.

118. Scott and Marshall, *Cocaine Politics*; Reiss, *We Sell Drugs*, 220–21.

119. Young, *Forever Prisoners*, 131–32.

120. Cuban-American National Foundation, *Report of the Commission on a Free Cuba*.

121. Hamm, *Abandoned Ones*, 73. See chapter 1, as well as Kanstroom, *Deportation Nation*, for an explanation of the judicial branch's increasing deference to the executive in the history of immigration enforcement.

122. "Cubans Jailed in US Start a Court Fight," *Wall Street Journal*, January 23, 1981, box 3, AFA. See also Erickson, "Saga of Indefinitely Detained Mariel Cubans."

123. Capó, "Queering Mariel," 99–100.

124. "Clinton Criticizes White on Cubans," Associated Press, n.d. (1982), folder "RS/INS—Detention Facilities," box 51, SFRG.

CHAPTER 3

1. "Bahamians Agree to Rescue 102 Haitians Marooned for a Month," *New York Times*, November 9, 1980, sec. A1; J. Miller, *Plight of Haitian Refugees*, 69.

2. Jo Thomas, "Sadly, the Marooned Haitians Return Home: Some Will Be Hospitalized Vessel Is Delayed," *New York Times*, November 17, 1980.

3. "Marooned Haitians Resist Rescue, Bahamians Say: A Radio Call for Help," *New York Times*, November 12, 1980; J. Miller, *Plight of Haitian Refugees*, 71.

4. "Bahamians Agree to Rescue 102 Haitians Marooned for a Month."

5. "The Horror of Cayo Lobos Must Shake the Conscience," *Miami Herald*, November 15, 1980; "The Significance of Cayo Lobos," *Miami Herald*, November 29, 1980.

6. Desperate economic and political conditions in Haiti drove the number of Haitian arrivals from 3,859 in 1979 to 22,499 in 1980 and 9,505 in 1981, with a total of 60,000 arrivals between 1977 and 1981. J. Miller, *Plight of Haitian Refugees*, xii; Portes and Stepick, *City on the Edge*, 51.

7. "Federal Correctional Institute, Miami Florida, U.S. Immigration and Naturalization Service," March 5, 1980, folder "Fort McCoy [2]," box 4, CHTF; Lindskoog, *Detain and Punish*, 33.

8. Ronald Reagan, "Executive Order 12324—Interdiction of Illegal Aliens," September 29, 1981, Ronald Reagan Presidential Library, https://www.reaganlibrary.gov/archives/speech/executive-order-12324-interdiction-illegal-aliens; Laguerre, *Diasporic Citizenship*, 82.

9. Gregory Jaynes, "33 Haitians Drown as Boat Capsizes Off Florida," *New York Times*, October 27, 1981, sec. 1A; Stuart Taylor Jr., "Deciding How to Stop Haitians—and Why," *New York Times*, November 1, 1981, sec. E4.

10. Taylor, "Deciding How to Stop Haitians"; Benjamin Hooks, telegram to Ronald Reagan, November 6, 1981, folder "December '81 (2 of 2)," box 3, CFRG.

11. J. Miller, *Plight of Haitian Refugees*, 129.

12. Lipman, "Fish Trusts the Water," 117. See also Lindskoog, *Detain and Punish*; and the chapter "America's Boat People" in Loyd and Mountz, *Boats, Borders, and Bases*.

13. "FCO Report—May 26, 1980," box 1, FCC. See also Lipman, "Fish Trusts the Water," for more on the Cold War origins of the Krome detention facility.

14. Laguerre, *Diasporic Citizenship*, 82.

15. On the unique discrimination facing Haitian migrants, see J. Kahn, *Islands of Sovereignty*; Laguerre, *Diasporic Citizenship*; Lindskoog, *Detain and Punish*; J. Miller, *Plight of Haitian Refugees*; and Stepick, "Unintended Consequences."

16. Lindskoog, *Detain and Punish*; Ordaz, *Shadow of El Centro*.

17. W. Smith, *Law and Justice in the Reagan Administration*, 193.

18. Reagan, *Reagan Diaries*, 30.

19. J. Michael Dash is cited in Polyné, *From Douglass to Duvalier*, 186–93. For more on the era of US military occupation of Haiti, see Renda, *Taking Haiti*.

20. Quoted in Polyné, *From Douglass to Duvalier*, 186.

21. J. Kahn, *Islands of Sovereignty*, 100–101. See also Trouillot, *Haiti*.

22. Lindskoog, *Detain and Punish*, 15–17.

23. "Resolution in Support of Haitian Refugees," National Council of Churches of Christ in U.S.A., February 28, 1974, folder 17, box 21, HRC; Lindskoog, *Detain and Punish*, 18–19.

24. "Dear Friend" Newsletter, American Committee for the Protection of Foreign-Born, March 12, 1974, box 1, American Committee for the Protection of Foreign Born Papers, Special Collections, University of Miami.

25. Turenne Deville, "Testimony of the Deceased," March 23, 1974, box 1, American Committee for the Protection of Foreign Born Papers.

26. Flyer, US Committee for Justice to Latin American Political Prisoners, n.d., folder 7, box 34, HRC.

27. Jay Ressler, "Dragnets: A New Danger for Haitians," *Spirit Magazine*, Spring 1974, CUNY Digital History Archive, http://cdha.cuny.edu/files/original/06ae45f099ba6ee9e0dbc4fab7272f38.pdf.

28. Letter from Haitians at El Paso Camp, February 10, 1977, folder 5, box 31, HRC.

29. Lindskoog, *Detain and Punish*, 25–27. The Haitian Program was also a forebear of Operation Streamline, a program of expedited removal criminal proceedings adopted by the DHS in 2005.

30. "Priest Discovers 8-Year-Old Child of Haitian Refugee Jailed for Two Weeks by Immigration Authorities," Rescue Committee for Haitian Refugees, December 4, 1978, box 1, American Committee for the Protection of Foreign Born Papers.

31. "Seventy Jailed Haitians on Hunger Strike," Rescue Committee for Haitian Refugees, February 13, 1979, folder 6, box 28, HRC. For more on these events, see Lindskoog, *Detain and Punish*, 28–29.

32. Loescher and Scanlan, *Calculated Kindness*, 82–83.

33. Memo, Peter A. Schey to David Crosland, August 4, 1980, folder "Haitians," box 21, CHTF.

34. "State Department Study Team on Haitian Returnees," 1980, folder "Haitians 2nd File [1]," box 36; and Mario A. Rivera, "The Cuban and Haitian Influxes of 1980 and the American Response: Retrospect and Prospect," November 1980, folder "Cuban and Haitian Influxes," box 12, both in CHTF.

35. John Silva, "Court Told of Living Death in Haitian Prison," *Miami News*, April 9, 1980, 1B, 7B; Portes and Stepick, *City on the Edge*, 53.

36. J. Kahn, *Islands of Sovereignty*, 113–18.

37. Judge King cited in Margaret Louden, "Haitian Refugees: No Room for Them," *Judgment* 5, no. 2 (February 1982): 10, folder 8, box 36, HRC.

38. Laguerre, *Diasporic Citizenship*, 81; Stepick, "Unintended Consequences," 137.

39. It was not until the Immigration Reform and Control Act of 1986 that Haitian entrants who arrived during the boatlift were granted permanent status. Loescher and Scanlan, "Human Rights," 344; Stepick, "Unintended Consequences," 141.

40. Stepick, "Unintended Consequences," 188–89.

41. J. Miller, *Plight of Haitian Refugees*, 125–29.

42. "Memorandum of Points and Authorities in Support of Plaintiff's Motion for Temporary Restraining Order and Preliminary Injunction," Graham v. Smith, No. 81–1497-Civ. JE (S.D. FLa. n.d.), in appendix to US Congress, House, Subcommittee on Immigration and Refugee Policy of the Subcommittee Committee on the Judiciary, *United States as a Country of Mass First Asylum*.

43. Memo, James A. Baker to Ronald Reagan, March 13, 1981, folder "[Haitian Refugees] (5 of 6)," box 1, JMLF.

44. Larry L. Sims, "Memorandum for the Attorney General Re: Authority to return undocumented aliens to Haiti after interdiction of Haitians vessels on the high seas," April 10, 1981, folder "Interdiction of Haitian Vessels (1 of 4)," box 1, JMLF.

45. 8 U.S.C. § 1182(f) and 8 U.S.C. § 1185(a)(1).

46. United States ex rel. Knauff v. Shaughnessy, 338 U.S. 537 (1950). Also cited is Ekiu v. United States, 142 U.S. 651, 659 (1892).

47. Sims, "Memorandum for the Attorney General," April 10, 1981, JMLF.

48. As the report admitted, "There is some doubt whether anyone would be able to challenge the plan. It is possible, as recognized by the Criminal Division, that the district court in Florida might be sympathetic to suits filed by third parties challenging the plan. Although the Haitians returned to Haiti would probably lack standing to sue . . . there is a statute which permits aliens permission to sue for torts committed in violation of the law of nations." Sims, "Memorandum for the Attorney General," April 10, 1981, JMLF.

49. Zolberg's *Nation by Design* and Kanstroom's *Deportation Nation* acknowledge the larger trend of Congress and the Supreme Court gradually ceding authority over immigration enforcement to the executive branch over the past century and a half but fail to take the significance of the Reagan administration's expansion of executive authority through Haitian interdiction into account. For a more detailed legal account of challenges to Haitian interdiction concluding in the Supreme Court confirming executive authority in immigration enforcement on the high seas, see Ralph, "Haitian Interdiction on the High Seas."

50. Charles R. Babcock, "Immigration Plan Includes Amnesty, Tighter Controls," *Washington Post*, sec. A, July 31, 1981; Dunn, *Militarization of the U.S.-Mexico Border*, 46.

51. Tennis, "Offshoring the Border," 174, 184.

52. US House, Subcommittee on Immigration, Refugees, and International Law, Senate, Subcommittee on Immigration and Refugee Policy. *Administration's Proposals on Immigration and Refugee Policy*, 11.

53. US Congress, House, Subcommittee on Immigration, Refugees, and International Law, 11. This intention foreshadows Operation Safe Haven of 1994 and accompanying plans to foster interagency and international cooperation to keep Haitians and other Caribbean migrants from arriving on US shores, including the detention of Cubans and Haitians at Guantánamo Bay in the early 1990s.

54. Theodore B. Olson, "Memorandum for the Attorney General Re: Proposed interdiction of Haitian flag vessels," August 11, 1981, folder "Interdiction of Haitian Vessels (1 of 4)," box 1, JMLF.

55. Despite challenges claiming Haitian interdiction violated the United Nations 1967 *Convention and Protocol Relating to the Status of Refugees* and the Refugee Act of 1980, which states that "no contacting state shall expel or return" asylum seekers, interdiction has been upheld by the Supreme Court on the grounds that prohibitions against the forced return of refugees do not apply outside of the territory of the United States. See Haitian Refugee Center, Inc. v. Gracey, 600 F. Supp. 1396 (D.D.C. 1985); Haitian Refugee Center, Inc. v. Baker, 789 F. Supp. 1552 (S.D. Fla. 1991) and 112 S. Ct. 1245 (1992); Haitian Centers Council v. McNary, 789 F. Supp. 541 (E.D.N.Y. 1992); and Sale v. Haitian Centers Council, Inc., 509 U.S. 155 (1993). See also Ralph, "Haitian Interdiction on the High Seas."

56. Handwritten notes by J. Michael Luttig, August 1981, folder "Interdiction of Haitian Vessels (2 of 4)," box 1, JMLF.

57. Handwritten notes by J. Michael Luttig, JMLF.

58. Handwritten notes by J. Michael Luttig, JMLF.

59. This agreement was forged by way of an exchange of diplomatic letters between US ambassador to Haiti Ernest Preeg and Haiti's Secretary of State for Foreign Affairs Edouard Francisque. Haiti agreed to "stop the clandestine migration of numerous residents of Haiti to the United States" in exchange for the United States aiding in enforcing Haiti's emigration laws. The agreement also acknowledged that it is "understood that the United States, having regard for its international obligations pertaining to refugees, does not intend to return to Haiti any Haitian migrants the United States determines qualify for refugee status," while Haiti assured "that Haitians returned to their country and who are not traffickers in illegal migration will not be subject to prosecution for illegal departure." Inter-American Commission on Human Rights, "Report No. 28/93, Case 10.675, United States Decision of the Commission as to the Admissibility."

60. See Motomura, "Haitian Asylum Seekers," for more historical context on the "plenary power doctrine" and evolution of immigration enforcement falling increasingly under the purview of the executive branch over time.

61. "To amend the Immigration and Nationality Act, and for other purposes," U.S. Department of Justice Office of Legislative Affairs, folder "Interdiction of Haitian Vessels (3 of 4)," box 1, JMLF.

62. Mary Thornton, "Reagan Wants Emergency Power: Bars to Immigration Sought," *Washington Post*, October 22, 1981, sec. A, folder "Immigration: Press and Clippings," box OA9445, Michael Ulman Files, Ronald Reagan Presidential Library and Museum, Simi Valley, CA.

63. W. Smith, *Law and Justice in the Reagan Administration*, 196.

64. W. Smith, 194–95, 197.

65. W. Smith, 199.

66. Rudolph W. Giuliani, "The Interdiction Program," *INS Reporter*, Summer 1982, 3–4.

67. Letter, Kenneth W. Dam to William French Smith, December 18, 1982, folder "December 1982," box 1, CFRG.

68. "Around the Nation; Stowaway's Deportation Is Protested in Miami," *New York Times*, January 17, 1982, sec. A.

69. Memorandum, Rudolph W. Giuliani to William French Smith, January 28, 1982, folder "January '82," box 3, CFRG.

70. *Voyage of Dreams.*

71. Jo Thomas, "Racism Is Charged in Fort Drum Plan: Attorneys and Mayor of Miami Criticize Decisions to Move Haitians to Army Post," *New York Times*, November 12, 1981, sec. B14.

72. A 1979 essay by Jeane J. Kirkpatrick, foreign policy advisor to Reagan, is well known for influencing Reagan's foreign policy stance and outlining the Reagan Doctrine, which advocated allying with authoritarian regimes in the fight against communism. Kirkpatrick, "Dictatorships and Double Standards," *Commentary*, November 1979.

73. Reagan, *Reagan Diaries*, 6.

74. Stepick, "Unintended Consequences," 144.

75. Rudolph W. Giuliani, "Memorandum to Files: Visit to Haiti, March 14–16, 1982," April 7, 1982, folder "April '82," box 3, CFRG.

76. "U.S. Official Finds No Repression in Haiti," *New York Times*, April 3, 1982; letter, D. Raphael to Giuliani, n.d., folder "Citizen Mail," box 3, SFRG.

77. Letter, Rudolph W. Giuliani to Louis Casale, March 29, 1982, folder "March '82," box 3, CFRG.

78. Letter, Rudolph W. Giuliani to Peter McPherson, May 13, 1983, folder "May '83 (2 of 2)," box 1, CFRG. The Reagan administration also pushed the Caribbean Basin Initiative to foster business partnerships and open Haiti further to US interests.

79. Polyné, *From Douglass to Duvalier*, 3, 207. For more on the Mica Amendment, see Tennis, "Offshoring the Border," 187.

80. Potoker and Borgman, "Economic Impact of the Caribbean Basin Initiative," 79–80.

81. In the end, the CBI disadvantaged participating economies, including the program's donor partners, Canada, Mexico, and Venezuela. Bakan, Cox, and Leys, *Imperial Power and Regional Trade*, 4–6, 24–32. See also LaFeber, *Inevitable Revolutions*, 286–91.

82. Jimmy Carter, "Caribbean/Central American Action," April 9, 1980, *Administration of Jimmy Carter, 1980*, 624–27, Jimmy Carter Presidential Library and Museum, Atlanta.

83. Bakan, Cox, and Leys, *Imperial Power and Regional Trade*, 29.

84. Memo, Richard V. Allen to Pendleton James, August 28, 1981, #039000–045999, box 23, CO.

85. Memo, Steve Saunders to William E. Brock, January 25, 1982, #204542–219789, box 27, CO.

86. Memo, Thomas O. Enders to Kenneth Duberstein, "Talking Points for Congressional Contacts on CBI," February 2, 1982, #039000–045999, box 23, CO.

87. Memo, Jim Cicconi to James A. Baker III, February 19, 1982, #204542–219780, box 27, CO.

88. Memo, Thomas O. Enders to Kenneth Duberstein, "Talking Points for Congressional Contacts on CBI," CO; Bakan, Cox, and Leys, *Imperial Power and Regional Trade*, 27.

89. Stepick, "Unintended Consequences," 155; Mitchell, "U.S. Policy toward Haitian Boat People," 78.

90. See *Haitian Refugee Center v. Civiletti, Louis v. Nelson,* and *Jean v. Nelson* (see n. 108 below); Stepick, "Unintended Consequences," 137–42; and Loescher and Scanlan, "Human Rights," 339–40.

91. Quoted in Pamphile, *Haitians and African Americans,* 178–80.

92. Pamphile, 181; *Crisis Magazine,* December 1981, 504.

93. Telegram to President Reagan from William Brown and the NAACP, March 24, 1982, folder "Subject Files: Correspondence and Newspaper Clippings about Krome Detention Center," box 2548, Dante B. Fascell Papers, Special Collections, University of Miami.

94. This "familiar struggle" also drew upon a longer discourse in African American thought concerning US policies in Haiti dating back to the 1800s and early 1900s. See Sommers, *Race, Reality, and Realpolitik*; Plummer, *In Search of Power*; Renda, *Taking Haiti*; and Rosenberg, *Financial Missionaries.* This broader conception of an enduring imperial US-Haiti relationship may also help explain the higher level of advocacy efforts made on behalf of Haitian migrants as opposed to Mariel Cubans.

95. Memo, Alan Nelson to Giuliani, March 1, 1982, folder "RS/INS—Organization of American States," box 53, SFRG.

96. Margaret Louden, "Haitian Refugees," *Judgment: Alderson Hospitality House* vol. 5, no. 2 (February 1982), folder 8, box 36, HRC.

97. Roz Dixon, "No Refuge for Haitian Women," *Off Our Backs* 12, no. 3 (March 1982): 12.

98. Lani Davidson, "Haitian Women Prisoners Stand Strong," *Off Our Backs* 12, no. 4 (April 1982): 15, 27.

99. Dixon, "No Refuge for Haitian Women," 12.

100. Davidson, "Haitian Women Prisoners Stand Strong," 27.

101. Davidson, "Haitian Women Prisoners Stand Strong," 15.

102. Maya Spencer, "Haitian Prisoners Stage Hunger Strike," *Off Our Backs* 12, no. 6 (June 1982): 12.

103. Portes and Stepick, *City on the Edge,* 53; Pamphile, *Haitians and African Americans,* 181.

104. Pamphile, *Haitians and African Americans,* 181.

105. Jesse Jackson, "White House Discriminates against Haitian Refugees," *Gainesville Sun,* June 3, 1982, sec. A. For more on the red ribbon campaign, see also "Free Haitians from Camps, Jackson Asks," *Washington Post,* April 5, 1982, sec. B.

106. McCarthy quoted in William Raspberry, "Why Are We Locking Up Haitians?," *Washington Post,* March 15, 1982, sec. A.

107. Memo, Alan C. Nelson to T. Kenneth Cribb, April 9, 1982, folder "Immigrants/ Refugees (2)," box 3, Richard Williamson Sr. Files, Reagan Presidential Library.

108. W. Smith, *Law and Justice in the Reagan Administration,* 196.

109. Lindskoog, *Detain and Punish,* 93–94.

110. Louis v. Nelson, 570 Supp. 1364 (1983); Jean v. Nelson, 711 F.2nd 1455 (1983). While Haitian advocates made some inroads in the early 1980s by challenging the discriminatory treatment of Haitians in US courts, the constitutionality of the extension of executive power through interdiction was not challenged until President H. W. Bush issued Executive Order 12807 in 1992, eliminating asylum screenings on board Haitian vessels in response to new migrant arrivals after the overthrow of Jean-Bertrand Aristide in 1991. This order was challenged yet upheld in *Sale v. Haitian Centers Council, Inc.,* 509 US 155 (1993). The Supreme Court ruled that provisions against the forced return of refugees did

not apply outside of US territory, despite the language of the Refugee Act of 1980. See T. Jones, "Sale v. Haitian Centers Council, Inc."; Nessel, "Externalized Borders"; and Pizor, "Sale v. Haitian Centers Council."

111. Memorandum, Mike Horowitz to Ed Harper, "Re: Haitian Refugees," September 16, 1981, folder "Immigration and Refugee Matters (5)," box 21, Edwin Meese III Files, Ronald Reagan Presidential Library and Museum, Simi Valley, CA.

112. Memo, Mike Horowitz to Ed Harper, September 16, 1981, box 21, Edwin Meese III Files, Ronald Reagan Presidential Library.

113. W. Smith, *Law and Justice in the Reagan Administration*, 199.

114. Memo, Max Friedersdorf to Jim Baker et al., July 21, 1981, box 8, FHF.

115. "Federal Prison and Alien Detention Policy" from Edward C. Schmults to James A. Baker III, Edwin L. Harper, Annelise Anderson, and James W. Cicconi, March 10, 1982, folder "Immigration Policy: Cubans and Haitians," box 10, JCF.

116. "Mass Immigration Emergency Plan," August 20, 1982, ID #101591, IM.

117. Memo, Annelise Anderson to Jim Cicconi, March 9, 1982, box 10, JCF.

118. General Accounting Office, *Detention Policies Affecting Haitian Nationals*, iv.

CHAPTER 4

1. "El Centro Report to Senator Dennis DeConcini," October 29, 1981, folder "RS/ INS—Detention Facilities," box 51, SFRG.

2. Letter, Dennis DeConcini to William French Smith, January 4, 1982, folder "RS/ INS—Detention Facilities," box 51, SFRG.

3. Letter, Dennis DeConcini to William French Smith, January 4, 1982, SFRG; memo, Alan Nelson to William French Smith, March 23, 1982, folder "INS," box 8, SFRG; Dan Balz, "Another War, Another Wave of Refugees," *Washington Post*, March 15, 1982, A1.

4. "El Centro Report to Senator Dennis DeConcini."

5. Ordaz, *Shadow of El Centro*, 11–12.

6. "El Centro Report to Senator Dennis DeConcini."

7. R. Kahn, *Other People's Blood*, 15.

8. "El Centro Report to Senator Dennis DeConcini."

9. John M. Crewdson, "Salvadoran Says Fear of Death Pushed Him on Hard Trek North," *New York Times*, March 6, 1981, A10.

10. "El Centro Report to Senator Dennis DeConcini."

11. Laurie Becklund, "Hopes for Asylum Wither in Hot, Dusty Immigrant Camp," *Los Angeles Times*, February 28, 1982, A3.

12. Ordaz, *Shadow of El Centro*; Cullison, "Valley of Caged Immigrants." For more on Chicanx resistance movements against border enforcement in the 1970s and 1980s, see Patiño, *Raza Sí, Migra No*.

13. Perla, "Central American Counter Public Mobilization"; Ordaz, *Shadow of El Centro*.

14. "Truth Commission: El Salvador."

15. Memo, Alan Nelson to Rudolph Giuliani, March 31, 1983, folder "Attorney General's Office," box 1, SFRG.

16. Quoted in Crandall, *Salvador Option*, 208.

17. Dunn, *Militarization of the U.S.-Mexico Border*, 20, 35.

18. R. Kahn, *Other People's Blood*, 53–54; McClintock, *American Connection*, 59–61, 215, 218–21.

19. Ronald Reagan, "Meeting Castro's Challenge in Central America," March 10, 1983, *Public Papers of President Ronald Reagan*. In this speech, Reagan referred to the region as the nation's "fourth border," but White House discussions of the Caribbean Basin Initiative often referred to it as the "third border." On the influence of global counterinsurgency on US policing and US-Mexico border militarization, see Schrader, *Badges without Borders*; Seigel, *Violence Work*; and Dunn, *Militarization of the U.S.-Mexico Border*.

20. Grandin, *End of the Myth*, 226–29.

21. Martinez, *Injustice Never Leaves You*.

22. Alexander, *New Jim Crow*; Hinton, *From the War on Poverty to the War on Crime*; Erlichman quoted in Dan Baum, "Legalize It All," *Harper's*, April 2016.

23. Cullison, "Valley of Caged Immigrants," 233; Kang, *INS on the Line*; Goodman, *Deportation Machine*; K. Hernández, *Migra!*

24. K. Hernández, *Migra!*, 205.

25. Grandin, *End of the Myth*, 222. See also L. Chavez, *Latino Threat*.

26. Felker-Kantor, *Policing Los Angeles*, 162–63.

27. Cullison, "Valley of Caged Immigrants," 238.

28. Grandin, *End of the Myth*, 223; Patiño, *Raza Sí, Migra No*.

29. "In Depth: Crime," Gallup, 2021, https://news.gallup.com/poll/1603/crime.aspx; Selman and Leighton, *Punishment for Sale*, 35.

30. Rudolph W. Giuliani, "Keynote: Facing the Here and Now," *Corrections Today* (September/October 1981), folder "Bureau of Prisons," box 3, SFRG.

31. Seigel, *Violence Work*, 34.

32. Letters to Rudolph Giuliani, folder "December 1982," box 1, CFRG; folder "Citizen Mail," box 3, SFRG.

33. Selman and Leighton, *Punishment for Sale*, 40–42.

34. Felker-Kantor, *Policing Los Angeles*, 163.

35. George L. Kelling and James Q. Wilson, "Broken Windows," *Atlantic*, March 1982. For a recent debunking of broken windows theory, see O'Brien, Farrell, and Welsh, "Looking through Broken Windows."

36. Grandin, *End of the Myth*, 225.

37. Quoted in "80% of Callers Approve of Raids on Aliens," *Los Angeles Herald Examiner*, May 6, 1982. Article and statistics found in folder "INS," box 8, SFRG.

38. Telegram, Edward R. Roybal to Ronald Reagan, May 4, 1982; Letter, Alan C. Nelson to Edward R. Roybal, May 26, 1982, ID #076632, IM.

39. Letter, American GI Forum to INS, January 26, 1982, #149999, box 18, Federal Government Organizations (FG), White House Office Records Management Central Files (WHORM) Subject Files, Ronald Reagan Presidential Library and Museum, Simi Valley.

40. "Brooklyn SPC" graph, folder "RS/INS—Detention Facilities," box 51, SFRG.

41. Memo, "Justification for a new federal correctional institution in Phoenix," March 9, 1982; and memo, "Transfer of BofP Facility to INS," April 8, 1983, both in folder "Bureau of Prisons," box 3, SFRG.

42. Ronald Reagan, "Meeting Castro's Challenge in Central America," March 10, 1983, *Public Papers of President Ronald Reagan*.

43. Dunn, *Militarization of the U.S.-Mexico Border*, 106–7.

44. Memo, "Comments by DOJ on Miami Action Plan," January 18, 1982, folder "January '82," box 3, CFRG. For more on Miami as a central node in the War on Drugs, see Stephens, "Making Migrants 'Criminal.'"

45. E. González, "Cuban Connection"; *Washington Post*, May 10, 1983, A10.

46. Giuliani, "Keynote: Facing the Here and Now," SFRG.

47. Overturning a Carter administration ban on the use of herbicides overseas and ignoring a 1977 UN ban on the use of herbicides in warfare, the Reagan administration expanded the practice of applying deadly herbicides throughout Central and South America in attempts to target and eradicate marijuana and cocaine crops with devastating environmental and human cost. See Jesse Kornbluth, "Poisonous Fallout from the War on Marijuana," *New York Times*, November 19, 1978; and del Olmo, "Aerobiology and the War on Drugs," 31.

48. Grandin, *End of the Myth*, 223–29. See also Martinez, *Injustice Never Leaves You*; and Belew, *Bring the War Home*.

49. M. C. García, *Seeking Refuge*, 1.

50. Striffler, *Solidarity*, 126; Lovato, *Unforgetting*.

51. LeoGrande, *Our Own Backyard*, 60–67; Rabe, *Killing Zone*, 159–74.

52. Grandin, *Empire's Workshop*, 67–68; Wiarda, *American Foreign Policy*, 21–22.

53. Documents shaping Reagan's Central American foreign policy included Nixon's Cold War handbook, Heritage Foundation reports, a document by the Committee of Santa Fe of the Council for Inter-American Security, and the writings of national security advisor Jeane Kirkpatrick. Grandin, *Empire's Workshop*, 70–71; LeoGrande, *Our Own Backyard*, 54–56.

54. Jeane Kirkpatrick, "U.S. Role in Latin America," #145500–219999, box 69, CO; "Reduce State Department Focus on Rights, Reagan Urged," *Miami Herald*, December 5, 1980.

55. LeoGrande, *Our Own Backyard*, 80–81; Rabe, *Killing Zone*, 158.

56. Rabe, *Killing Zone*, 167; Crandall, *Salvador Option*, 217; Abrego, "On Silences," 74–75.

57. LaFeber, *Inevitable Revolutions*, 284–91.

58. Abrams quoted in Grandin, *Empire's Workshop*, 80; Steven Strasser, "Teaching the ABC's of War," *Newsweek*, March 28, 1983.

59. "Communist Interference in El Salvador: The U.S. State Department White Paper," in Gettleman, et al., *El Salvador*, 314–15; LeoGrande, *Our Own Backyard*, 86–87.

60. Jonathan Kwitney, "Apparent Errors Cloud US 'White Paper' on Reds in El Salvador," *Wall Street Journal*, June 8, 1981; LaFeber, *Inevitable Revolutions*, 285.

61. Grandin, *Empire's Workshop*, 100.

62. Jarquín, "Red Christmases," 92–93. Jarquín shows how Indigenous action and foreign intervention, especially by Honduras and Argentina prior to US involvement, were pivotal in Nicaragua's slide into civil war after these events. Dunbar-Ortiz's firsthand account charges US and Contra propaganda of stoking fears of Cuban concentration camps for Miskito people as prompting the resettlement effort, labeling Red Christmas as the "opening salvo of the US-organized and financed Contra war." *Blood on the Border*, 118.

63. Dunbar-Ortiz, *Blood on the Border*, 94–101. See also Jarquín, "Red Christmases"; Martin Diskin's chapter, "The Manipulation of Indigenous Struggles," in Walker, *Reagan versus the Sandinistas*; and Moore, "Rights or Wishes?" 716–18.

64. "Nicaraguan Repression of Miskito Indians: The Christmas Exodus," February 22, 1984; and "The Sandinista War on Human Rights," Heritage Foundation Backgrounder, July 19, 1983, #174500–204541, box 26, CO.

65. Dunbar-Ortiz, *Blood on the Border*, 130–31; "The Use and Abuse of the Miskito Indians," *Washington Post*, March 28, 1982. Charged with accusations of genocide that did

not stick in subsequent international forums, Sandinista leaders have since apologized for what they called a military "miscalculation" born out of cultural misunderstanding. One upside of the international attention wrought by these incidents was Nicaragua's adoption of a constitutional amendment in 1986 affirming ethnic pluralism and Indigenous self-determination. See Jarquín, "Red Christmases," 99–105.

66. Lovato, *Unforgetting*, 154–55.

67. Compher and Morgan, *Going Home*, 14–15.

68. "The Human Rights Situation in El Salvador in Light of the Geneva Conventions," FMLN, September 1983; and memo, Robert M. Kimmitt to John Norton Moore, February 28, 1984, #145500–219999, box 69, CO.

69. Alma Guillermoprieto, "Salvadoran Peasants Describe Mass Killing," *Washington Post*, January 27, 1982.

70. "Truth Commission: El Salvador"; Rauda and Gressier, "U.S. Government Has Presence of U.S. Advisor in El Mozote Massacre, Expert Says," *El Faro*, April 27, 2021. See also Danner, *Massacre at El Mozote*; and Rabe, *Killing Zone*, 166–70.

71. Telegram, Jerry Falwell to Ronald Reagan, September 15, 1983; letter, Shosana Bryen to Faith R. Whittlesey, September 7, 1983; "The Sandinistas and the Jews," *Wall Street Journal*, August 24, 1983; *Israel Today*, August 30, 1983; letter, Robert Gibbons to Ronald Reagan, August 22, 1983, #157200–174499, all in box 25, CO.

72. Perla, "Central American Counter Public Mobilization," 185.

73. "Summary of Working Group Activity," n.d., #157200–174499, box 25, CO.

74. "The Reality Report," Citizens for America, September 2, 1983, #157200–174499, box 25, CO.

75. Ronald Reagan, "Meeting Castro's Challenge in Central America," March 10, 1983, *Public Papers of President Ronald Reagan*.

76. Sharon Tosi Lacey, "How the Invasion of Grenada Was Planned with a Tourist Map and a Copy of 'The Economist,'" *Military Times*, October 25, 2018.

77. Gosse, "North American Front," 12.

78. Memo, Thomas O. Enders to Kenneth Duberstein, "Talking Points for Congressional Contacts on CBI," February 2, 1982, ID #039000–045999, box 23, CO.

79. "Presidential Address to OAS," February 18, 1982, #063500–064999, box 23, CO.

80. Letter, Charles H. Percy to Ronald Reagan, February 2, 1982, #061000–063499, box 23, CO.

81. Letter, Ronald Reagan to Douglas Morrow, July 6, 1981, #001000–0199999, box 22, CO; letter, Asia A. Bennett to Ronald Reagan, March 22, 1982, #067400–074999, box 23, CO. Douglas Morrow's initial letter to Reagan is redacted in Reagan Presidential Library files.

82. Author's summation of Reagan's letters, box 22–23, CO. See also Bakan, Cox, and Leys, *Imperial Power and Regional Trade*, 27.

83. Bakan, Cox, and Leys, *Imperial Power and Regional Trade*, 21.

84. Bakan, Cox, and Leys, 38.

85. George D. Moffett III, "The Debt Crisis: Despite Reagan Initiative, Caribbean Basin Trade Woes Worsen," *Christian Science Monitor*, March 19, 1987; Bakan, Cox, and Leys, *Imperial Power and Regional Trade*, 206–10.

86. Seigel, *Violence Work*, 27–28.

87. LaFeber, *Inevitable Revolutions*, 289–90.

88. Ronald Reagan, "Address on Central America," April 27, 1983, Miller Center for Public Affairs, https://millercenter.org/the-presidency/presidential-speeches/april-27-1983-address-central-america; University of Virginia; and memo, Oliver L. North to William P. Clark, August 4, 1983, #145500–219999, box 69, CO.

89. Abrams quoted in US Department of State, *Bulletin* 82 (September 1982): 44; Lars Schoultz, "Central America and the Politicization of U.S. Immigration Policy," in Mitchell, *Western Hemisphere Immigration*, 158.

90. *Weekly Compilation of Presidential Documents* 19 (June 27, 1983): 901, Reagan Presidential Library.

91. Balz, "Another War, Another Wave of Refugees."

92. Ernest Graves, "U.S. Policy toward Central America and the Caribbean," in Lowenthal and Wells, *Central American Crisis*, 19.

93. Schoultz, "Central America and the Politicization of U.S. Immigration Policy," 158.

94. Letter, Tony Abril to Ronald Reagan, March 26, 1981, #001000–0199999, box 22, CO.

95. Memo, "CHEP-Immigration Notes," Department of Justice Community Relations Service, June 13, 1984, AFP.

96. Lee, *America for Americans*, 158–59; Denvir, *All-American Nativism*.

97. Memo, Judge William P. Clark to Faith Ryan Whittlesey, September 21, 1983; memo, Alfonso Sapia-Bosh to William P. Clark, September 19, 1983; and "Central America: The Refugee Crisis," #174500–204541, all in box 26, CO.

98. "Address to the Nation on United States Police in Central America," May 9, 1984, *Public Papers of President Ronald Reagan*.

99. Ronald Reagan, "Remarks at a Joint German-American Military Ceremony at Bitburg Air Base in the Federal Republic of Germany," May 5, 1985, *Public Papers of President Ronald Reagan*.

100. "Matter of Conscience—Civil Disobedience," *Los Angeles Times*, September 4, 1981.

101. Author interview with Mayra Novello, September 17, 2021.

102. C. Hernández, *Migrating to Prison*, 63; Moore, "Rights or Wishes?," 718; Riosmena, "Policy Shocks," 275.

103. M. C. García, *Seeking Refuge*.

104. Tomsho, *American Sanctuary Movement*, foreword, 2–4.

105. "El Centro Report to Senator Dennis DeConcini."

106. Gosse, "North American Front," 14; Perla, "Central American Counter Public Mobilization."

107. Lovato, *Unforgetting*, 143.

108. Parallel yet distinct from the formation of Black liberation theology in the United States, Latin American liberation theology is rooted in socioeconomic analysis and anti-imperialism. It has also driven the formation of "base communities" that have built solidarities and grassroots social change. See Levine, *Popular Voices in Latin American Catholicism*, 31–32; and Tombs, *Latin American Liberation Theology*.

109. Gosse, "North American Front," 16–19. See also Striffler, *Solidarity*, 126–27; and Gosse, "El Salvador Is Spanish for Vietnam," 318.

110. Gosse, "North American Front," 33. See Luke Hauser, *Direct Action: An Historical Novel*, for an original copy of a Pledge of Resistance manual published by the Emergency Response Network in San Francisco in 1986, http://www.reclaimingquarterly.org/web/handbook/DA-Handbk-Pledge86-lo.pdf.

111. Correspondence, flyers, and petitions, 1981–83, #017090, box 67, CO. See also Gosse, "El Salvador Is Spanish for Vietnam," 318; and Perla, "Central American Counter Public Mobilization," 167.

112. Crittenen, *Sanctuary*, 26–27.

113. Ursula Vils, "Relieving Plight of the Salvadorans: L.A.'s El Rescate Provides Legal and Social Aid to Refugees," *Los Angeles Times*, February 12, 1982, p. OC-D28.

114. Tomsho, *American Sanctuary Movement*, 119; R. Kahn, *Other People's Blood*, 17.

115. R. Kahn, *Other People's Blood*, 17.

116. Golden and McConnell, *Sanctuary*, 1–2; Chinchilla, Hamilton, and Loucky, "Sanctuary Movement."

117. Abrams quoted in Kahn, *Other People's Blood*, 40–41; Tomsho, *American Sanctuary Movement*, 108; Ordaz, "Protesting Conditions inside El Corralón," 73.

118. EVD had also been granted to Afghan, Iranian, and Ethiopian nationals during this time; however, the State Department began to increasingly resist awarding the status to new groups after 1979 in fear that the list would be ever-expanding. EVD was a precursor to today's Temporary Protected Status, first extended to Hondurans in the wake of Hurricane Mitch in 1999, a liminal legal status that continues to be politicized and weaponized against migrant groups. See Oswald, "Extended Voluntary Departure," 152–54; and Yarnold, *Refugees without Refuge*.

119. Brown, *Undoing the Demos*, 151–52.

120. Letter, Armando Laguardia to the Honorable Victor Atiyeh, Governor of Oregon, and forwarded to the White House for response, January 28, 1981, ID #006089, IM.

121. Letter, David H. Shinn to Wally Priestly, April 16, 1981, ID #006089, IM.

122. Cable, Immigration and Naturalization Service, April 27, 1981; and "Asylum Applications Submitted by Nationals from El Salvador," February 3, 1982, folder "INS," box 8, SFRG.

123. Letter, Richard Fairbanks to Clement J. Zablocki, June 1, 1981, #020000–038999, box 23, CO.

124. Report by Immigration Examiner Richard R. Spurlock, August 26, 1981, folder "INS," box 8, SFRG. See also M. C. García, *Seeking Refuge*, 88–91; and Yarnold, *Refugees without Refuge*.

125. Letter, Bruce A. Morrison to Ronald Reagan, June 30, 1983, ID #149458, IM.

126. R. Kahn, *Other People's Blood*, 44. See also M. C. García, *Seeking Refuge*, 84–118.

127. "Salvador's Refugees May Face U.S. Detention, Official Says," *Miami Herald*, March 11, 1982; memo, Rudy Giuliani to Alan Nelson, March 18, 1982, folder "March 1982," box 3, CFRG.

128. Rudolph W. Giuliani, "Statement before the House Committee on Judiciary Subcommittee on Courts, Civil Liberties and the Administration of Justice on 'Construction of Alien Detention Facilities,'" June 23, 1982, folder "Speeches by RWG," box 16, SFRG.

129. "Issue Paper: To justify and outline the rationale of pursuing the acquisition of the former Radar Air Defense Unit, known as Mt. Laguna, for use as a detention facility by INS," folder "RS/INS—Detention Facilities," box 51, SFRG.

130. Orantes-Hernandez v. Smith, 541 F.Supp. 351 (C.D. Cal. 1982).

131. John M. Crewdson, "Salvadoran Says Fear of Death Pushed Him on Hard Trek North," *New York Times*, March 6, 1981, A10.

132. "Information furnished to the Department of State for their response to UNHCR cable, Geneva," August 26, 1981, folder "INS," box 8, SFRG.

133. Mark Forster, "Judge to Tour Salvadorans' Detention Site," *Los Angeles Times*, January 15, 1982, SD-A1; *Orantes-Hernandez v. Smith.*

134. Orantes-Hernandez v. Thornburgh, 919 F.2d 549 (9th Cir. 1990). See also Loyd and Mountz, *Boats, Borders, and Bases*, 105–6.

135. R. Kahn, *Other People's Blood*, 1, 14–15, 18, 22.

136. See *Hotel and Restaurant Employees Union, Local 25, et al v. William French Smith, Nabor Ortega, Aurelio Gonzalez, et al v. Bill M. Rowe*, and *Rafael Fernandez-Roque, et al v. William French Smith*; Macías-Rojas, *From Deportation to Prison*, 57–59.

137. Ordaz, *Shadow of El Centro*, 83.

138. H. G. Reza, "300 Aliens on Hunger Strike at El Centro INS Detention Center," *Los Angeles Times*, May 28, 1985.

139. For a more detailed recounting of the 1985 hunger strike, see Ordaz, *Shadow of El Centro*, 79–84.

140. Elizabeth Kennedy has counted at least eighty-three deaths of Central American migrants upon deportation in the 1980s. Cited in Loyd and Mountz, *Boats, Borders, and Bases*, 222.

141. Abrego, "On Silences," 76.

142. Moffett III, "The Debt Crisis," *Christian Science Monitor*, March 19, 1987.

143. Zilberg, *Space of Detention*; Lovato, *Unforgetting*.

144. Some expanded "tent" facilities erected during this time such as at Port Isabel, Texas, which at one time in the late 1980s had a capacity of 10,000, still operate today.

145. Memo, Rudolph W. Giuliani to Al Nelson, March 28, 1983, folder "March 1983," box 1, SFRG.

146. Memo, Rudolph W. Giuliani to Alan Nelson and Norm Carlson, "Identification of Contingency Space at Department of Justice Facilities," April 13, 1983, folder "April 1983," box 1, CFRG.

147. Alfonso Chardy, "Reagan Aides and the 'Secret Government,'" *Miami Herald*, July 5, 1987. See also Christopher Ketcham, "The Last Roundup," *Radar Magazine*, June 6, 2008; Michael Grasso, "'Look It Up, Check It Out': REX 84 and the History of an American Conspiracy," *We Are the Mutants*, March 13, 2017; and Reynolds, "Rise of the National Security State." Apparently, Attorney General Smith curbed plans for Rex84, thinking it beyond FEMA's mandate, while Ollie North was transferred from FEMA contingency planning to oversee international covert management of the Contras, leading into the Iran-Contra scandal. Reagan's "Armageddon Plan," another highly classified plan for the event of nuclear war, ran adjacent to Rex84, both inspiring the George W. Bush administration's Continuity of Operations Exercises in 2003. See James Mann, "The Armageddon Plan," *Atlantic*, March 2004.

148. Rex84 also harkens back to Operation Garden Plot, a Department of Defense response drafted after the Watts and Detroit uprisings in the 1960s to activate military and law enforcement cooperation to restore order after civil disturbances. When Garden Plot was revealed publicly, it fueled activism leading to the repeal of the Emergency Detention Act in 1971. See Izumi, "Prohibiting 'American Concentration Camps.'"

CHAPTER 5

1. John McCoy, "Refugees Arrive Here for Sanctuary," *Seattle Post-Intelligencer*, July 5, 1984; and Carol M. Ostrom, "Underground Railroad for Central America Refugees Going Public," *Seattle Times*, n.d. [1984], both in folder 12, "Clippings, 1982–1989," box 3, UBC.

2. McCoy, "Refugees Arrive Here for Sanctuary."

3. Stuart Taylor Jr., "16 Indicted by U.S. in Bid to End Church Smuggling of Latin Aliens," *New York Times*, January 15, 1985.

4. "Pilar," n.d., folder 3, "Testimonies of Refugees, 1983–1988," box 3, UBC.

5. Carey Quan Gelerntner, "Salvadoran Vow to Fight Deportation," *Seattle Times*, n.d. [January 1985]; and Gigi Peterson, "Refugee Crackdown," *Northwest Passage*, February 1985, both in folder 12, "Clippings, 1982–1989," box 3, UBC.

6. Steve Maynard, "Refugee: Salvadoran Woman Finds Safety in Church Sanctuary Program," *Walla Walla Union-Bulletin*, November 25, 1983; Gelerntner, "Salvadoran Vow to Fight Deportation"; "History of UBC Sanctuary," folder "Features and Letters," box 1, UBC.

7. Heather McCarty, "Blood In, Blood Out," in Chase, *Caging Borders*, 245.

8. M. C. García, *Seeking Refuge*, 5; Ordaz, "Protesting Conditions inside El Corralón."

9. Michel, Haitian detained in US federal prison in Otisville, NY, November 1981, in *Voyage of Dreams*.

10. "FCO Report—May 26, 1980," folder "Gastón A. Fernández: Federal Coordinating Office Reports, 1980," box 1, FCC.

11. Larry Mahoney, "Welcome to Camp Krome," *Miami Herald Tropic*, January 10, 1982. This is the source for the quotes in the next paragraph as well.

12. *Miami Herald*, September 7, 1981; Paul Maroon, "Haitians Fight Back," *Overthrow* 4, no. 1 (March 1982); J. Miller, *Plight of Haitian Refugees*, 127–29.

13. *Miami Herald*, September 7, 1981.

14. Of the 150 Haitians who initially escaped, 115 remained at large. "Status Report on Krome Escapes," December 29, 1981, folder "RS/Krome—INS," box 51, SFRG; "Camp Disturbance Staged by Haitians," *New York Times*, December 28, 1981, B16; "Immigration Service Says Over 100 Fled from Haitian Camp," *New York Times*, December 29, 1981.

15. Maroon, "Haitians Fight Back."

16. Memo, Alan C. Nelson to Rudolph Giuliani, January 11, 1982, folder "RS/Krome—INS," box 51, SFRG.

17. Letter, Giuliani to Lawrence S. Eagleburger, April 5, 1982; and letter, Giuliani to FBI director Judge William H. Webster, "December 29, 1981," folder "April '82," box 3, CFRG.

18. "After Action Report—Miami, Florida (Krome Site)," January 27, 1982, folder "RS/Krome—INS," box 51, SFRG.

19. "Miami PIO," January 6, 1982, folder "INS," box 8, SFRG.

20. *Newsweek*, February 1, 1982, 25; *Miami Herald*, December 30, 1981; J. Miller, *Plight of Haitian Refugees*, 127; Mike Clary, "No Way Out," *Miami Herald*, n.d., folder "RS/Krome—INS," box 51, SFRG.

21. Letter, Rudolph Giuliani to Congressman Larry J. Hopkins, July 31, 1981, folder "RS/Krome—INS," box 51, SFRG; J. Miller, *Plight of Haitian Refugees*, 130.

22. Art Harris and Harold Lidin, "Refugees in Puerto Rico Sink Deeper into Despair," *Washington Post*, December 25, 1981.

23. "Puerto Rico and the Refugee Issue: Statement by the Honorable Hernán Padilla," October 16, 1980, folder "RS/Fort Allen—INS," box 52, SFRG.

24. Harold Lidin, "Future Brightens for Haiti Refugees as Sympathy Grows in Puerto Rico," *Washington Post*, August 20, 1981.

25. J. Miller, *Plight of Haitian Refugees*, 130–33.

26. Bar Association of Puerto Rico Resolution No. 21, August 15, 1981, Series III, Subseries A, Ana Livia Cordero Papers, Schlesinger Library, Harvard University, Cambridge, MA.

27. Jo Thomas, "778 Haitians See No End to Odyssey," *New York Times*, November 15, 1981, 1; "Haitians: We'll Kill Ourselves," *New York Times*, November 29, 1981, sec. E; Lani Davidson, "Haitian Women Prisoners Stand Strong," *Off Our Backs* 12, no. 4 (April 1982): 15, 27.

28. Davidson, "Haitian Women Prisoners Stand Strong"; "Open Letter from a Group of Refugees to the President of the United States," Series III, Subseries A, Ana Livia Cordero Papers.

29. "U.S. Aides and Haitians' Lawyers Discuss Riot in Puerto Rico Camp," *New York Times*, December 22, 1981, A16.

30. "Sit-Down at Fort Allen," April 5, 1982, folder "Misc. Renee," box 11; and "Fort Allen Disturbance during the Period of April 4, 1982 through April 15, 1982," April 23, 1982, folder "RS/Fort Allen—INS," box 52, both in SFRG.

31. "Memorandum of Information RE: Suicide at Fort Allen, Puerto Rico," August 10, 1982, folder "RS/Fort Allen—INS," box 52, SFRG.

32. "Memorandum of Information RE: Suicide at Fort Allen, Puerto Rico," SFRG; Harris and Lidin, "Refugees in Puerto Rico Sink Deeper into Despair."

33. J. Miller, *Plight of Haitian Refugees*, 131.

34. Thomas, "778 Haitians See No End to Odyssey."

35. "Mental Health Conditions Ft. Allen and Krome North," March 29, 1982, folder "RS/Krome—INS," box 51, SFRG.

36. US Centers for Disease Control and Prevention, "Gynecomastia in Haitians—Puerto Rico, Florida, Texas, New York," *Morbidity and Mortality Weekly Report*, April 30, 1982, 205–6. See also J. Kahn, *Islands of Sovereignty*.

37. Maya Spencer, "Haitian Prisoners Stage Hunger Strike," *Off Our Backs* 12, no. 6 (June 1982): 12.

38. "Puerto Rico and the Refugee Issue: Statement by the Honorable Hernán Padilla," SFRG.

39. Letter, Hernán Padilla to Honorable William French Smith, January 12, 1982; and draft, letter, Rudolph W. Giuliani to Mayor Padilla, February 5, 1982, both in folder "RS/Fort Allen—INS," box 52, SFRG.

40. Citizens United in Support of the Haitian People, "Press Release," December 11, 1981, Series III, Subseries A, Ana Livia Cordero Papers.

41. Vega, *El Tramo ancla*, 75; N'Zengou-Tayo, "Ana Lydia Vega and Haiti," 49–50.

42. Steve VanderStaay, "Tales of El Salvador," *Daily of the University of Washington*, March 1, 1983, folder 3, "Testimonies-Refugee," box 3, UBC.

43. Perla, "Central American Counter Public Mobilization," 167–69; see also Perla, "Si Nicaragua Venció."

44. Coutin, *Exiled Home*, 6.

45. Lovato, *Unforgetting*, xxiii–xxiv; Abrego, "On Silences."

46. C. Smith, *Resisting Reagan*, xvi–xviii. For more histories of Sanctuary, see Crittenden, *Sanctuary*; Davidson, *Convictions of the Heart*; Golden and McConnell, *Sanctuary*; Lorentzen, *Women in the Sanctuary Movement*; Tomsho, *American Sanctuary Movement*; Coutin, *Culture of Protest*; and Paik, "Abolitionist Futures."

47. Author interview with Renny Golden, September 18, 2020.

48. Crittenden, *Sanctuary*, 28–30; C. Smith, *Resisting Reagan*, 60–62.

49. Christina Ravashiere, "Salvador Refugees: Shipped from US Back into Civil War at 'Home,'" *Christian Science Monitor*, February 5, 1982.

50. Jim Corbett, "One Year After," n.d., folder "Chicago Religious Task Force on Central America. Sanctuary: A Justice Ministry circa 1983–1986," box 2, DNP; Crittenden, *Sanctuary*, 30–31; C. Smith, *Resisting Reagan*, 62–64; Tomsho, *American Sanctuary Movement*, 14–15. See Lorentzen, *Women in the Sanctuary Movement*, 55–60, for more on ideological splits within the movement.

51. The 1980s Sanctuary movement was the first to revive the term in order to relate "sanctuary" for migrants to Quakers' assistance of people escaping slavery on the Underground Railroad of the pre–Civil War era. See Crittenden, *Sanctuary*, 62–63.

52. Crittenden, *Sanctuary*, 5–11; Gosse, "North American Front," 34.

53. Quoted in Golden and McConnell, *Sanctuary*, 47.

54. "Conspiracy of Compassion: Four Indicted Leaders Discuss the Sanctuary Movement," *Sojourners*, March 1985, folder 52, box 2, DNP.

55. James R. Wyckoff, "Church Goes Public with Sanctuary Offer," *Tucson Citizen*, March 24, 1982.

56. Quoted in Golden and McConnell, *Sanctuary*, 47–48.

57. Crittenden, *Sanctuary*, 72–73. For a history of the clandestine Sanctuary movement in Mexico, see Golden and McConnell, *Sanctuary*, 95–123. For more on the role of women in the movement, especially as it operated from Chicago, see Lorentzen, *Women in the Sanctuary Movement*.

58. Author interview with Golden.

59. Although Southside Presbyterian declared itself as the first sanctuary church to the US government, Sacred Heart in Nogales had been effectively operating as a sanctuary church before Corbett and Fife's announcement.

60. Cunningham, *God and Caesar at the Rio Grande*, 26; Crittenden, *Sanctuary*, 87. On Sanctuary's efforts to move migrants to Canada, see Lippert, *Sanctuary, Sovereignty, Sacrifice*.

61. Gosse, "North American Front," 28.

62. "Media Relations Policy Guidance," folder "Alan C. Nelson, Commissioner 1985," box 34, CCEM.

63. Kevin Drew, "Fleeing Refugees Plead for End to Arms Supply," *Ashland Daily Tidings*, July 4, 1985; and Ashley Dunn, "Scarred Guatemalan Refugee Speaks for Seattle Sanctuary," *Seattle Post-Intelligencer*, July 26, 1985, both in folder "Clippings, 1982–1989," box 3, UBC.

64. Lorentzen, *Women in the Sanctuary Movement*, 54–56; Yukich, "Constructing the Model Immigrant." See also Paik, "Abolitionist Futures."

65. Paik, "Abolitionist Futures"; Yukich, "Constructing the Model Immigrant."

66. Quoted in Crittenden, *Sanctuary*, 172–74.

67. *Sanctuary Perspectives*, Task Force for Central America, Tucson Ecumenical Council, January 1985, folder 47, box 2, DNP.

68. *Sanctuary Perspectives*, DNP.

69. "Offered Sanctuary: Scores of U.S. Churches Take In Illegal Aliens Fleeing Latin America," *Wall Street Journal*, June 21, 1984, folder "Clippings, 1982–1989," box 3, UBC.

70. Quoted in Crittenden, *Sanctuary*, xv.

71. Paul Andres, "Captive: Seattle Man Felt as If He Was Reliving Film 'Missing,'" *Seattle Times*, August 27, 1983, folder "Clippings, 1982–1989," box 3, UBC.

72. *Sanctuary Perspectives*, DNP.

73. Cited in Ortiz, *African American and Latinx History*, 162.

74. Walters and Barker, *Jesse Jackson's 1984 Presidential Campaign*, 115–23.

75. "Chicago Religious Task Force on Central America 1984–1987," folder 12, box 2, DNP.

76. "Chicago Religious Task Force on Central America 1984–1987."

77. Corbett, "One Year After," DNP.

78. Crittenden, *Sanctuary*, 77.

79. Author interview with Golden; Gosse, "North American Front," 35–40.

80. Author interview with Golden; "Guatemalan Family Reaches Refuge," *New York Times*, March 25, 1984; *Sanctuary Perspectives*, DNP.

81. A dissenting member of Southside Presbyterian had in fact informed the FBI of Corbett and Fife's intentions before their official declaration of sanctuary in March 1981. Crittenden, *Sanctuary*, 69–70.

82. Nelson's *Frontline* comments quoted in Tomsho, *American Sanctuary Movement*, 93–94; "Church Sanctuary for Nationals of El Salvador Illegally in the U.S.," memo, Alan C. Nelson to William French Smith, March 25, 1983, folder "March 1983," box 8, SFRG.

83. Golden and McConnell, *Sanctuary*, 71–72.

84. Golden and McConnell, 71–72; Tomsho, *American Sanctuary Movement*, 93.

85. "Operational and Policy Issues at Fort Chaffee," March 5, 1981, folder "Barbara Lawson: Cuban-Haitian Task Force Documents, 1980–1981," box 1, FCC.

86. Renee L. Szybala, "Summary of Cases," August 24, 1981, folder "Misc. Renee," box 8, SFRG.

87. "Issue Paper—Detention Options," US Department of Justice, March 18, 1982, folder "RS/INS—Detention BOP," box 51, SFRG.

88. "Responsibility for Alien Detention," memo, Renee L. Szybala to Rudolph W. Giuliani, March 26, 1982, folder "RS/INS—Detention BOP," box 51, SFRG.

89. As the decade progressed, public support for prison-building grew. See Gilmore, *Golden Gulag*.

90. "After Action Report—Miami, Florida (Krome Site)," SFRG.

91. "Statement of Arthur C. Helton of the Lawyers Committee for International Human Rights on the Haitian Detention Program," June 23, 1982, folder "RS/INS—Detention BOP," box 51, SFRG.

92. Letter, Rudolph W. Giuliani to Congressman Hopkins, July 31, 1981; and letter, Rudolph W. Giuliani to Senator Bentsen, July 24, 1981, folder "RS/Krome—INS," box 51, SFRG.

93. "Immigration and Naturalization Service Standards for Detention," August 1, 1980, USCIS.

94. *New York Times*, August 30, 1981; J. Miller, *Plight of Haitian Refugees*, 134.

95. "Statement of Arthur C. Helton," SFRG.

96. According to Human Rights Watch, subjecting anyone with mental health conditions to solitary confinement violates the UN Convention against Torture, to which the United

States is a signatory. See Grace Meng, "Stint in Solitary Preceded Death in Immigration Detention," Human Rights Watch, July 31, 2018, https://www.hrw.org/news/2018/07/31 /stint-solitary-preceded-death-us-immigration-detention.

97. "Joint Security Plan," folder "Gastón A. Fernández: Security Reports and Memoranda, 1980," box 2, FCC.

98. *New York Times,* August 30, 1981.

99. R. M. Kisnor, "Uniform Disciplinary Procedures at All Service Processing Centers," August 1, 1984, USCIS.

100. Quoted in Ordaz, *Shadow of El Centro,* 83–88.

101. "Immigration and Naturalization Service Standards for Detention," USCIS; *Immigration Detention Officer Handbook,* United States Department of Justice Immigration and Naturalization Service, USCIS.

102. "Hiring at Krome," memo, Giuliani to Nelson, April 5, 1982, folder "Budget—INS," box 1, SFRG.

103. Hefner, *Between the Fences,* 16, 33.

104. Hefner, 35, 42–43.

105. "New Trial Set in Salvadoran Tour Case," *Overthrow* 4, no. 1 (March 1982): 2; Don Hayden, "Defense Seeks to Move Alien Smuggling Case," *Oklahoman,* December 24, 1981.

106. R. Kahn, *Other People's Blood,* 54–56.

107. Gelbspan, *Break-Ins, Death Threats, and the FBI,* 36–37.

108. Executive Order 12333, "United States Intelligence Activities," December 4, 1981. See Parts 1.8(e) and 3.4(h). National Archives and Records Administration, https://www .archives.gov/federal-register/codification/executive-order/12333.html.

109. Glick, *War at Home,* 30–37.

110. Wyckoff, "Church Goes Public with Sanctuary Offer."

111. Quoted in Crittenden, *Sanctuary,* 75–76.

112. "FBI Surveillance Continues," *Basta!,* March 1987, folder "Sanctuary break-ins," box 2, UBC; Gelbspan, *Break-Ins, Death Threats, and the FBI,* 97–99.

113. Golden and McConnell, *Sanctuary,* 64–73; Crittenden, *Sanctuary,* 139–48.

114. Sandy Tolan and Carol Ann Bassett, "Informers in the Sanctuary Movement," *The Nation,* July 20, 1985, 40–43, folder "Clippings, 1982–1989," box 3, UBC.

115. "Sanctuary Groups File Suit to Bar Prosecution by U.S.," *New York Times,* May 8, 1985; Crittenden, *Sanctuary,* 172–74.

116. Gelbspan, *Break-Ins, Death Threats, and the FBI,* 197–205; "Sanctuary Break-Ins," map, n.d., folder "Sanctuary break-ins," box 2, UBC; Carol M. Ostrom, "U.S. Harassment of Sanctuary Workers?," *Seattle Times,* October 7, 1985, folder "Clippings, 1982–1989," box 3, UBC.

117. *Deportation Officer's Handbook,* United States Department of Justice Immigration and Naturalization Service, USCIS.

118. *Media Relations Policy Guidance,* Immigration and Naturalization Service, May 31, 1985, folder "Alan C. Nelson, Commissioner 1985," box 34, CCEM.

119. Carol M. Ostrom, "Sanctuary Activists 'Greet' New Immigration Prosecutor," *Seattle Times,* June 9, 1987, folder "Clippings, 1982–1989," box 3, UBC.

120. Author interview with Golden.

121. Gosse, "North American Front," 19–29.

122. West, "Reconstructing the American Left." See also Ortiz, *African American and Latinx History,* 161–62.

123. Gosse, "North American Front," 15.

124. Quoted in Tomsho, *American Sanctuary Movement*, 5–6.

125. "Refugee Tells of Torture, Escape to U.S.," September 1985, folder "Clippings, 1982–7," box 3, UBC.

126. *Sanctuary Perspectives*, DNP.

CHAPTER 6

1. Associated Press Briefing, November 23, 1987; and David Maraniss, "Cuba Exiles Holding 20 as Hostages," *Washington Post*, November 23, 1987, both in folder "23–02," box 1, OAPR.

2. Loyd and Mountz, *Boats, Borders, and Bases*, 87.

3. Macías-Rojas, *From Deportation to Prison*, 56; Hamm, *Abandoned Ones*, 81.

4. Dunn, *Militarization of the U.S.-Mexico Border*, 48–49. The average length of detention also increased during the Reagan years from 3.6 days in 1981 to 15.2 days in 1988, evidencing the punitive shift in detention's intent.

5. Memo, Alan Nelson to Edwin Meese, December 14, 1985, folder "Immigration and Naturalization Service (INS) (1985) 3 of 3," box 34, CCEM.

6. Cited in Macías-Rojas, *From Deportation to Prison*, 57.

7. Batsalel, "Limit(s) of Commitment," 100. See also Parsons, *From Asylum to Prison*, on how Reagan's deinstitutionalization of mental health facilities contributed to prison overcrowding.

8. Kornbluh and LeoGrande, *Back Channel to Cuba*, 238–40.

9. Letter, Bill McCollum to Ronald Reagan, October 26, 1983; and telegram, Lawton Chiles to Ronald Reagan, October 28, 1983, both in #182499, box 60, CO.

10. Telegram, Jesse Jackson to Ronald Reagan, July 27, 1984, #182500–564999, box 61, CO. See also Walters and Barker, *Jesse Jackson's 1984 Presidential Campaign*, 115–23.

11. In negotiations, the United States also wanted Cuba to withdraw from Central America and sever ties with the Soviet Union, but for Castro this was "not for negotiation." Kornbluh and LeoGrande, *Back Channel to Cuba*, 240–44. For more on prisoner exchanges between Cuba and the United States, see Latner, *Cuban Revolution in America*.

12. Young, *Forever Prisoners*, 128–32.

13. Minian, *Undocumented Lives*, 215–19; Cohen, *Illegal*, 157; Denvir, *All-American Nativism*, 45.

14. INS handbook cited in Macías-Rojas, *From Deportation to Prison*, 59–60.

15. Gregory Jaynes, "Fort Smith Has a Bad Morning After," *New York Times*, February 12, 1982, A16.

16. Loyd and Mountz, *Boats, Borders, and Bases*, 88.

17. Letter, William French Smith to David A. Stockman, undated, folder "INS," box 8, SFRG.

18. "Responsibility for Proposed Alien Detention Facility," memo, Rudolph W. Giuliani to Alan C. Nelson, April 14, 1982, folder "RS/INS—Detention BOP," box 51, SFRG.

19. Memo, Edward C. Schmults to James A. Baker III, January 8, 1982, folder "RS/INS—Glasgow," box 52, SFRG; Robert D. Shaw Jr., "Carter Team Reportedly Rejected Montana for Refugees," *Washington Post*, September 3, 1981; letter, D. C. Beckman to James A. Baker, December 3, 1981, ID #052812, IM.

20. Doris Meissner, "Cost and Staffing Analysis for Glasgow, Montana AFB," folder "RS/INS—Glasgow," box 52, SFRG.

21. "A Proposal to Operate a Transitional Center at Valley Industrial Park Montana," PHP Corporation, February 22, 1982, folder "RS/INS—Glasgow," box 52, SFRG.

22. Memo, Kathryn A. Oberly to David Crosland, September 21, 1981, folder "RS/INS—Glasgow," box 52, SFRG.

23. Letter, D. C. Beckman to Craig Fuller, January 20, 1982, folder "February '82," box 3, CFRG; letter, Rudolph W. Giuliani to Ronald C. Marlenee, July 16, 1982, folder "RS/INS—Glasgow," box 52, SFRG.

24. Memo, Rudolph W. Giuliani to William French Smith, May 5, 1982, "Site Selection for INS Detention Facility," folder "RS/INS—Glasgow," box 52, SFRG.

25. Letter, John W. Warner Jr., Harry F. Bird Jr., and Robert W. Daniel Jr. to William French Smith, July 26, 1982, folder "RS/INS—El Reno/Petersburg," box 51, SFRG.

26. Letters, Frank Harbin to William French Smith and William French Smith to Frank Harbin, December 28, 1981, and February 9, 1982, folder "RS/INS—McAlister [sic]," box 53, SFRG; letter, William French Smith to Commissioners, December 16, 1981, folder "Attorney General's Office," box 1, SFRG.

27. US Congress, House, Subcommittee of the Committee on Government Operations, *Hearings on a Proposal for Detention Center for Illegal Aliens in El Reno, Okla*, 2–4.

28. US Congress, House, Subcommittee of the Committee on Government Operations, 29–31, 21–23.

29. US Congress, House, Subcommittee of the Committee on Government Operations, 26–27, 33–34.

30. Letter, Don Nickles to William French Smith, December 16, 1982, folder "RS/INS—El Reno/Petersburg," box 51, SFRG.

31. Memo, Renee L. Szybala to Ron Waldron, "Oakdale Louisiana," April 30, 1982, folder "RS/INS—Oakdale," box 53, SFRG.

32. Reagan sought no tax increases in 1982, which arguably exacerbated the recession further. See Wilentz, *Age of Reagan*, 96, 147–48; Collins, "Reagan Revolution"; and Sam LaSpada, "Center for Aliens Town's Salvation?," *USA Today*, February 17, 1983.

33. "Talking Points for the Attorney General: Selection of Oakdale, Louisiana as a Site for 1,000 Bed Alien Detention Facility," n.d.; and memo, Rudolph W. Giuliani to the Attorney General, "Site Selection for New Alien Detention Facility," n.d., both in folder "RS/INS—Oakdale," box 53, SFRG.

34. "Site Selection Analysis for the Alien Detention Center," n.d., US Department of Justice, folder "RS/INS—Oakdale," box 53, SFRG.

35. Memo, Alan C. Nelson to Rudolph W. Giuliani, "Meeting with Oakdale, Louisiana officials on Proposed Detention Center," February 9, 1983, folder "RS/INS—Oakdale," box 53, SFRG.

36. Loyd and Mountz, *Boats, Borders, and Bases*, 107.

37. LaSpada, "Center for Aliens Town's Salvation?"; Loyd and Mountz, *Boats, Borders, and Bases*, 100–102.

38. "Legal Groups Protest Construction of Massive Immigration Jail," *El Renacimiento* 15, no. 208, August 27, 1984.

39. Frances Frank Marcus, "Prison for Aliens Opens in Louisiana," *New York Times*, April 8, 1986.

40. "Federal Detention Center, Oakdale, Louisiana: Dedication, March 21, 1986," video 208, USCIS.

41. Marcus, "Prison for Aliens Opens in Louisiana." This wage is even lower than the one dollar a day wage set by Congress in 1979 in an appropriations act and has not been raised since. Sinha, "Slavery by Another Name," 30.

42. "Department of Justice: For Immediate Release," February 11, 1983, folder "RS/INS—Oakdale," box 53, SFRG.

43. Nancy Stancill, "Ruling Clouds INS Plan for Private Jails," *Houston Chronicle*, May 8, 1984, folder "Alan C. Nelson, Commissioner 1985," box 34, CCEM; Martin Tolchin, "As Privately-Owned Prisons Increase, So Do Their Critics," *New York Times*, February 11, 1985.

44. Tolchin, "As Privately-Owned Prisons Increase, So Do Their Critics."

45. Tolchin, "As Privately-Owned Prisons Increase, So Do Their Critics."

46. Wayne King, "Contracts for Detention Raise Legal Questions," *New York Times*, March 6, 1984, A10; "Private Firms Operate Jails, Legality Challenged," *Washington Post*, December 20, 1984, E1.

47. "Media Relations Policy Guidance," INS, May 31, 1985, folder "Alan C. Nelson, Commissioner 1985," box 34, CCEM.

48. Selman and Leighton, *Punishment for Sale*, 60.

49. Nickerson and Dochuck, *Sunbelt Rising*, 4; Volker Janssen, "Private Prisons," in Chase, *Caging Borders*.

50. "Prisons for Profit," NPR radio transcript, January 31, 1984, folder "Alan C. Nelson, Commissioner 1985," box 34, CCEM.

51. Hallett, *Private Prisons in America*.

52. Young, *Forever Prisoners*.

53. Robbins, *The Legal Dimensions of Private Incarceration*; Selman and Leighton, *Punishment for Sale*, 55. For more on the debate over prison privatization, see also Shichor, *Punishment for Profit*; and Eisen, *Inside Private Prisons*.

54. William C. Toney, "The Privatization of Corrections," Annual Training Conference of the Washington Correctional Association, Yakima, WA, October 16, 1985, in the author's possession; Shichor, *Punishment for Profit*, 15–17.

55. Peter Greenwood, "Private-Enterprise Prisons? Why Not? The Job Would Be Done Better and at Less Cost," *Los Angeles Times*, May 11, 1981, C5. See Fixler and Poole Jr., "The Privatization Revolution," for arguments in favor of privatization from the Reason Foundation.

56. Shichor, *Punishment for Profit*, 14.

57. In 1981, Florida became the first state to contract out its entire prison labor industry to the management of Prison Rehabilitative Industries and Diversified Enterprises, Inc. (PRIDE). Janssen, "Private Prisons," 285; Sinha, "Slavery by Another Name," 30; Dana Joel, "A Guide to Prison Privatization," *Heritage Foundation*, May 24, 1988, https://www .heritage.org/political-process/report/guide-prison-privatization.

58. Judith Greene, "Entrepreneurial Corrections: Incarceration as a Business Opportunity," in Mauer and Chesney-Lind, *Invisible Punishment*, 96. The first private contract at the state level in the late twentieth century was the Weaversville Intensive Treatment Unit for juveniles in Pennsylvania in 1975. Logan, *Private Prisons*, 17–19; Janssen, "Private Prisons," 289. See also Goffman, "On the Characteristics of Total Institutions," in *Asylums*.

59. Selman and Leighton, *Punishment for Sale*, 53–54.

60. Eisen, *Inside Private Prisons*, 39–40.

61. Selman and Leighton, *Punishment for Sale*, 60–61; Patt Morrison, "Alien Families Find a Refuge from Fear at Detention Center," *Los Angeles Times*, April 10, 1981, B3.

62. "Prisons for Profit," NPR, January 31, 1984; "Media Relations Policy Guidance," INS, May 31, 1985, folder "Alan C. Nelson, Commissioner 1985," box 34, CCEM.

63. Memo, Doris M. Meissner to Rudolph W. Giuliani, "Start-Up Contracts in Support of Fort Allen, Puerto Rico," September 8, 1981, folder "RS/Fort Allen—INS," box 52, SFRG.

64. Letter, Thomas F. Keohane Jr. to Stanley McKinley, November 3, 1981, folder "RS/Fort Allen—INS," box 52, SFRG.

65. Memo, Renee L. Syzbala to Rudolph W. Giuliani, "Responsibility for Alien Detention," March 26, 1982, folder "RS/INS—Detention BOP," box 51, SFRG.

66. Memo, Norman A. Carlson and Alan C. Nelson to Rudolph W. Giuliani, "Proposed Transfer of the Federal Detention Center, Florence, Arizona from the Bureau of Prisons to the Immigration and Naturalization Service," folder "Bureau of Prisons," box 3, SFRG; Loyd and Mountz, *Boats, Borders, and Bases*, 125–33.

67. Memo, Alan C. Nelson to Rudolph W. Giuliani, "Contingency Detention Space at BOP/INS Facilities," May 20, 1983, folder "RS/INS—Detention Facilities," box 51, SFRG.

68. Today, the Corrections Corporation of America (now rebranded as CoreCivic since 2017) is the largest private prison contractor in the United States, and the Wackenhut Corporation (now the GEO Group, Inc.) is the largest private prison contractor in the world.

69. Tanya Golash-Boza defines "immigration-industrial complex" (first coined by Deepa Fernandes) as "the public and private sector interests in the criminalization of undocumented migration, immigration law enforcement, and the promotion of 'anti-illegal' rhetoric." Golash-Boza, "Immigration Industrial Complex," 296; Fernandes, *Targeted*.

70. Selman and Leighton, *Punishment for Sale*, 55–56; Guenther, "Prison Beds and Compensated Man-Days," 33.

71. Selman and Leighton, *Punishment for Sale*, 56; Tina Grant, "History of Corrections Corporation of America," in *International Directory of Business Histories*, vol. 23, edited by Tina Grant (Farmington Hills, MI: St. James Press, 1998), 158.

72. *Report of the Secretary of Transportation and Public Safety on Privatization in Corrections*, House Document No. 7 (Richmond: Commonwealth of Virginia, 1987), 70.

73. Hutto v. Finney, 437 U.S. 678 (1978). See also Selman and Leighton, *Punishment for Sale*, 56–58; Craig Becker and Amy Dru, "The Downside of Private Prisons," *Nation*, June 15, 1985, 728; and Mattera and Khan, *Corrections Corporation of America*.

74. Bauer, *American Prison*, 14–15.

75. Selman and Leighton, *Punishment for Sale*, 58–59.

76. Grant, "History of Corrections Corporation of America," 158.

77. The video interview of CCA founders Tom Beasley and Don Hutto is no longer publicly available but was accessed by the author on *The Nation*'s YouTube channel on September 4, 2019, and it is also described in Shane Bauer, "Today it Locks Up Immigrants. But CoreCivic's Roots Lie in the Brutal Past of America's Prisons," *Mother Jones*, September/October 2018, https://www.motherjones.com/crime-justice/2018/09/corecivic-private-prison-shane-bauer-book/.

78. Mattera and Khan, *Jail Breaks*.

79. King, "Contracts for Detention Raise Legal Questions."

80. Vicki Quade, "Jail Business: Private Firm Breaks In," *American Bar Association Journal* 69, no. 11 (November 1983): 1611.

81. "Prisons for Profit: A Growing Business," *U.S. News & World Report*, July 2, 1984, 45.

82. Marjorie Anders, "Profiting from Prisons," *State Magazine*, August 11, 1985.

83. Randy Fitzgerald, "Free Enterprise Jails: Key to Our Prison Dilemma?," *Reader's Digest*, March 1986, 86.

84. Tolchin, "As Privately-Owned Prisons Increase, So Do Their Critics."

85. Philip E. Fixler Jr., "Behind Bars We Find an Enterprising Zone," *Wall Street Journal*, November 29, 1984, 34.

86. Grant, "History of Corrections Corporation of America," 158; Janssen, "Private Prisons," 291.

87. Logan, *Private Prisons*, 22; Grant, "History of Corrections Corporation of America."

88. Author interview with Mayra Novello, September 17, 2021.

89. Greene, "Banking on the Prison Boom," in Herivel and Wright, *Prison Profiteers*, 13; Janssen, "Sunbelt Lock-Up," 230–31.

90. See Clayton Mosher, Gregory Hooks, and Peter B. Wood, "Don't Build It Here: The Hype Versus the Reality of Prisons and Local Employment," in Herivel and Wright, *Prison Profiteers*, 90–97.

91. Janssen, "Private Prisons." See also Janssen, "Sunbelt Lock-Up," 219.

92. RG 519, Presbyterian Historical Society, Philadelphia, PA.

93. Quoted in Loyd and Mountz, *Boats, Borders, and Bases*, 128.

94. Fred Grimm, "Inmate Advocates Forgotten, Nearly Broke as Cause Wanes," *Miami Herald*, December 20, 1987, A14.

95. Young, *Forever Prisoners*, 135.

96. Schoultz, *That Infernal Little Cuban Republic*, 415; Kornbluh and LeoGrande, *Back Channel to Cuba*, 245.

97. Ann Woolner, "Hope Wanes for Cubans at the Pen," *Atlanta Constitution*, September 15, 1985, recounted in Young, *Forever Prisoners*, 136–37.

98. Ari L. Goldman, "From Tiny Port to Louisiana Rampage," *New York Times*, November 23, 1987, folder "23–02," box 1, OAPR.

99. Loyd and Mountz, *Boats, Borders, and Bases*, 112.

100. "Cuban Prisoners in Rebellion," Presbyterian Historical Society blog, accessed February 26, 2021, https://www.history.pcusa.org/blog/2019/10/cuban-prisoners-rebellion.

101. US Congress, *Atlanta Federal Penitentiary*.

102. "Cuban Prisoners in Rebellion"; Hamm, *Abandoned Ones*, 97–100.

103. Loyd and Mountz, *Boats, Borders, and Bases*, 102, 114; R. Kahn, *Other People's Blood*, 169.

104. "ACLU Challenges Opening of Immigrant Detention Center," *El Renacimiento* 16, no. 228, April 28, 1986.

105. Hamm, *Abandoned Ones*, 80.

106. Young, *Forever Prisoners*, 125.

107. Goldman, "From Tiny Port to Louisiana Rampage." Making matters worse, the State Department told BOP wardens and staff at Atlanta and Oakdale about the repatriation agreement only the morning after; the outbreak of rebellion came as a surprise to all.

108. November 23, 1987, folder "25–03," box 1, OAPR.

109. Ramon Bracamontes, "Prisons across USA are isolating Cubans," November 25, 1987, folder "25–16," box 1, OAPR.

110. Hamm, *Abandoned Ones*, 18, 31–33; "Hostages Recall Fright as Well as Inmates' Discipline and Consideration," *New York Times*, December 5, 1987; "Freedom, Lost and Found: Guard, as Captive, Came to Embrace Cubans' Hopes," *Sun*, December 6, 1987, folder "D-07–01," box 1, OAPR.

111. Young, *Forever Prisoners*, 144–45.

112. "Justice Command Center Prison Status Report," November 24, 1987, folder "24–05," box 1, OAPR; Lindsey Gruson, "Talks with Cubans in Louisiana Go On as Siege Is Said to Stabilize," *New York Times*, November 26, 1987, D17; Hamm, *Abandoned Ones*, 22–26.

113. "Cuban Prisoners in Rebellion."

114. Handwritten letter, Steve Martin to Alan Nelson, November 25, 1987, folder "25–03," box 1, OAPR.

115. Hamm, *Abandoned Ones*, 26; Michael Rezendes, "Miami Prelate May Be Key in Oakdale," *Washington Post*, November 29, 1987, folder "29–03," box 1, OAPR; Young, *Forever Prisoners*, 144–45.

116. Young, *Forever Prisoners*, 147.

117. "A Mariel Thanksgiving," *Washington Times*, November 26, 1987; and Michael Kinsley, "Wretched Refuse," *Washington Post*, November 26, 1987, both in folder "27–20," box 1, OAPR.

118. Pierre DeGruy, "The Press Held Hostage," *Gambit* (New Orleans), December 8, 1987, folder "D-07–01," box 1, OAPR.

119. Young, *Forever Prisoners*, 149.

120. Hamm, *Abandoned Ones*, 28–29.

121. Young, *Forever Prisoners*, 151–52.

122. *U.S. News and World Report*, December 28, 1987, 19, folder "D-07–01," box 1, OAPR.

123. "Crime Codes," National Crime Information Center, November 30, 1987, folder "30–03"; and FBI memo, O. B. Revell and F. I. Clarke to the Director, November 29, 1987, folder "29–04," box 1, OAPR.

124. Memo, O. B. Revell and F. I. Clarke to FBI Director, November 29, 1987, folder "30–03," box 1, OAPR.

125. Guy Coates, "Meese Says Riot Ringleaders Will Be Punished," Associated Press, December 16, 1987, folder "D-07–01"; and Levin notes, folder "25–04," both in box 1, OAPR.

126. Loyd and Mountz, *Boats, Borders, and Bases*, 115; Young, *Forever Prisoners*, 153; Rivas quoted in "Transferred Detainees Detail Abuse," *Chicago Tribune*, December 29, 1987, sec. 1–8, folder "D-07–01," box 1, OAPR.

127. Liz Sly, "Cuban Inmates Complain of Isolation, Abuse," *Newsday*, December 23, 1987, 3, folder "D-07–01," box 1, OAPR.

128. "Transferred Detainees Detail Abuse," *Chicago Tribune*, December 29, 1987, A8; Jacquelyn Swearingen, "Rights Sought for Cuban Inmates," *Miami Herald*, December 29, 1987, A6; Carlos Harrison, "Guards Beat Us, Krome Inmates Say," *Miami Herald*, December 14, 1987, B2; "Cuban Inmates Complain of Isolation, Abuse"; Marshall Ingwerson, "Cubans Await Details of Promised Hearings," *Christian Science Monitor*, December 7, 1987; and Fred Grimm, "Inmate Advocates Forgotten, Nearly Broke as Cause Wanes," *Miami Herald*, December 20, 1987, 14-A, all in folder "D-07–01," box 1, OAPR.

129. Hamm, *Abandoned Ones*, 170–71.

130. Quoted in Loyd and Mountz, *Boats, Borders, and Bases*, 114.

131. US Congress, House, Judiciary Subcommittee on Courts, Civil Liberties, and the Administration of Justice, *Hearings on the Mariel Cuban Prison Riots*, 5.

132. Young, *Forever Prisoners*, 126.

133. Batsalel, "Limit(s) of Commitment," 101.

134. "Cuban Prisoners in Rebellion."

135. Robert L. Jackson, "15 Cubans Involved in Prison Riots Face Deportation as Incorrigibles," *Los Angeles Times*, November 18, 1988.

136. Batsalel, "Limit(s) of Commitment," 90–94.

137. Batsalel, "Limit(s) of Commitment," 97–100.

138. Batsalel, "Limit(s) of Commitment," 103–4.

139. Quoted in Hamm, *Abandoned Ones*, 64–65.

140. Young, *Forever Prisoners*, 121.

141. "Senator: Keep Cubans Out of Rebuilt Oakdale Prison," *Miami Herald*, December 15, 1987, 8A, folder "D-07-01," box 1, OAPR.

142. Loyd and Mountz, *Boats, Borders, and Bases*, 115.

143. Loyd and Mountz, 111.

144. C. Hernández, *Migrating to Prison*, 67.

145. Macías-Rojas, *From Deportation to Prison*, 75.

146. Latin American Studies Association annual meeting, Vancouver, Canada, May 28, 2021.

POSTSCRIPT

1. Guha, "Prose of Counter-Insurgency"; Chavez, *Latino Threat*.

2. Volker Janssen, "Private Prisons," in Chase, *Caging Borders*, 294.

3. Ashley Dunn, "Harsh Memories of Detention Center," *New York Times*, June 19, 1995; Rizzo, "Reading against the Grain."

4. Rizzo, "Reading against the Grain," 29.

5. Lisa Peterson, "Detainee Still Hears the Crash of Glass in 'Night of Screams,'" *Star-Ledger*, June 23, 1995; David M. Levitt, "Lawyers Looking for Ex-Esmor Clients," *News Tribune*, June 23, 1995, A-3; "Guards Charged with Mistreating Migrants," United Press International, October 13, 1995.

6. "The Elizabeth, New Jersey Contract Detention Facility Operated by ESMOR Inc. Interim Report Executive Summary," USCIS; "Detention Center Ban a Must," *Elizabeth Reporter*, June 23–29, 1995.

7. Pauline Daniels, "The Ins and Outs of the Jama Case, Part I," States of Incarceration, accessed January 2, 2022, https://statesofincarceration.org/story/ins-and-outs-jama-case-part-i; Rizzo, "Reading against the Grain," 27, 31.

8. Booth, "Ending Forced Labor."

9. Eisen, *Inside Private Prisons*, 24–25; C. Hernández, *Migrating to Prison*, 68–69.

10. Chan, "Immigration Detention Bed Quota Timeline."

11. *IMM Print* is a digital archive of stories from immigration detention conceived and launched by the author in 2017.

12. The nonprofit Freedom for Immigrants was formerly Community Initiatives for Visiting Immigrants in Confinement (CIVIC), changing its name after the Corrections Corporation of America rebranded itself as CoreCivic in 2017.

13. An Xiao, "On the Origins of 'They Tried to Bury Us, They Didn't Know We Were Seeds,'" Hyperallergic, July 3, 2018, https://hyperallergic.com/449930/on-the-origins-of-they-tried-to-bury-us-they-didnt-know-we-were-seeds/.

14. "RE: A Wisconsin Prisoner requests deportation," Letter, Peg Swan to President Donald Trump, July 25, 2018, https://casesprison.files.wordpress.com/2018/12/Lene

-Cepedes-Torres-App-for-deportation.pdf. I have so far been unable to reach Lenin for comment. Thanks to Omar Granados at the University of Wisconsin–La Crosse and Peg Swan at Forum for Understanding Prisons who brought his case to my attention. Granados says that multiple versions of Lenin's story continue to circulate locally.

15. Granados, "Cubans in the Tundra"; Young, *Forever Prisoners*, 122.

16. Alexander M. Stephens, "Wet Foot, Dry Foot: The Mariel Boatlift and the Dangerous Persistence of Memory," IEHS Online, February 21, 2018, https://iehs.org/alexander-stephens-wet-foot-dry-foot/.

17. Dow, *American Gulag*, 16, 297; Mirta Ojito, "The Long Voyage from Mariel Ends," *New York Times*, January 16, 2005.

18. Schoultz, *That Infernal Little Cuban Republic*, 415.

19. Liz Vinson, "Immigrant Prison 'Driving Him Crazy,'" Southern Poverty Law Center, April 8, 2019, https://www.splcenter.org/attention-on-detention/immigrant-prison-'driving-him-crazy'.

20. J. García, *Voices from Mariel*; "The Lost Voices of Mariel," University of Wisconsin–La Crosse Campus Connection, April 19, 2021; "With Open Heart and Open Arms"; *Lene Stranded from Cuba* (blog), accessed January 2, 2022, http://lenescespedes.blogspot.com/.

21. Silky Shah, "Number of Immigrants Detained by ICE Has Increased 70% under Biden," *Truthout*, September 21, 2021, https://truthout.org/articles/number-of-immigrants-detained-by-ice-has-increased-70-percent-under-biden/.

22. "A Cuban Asylum-Seeker in Detention Speaks Out," *IMM Print*, November 4, 2020, https://imm-print.com/a-cuban-asylum-seeker-in-detention-speaks-out/.

23. *Lene Stranded from Cuba*, accessed January 2, 2022, http://lenescespedes.blogspot.com/.

24. Paik, "Carceral Quarantine at Guantánamo," 155.

25. Chávez, "ACT UP, Haitian Migrants, and Alternative Memories of HIV/AIDS." See also Guantánamo Public Memory Project.

26. Chávez, "ACT UP, Haitian Migrants, and Alternative Memories of HIV/AIDS," 66.

27. Ronald Aubourg oral history, Guantánamo Public Memory Project.

28. Paik, "Carceral Quarantine at Guantánamo," 159.

29. Ratner, "How We Closed the Guantanamo HIV Camp," 211. See also Goldstein, *Storming the Court*.

30. "In Tijuana, Deep Need Meets Radical Hope," *IMM Print*, March 13, 2017, https://imm-print.com/in-tijuana-deep-need-meets-radical-hope-f376c0911bcd/.

31. Jasmine Aguilera, "Caught between U.S. Policies and Instability at Home, Haitian Migrants in Tijuana Are in a State of Limbo," *Time*, July 22, 2021.

32. Molly O'Toole, "ICE Is Deporting Women at Irwin amid Criminal Investigation into Georgia Doctor," *Los Angeles Times*, November 18, 2020; Project South et al., *Violence and Violation: Medical Abuse of Immigrants Detained at the Irwin County Detention Center*.

33. Emily Green, "US Border Agents Are Removing Haitians Using Horses and Whips," *Vice*, September 20, 2021, https://www.vice.com/en/article/k78vdm/us-border-agents-are-removing-haitian-migrants-using-horses-and-whips.

34. Anna Giaritelli, "Haitian Migrants Revolt in Custody and Seize Control of Privately Contracted Bus," *Washington Examiner*, September 21, 2021.

35. Todd Miller, "What Will Climate Change Do to the U.S.-Mexico Border?," *Yes! Magazine*, September 26, 2018.

36. "New INS Policies Deny Refugee Rights," *Amparo Puget Sound Sanctuary News* 5, no. 1 (June 1989), folder 8, box 1, UBC; Loyd and Mountz, *Boats, Borders, and Bases*, 137–39.

37. S. Shah, "Number of Immigrants Detained by ICE Has Increased."

38. Jason Buch, "ICE Drops Plans for Texas Family Detention Center," *Express News*, February 7, 2012.

39. Julia Preston, "Snakes and Thorny Brush, and Children at the Border Alone," *New York Times*, June 25, 2014.

40. "Report: Migrant Children Detention Center Could Be Built on Chemical-Riddled Landfill."

41. Daniel Halper, "Obama: 'Don't Send Your Children Unaccompanied,'" *Weekly Standard*, June 27, 2014.

42. T. Miller, *Empire of Borders*; Nicole Narea, "Mexico Is Cracking Down on Another US-Bound Migrant Caravan," *Vox*, January 21, 2021.

43. "An Immigrant's Story: Behind the Walls of Adelanto," *IMM Print*, November 14, 2019, https://imm-print.com/an-immigrants-story-behind-the-walls-of-adelanto/.

44. Alejandra Molina, "Why One Former Immigrant Detainee Says Detention Centers Should Be Called Prisons," *Orange County Register*, January 28, 2018.

45. "Carlos Hidalgo from Adelanto Detention Center," California's New Angel Island, Freedom for Immigrants, accessed January 2, 2022, https://www.freedomforimmigrants.org/californias-new-angel-island.

46. *Call Me Libertad: Poems between Borders*, Freedom for Immigrants, 2016, accessed January 2, 2022, https://www.freedomforimmigrants.org/poetry.

47. Tom Driesbach, "Exclusive: Video Shows Controversial Use of Force inside an ICE Detention Center," NPR, February 6, 2020.

48. "Judge Stops ICE from Destroying Records of Abuse," CREW, March 12, 2021, https://www.citizensforethics.org/news/press-releases/ice-records-destruction-victory/.

Bibliography

ARCHIVAL AND MANUSCRIPT COLLECTIONS

Arkansas
    Special Collections, University of Arkansas Libraries, Fayetteville
        Alina Fernandez Addendum
        Alina Fernandez Papers
California
    Honnold/Mudd Library, Claremont University Consortium, Claremont
        Darlene Nicgorski Papers on the Sanctuary Movement
    ONE National Gay and Lesbian Archives, Los Angeles
        ACT UP Los Angeles Records
    Ronald Reagan Presidential Library and Museum, Simi Valley
        Edwin Meese III Files
        Francis S. M. (Frank) Hodsoll Files
        James Cicconi Files
        J. Michael Luttig Files
        Margaret D. Tutwiler Files
        Michael K. Deaver Files
        Michael Ulman Files
        Nancy Risque Files
        Richard Williamson Sr. Files
        Weekly Compilation of Presidential Documents
        White House Office Records Management Central
            Files (WHORM) Subject Files Countries
          Federal Government Organizations
          Immigration/Naturalization
          Public Relations
Florida
    Cuban Heritage Collection, University of Miami
        Exile Journals
        Fort Chaffee Collection
    Special Collections, University of Miami
        American Committee for the Protection of Foreign Born Papers
        Dante B. Fascell Papers

Georgia
    Jimmy Carter Presidential Library and Museum, Atlanta
        Cuban-Haitian Task Force Files
Maryland
    Records of the Bureau of Prisons, Record Group 129,
        National Archives and Records Administration at College Park
    Records of the Department of Justice, Record Group 60,
        National Archives and Records Administration at College Park
        Chronological Files of Associate Attorney General Rudolph W. Giuliani
        Component Correspondence Files of the Attorney General;
            Edwin Meese, 1985–1988
        Records Relating to the Oakdale and Atlanta Prison Riots, 11/23/1987–12/4/19,
            FOIA Request #60856
        Subject Files of Rudolph W. Giuliani, 1981–1983
Massachusetts
    Schlesinger Library, Harvard University, Cambridge
        Ana Livia Cordero Papers
    Special Collections, University of Massachusetts at Amherst
        Cynthia Miller Papers
        W. E. B. DuBois Papers
New York
    Schomburg Center for Research in Black Culture, New York Public Library
        Haitian Refugee Collection
Pennsylvania
    Presbyterian Historical Society, Philadelphia
        Presbyterian Church (U.S.A.)
            Social Justice and Peacemaking Ministry Unit Records
Washington
    Special Collections, University of Washington, Seattle
        University Baptist Church Sanctuary Movement Records
Washington, DC
    USCIS History Office and Library

GOVERNMENT PUBLICATIONS

California Governor's Commission on the Los Angeles Riots. *Reports of Consultants*. Vol. 17. Sacramento, State of California, 1965.

General Accounting Office. *Detention Policies Affecting Haitian Nationals*. Washington, DC, June 16, 1983.

Immigration and Customs Enforcement data, 2018–21, https://www.ice.gov/.

INS Reporter, 1980–83.

The President's Commission on Privatization. *Privatization: Toward More Effective Government*. March 1988.

Reagan, Ronald. *The Public Papers of President Ronald Reagan*. Ronald Reagan Presidential Library and Museum. https://www.reaganlibrary.gov/archives/public-papers -president-ronald-reagan.

Report of the Secretary of Transportation and Public Safety on Privatization in Corrections,
    House Document No. 7. Richmond: Commonwealth of Virginia, 1987.
US Congress, *Atlanta Federal Penitentiary: Report of the Subcommittee on Courts, Civil
    Liberties, and the Administration of Justice,* 99th Cong, 2nd sess. Washington DC: US
    Government Printing Office, 1986.
US Congress, House, Judiciary Subcommittee on Courts, Civil Liberties, and the Ad-
    ministration of Justice. *Hearings on the Mariel Cuban Prison Riots.* February 4, 1988.
    https://www.c-span.org/video/?707-1/mariel-cuban-prison-riots.
US Congress, House, Subcommittee of the Committee on Government Operations. *Hear-
    ings on a Proposal for Detention Center for Illegal Aliens in El Reno, Okla.* 97th Congress,
    2nd sess., July 8, 1982. Washington, DC: US Government Printing Office, 1982.
US Congress, House, Subcommittee on Immigration and Refugee Policy of the Subcom-
    mittee Committee on the Judiciary. *Hearings on the United States as a Country of Mass
    First Asylum.* 97th Congress, 1st sess., August 6, 1981. Washington, DC: US Govern-
    ment Printing Office, 1982.
US Congress, House, Subcommittee on Immigration, Refugees, and International Law,
    Senate, Subcommittee on Immigration and Refugee Policy. *Administration's Proposals
    on Immigration and Refugee Policy.* 97th Congress, 1st sess., July 30, 1981. Washington,
    DC: US Government Printing Office, 1982.
US Department of State, *Cuban Refugees.* Washington, DC: US Government Printing
    Office, 1980.
US Department of State Bulletin 82 (September 1982).

SELECTED NEWSPAPERS AND OTHER PERIODICALS

Arkansas Democrat (Little Rock, AR)
Atlantic
Chicago Sun-Times
Christian Science Monitor
Crisis Magazine
El Faro (San Salvador)
El Nuevo Herald (Doral, FL)
El Renacimiento (Lansing, MI)
Express News (San Antonio, TX)
Harper's
Los Angeles Times
Miami Herald
Miami Herald Tropic
Miami News
Nation
New Yorker
New York Times
Newsweek
Off Our Backs
Oklahoman
Orange County Register
Overthrow
Palm Beach Post
People
Radar Magazine
Reader's Digest
San Diego Union-Tribune
Seattle Post-Intelligencer
Spirit Magazine
State Magazine
Time
Tucson Citizen
US News & World Report
USA Today
Vox
Wall Street Journal
Washington Examiner
Washington Post

MULTIMEDIA AND DIGITAL ARCHIVES

"California's New Angel Island." Freedom for Immigrants, 2014. https://www.freedomfor immigrants.org/californias-new-angel-island.

Cocaine Cowboys. Directed by Billy Corben. New York: Magnolia Pictures, 2016. DVD.

Cuban-American National Federation Archives. https://www.canf.org/the-archive/. Accessed December 14, 2021.

El Salvador: Another Vietnam. Directed by Glenn Silber. New York: Icarus Films, 1981. DVD.

Gary Monroe Photographs, 1980–1988. Duke University Digital Repositories. https:// repository.duke.edu/dc/garymonroe. Accessed December 14, 2021.

Guantánamo Public Memory Project. https://gitmomemory.org/timeline/resisting-and -protesting-guantanamo/act-up-turns-to-hiv-positive-haitian-detainees/. Accessed December 14, 2021.

IMM Print. https://imm-print.com/. Accessed December 14, 2021.

Lost in Detention: President Obama's Tough Immigration Enforcement. Directed by Rick Young. Boston: WGBH Educational Foundation, 2012. DVD.

ONE National Gay and Lesbian Archives, University of Southern California. https://one .usc.edu/. Accessed December 14, 2021.

Presidential Speeches. Miller Center for Public Affairs, University of Virginia. https:// millercenter.org/the-presidency/presidential-speeches. Accessed December 31, 2021.

States of Incarceration. https://statesofincarceration.org/. Accessed December 14, 2021.

Voyage of Dreams: A Documentary Essay. Directed by Collis Davis. New York: Cinema Guild, 1983. DVD.

"With Open Heart and Open Arms: LGBTQ Cuban Refugees and Our Community's Response to the Mariel Boatlift." LGBT Center, Harrisburg, PA. https:// centralpalgbtcenter.org/withopenheart. Accessed December 14, 2021.

INTERVIEWS, ORAL HISTORIES, AND MEMOIRS

ACT UP Oral History Project. https://actuporalhistory.org/. Accessed December 14, 2021.

Arenas, Reinaldo. *Before Night Falls.* New York: Penguin, 1994.

Clinton, Bill. *My Life.* New York: Vintage Books, 2004.

Dunbar-Ortiz, Roxanne. *Blood on the Border: A Memoir of the Contra War.* Cambridge, MA: South End Press, 2005.

García, José Manuel. *Voices from Mariel: Oral Histories of the 1980 Cuban Boatlift.* Gainesville: University of Florida Press, 2018.

Golden, Renny. Phone interview with the author. September 18, 2020.

Hefner, Tony. *Between the Fences: Before Guantanamo, There Was the Port Isabel Service Processing Center.* New York: Seven Stories Press, 2010.

Jozef, Guerline. Phone interview with the author. September 11, 2021.

LGBTQ Marielitos Oral History Project. John J. Wilcox, Jr. Archives, William Way LGBT Community Center, Philadelphia, PA. https://www.waygay.org/archives/.

Lovato, Roberto. *Unforgetting: A Memoir of Family, Migration, Gangs, and Revolution in the Americas.* New York: Harper, 2020.

Mayra. Phone interview with the author. September 17, 2021.

Reagan, Ronald. *An American Life.* New York: Simon and Schuster, 1990.

———. *The Reagan Diaries*. New York: HarperCollins, 2009.

Smith, William French. *Law and Justice in the Reagan Administration: The Memoirs of an Attorney General*. Stanford: Stanford University Press, 1991.

NONGOVERNMENTAL ORGANIZATION REPORTS

"Attorney General Reveals Abuses in Immigration Detention Conditions Report." Immigrant Legal Resource Center, February 26, 2019. https://www.ilrc.org/california%E2%80%99s-attorney-general-reveals-abuses-immigration-detention-conditions-report.

Bacevich, A. J., James D. Hallums, Richard H. White, and Thomas F. Young. *American Military Policy in Small Wars: The Case of El Salvador*. Washington, DC: Pergamon-Brassey's International Defense Publishers, Institute for Foreign Policy Analysis, 1988.

Center for Migration Studies of New York, Inc. *In Defense of the Alien*. Vols. 3–11 (1980–88). https://www.jstor.org/journal/indefensealien.

Chan, Jennifer. "Immigration Detention Bed Quota Timeline." National Immigrant Justice Center, January 13, 2017. https://www.immigrantjustice.org/staff/blog/immigration-detention-bed-quota-timeline.

Cuban-American National Foundation. *Report of the Commission on a Free Cuba*. June 1990. https://www.canf.org/the-archive/archive-search/Report%20of%20the%20Commission%20on%20a%20Free%20Cuba%201990/400-report-of-the-commission-on-a-free-cuba.

Detention Watch Network. *The Influence of the Private Prison Industry in Immigration Detention*. May 2011. http://www.detentionwatchnetwork.org/privateprisons.

Flynn, Michael, and Cecilia Cannon. "The Privatization of Immigration Detention: Towards a Global View." *Global Detention Project*. Geneva, Switz.: Graduate Institute of International Studies, September 2009. https://www.refworld.org/docid/545b37394.html.

Inter-American Commission on Human Rights. "Report No. 28/93, Case 10.675, United States Decision of the Commission as to the Admissibility." October 13, 1993. http://cidh.org/annualrep/93eng/USA.10675.htm.

Mattera, Philip, and Mafruza Khan. *Corrections Corporation of America: A Critical Look at Its First Twenty Years*. Grassroots Leadership, Good Jobs First, and Prison Privatisation Report International, December 2003. http://www.goodjobsfirst.org/sites/default/files/docs/pdf/CCA%20Anniversary%20Report.pdf.

———. *Jail Breaks: Economic Development Subsidies Given to Private Prisons*. Washington, DC: Good Jobs First, October 2001. http://www.opensocietyfoundations.org/sites/default/files/jb_complete.pdf.

Migration Policy Institute. *Immigration Enforcement Spending Since IRCA*. No. 10 (November 2005). https://www.migrationpolicy.org/sites/default/files/publications/FactSheet_Spending.pdf.

"Monitoring and Investigations." Freedom for Immigrants. https://www.freedomforimmigrants.org/monitoring-investigations. Accessed December 14, 2021.

Project South et al. *Violence and Violation: Medical Abuse of Immigrants Detained at the Irwin County Detention Center*. September 2021. https://projectsouth.org/wp-content/uploads/2021/09/IrwinReport_14SEPT21.pdf.

"Report: Migrant Children Detention Center Could Be Built on Chemical-Ridden Landfill." Earthjustice, February 12, 2019. https://earthjustice.org/news/press/2019/report-migrant-children-detention-center-to-be-built-on-chemical-riddled-landfill.

Reynolds, Diana. "The Rise of the National Security State: FEMA and the NSC." Political Research Associates. http://www.publiceye.org/liberty/fema/Fema_3.html. Accessed December 14, 2021.

"Systemic Indifference: Dangerous and Substandard Medical Care in US Immigration Detention." Human Rights Watch, May 8, 2017. https://www.hrw.org/report/2017/05/08/systemic-indifference/dangerous-substandard-medical-care-us-immigration-detention#.

"Truth Commission: El Salvador." United States Institute of Peace, July 1, 1992. https://www.usip.org/publications/1992/07/truth-commission-el-salvador.

United Nations General Assembly. *Convention and Protocol Relating to the Status of Refugees.* January 31, 1967. https://www.ohchr.org/EN/ProfessionalInterest/Pages/ProtocolStatusOfRefugees.aspx.

THESES AND DISSERTATIONS

Capó, Julio, Jr. "It's Not Queer to be Gay: Miami and the Emergence of the Gay Rights Movement, 1945–1995." PhD diss., Florida International University, 2011.

Cullison, Jennifer L. "The Growth of Immigrant Caging in Postwar America: National Immigration Policy Choices, Regional Shifts toward Greater Carceral Control, and Continuing Legal Resistance in the US and South Texas." PhD diss., University of Colorado, Boulder, 2018.

Fowler, Rebecca A. "Water in the Desert or 'The Sanctuary Movement Never Ended': An Examination of Humane Borders, Tucson Samaritans, and No More Deaths Counter-Conducts." PhD diss., Washington State University, 2016.

González, Sergio. "'I Was a Stranger and You Welcomed Me': Latino Immigration, Religion, and Community Formation in Milwaukee, 1920–1990." PhD diss., University of Wisconsin-Madison, 2018.

Nofil, Brianna. "Detained Immigrants, Excludable Rights: The Strange Devolution of Immigration Authority." MA thesis, Duke University, 2012.

Shull, Kristina. "'Nobody Wants These People': Reagan's Immigration Crisis and America's First Private Prisons." PhD diss., UC Irvine, 2014.

Smith, Renaldo A. "The Cuban Detainee Uprising and Riot at the Atlanta Penitentiary, November 23, 1987." MA thesis, Atlanta University, 1988.

Stephens, Alexander. "'I Hope They Don't Come to Plains': Race and the Detention of Mariel Cubans, 1980–1981." MA thesis, University of Georgia, 2016.

Vong, Sam. "Compassion Politics: The History of Indochinese Refugees and the Transnational Networks of Care, 1975–1994." PhD diss., Yale University, 2013.

ARTICLES, BOOKS, AND CHAPTERS

Abrego, Leisy J. "On Silences: Salvadoran Refugees Then and Now." *Latino Studies* 15, no. 1 (2017): 73–85.

Abrego, Leisy J., and Genevieve Negrón-Gonzales, eds. *We Are Not Dreamers: Undocumented Scholars Theorize Undocumented Life in the United States.* Durham, NC: Duke University Press, 2020.

Achiume, E. Tendayi. "Migration as Decolonization." *Stanford Law Review* 71 (June 2019): 1509–73.

Agamben, Giorgio. *Homo Sacer: Sovereign Power and Bare Life*. Stanford: Stanford University Press, 1998.

Aguirre, Benigno E. "Cuban Mass Migration and the Social Construction of Deviants." *Bulletin of Latin American Research* 13 (1994): 155–83.

Aguirre, Benigno E., Rogelio Sáenz, and Brian Sinclair James. "Marielitos Ten Years Later: The Scarface Legacy." *Social Science Quarterly* 78, no. 2 (June 1997): 487–507.

Aja, Alan A. *Miami's Forgotten Cubans: Race, Racialization, and the Miami Afro-Cuban Experience*. New York: Palgrave Macmillan, 2016.

Alamo-Pastrana, Carlos. *Seams of Empire: Race and Radicalism in Puerto Rico and the United States*. Gainesville: University Press of Florida, 2016.

Alexander, Michelle. *The New Jim Crow: Mass Incarceration in the Age of Colorblindness*. New York: New Press, 2010.

Arnold, Kathleen R., ed. *Anti-immigration in the United States: A Historical Encyclopedia*. Santa Barbara, CA: Greenwood Press, 2011.

Avila, Eric. *Popular Culture in the Age of White Flight: Fear and Fantasy in Suburban Los Angeles*. Berkeley: University of California Press, 2006.

Bach, Robert L. "Immigration and U.S. Foreign Policy in Latin America and the Caribbean." In *Immigration and U.S. Foreign Policy*, edited by Robert W. Tucker, Charles B. Keely, and Linda Wrigley, 123–49. Boulder, CO: Westview Press, 1990.

Bailey, Beth. *America's Army: Making the All-Volunteer Force*. Cambridge, MA: Belknap Press, 2009.

Bakan, Abigail B., David Cox, and Colin Leys, eds. *Imperial Power and Regional Trade: The Caribbean Basin Initiative*. Waterloo, ON: Wilfrid Laurier University Press, 1993.

Balderrama, Francisco E. *Decade of Betrayal: Mexican Repatriation in the 1930s*. Albuquerque: University of New Mexico Press, 1995.

Banham, Reynor. *Los Angeles: The Architecture of Four Ecologies*. Berkeley: University of California Press, 1971.

Bardacke, Frank. "César Chávez: The Serpent and the Dove." In *The Human Tradition in California*, edited by Clark Davis and David Igler, 209–24. Wilmington: Scholarly Resources, 2002.

Batsalel, Kenneth Aaron. "The Limit(s) of Commitment: Journal Reflections on the Mariel Cuban Repatriation Panel Review Hearings." *Dialectical Anthropology* 17, no. 1 (1992): 85–111.

Bauer, Shane. *American Prison: A Reporter's Undercover Journey into the Business of Punishment*. New York: Penguin, 2018.

Beckett, Katherine. *Making Crime Pay: Law and Order in Contemporary American Politics*. Oxford: Oxford University Press, 1997.

Belew, Kathleen. *Bring the War Home: The White Power Movement and Paramilitary America*. Cambridge, MA: Harvard University Press, 2019.

Berger, Dan. *Captive Nation: Black Prison Organizing in the Civil Rights Era*. Chapel Hill: University of North Carolina Press, 2014.

———. *The Struggle Within: Prisons, Political Prisoners, and Mass Movements in the United States*. Montreal: PM Press, 2014.

Blackmon, Douglas A. *Slavery by Another Name*. New York: Random House, 2008.

Bodnar, John. *The Transplanted: A History of Immigrants in Urban America*. Bloomington: Indiana University Press, 1995.

Bon Tempo, Carl J. *Americans at the Gate: The United States and Refugees during the Cold War*. Princeton: Princeton University Press, 2008.

Booth, Jonathon. "Ending Forced Labor in ICE Detention Centers: A New Approach." *Georgetown Immigration Law Journal* 573 (August 2020): 573–611.

Boswell, Thomas D., and James R. Curtis. *The Cuban-American Experience: Culture, Images and Perspectives*. Lanham, MD: Rowman and Littlefield, 1984.

Brown, Wendy. *Undoing the Demos: Neoliberalism's Stealth Revolution*. New York: Zone Books, 2015.

Buff, Rachel Ida. *Against the Deportation Terror: Organizing for Immigrant Rights in the Twentieth Century*. Philadelphia: Temple University Press, 2018.

Bustamante, Michael J. "Anti-Communist Anti-Imperialism? Agrupación Abdala and the Shifting Contours of Cuban Exile Politics, 1968–1986." *Journal of American Ethnic History* 35, no. 1 (Fall 2015): 71–99.

Cacho, Lisa Marie. *Social Death: Racialized Rightlessness and the Criminalization of the Unprotected*. New York: New York University Press, 2012.

Cadava, Geraldo. *The Hispanic Republican: The Shaping of an American Political Identity, from Nixon to Trump*. New York: HarperCollins, 2020.

Camacho, Alicia Schmidt. *Migrant Imaginaries: Latino Cultural Politics in the US-Mexico Borderlands*. New York: New York University Press, 2008.

Camp, Jordan T. *Incarcerating the Crisis: Freedom Struggles and the Rise of the Neoliberal State*. Berkeley: University of California Press, 2016.

Capó, Julio, Jr. "Queering Mariel: Mediating Cold War Foreign Policy and US Citizenship among Cuba's Homosexual Exile Community, 1978–1994." *Journal of American Ethnic History* 29, no. 4 (Summer 2010): 78–106.

———. *Welcome to Fairyland: Queer Miami before 1940*. Chapel Hill: University of North Carolina Press, 2017.

Casavantes Bradford, Anita. "Remembering Pedro Pan: Childhood and Collective Memory-Making in Havana and Miami, 1960–2000." *Cuban Studies* 44 (2016): 283–308.

Chacón, Justin Akers, and Mike Davis. *No One Is Illegal: Fighting Racism and State Violence on the U.S.-Mexico Border*. Chicago: Haymarket Books, 2006.

Chase, Robert T., ed. *Caging Borders and Carceral States: Incarcerations, Immigration Detentions, and Resistance*. Chapel Hill: University of North Carolina Press, 2019.

Chávez, Karma R. "ACT UP, Haitian Migrants, and Alternative Memories of HIV/AIDS." *Quarterly Journal of Speech* 98, vol. 1 (2012): 63–68.

Chavez, Leo R. *Covering Immigration: Popular Images and the Politics of the Nation*. Berkeley: University of California Press, 2001.

———. *The Latino Threat: Constructing Immigrants, Citizens, and the Nation*. Stanford: Stanford University Press, 2008.

Chinchilla, Norma Stoltz, Nora Hamilton, and James Loucky. "The Sanctuary Movement and Central American Activism in Los Angeles." *Latin American Perspectives* 36, no. 6 (November 2009): 101–26.

Cleek, Todd. "The Legal Standards behind the Marielito Detentions." *Willamette Bulletin of Law and Policy* 1, no. 1 (1993): 127–37.

Cohen, Elizabeth F. *Illegal: How America's Lawless Immigration Regime Threatens Us All*. New York: Basic Books, 2020.

Cohen, Stanley. *Folk Devils and Moral Panics*. London: Routledge, 1972.

Collins, Robert M. "The Reagan Revolution and Antistatist Growthsmanship." Chap. 6 in *More: The Politics of Economic Growth in Postwar America*. New York: Oxford University Press, 2000.

Compher, Vic, and Betsy Morgan, eds. *Going Home: Building Peace in El Salvador; The Story of Repatriation*. New York: Apex Press, 1991.

Coutin, Susan Bibler. *The Culture of Protest: Religious Activism and the U.S. Sanctuary Movement*. Boulder, CO: Westview Press, 1993.

——. *Exiled Home: Salvadoran Transnational Youth in the Aftermath of Violence*. Durham, NC: Duke University Press, 2016.

——. *Legalizing Moves: Salvadoran Immigrants' Struggle for U.S. Residency*. Ann Arbor: University of Michigan Press, 2003.

Crandall, Russell. *The Salvador Option: The United States in El Salvador, 1977–1992*. Cambridge: Cambridge University Press, 2016.

Crittenden, Ann. *Sanctuary: A Story of American Conscience and the Law in Collision*. New York: Weidenfeld and Nicolson, 1988.

Cullison, Jennifer. "Valley of Caged Immigrants: Punishment, Protest, and the Rise of the Port Isabel Detention Center." *Tabula Rasa* 33 (2020): 225–69.

Cunningham, Hilary. *God and Caesar at the Rio Grande: Sanctuary and the Politics of Religion*. Minneapolis: University of Minnesota Press, 1995.

Danner, Mark. *The Massacre at El Mozote*. New York: Vintage Books, 1993.

Das, Alina. *No Justice in the Shadows: How America Criminalizes Immigrants*. New York: Bold Type Books, 2020.

Das Gupta, Monisha. *Unruly Immigrants: Rights, Activism, and Transnational South Asian Politics in the United States*. Durham, NC: Duke University Press, 2006.

Davidson, Miriam. *Convictions of the Heart: Jim Corbett and the Sanctuary Movement*. Tucson: University of Arizona Press, 1988.

Davis, Angela Y. *Are Prisons Obsolete?* New York: Seven Stories Press, 2003.

De Genova, Nicholas, and Nathalie Peutz, eds. *The Deportation Regime: Sovereignty, Space, and the Freedom of Movement*. Durham, NC: Duke University Press, 2010.

De Leon, Jason, and Michael Wells. *Land of Open Graves: Living and Dying on the Migrant Trail*. Berkeley: University of California Press, 2015.

del Olmo, Rosa. "Aerobiology and the War on Drugs: A Transnational Crime." *Crime and Social Justice* 30 (1987): 28–44.

Denvir, Daniel. *All-American Nativism: How the Bipartisan War on Immigrants Explains Politics as We Know It*. London: Verso, 2020.

Dow, Mark. *American Gulag: Inside U.S. Immigration Prisons*. Berkeley: University of California Press, 2004.

Du Bois, W. E. B. "The Spawn of Slavery: The Convict-Lease System in the South." *Missionary Review of the World* 14 (1901): 737–45.

Dunn, Timothy J. *Blockading the Border and Human Rights: The El Paso Operation That Remade Immigration Enforcement*. Austin: University of Texas Press, 2010.

——. *The Militarization of the U.S.-Mexico Border, 1978–1992: Low-Intensity Conflict Doctrine Comes Home*. Austin: University of Texas Press, 1996.

Eisen, Lauren. *Inside Private Prisons: An American Dilemma in the Age of Mass Incarceration*. New York: Columbia University Press, 2018.

Ellinghaus, Katherine. *Blood Will Tell: Native Americans and Assimilation Policy*. Lincoln: University of Nebraska Press, 2017.

Engstrom, David W. *Presidential Decision Making Adrift: The Carter Administration and the Mariel Boatlift*. Lanham, MD: Rowman and Littlefield, 1997.

Enns, Peter K. *Incarceration Nation: How the United States Became the Most Punitive Democracy in the World*. New York: Cambridge University Press, 2016.

Erickson, Philip. "The Saga of Indefinitely Detained Mariel Cubans: Garcia Mir v. Meese." *Loyola Los Angeles International and Comparative Law Review* 10, no. 271 (1988): 271–98.

Escobar, Martha D. *Captivity beyond Prisons: Criminalization Experiences of Latina (Im)migrants*. Austin: University of Texas Press, 2016.

Espiritu, Yến Lê. *Body Counts: The Vietnam War and Militarized Refugees*. Berkeley: University of California Press, 2014.

———. "Toward a Critical Refugee Study: The Vietnamese Refugee Subject in US Scholarship." *Journal of Vietnamese Studies* 1, no. 1–2 (February/August 2006): 410–33.

Estes, Nick. *Our History Is the Future: Standing Rock versus the Dakota Access Pipeline, and the Long Tradition of Indigenous Resistance*. London: Verso, 2019.

Felber, Garrett. *Those Who Know Don't Say: The Nation of Islam, the Black Freedom Movement, and the Carceral State*. Chapel Hill: University of North Carolina Press, 2020.

Felker-Kantor, Max. *Policing Los Angeles: Race, Resistance, and the Rise of the LAPD*. Chapel Hill: University of North Carolina Press, 2018.

Fernandes, Deepa. *Targeted: Homeland Security and the Business of Immigration*. New York: Seven Stories Press, 2007.

Fernández, Gastón A. *The Mariel Exodus: Twenty Years Later; A Study on the Politics of Stigma and a Research Bibliography*. Miami: Ediciones Universal, 2002.

Fierce, Mildred C. *Slavery Revisited: Blacks and the Southern Convict Lease System, 1865–1833*. Brooklyn: Africana Studies Research Center, Brooklyn College, 1994.

FitzGerald, David Scott. *Refuge beyond Reach: How Rich Democracies Repel Asylum Seekers*. Oxford: Oxford University Press, 2019.

Fixler, Philip E. and Robert W. Poole Jr. "The Privatization Revolution: What Washington Can Learn from State and Local Government." *Policy Review* (June 1986): 68–73.

Flynn, Michael J., and Matthew B. Flynn. *Challenging Immigration Detention: Academics, Activists, and Policy-Makers*. Northampton, MA: Edward Elgar, 2017.

Foucault, Michel. *Discipline and Punish: The Birth of the Prison*. 2nd ed. New York: Random House, 1995. Originally published in French in 1975 by Editions Gallimard.

Galeano, Eduardo. "The Invisible Sources of Power." Chap. 3 in *Open Veins of Latin America: Five Centuries of the Pillage of a Continent*. New York: Monthly Review Press, 1997.

Garcia, Margarita. "The Last Days in Cuba: Personal Accounts of the Circumstances of the Exit." *Migration Today* 11, no. 4–5 (1983): 13–22.

García, María Cristina. *Havana USA: Cuban Exiles and Cuban Americans in South Florida, 1959–1994*. Berkeley: University of California Press, 1996.

———. *The Refugee Challenge in Post–Cold War America*. Oxford: Oxford University Press, 2017.

———. *Seeking Refuge: Central American Migration to Mexico, the United States, and Canada*. Berkeley: University of California Press, 2006.

Gelbspan, Ross. *Break-Ins, Death Threats, and the FBI: The Covert War against the Central America Movement*. Boston: South End Press, 1991.

Gettleman, Marvin E., Patrick Lacefield, Louis Menashe, David Mermelstein, and Ronald Radosh, eds. *El Salvador: Central America in the New Cold War*. New York: Grove Press, 1987.

Gill, Lesley. *The School of the Americas: Military Training and Political Violence in the Americas*. Durham, NC: Duke University Press, 2004.

Gilmore, Ruth Wilson. *Golden Gulag: Prisons, Surplus, Crisis, and Opposition in Globalizing California*. Berkeley: University of California Press, 2007.

Glick, Brian. *The War at Home*. Boston: South End Press, 1989.

Goffman, Erving. *Asylums: Essays on the social situations of mental patients and other inmates*. London: Routledge, 2007.

Golash-Boza, Tanya. *Deported: Immigrant Policing, Disposable Labor and Global Capitalism*. New York: New York University Press, 2015.

———. "The Immigration Industrial Complex: Why We Enforce Immigration Policies Destined to Fail." *Sociology Compass* 3, no. 2 (2009): 295–309.

Golden, Renny, and Michael McConnell. *Sanctuary: The New Underground Railroad*. Maryknoll, NY: Orbis Books, 1986.

Goldstein, Brandt. *Storming the Court: How a Band of Law Students Fought the President—and Won*. New York: Scribner, 2005.

Gómez, Alan Eladio. "'*Nuestras vidas corren casi paralelas*': Chicanos, *Independentistas*, and the Prison Rebellions in Leavenworth, 1969–72." In *Behind Bars: Latino/as and Prison in the United States*, edited by Suzanne Oboler, 67–96. New York: Palgrave Macmillan, 2009.

Gonzales, Alfonso. *Reform without Justice: Latino Migrant Politics and the Homeland Security State*. Oxford: Oxford University Press, 2013.

González, Emilio T. "The Cuban Connection: Drug Trafficking and the Castro Regime." *Cuban Studies Association Occasional Paper Series* 2, no. 6 (July 1997): 1–19.

Gonzalez-Pando, Miguel. *The Cuban Americans*. Westport, CT: Greenwood Press, 1998.

Goodman, Adam. *The Deportation Machine: America's Long History of Expelling Immigrants*. Princeton: Princeton University Press, 2020.

Gosin, Monika. *The Racial Politics of Division: Interethnic Struggles for Legitimacy in Multicultural Miami*. Ithaca: Cornell University Press, 2019.

Gosse, Van. "'El Salvador Is Spanish for Vietnam': The Politics of Solidarity and the New Immigrant Left, 1955–1993." In *The Immigrant Left in the United States*, edited by Paul Buhle and Dan Georgakas, 308–29. Albany: State University of New York Press, 1996.

———. "The North American Front: Central American Solidarity in the Reagan Era." In *Reshaping the US Left: Popular Struggles in the 1980s*, edited by Mike Davis and Michael Sprinkler, 11–50. New York: Verso, 1988.

———. *Where the Boys Are: Cuba, Cold War America, and the Making of a New Left*. New York: Verso, 1993.

Granados, Omar. "Cubans in the Tundra: The 1980 Cuban Refugee Program of Fort McCoy." *Cuban Counterpoints*, September–October 2016. https://cubacounterpoints.com/archives/3400.html.

Grandin, Greg. *Empire's Workshop: Latin America, the United States, and the Rise of the New Imperialism*. New York: Metropolitan Books, 2006.

———. *The End of the Myth: From the Frontier to the Border Wall in the Mind of America*. New York: Macmillan, 2019.

Grasso, Michael. "'Look It Up, Check It Out': REX 84 and the History of an American Conspiracy." *We are the Mutants*, March 13, 2017. https://wearethemutants.com/2017/03/13/look-it-up-check-it-out-rex-84-and-the-history-of-an-american-conspiracy/.

Greene, Judith A., Bethany Carson, and Andrea Black. *Indefensible: A Decade of Mass Incarceration of Migrants Prosecuted for Crossing the Border*. Austin, TX: Grassroots Leadership and Justice Strategies, 2016.

Greenhill, Kelly M. *Weapons of Mass Migration: Forced Displacement, Coercion, and Foreign Policy*. Cornell: Cornell University Press, 2010.

Guenther, Lisa. "Prison Beds and Compensated Man-Days: The Spatio-temporal Order of Carceral Neoliberalism." *Social Justice* 44, no. 2–3 (2017): 31–54.

Guerrero, Perla M. "A Tenuous Welcome for Latinas/os and Asians: States' Rights Discourse in Late 20th Century Arkansas." In *Race and Ethnicity in Arkansas: Perspectives on the African American and Latino/a Experience*, edited by John Kirk, 141–52. Little Rock: University of Arkansas Press, 2014.

Guha, Ranajit. "The Prose of Counter-Insurgency." In *Selected Subaltern Studies*, edited by Ranajit Guha and Gayatri Chakravorty Spivak, 45–84. Oxford: Oxford University Press, 1988.

Haley, Sarah. *No Mercy Here: Gender, Punishment, and the Making of Jim Crow Modernity*. Chapel Hill: University of North Carolina Press, 2016.

Hall, Stuart, Charles Critcher, Tony Jefferson, John Clarke, and Brian Roberts. *Policing the Crisis: Mugging, the State, and Law and Order*. London: Red Globe Press, 1978.

Hallett, Michael A. *Private Prisons in America: A Critical Race Perspective*. Urbana: University of Chicago Press, 2006.

Hamm, Mark S. *The Abandoned Ones: The Imprisonment and Uprising of the Mariel Boat People*. Boston: Northeastern University Press, 1995.

Haney, Patrick J., and Walt Vanderbush. "The Role of Ethnic Interest Groups in US Foreign Policy: The Case of the Cuban American National Foundation." *International Studies Quarterly* 43, no. 2 (June 1999): 341–61.

Hay, Michelle A. *"I've Been Black in Two Countries": Black Cuban Views on Race in the United States*. El Paso: LFB Scholarly Publishing, 2009.

Heclo, Hugh. "Ronald Reagan and the American Public Philosophy." In *The Reagan Presidency: Pragmatic Conservatism and Its Legacies*, edited by W. Elliot Brownlee and Hugh Davis Graham, 17–39. Lawrence: University Press of Kansas, 2003.

Hedge, Radha S. *Mediating Migration*. Malden, MA: Polity Press, 2016.

Heidbrink, Laura. *Migranthood: Youth in a New Era of Deportation*. Palo Alto: Stanford University Press, 2020.

Herivel, Tara, and Paul Wright, eds. *Prison Profiteers: Who Makes Money from Mass Incarceration*. New York: New Press, 2007.

Hernández, César Cuauhtémoc García. *Migrating to Prison: America's Obsession with Locking Up Immigrants*. New York: New Press, 2019.

Hernández, David Manuel. "Carceral Shadows." In *Caging Borders and Carceral States: Incarcerations, Immigration Detentions, and Resistance*, edited by Robert T. Chase, 57–92. Chapel Hill: University of North Carolina Press, 2019.

———. "Undue Process: Racial Genealogies of Immigrant Detention." In *Constructing Borders/Crossing Boundaries: Race, Ethnicity, and Immigration*, edited by Caroline B. Brettell, 59–88. Lanham, MD: Rowman and Littlefield, 2007.

Hernández, Kelly Lytle. *City of Inmates: Conquest, Rebellion, and the Rise of Human Caging in Los Angeles, 1771–1965*. Chapel Hill: University of North Carolina Press, 2017.

———. *Migra! A History of the U.S. Border Patrol*. Berkeley: University of California Press, 2010.

Hernández, K. L., K. G. Muhammad, and H. A. Thompson. "Introduction: Constructing the Carceral State." *Journal of American History* 102, no. 1 (2015): 18–24.

Hester, Torrie. *Deportation: Origins of US Policy.* Philadelphia: University of Pennsylvania Press, 2017.

Higashide, Seiichi. *Adios to Tears: The Memoirs of a Japanese-Peruvian Internee in US Concentration Camps.* Seattle: University of Washington Press, 1993.

Hing, Bill Ong. *American Presidents, Deportations, and Human Rights Violations.* Cambridge: Cambridge University Press, 2019.

Hinton, Elizabeth. *America on Fire: The Untold History of Police Violence and Black Rebellion since the 1960s.* New York: W. W. Norton, 2021.

———. *From the War on Poverty to the War on Crime: The Making of Mass Incarceration in America.* Cambridge, MA: Harvard University Press, 2016.

Hirabayashi, Gordon K. *A Principled Stand: The Story of Hirabayashi v. United States.* Seattle: University of Washington Press, 2013.

Hirota, Hidetaka. *Expelling the Poor: Atlantic Seaboard States and the Nineteenth-Century Origins of American Immigration Policy.* Oxford: Oxford University Press, 2017.

Holmes, Todd. "The Economic Roots of Reaganism: Corporate Conservatives, Political Economy, and the United Farm Workers Movement, 1965–1970." *Western Historical Quarterly* 41, no. 1 (Spring 2010): 55–80.

Hoxie, Frederick E. *The Campaign to Assimilate the Indians, 1880–1920.* Lincoln: University of Nebraska Press, 1984.

Hsu, Madeline Y. *Dreaming of Gold, Dreaming of Home: Transnationalism and Migration between the United States and South China, 1882–1943.* Palo Alto: Stanford University Press, 2000.

Hufker, Brian, and Gray Cavender. "From Freedom Flotilla to America's Burden: The Social Construction of the Mariel Immigrants." *Sociological Quarterly* 31, no. 2 (1990): 321–35.

Inda, J. X. "Borderzones of Enforcement: Criminalization, Workplace Raids, and Migration Counterconducts." In *The Contested Politics of Mobility: Borderzones and Irregularity,* edited by V. Squire, 74–90. New York: Routledge, 2011.

Izumi, Masumi. "Prohibiting 'American Concentration Camps': Repeal of the Emergency Detention Act and the Public Historical Memory of the Japanese American Internment." *Pacific Historical Review* 74, no. 2 (May 2005): 165–94.

Jacklin, Jillian Marie. "Dangerous Marielitos: Wisconsin Newspapers and the Proliferation of a Negative Representation." *International Journal of Cuban Studies* 10, no. 1 (Spring 2018): 30–52.

Janssen, Volker. "Sunbelt Lock-Up: Where the Suburbs Met the Super-Max." In *Sunbelt Rising: The Politics of Place, Space, and Region,* edited by Michelle Nickerson and Darren Dochuk, 217–39. Philadelphia: University of Pennsylvania Press, 2011.

Jarquín, Mateo Cayetano. "Red Christmases: The Sandinistas, Indigenous Rebellion, and the Origins of the Nicaraguan Civil War, 1981–82." *Cold War History* 18, no. 1 (2018): 91–107.

Jones, Reece. *Violent Borders: Refugees and the Right to Move.* New York: Verso Books, 2017.

———. *White Borders: The History of Race and Immigration in the United States from Chinese Exclusion to the Border Wall.* New York: Penguin, 2021.

Jones, Thomas David. "Sale v. Haitian Centers Council, Inc." *American Journal of International Law* 88, no. 1 (January 1994): 114–26.

Juhasz, Alexandra. "Video Remains: Nostalgia, Technology, and Queer Archive Activism." *GLQ: A Journal of Gay and Lesbian Studies* 12 (2006): 319–28.

Kaba, Mariame. *We Do This 'til We Free Us: Abolitionist Organizing and Transforming Justice.* Chicago: Haymarket Books, 2021.

Kahn, Jeffrey S. *Islands of Sovereignty: Haitian Migration and the Borders of Empire.* Chicago: University of Chicago Press, 2019.

Kahn, Robert S. *Other People's Blood: Immigration Prisons in the Reagan Decade.* New York: Westview Press, 1996.

Kami, Hideaki. *Diplomacy Meets Migration: US Relations with Cuba during the Cold War.* Cambridge: Cambridge University Press, 2018.

Kang, S. Deborah. *The INS on the Line: Making Immigration Law on the US-Mexico Border, 1917–1954.* Oxford: Oxford University Press, 2017.

Kanstroom, Dan. *Deportation Nation: Outsiders in American History.* Cambridge, MA: Harvard University Press, 2007.

Khalili, Laleh. *Time in the Shadows: Confinement in Counterinsurgencies.* Redwood City: Stanford University Press, 2012.

Kim, Alice, Erica R. Meiners, Jill Petty, Audrey Petty, Beth E. Richie, and Sarah Ross, eds. *The Long Term: Resisting Life Sentences, Working toward Freedom.* Chicago: Haymarket Books, 2018.

King, Martin Luther Jr., "Beyond Vietnam—A Time to Break Silence." Speech, New York, April 4, 1967. American Rhetoric. https://www.americanrhetoric.com/speeches /mlkatimetobreaksilence.htm.

Klein, Naomi. *The Shock Doctrine: The Rise of Disaster Capitalism.* New York: Henry Holt, 2007.

Kornbluh, Peter. *Nicaragua, the Price of Intervention: Reagan's Wars against the Sandinistas.* Washington, DC: Institute for Policy Studies, 1987.

Kornbluh, Peter, and William M. LeoGrande. *Back Channel to Cuba: The Hidden History of Negotiations between Washington and Havana.* Chapel Hill: University of North Carolina Press, 2014.

Kunzel, Regina. *Criminal Intimacy: Prison and the Uneven History of Modern American Sexuality.* Chicago: University of Chicago Press, 2008.

Kuzmarov, Jeremy. *Modernizing Repression: Police Training and Nation-Building in the American Century.* Amherst: University of Massachusetts Press, 2012.

LaFeber, Walter. *Inevitable Revolutions: The United States in Central America.* 2nd ed. New York: W. W. Norton, 1993.

Laguerre, Michel S. *Diasporic Citizenship: Haitian Americans in Transnational America.* New York: St. Martin's Press, 1998.

Lal, Prerna. *Unsung America: Immigrant Trailblazers and Our Fight for Freedom.* Coral Gables, FL: Mango Publishing, 2019.

Larzelere, Alex. *The 1980 Cuban Boatlift: Castro's Ploy—America's Dilemma.* Washington, DC: National Defense University Press, 1988.

Latner, Teishan. "'Agrarians' or 'Anarchists'? The Venceremos Brigades to Cuba, State Surveillance, and the FBI as Biographer and Archivist." *Journal of Transnational American Studies* 9, no. 1 (2018): 119–40.

———. *Cuban Revolution in America: Havana and the Making of a United States Left, 1968–1992.* Chapel Hill: University of North Carolina Press, 2018.

Law, Anna O. "Lunatics, Idiots, Paupers, and Negro Seamen—Immigration Federalism and the Early American State." *Studies in American Political Development* 28, no. 2 (2014): 107–28.

Lee, Erika. *America for Americans: A History of Xenophobia in the United States*. New York: Basic Books, 2019.

———. *At America's Gates: Chinese Immigration during the Exclusion Era, 1882–1943*. Chapel Hill: University of North Carolina Press, 2003.

———. "'The Yellow Peril' and Asian Exclusion in the Americas." *Pacific Historical Review* 76, no. 4 (November 2007): 537–62.

Leffler, Melvyn, and David Painter, eds. *Origins of the Cold War: An International History*. London: Routledge, 2005.

LeFlouria, Tabitha L. *Chained in Silence: Black Women and Convict Labor in the New South*. Chapel Hill: University of North Carolina Press, 2016.

LeoGrande, William M. *Our Own Backyard: The United States in Central America, 1977–1992*. Chapel Hill: University of North Carolina Press, 1998.

Levine, Daniel H. *Popular Voices in Latin American Catholicism*. Princeton: Princeton University Press, 1992.

Lewis, William F. "Telling America's Story: Narrative Form and the Reagan Presidency." *Quarterly Journal of Speech* 73, no. 3 (1987): 280–302.

Light, Jennifer S. *From Warfare to Welfare: Defense Intellectuals and Urban Problems in Cold War America*. Baltimore: Johns Hopkins University Press, 2005.

Lindskoog, Carl. *Detain and Punish: Haitian Refugees and the Rise of the World's Largest Immigration Detention System*. Gainesville: University of Florida Press, 2018.

Lipman, Jana K. "The Fish Trusts the Water, and It Is in the Water That It Is Cooked." *Radical History Review* 115 (Winter 2013): 115–41.

———. *Guantánamo: A Working-Class History between Empire and Revolution*. Berkeley: University of California Press, 2008.

———. *In Camps: Vietnamese Refugees, Asylum Seekers, and Repatriates*. Berkeley: University of California Press, 2020.

———. "'A Precedent Worth Setting . . .' Military Humanitarianism: The US Military and the 1975 Vietnamese Evacuation." *Journal of Military History* 79, no. 1 (January 2015): 151–79.

———. "A Refugee Camp in America: Fort Chaffee and Vietnamese and Cuban Refugees, 1975–1982." *Journal of American Ethnic History* 33, no. 2 (Winter 2014): 57–87.

Lippert, Randy K. *Sanctuary, Sovereignty, Sacrifice: Canadian Sanctuary Incidents, Power and Law*. Vancouver: University of British Columbia Press, 2005.

Llanes, José. *Cuban Americans: Masters of Survival*. Cambridge, MA: Abt Books, 1982.

Loescher, Gil, and John A. Scanlan. *Calculated Kindness: Refugees and America's Half-Open Door, 1945 to the Present*. New York: Free Press, 1986.

———. "Human Rights, U.S. Foreign Policy, and Haitian Refugees." *Journal of Interamerican Studies and World Affairs* 26, no. 3 (August 1984): 313–56.

Logan, Charles H. *Private Prisons: Cons and Pros*. Oxford: Oxford University Press, 1990.

Longley, Kyle, ed. *Deconstructing Reagan: Conservative Mythology and America's Fortieth President*. London: Routledge, 2006.

López, Ian Haney. *Dog Whistle Politics: How Coded Racial Appeals Have Reinvented Racism and Wrecked the Middle Class*. Oxford: Oxford University Press, 2013.

Lopez, William D. *Separated: Family and Community in the Aftermath of an Immigration Raid*. Baltimore: Johns Hopkins University Press, 2019.

Lorentzen, Robin. *Women in the Sanctuary Movement*. Philadelphia: Temple University Press, 1991.

Lowenthal, Abraham F., and Samuel F. Wells Jr., eds. *The Central American Crisis: Policy Perspectives*. Working Papers 119. Washington, DC: Latin American Program, the Wilson Center, 1982.

Loyd, Jenna M., and Alison Mountz. *Boats, Borders, and Bases: Race, the Cold War, and the Rise of Migrant Detention in the United States*. Berkeley: University of California Press, 2018.

Loza, Mireya. *Defiant Braceros: How Migrant Workers Fought for Racial, Sexual, and Political Freedom*. Chapel Hill: University of North Carolina Press, 2016.

Luibhéid, Eithne, and Karma R. Chávez. *Queer and Trans Migrations: Dynamics of Illegalization, Detention, and Deportation*. Urbana: University of Illinois Press, 2020.

Macías-Rojas, Patrisia. *From Deportation to Prison: The Politics of Immigration Enforcement in Post–Civil Rights America*. New York: New York University Press, 2016.

Madero, Abel Sierra. *Del otro lado del espejo: La sexualidad en la construcción de la nación cubana*. Havana: Casas de las Américas, 2006.

Martin, Bradford. *The Other Eighties: A Secret History of America in the Age of Reagan*. New York: Hill and Wang, 2011.

Martinez, Monica Muñoz. *The Injustice Never Leaves You: Anti-Mexican Violence in Texas*. Cambridge, MA: Harvard University Press, 2018.

Masud-Piloto, Felix. *From Welcomed Exiles to Illegal Immigrants: Cuban Migration to the U.S., 1959–1995*. Lanham, MD: Rowman and Littlefield, 1996.

Mauer, Marc, and Meda Chesney-Lind, eds. *Invisible Punishment: The Collateral Consequences of Mass Imprisonment*. New York: New Press, 2003.

McAlister, Melani. *Epic Encounters: Culture, Media, and U.S. Interests in the Middle East since 1945*. Berkeley: University of California Press, 2001.

McClintock, Michael. *The American Connection: State Terror and Popular Resistance in El Salvador*. Avon, UK: Zed Books, 1985.

Miller, Jake C. *The Plight of Haitian Refugees*. New York: Praeger, 1984.

Miller, Stuart Creighton. *The Unwelcome Immigrant: The American Image of the Chinese, 1785–1882*. Berkeley: University of California Press, 1969.

Miller, Todd. *Empire of Borders: The Expansion of the US Border around the World*. New York: Verso, 2019.

Minian, Ana Raquel. *Undocumented Lives: The Untold Story of Mexican Migration*. Cambridge, MA: Harvard University Press, 2018.

Mitchell, Christopher. "U.S. Policy toward Haitian Boat People, 1972–93." *Annals of the American Academy of Political and Social Science* 534, no. 1 (1994): 69–80.

———, ed. *Western Hemisphere Immigration and United States Foreign Policy*. Philadelphia: University of Pennsylvania Press, 2005.

Molina, Natalie. *Fit to Be Citizens? Public Health and Race in Los Angeles, 1879–1939*. Berkeley: University of California Press, 2006.

Moore, Erik A. "Rights or Wishes? Conflicting Views over Human Rights and America's Involvement in the Nicaraguan Contra War." *Diplomacy and Statecraft* 29, no. 4 (2018): 716–37.

Motomura, Hiroshi. "Haitian Asylum Seekers: Interdiction and Immigrant Rights." *Cornell International Law Journal* 26, no. 3 (1996): 695–717.

Muhammad, Khalil G. *The Condemnation of Blackness: Race, Crime, and the Making of Modern Urban America*. Cambridge, MA: Harvard University Press, 2010.

Murukawa, Naomi. *The First Civil Right: How Liberals Built Prison America*. Oxford: Oxford University Press, 2014.

Nebolon, Juliet. "'Life Given Straight from the Heart': Settler Militarism, Biopolitics, and Public Health in Hawai'i during World War II." *American Quarterly* 69, no. 1 (March 2017): 23–45.

Nessel, Lori A. "Externalized Borders and the Invisible Refugee." *Columbia Human Rights Law Review* 40, no. 625 (Spring 2009): 625–29.

Nethery, Amy, and Stephanie J. Silverman, eds. *Immigration Detention: The Migration of a Policy and Its Human Impact*. London: Routledge, 2017.

Nevins, Joseph. *Operation Gatekeeper and Beyond: The War on "Illegals" and the Remaking of the U.S.-Mexico Boundary*. New York: Routledge, 2010.

Ngai, Mae M. *Impossible Subjects: Illegal Aliens and the Making of Modern America*. Princeton: Princeton University Press, 2003.

Nguyen, Mimi Thi. *The Gift of Freedom: War, Debt, and Other Refugee Passages*. Durham, NC: Duke University Press, 2012.

Nickerson, Michelle, and Darren Dochuk. *Sunbelt Rising: The Politics of Space, Place, and Region*. Philadelphia: University of Pennsylvania Press, 2014.

N'Zengou-Tayo, Marie-José. "Ana Lydia Vega and Haiti: Between Fascination and Rejection." *Journal of Haitian Studies* 13, no. 1 (Spring 2007): 42–60.

O'Brien, Daniel T., Chelsea Farrell, and Brandon C. Welsh. "Looking through Broken Windows: The Impact of Neighborhood Disorder on Aggression and Fear of Crime Is an Artifact of Research Design." *Annual Review of Criminology* 2 (January 2019): 53–71.

Ordaz, Jessica. "Protesting Conditions inside El Corralón: Immigration Detention, State Repression, and Transnational Migrant Politics in El Centro, California." *Journal of American Ethnic History* 38, no. 2 (Winter 2019): 65–93.

———. *The Shadow of El Centro*. Chapel Hill: University of North Carolina Press, 2021.

Ortiz, Paul. *An African American and Latinx History of the United States*. Boston: Beacon Press, 2018.

Osgood, Kenneth. *Total Cold War: Eisenhower's Secret Propaganda Battle at Home and Abroad*. Lawrence: University Press of Kansas, 2006.

Oswald, Lynda J. "Extended Voluntary Departure: Limiting the Attorney General's Discretion in Immigration Matters." *Michigan Law Review* 85, no. 1 (1986): 152–90.

Paik, A. Naomi. "Abolitionist Futures and the US Sanctuary Movement." *Race and Class* 59, no. 2 (2017): 3–15.

———. *Bans, Walls, Raids, Sanctuary: Understanding U.S. Immigration for the Twenty-First Century*. Berkeley: University of California Press, 2020.

———. "Carceral Quarantine at Guantánamo: Legacies of US Imprisonment of Haitian Refugees, 1991–1994." *Radical History Review* 115 (Winter 2013): 142–68.

———. "Guantánamo Bay: A Palimpsest of Carceral Violence." *The Funambulist*, April 2016. https://thefunambulist.net/magazine/04-carceral-environments/guantanamo-bay-palimpsest-carceral-violence-naomi-paik.

———. *Rightlessness: Testimony and Redress in U.S. Prison Camps since World War II*. Chapel Hill: University of North Carolina Press, 2016.

Pamphile, Leon D. *Haitians and African Americans: A Heritage of Tragedy and Hope*. Gainesville: University Press of Florida, 2001.

Parsons, Anne E. *From Asylum to Prison: Deinstitutionalization and the Rise of Mass Incarceration after 1945*. Chapel Hill: University of North Carolina Press, 2018.

Patiño, Jimmy. *Raza Sí, Migra No: Chicano Movement Struggles for Immigrant Rights in San Diego*. Chapel Hill: University of North Carolina Press, 2017.

Patler, Caitlin, Kristina Shull, and Katie Dingeman. "Detention and Deportation." In *The Routledge International Handbook of Migration Studies*. 2nd ed., edited by S. J. Gold and S. J. Nawyn, 382–94. London: Routledge, 2019.

Pawel, Miriam. *The Union of Their Dreams: Power, Hope, and Struggle in Cesar Chavez's Farm Worker Movement*. New York: Bloomsbury, 2010.

Peña, Susana. "'Obvious Gays' and the State Gaze: Cuban Gay Visibility and U.S. Immigration Policy during the Mariel Boatlift." *Journal of the History of Sexuality* 16, no. 3 (September 2007): 482–514.

———. *¡Oye Loca! From the Mariel Boatlift to Gay Cuban Miami*. Minneapolis: University of Minnesota Press, 2013.

Perkinson, Robert. *Texas Tough: The Rise of America's Prison Empire*. New York: Macmillan, 2010.

Perla, Héctor. "Central American Counter Public Mobilization: Transnational Social Movement Opposition to Reagan's Foreign Policy toward Central America." *Latino Studies* 11, no. 2 (2013): 167–89.

———. "Si Nicaragua Venció, El Salvador Vencerá: Central American Agency in the Creation of the U.S.-Central American Peace and Solidarity Movement." *Latin American Research Review* 43, no. 2 (2008): 136–58.

Perlstein, Rick. *The Invisible Bridge: The Fall of Nixon and the Rise of Reagan*. New York: Simon and Schuster, 2015.

———. *Reaganland: America's Right Turn, 1976–1980*. New York: Simon and Schuster, 2020.

Phillips, Kevin. *The Emerging Republican Majority*. New Rochelle, NY: Arlington House, 1969.

Pizor, Andrew G. "Sale v. Haitian Centers Council: The Return of Haitian Refugees." *Fordham International Law Journal* 17, no. 4 (1993): 1062–114.

Plummer, Brenda Gayle. *In Search of Power: African Americans in the Era of Decolonization, 1956–1974*. Cambridge: Cambridge University Press, 2012.

Polyné, Millery. *From Douglass to Duvalier: U.S. African Americans, Haiti, and Pan Americanism, 1870–1964*. Gainesville: University Press of Florida, 2010.

Portes, Alejandro, and Alex Stepick. *City on the Edge: The Transformation of Miami*. Berkeley: University of California Press, 1993.

———. "Unwelcome Immigrants: The Labor Market Experiences of 1980 (Mariel) Cuban and Haitian Refugees in South Florida." *American Sociological Review* 50, no. 4 (August 1985): 493–514.

Potoker, Elaine, and Richard H. Borgman. "The Economic Impact of the Caribbean Basin Initiative: Has It Delivered Its Promise?" *Canadian Journal of Latin American and Caribbean Studies* 32, no. 64 (2007): 79–80.

Rabe, Stephen. *The Killing Zone: The United States Wages Cold War in Latin America*. Oxford: Oxford University Press, 2015.

Ralph, David E. "Haitian Interdiction on the High Seas: The Continuing Saga of the Rights of Aliens outside United States Territory." *Maryland Journal of International Law* 17, no. 2 (1993): 227–51.

Bibliography

Ramírez, Marla Andrea. "The Making of Mexican Illegality: Immigration Exclusions Based on Race, Class Status, and Gender." *New Political Science* 40, no. 2 (2018): 317–35.

Ratner, Michael. "How We Closed the Guantanamo HIV Camp: The Intersection of Politics and Litigation." *Harvard Human Rights Journal* 11, no. 187 (1998): 187–220.

Regan, Margaret. *Detained and Deported: Stories of Immigrant Families under Fire*. Boston: Beacon Press, 2015.

Reiss, Susanna. *We Sell Drugs: The Alchemy of US Empire*. Berkeley: University of California Press, 2014.

Reiter, K., and A. Koenig, eds. *Extreme Punishment: Comparative Studies in Detention, Incarceration and Solitary Confinement*. London: Palgrave Macmillan, 2015.

Renda, Mary A. *Taking Haiti: Military Occupation and the Culture of US Imperialism*. Chapel Hill: University of North Carolina Press, 2001.

Riosmena, Fernanda. "Policy Shocks: On the Legal Auspices of Latin American Migration to the United States." *Annals of the American Academy* 630 (July 2010): 270–93.

Rivera, Mario Antonio. *Decision and Structure: U.S. Refugee Policy in the Mariel Crisis*. Lanham, MD: University Press of America, 1991.

Rizzo, Mary. "Reading against the Grain, Finding the Voices of the Detained." *Museums and Social Issues* 12, no. 1 (2017): 26–32.

Robbins, Ira. *The Legal Dimensions of Private Incarceration*. Washington, DC: American Bar Association, 1988.

Rodríguez, Dylan. *Forced Passages: Imprisoned Radical Intellectuals and the U.S. Prison Regime*. Minneapolis: University of Minnesota Press, 2005.

———. *White Reconstruction: Domestic Warfare and the Logics of Genocide*. New York: Fordham University Press, 2021.

Romero, Robert Chao. *The Chinese in Mexico, 1882–1940*. Tucson: University of Arizona Press, 2010.

Rosas, Ana. *Abrazando el Espíritu: Bracero Families Confront the US-Mexico Border*. Berkeley: University of California Press, 2014.

Rosenberg, Emily S. *A Date Which Will Live: Pearl Harbor in American Memory*. Durham, NC: Duke University Press, 2003.

———. *Financial Missionaries to the World: The Politics and Culture of Dollar Diplomacy, 1900–1930*. Durham, NC: Duke University Press, 2004.

Saadi, Altaf, Maria-Elena De Trinidad Young, Caitlin Patler, Jeremias Leonel Estrada, and Homer Venters. "Understanding U.S. Immigration Detention: Reaffirming Rights and Addressing Social-Structural Determinants of Health." *Health and Human Rights Journal* 22, no. 1 (June 2020): 187–98.

Saavedra, Marco, Claudia Muñoz, Mariela Nuñez-Janes, and Stephen Pavey. *Eclipse of Dreams: The Undocumented-Led Struggle for Freedom*. Chico, CA: AK Press, 2020.

Sampaio, Anna. *Terrorizing Latina/o Immigrants: Race, Gender, and Immigration Politics in the Age of Security*. Philadelphia: Temple University Press, 2015.

Sassen, Saskia. *Expulsions: Brutality and Complexity in the Global Economy*. Cambridge, MA: Belknap Press, 2014.

Schoultz, Lars. *That Infernal Little Cuban Republic: The United States and the Cuban Revolution*. Chapel Hill: University of North Carolina Press, 2011.

Schrader, Stuart. *Badges without Borders: How Global Counterinsurgency Transformed American Policing*. Berkeley: University of California Press, 2019.

Scott, Peter Dale, and Jonathan Marshall. *Cocaine Politics: Drugs, Armies, and the CIA in Central America.* Berkeley: University of California Press, 1991.

Seigel, Micol. *Violence Work: State Power and the Limits of Police.* Durham, NC: Duke University Press, 2018.

Self, Robert O. *All in the Family: The Realignment of American Democracy since the 1960s.* New York: Hill and Wang, 2012.

Sellers, Martin P. *The History and Politics of Private Prisons: A Comparative Analysis.* Madison, NJ: Fairleigh Dickinson University Press, 1993.

Selman, Donna, and Paul Leighton. *Punishment for Sale: Private Prisons, Big Business, and the Incarceration Binge.* Lanham, MD: Rowman and Littlefield, 2010.

Shah, Nayan. *Contagious Divides: Epidemics and Race in San Francisco's Chinatown.* Berkeley: University of California Press, 2005.

Shichor, David. *Punishment for Profit: Private Prisons/Public Concerns.* Thousand Oaks, CA: Sage, 1995.

Shull, Kristina. "'Nobody Wants These People': Reagan's Immigration Crisis and the Containment of Foreign Bodies." In *Body and Nation: The Global Realm of U.S. Body Politics in the Twentieth Century,* edited by Emily S. Rosenberg and Shanon Fitzpatrick, 241–63. Durham, NC: Duke University Press, 2014.

———. "Reagan's Cold War on Immigrants: Resistance and the Rise of a Detention Regime." *Journal of American Ethnic History* 40, no. 2 (Winter 2021): 5–51.

Simon, Jonathan. *Governing through Crime: How the War on Crime Transformed American Democracy and Created a Culture of Fear.* New York: Oxford University Press, 2007.

Sinha, Anita. "Slavery by Another Name: 'Voluntary' Immigrant Detainee Labor and the Thirteenth Amendment." *Stanford Journal of Civil Rights and Civil Liberties* 11, no. 1 (2015): 1–44.

Sommers, Jeffrey. *Race, Reality, and Realpolitik: U.S.-Haiti Relations in the Lead Up to the 1915 Occupation.* Lanham, MD: Lexington Books, 2016.

Smith, Christian. *Resisting Reagan: The U.S. Central America Peace Movement.* Chicago: University of Chicago Press, 1996.

Stanley, Eric A. *Captive Genders: Trans Embodiment and the Prison Industrial Complex.* Chico, CA: AK Press, 2015.

Statz, Michele. *Lawyering an Uncertain Cause: Immigration Advocacy and Chinese Youth in the U.S.* Nashville: Vanderbilt University Press, 2018.

Stephens, Alexander M. "Making Migrants 'Criminal': The Mariel Boatlift, Miami, and U.S. Immigration Policy in the 1980s." *Anthurium: A Caribbean Studies Journal* 17, no. 2 (2021): 4.

Stepick, Alex. "Haitian Boat People: A Study in the Conflicting Forces Shaping U.S. Immigration Policy." *Law and Contemporary Problems* 45, no. 2 (1982): 163–96.

———. "Unintended Consequences: Rejecting Haitian Boat People and Destabilizing Duvalier." In *Western Hemisphere Immigration and United States Foreign Policy,* edited by Christopher Mitchell, 125–56. University Park: Pennsylvania State University Press, 1992.

Stepick, Alex, Terry Rey, and Sarah J. Mahler. *Churches and Charity in the Immigrant City: Religion, Immigration, and Civic Engagement in Miami.* New Brunswick, NJ: Rutgers University Press, 2009.

Stern, Alexandra Minna. *Eugenic Nation: Faults and Frontiers of Better Breeding in Modern America.* Berkeley: University of California Press, 2005.

Stoler, Ann Laura, ed. *Haunted by Empire: Geographies of the Intimate in North American History*. Durham, NC: Duke University Press, 2006.

Striffler, Steve. *Solidarity: Latin America and the US Left in the Era of Human Rights*. London: Pluto Press, 2019.

Stumpf, Julie. "The Crimmigration Crisis: Immigrants, Crime, and Sovereign Power." *American University Law Review* 56, no. 2 (2006): 367–420.

Sudbury, Julia, ed. *Global Lockdown: Race, Gender, and the Prison-Industrial Complex*. New York: Routledge, 2005.

Tang, Irwin A., ed. *Asian Texans: Our Histories and Our Lives*. Scotts Valley, CA: CreateSpace, 2018.

Taparata, Evan. "'Refugees as You Call Them': The Politics of Refugee Recognition in the Nineteenth-Century United States." *Journal of American Ethnic History* 38, no. 2 (Winter 2019): 9–35.

Tazzioli, Martina, and Nicolas De Genova. "Kidnapping Migrants as a Tactic of Border Enforcement." *EPD: Society and Space* 38, no. 5 (2020): 1–20.

Tennis, Katherine H. "Offshoring the Border: The 1981 United States–Haiti Agreement and the Origins of Extraterritorial Maritime Interdiction." *Journal of Refugee Studies* 34, no. 1 (2019): 173–203.

Thompson, Heather Ann. *Blood in the Water: The Attica Prison Uprising of 1971 and Its Legacy*. New York: Pantheon, 2016.

———. "Why Mass Incarceration Matters: Rethinking Crisis, Decline, and Transformation in Postwar American History." *Journal of American History* 97, no. 3 (December 2010): 703–34.

Tombs, David. *Latin American Liberation Theology*. Boston: Brill Academic Publishers, 2002.

Tomsho, Robert. *The American Sanctuary Movement*. Austin: Texas Monthly Press, 1987.

Torres, Maria de los Angeles. *In the Land of Mirrors: Cuban Exile Politics in the United States*. Ann Arbor: University of Michigan Press, 1999.

Trouillot, Michel-Rolph. *Haiti: State against Nation; The Origins and Legacy of Duvalierism*. New York: Monthly Review Press, 1990.

———. *Silencing the Past: Power and the Production of History*. Boston: Beacon Press, 1995.

Troy, Gil. *Morning in America: How Ronald Reagan Invented the 1980s*. Princeton: Princeton University Press, 2005.

Tuck, Eve. "Suspending Damage: A Letter to Communities." *Harvard Educational Review* 79, no. 3 (Fall 2009): 409–27.

Turner, Jennifer, and Victoria Knight. *The Prison Cell: Embodied and Everyday Spaces of Incarceration*. London: Palgrave Macmillan, 2020.

Vega, Ana Lydia, ed. *El Tramo ancla*. San Juan: Editorial de la Universidad de Puerto Rico, 1993.

Vine, David. *Island of Shame: The Secret History of the U.S. Military Base on Diego Garcia*. Princeton: Princeton University Press, 2011.

Wacquant, Loïc. "From Slavery to Mass Incarceration: Rethinking the 'Race Question' in the US." *New Left Review* 13 (January–February 2002): 41–60.

———. "Race as Civic Felony." *International Social Science Journal* 57 (2005): 127–42.

Walker, D. R. *Penology for Profit: A History of the Texas Prison System, 1867–1912*. College Station: Texas A&M University Press, 1988.

Walker, Thomas W., ed. *Reagan versus the Sandinistas: The Undeclared War on Nicaragua*. London: Routledge, 1987.

Walters, Ronald, and Lucius J. Barker, eds. *Jesse Jackson's 1984 Presidential Campaign: Challenge and Change in American Politics.* Chicago: University of Illinois Press, 1989.

Wang, Jackie. *Carceral Capitalism.* Los Angeles: Semiotext(e), 2018.

Weber, Benjamin D. "Fearing the Flood: Prison Revolt and Counterinsurgency in the US-Occupied Philippines." *International Review of Social History* 63, S26 (August 2018): 191–210.

Welch, Michael. *Detained: Immigration Laws and the Expanding I.N.S. Jail Complex.* Philadelphia: Temple University Press, 2002.

Weld, Kirsten. *Paper Cadavers: The Archives of Dictatorship in Guatemala.* Durham, NC: Duke University Press, 2014.

West, Cornel. "Reconstructing the American Left: The Challenges of Jesse Jackson." *Social Text* 11 (Winter 1984–85): 3–19.

Wiarda, Howard J. *American Foreign Policy toward Latin America in the 80s and 90s: Issues and Controversies from Reagan to Bush.* New York: New York University Press, 1992.

Wilentz, Sean. *The Age of Reagan: A History, 1974–2008.* New York: Harper, 2008.

Wong, Tom K. *Rights, Deportation, and Detention in the Age of Immigration Control.* Palo Alto: Stanford University Press, 2015.

Yarnold, Barbara M. *Refugees without Refuge: Formation and Failed Implementation of U.S. Political Asylum Policy in the 1980s.* Lanham, MD: University Press of America, 1990.

Young, Elliott. *Alien Nation: Chinese Migration in the Americas from the Coolie Era through World War II.* Chapel Hill: University of North Carolina Press, 2014.

———. "Caging Immigrants at McNeill Island Federal Prison, 1880–1940." *Pacific Historical Review* 88, no. 1 (2019): 50–65.

———. *Forever Prisoners: How the United States Made the World's Largest Immigrant Detention System.* Oxford: Oxford University Press, 2021.

Yukich, Grace. "Constructing the Model Immigrant: Movement Strategy and Immigrant Deservingness in the New Sanctuary Movement." *Social Problems* 60, no. 3 (August 2013): 302–20.

Zaretsky, Natasha. *No Direction Home: The American Family and Fear of National Decline, 1968–1980.* Chapel Hill: University of North Carolina Press, 2007.

Zilberg, Elana. *Space of Detention: The Making of a Transnational Gang Crisis between Los Angeles and San Salvador.* Durham, NC: Duke University Press, 2011.

Zolberg, Aristide R. *A Nation by Design: Immigration Policy in the Fashioning of America.* Cambridge, MA: Harvard University Press, 2006.

Index

Page numbers in italics refer to illustrations.

abolition, prison, xiii, 4, 23, 233, 239
Abrams, Elliott, 120, 124, 129, 138
abuse: in Adelanto, xvii; at Atlanta penitentiary, 215; of civil rights, 150; in detention, 12, 56, 97, 137–38, 142, 184, 216, 239; in El Centro, 107; and human rights, 76, 108, 122, 124, 126, 135–38, 174; in immigration raids, 114; by INS, 198; at Irwin, 241; medical abuse, 207, 212; physical abuse, 104, 177; in private prisons, 211; psychological abuse, 150, 155, 176, 207; rape, 42, 111, 123, 147, 160, 166, 178, 186, 208, 216, 222, 227; sexual abuse, 177–78, 224, 245; of the state, 23, 160; in the Trump administration, 5
"A Day without Immigrants," xi
Adelanto detention facility, xiv–xvii, 236, 244
Adelanto 9, xiv–xvii, 241, 244–45; #Adelanto9, xiv, 245
Afghanistan, 132, 166, 200
African Americans: and criminalization, 36–37; and Mariel Cubans, 40; Reagan's anti-Black policies, 8; support of Haitians, 66–67, 70–71, 77, 88, 92–93, 97–99, 153, 240; views on immigration, 60. *See also* Congressional Black Caucus (CBC)
Alderson Hospitality House, 94–97
Alien and Sedition Acts (1798), 14
Alien Tort Claims Act, 234
Al Otro Lado, 241

American Civil Liberties Union (ACLU), 138, 200, 202, 214, 216, 227–28
American Committee for Protection of Foreign Born, 71–73
American Corrections Association, 208, 210
American Friends Service Committee, 127–28
American GI Forum, 114
American Legion, 124
American Legislative Exchange Council, 124
Americas Watch, 136
Amnesty International, 136
Angel Island, 17
Anti-Drug Abuse Acts, 230
Antiterrorism and Effective Death Penalty Act, 235
apartheid, xiii, 151, 170
ARENA Party, 120
Argentina, 119–20, 235
Aristide, Jean-Bertrand, 91
asylum: and Adelanto 9, xv–xvii, 245; architectures of, 32; Clinton administration and, 237; criminalization of, 52, 55–58, 60, 194; economically driven, 130, 139; and empire building, 15; alleged frivolousness, 147, 166; and GHW Bush administration, 242–43; and legal procedure, 81–84, 93, 100–102; Haitian asylum-seekers, 26–28, 36, 58, 66–69, 71–74, 77–80; homosexuals

asylum (*continued*)
  as persecuted group, 62–63; and ICE, 241; and medical danger, 239; and mentally ill individuals, 84–85; and non-refoulement, 20; political asylum, 106–7, 138, 141–43, 178, 206; and private prisons, 203, 238; and refugee arrival methods, 81; and resistance, 134–37, 147, 233–34; seekers, xiv, xviii, 2–5, 8–11; system of, 108; and transparency, 86; and trauma, 175; weaponization of, 232
Atlanta uprising, 12, 187, 190–92, 212–24

Bahamas, the, 64–65, 72
Bajeux, Jean-Claude, 157–58
Baker, James, 54, 60, 79, 90
Batsalel, Kenneth, 227–28
Beasley, Thomas, 208–10
Behavioral Systems Southwest, 202, 204, 206, 210
Big Springs, Texas, detention center in, 101–2, 174
Black nationalists, 24, 70, 145, 179
Blackness, 92, 96, 101; anti-Blackness, 8, 10, 27, 32, 40, 47, 101, 224 237; Jim Crow, 15, 17, 22–23
Black Panther Party, 9, 24
Border Association for Refugees from Central America (BARCA), 137
borders: borderlands, 7, 20, 109, 115, 243; Central America as third or fourth border, 2, 109, 127, 230; wall, xi, 16, 233, 243; war, 7, 115. *See also* US Border Patrol; US-Mexico border
Breaux, John, 220, 230
Brodyaga, Lisa, 137
budget: for anti-immigration measures, 91; and detention centers, 99–100, 188; increases, 9, 112–13, 189–90, 193, 211; and private prisons, 208, 226
Bureau of Prisons (BOP): detention of Cubans, 37, 46, 58–59, 116, 186, 214–21, 224–26; detention of Haitians, 66, 71, 92, 94–97, 173–76; facilities, 114, 145, 150, 153, 173–75, 188–89, 195–97, 207, 212; and resistance, 199, 201, 226, 228
Bush, George H. W., 54–55, 58, 116, 237–42

Bush, George W., 238, 243
Byrd, Robert, 235

Camp Libertad, 46
Canada, 17–18, 89–90, 162–63, 169
Canosa, Jorge Mas, 214, 220
capitalism: anti-capitalism, 23–24; and Cold War, 110, 118, 124, 133; and Cuban sponsorship cases, 49; dictatorships, 87; and neoliberalism, 22–23, 144; racial capitalism, 17, 22–25; and US colonialism, 88
caravans, xiv, xvi, 3–4, 244; La caravana Viacrusis de Refugiados, xiv; Freedom Train, 170; and Sanctuary movement, 12, 146–49, 159, 166, 170–71
carceral palimpsest: and Central Americans, 145; and counterinsurgency, 21–25, 232; and Cubans, 37, 188–189; definition, 5–6; and detention centers, 184; and Haitians, 69; historical origins, 17–21; and private prisons, 202–11; and resistance, 230; and Salvadorans, 105, 107; and the Vietnam War era, 26–28
Caribbeana Council, 89–90
Caribbean Basin Initiative (CBI), 9–10, 69, 85–91, 103, 108–9, 125–28, 140, 144
Caribbean Economic Recovery Act, 88, 128
Carlson, Norm, 214–15
Carter, Jimmy: and Haitians, 9, 13, 42, 74–77; and human rights, 6; and intent for detention, 5, 835; invisible bridge to Reagan, 52, 67–69, 86, 89, 101; and Mariel Cubans, 31, 34–36, 39, 45–46, 49, 116, 134, 155, 191; Reagan-Carter election, 49, 54. *See also* Cuban-Haitian Task Force
Castillo, Leo, 55–56, 210
Castillo, Mario, 146, 149, 167
Castro, Fidel: alleged Salvadoran interference, 121; May Day speech, 34; political prisoner exchange, 170, 191; regime, 74, 84–86; and Ronald Reagan, 52, 54, 214; and "undesirable" Mariel migrants, 29–37, 54, 60–61, 68, 102
Centers for Disease Control (CDC), 158

Central America: counterinsurgent warfare, 108, 110, 117–22, 128–29, 133; as feet people, 101, 129; Indigenous peoples in, 13, 118–24, 134–35, 146; as third or fourth border, 2, 109, 127, 230

Central Intelligence Agency (CIA), 9, 22, 61, 102, 109, 119–22, 134, 180

Chardy, Alfonso, 145

Chicago Religious Task Force on Central America (CRTFCA), 164–65, 168–71

Chicanx, 25, 41, 111

children: abuse, 123, 143, 178; of detained refugees, xii, xvi, 221, 227; in detention, xi, 97, 151–52, 243–44; at Fort Allen, 158; and Fort Chaffee media spectacle, 42, 44; imprisoned girls, 73; infantilization, 95; and Mariel criminalization, 216; Salvadoran refugees, 131–32, 147–49; in Sanctuary movement, 160, 168, 171; separated from parents, 114; sponsors' preference for, 48. See also fertility

Chile, 26, 72, 119

China, 142

Chinese, 7–8, 17–18, 85

Chisolm, Shirley, 92–93

Christian Democratic Party, 120

Christian Legal Aid, 123

Church World Service, 43–44, 48

CISPES (Committee in Solidarity with the People of El Salvador), 136, 142, 165, 178, 181

Citizens United in Support of Haitian People, 159

Civilian Matériel Assistance, 117

Civil Liberties Act, 23, 28

civil rights: complaint, xv; and Cuban support, 192, 216–17; era, 5; and Haitian support, 66–67, 70–71, 77, 88, 92–93, 97–99, 153, 240; movement, 21–24; post–civil rights era immigration opposition, 8, 28, 53, 188; reforms, 20; and resistance, 149–50, 163; violations, 177

climate change, xiii, xix, 36, 78, 90, 128, 195, 242

Clinton, Bill, xiii, 30–32, 37, 42, 53–54, 58, 63, 178, 233–39

Clinton, Hillary, 54–55

Coalition to Support Cuban Detainees, 213–17, 221, 224–27

Cold War: and capitalism, 110, 118, 124, 133; and communism, 24, 52, 117–21, 143; and Global South, 21; on immigrants, 4–11, 13, 15, 52, 149, 188, 232–33; and xenophobia, 31, 80

Committee in Solidarity with the People of El Salvador, 136, 142, 165, 178, 181

Committee of Santa Fe of the Council for Inter-American Security, 119

communism: African American opposition to, 92; aid to oppose, 22; anti-communist sentiment, 6, 12, 18, 81, 109; anti-Sandinista politics, 122; and the CBI, 10, 87–91, 125–29, 144; and Cold War, 24, 52, 117–21, 143; and criminalization, 65–67, 224; Cuban opposition to, 41, 49; and El Salvador, 108, 120–21, 134, 169; Haiti as bulwark against, 70–71, 87; and the KKK, 30; and refugee politics, 20, 26, 33–35, 74, 85–87, 129–32, 138; Revolutionary Communist Youth Brigade, 178; rights movements labeled as, 176; and the War on Drugs, 115

Congressional Black Caucus (CBC), 77, 88, 92–93

Convention and Protocol Relating to the Status of Refugees, 20, 73, 138

Cook, Donovan, 148–49, 166, 183

Corbett, Jim, 161–67, 171, 181–82

Cordero, Ana Livia, 159

CoreCivic. See Corrections Corporation of America (CCA)

Corrections Corporation of America (CCA), 203–4, 208–11, 234–35, 243

Costa Rica, 106, 170

counterinsurgency: against Jesse Jackson, 153; anti-communist methods, 109; and Central American warfare, 108, 110, 117–22, 128–29, 133; and Cuban crisis, 52; and Haitian immigration, 100–101; and migrant detention, 1–2, 5, 7, 11, 15–16, 149–50, 232–33; origins of mass incarceration, 21–25; prose of, xvii–xviii, 235; psychological effects, 158; and

counterinsurgency (*continued*)
    resistance, 142, 184; and the Sanctuary
    movement, 12–13, 145, 176, 180; and total
    war, 6; and War on Drugs, 9, 13, 143–44
COVID-19, xiii, xvii, 239
Crants, Doctor "Doc," 208–9
Criminal Alien Program, 10, 111, 230–31
crimmigration, 3, 5, 10, 16, 110, 188, 194, 224,
    229–30
Cuba: relationship with Soviet Union,
    52, 91, 115, 118, 120, 129; support of civil
    rights, 192, 216–17
Cubans: Abuelas, 49; Afro-Cubans, 33,
    40, 48, 227; as antisocial individuals,
    37, 41, 57, 196; and Catholicism, 47, 219,
    222, 228; and the Bureau of Prisons, 37,
    46, 58–59, 66, 116, 186, 214–21, 224–26;
    Coalition to Support Cuban Detainees,
    213–17, 221, 224–27; criminality
    narratives, 37–46, 52, 60, 212–17, 223–24;
    Cuban-Americans distancing from
    Marielitos, 41–42; Cuban/Haitian
    entrants, 35–36, 68, 77, 92, 196; and due
    process, 62, 192, 228; and the Freedom
    Flights, 33; opposition to civil rights, 41,
    49; protests at Krome I, 214, 216, 225. *See
    also* Cuban-Haitian Task Force; Mariel
    Cubans
Cuban Adjustment Act, 77, 238
Cuban American National Foundation
    (CANF), 41, 61–62, 220
Cuban-Haitian Task Force, 36, 39, 42–49,
    55, 61, 68, 74, 76, 152, 172
Customs and Border Protection, xv, 235,
    241

D'Aubuisson, Roberto, 109, 120
decolonization, 20–23, 135, 149
DeConcini, Dennis, 104–7, 135, 142
Department of Defense, 130; Department
    of Defense Authorization Act, 115–16
deportation: of Central Americans, 104–6,
    133–44, 149; and counterinsurgency, 25,
    170, 178; and detention transfers, 156–
    57; and federal immigration law, 17–20,
    234–35; of Haitians, 67–69, 72, 76–78,
    81–87, 92–93, 99; and ICE, xv, 241; and

immigration detention, 3, 16; and INS,
    187–92, 201–3; of Mariel Cubans, 10, 38,
    62, 101–2, 214, 221–22, 226–31, 238; of
    Mexicans, 110, 113, 115, 197; Obama as
    "Deporter in Chief," xiii, 243–44; and
    resistance, 12–15, 160–66, 185, 211–12
Deported Veterans, 241
Deville, Turenne, 72
disability, 216, 223–24, 237
disease: fear of, 196–97; outbreak, 12;
    pathology and criminalization, 17, 24,
    36, 42, 158, 216; skin, 73, 76; tuberculosis,
    42, 70, 76; venereal, 42, 76. *See also*
    Centers for Disease Control; COVID-
    19; HIV/AIDS
Displaced Persons Act (1948), 19
DIVA TV (Damned Interfering Video
    Activists), 240
Drug Enforcement Agency (DEA), 9, 61,
    111
drug trafficking, 9, 25, 54, 89, 110, 115–16, 230
Duarte, Jose Napoleon, 120
Dudeck, Carla, 213, 221, 225
due process: and Cubans, 62, 192, 228;
    denial of, xiv–xv, 137; and the Fifth
    Amendment, 140; and Haitians, 77,
    93–94, 100; and people of Japanese
    descent, 18; and private detention
    centers, 201; and Salvadorans, 107,
    140–142; violations of, 11
Duvalier, Francois ("Papa Doc"), 70
Duvalier, Jean-Claude ("Baby Doc"): and
    Carter administration, 74; deposed,
    91; and Haitian refugees' asylum
    cases, 70–71, 77, 85, 107; and human
    rights violations, 28, 65, 67, 92; Reagan
    administration and, 85–87, 93

Eglin Air Force Base, 31, 38
Eidenberg, Gene, 30–31, 46, 65
Eisenhower, Dwight D., 52, 131
El Centro detention facility, 199; abuses at,
    141, 162, 176, 202; Cubans rejected from,
    46; DeConcini's visit, 104–5, 135; hunger
    strikes at, 106–7, 137, 142; Salvadorans
    at, 12, 106–8, 135–37, 201
El Gran Paro Estadounidense, xi

Elizabeth Detention Center, xii, 233
Ellis Island, 20
El Mozote, 123
El Reno detention center, 196–99
El Rescate, 137, 142
El Salvador: and due process, 107,
    140–42; refugees from, 131–32, 147–49;
    Salvadoran National Guard, 119, 134,
    147; and silences, 143; Vietnam as, 121,
    160. See also Committee in Solidarity
    with the People of El Salvador
    (CISPES); Romero, Óscar
environmental issues: activism, 3, 23;
    anti-immigration policies based on,
    8; environmental disasters, xix, 2; and
    Haiti, 242; environmental laws, 56, 83;
    environmental racism, 73, 170. See also
    climate change
erasure: and Cold War on immigrants,
    107, 123, 134; need to reverse, xviii; and
    private prisons, 188, 204, 229–31; and
    the state, xvii, 15, 23, 26, 184, 232–33, 237
Esmor Correctional Services, 233–35
eugenics, 8, 17–18
Excot family, 171–72
Executive Office of Immigration Review,
    230
executive orders, 66, 83, 104; Order 9066,
    18; Order 12333, 9, 179–80; Order 12324,
    82
Ezell, Harold W., 176

Falwell, Jerry, 124
Farabundo Martí National Liberation
    Front (FMLN), 118, 123–25
Federal Bureau of Investigation (FBI):
    COINTELPRO, 9, 24, 179; federal
    law enforcement, 9, 25, 61, 102, 111, 150,
    154, 187, 218–19, 222, 228; psychological
    profiling, 223; and the Sanctuary
    movement, 172, 179–81
Federation for American Immigration
    Reform (FAIR), 8, 41, 183
Fernandez, Alina, 55
fertility, 130; birth rates, 130, 158; hyper-
    reproductivity, 2; pregnancy, xv, 45, 65,
    94, 114, 158, 178

Fife, John, 147, 163–67, 180–81
Flores, Héctor Efrén, 3–4
foreign policy: anti-Black, 133; CANF,
    41; and Central American refugees,
    107, 117–20, 124, 131, 135–38, 166; Cold
    War, 1–2, 5–10, 85, 98; development,
    10, 22–23, 41, 89–91, 122, 128, 144;
    dichotomous views, 101; dollar
    diplomacy, 22; and federal law
    enforcement, 179–80; and Haitians,
    36, 67–71, 74, 77–78, 82, 86, 93; and
    immigration, xviii; and Jesse Jackson,
    170, 191; and Mariel Cubans, 28, 36;
    and Obama administration, 243–44;
    and racial hierarchies, 22; and refugee
    politics, 20, 26, 33–35, 74, 85–87, 129–32,
    138; and resistance, 150, 161, 172, 176; and
    the CBI, 88–90, 127–28; and Vietnam
    War, 26. See also Caribbean Basin
    Initiative (CBI); Cold War
Fort Allen, 93, 100; and Haitians, 155–59;
    hunger strikes at, 150–51; and prison
    privatization, 195, 206–7
Fort Chaffee: close of, 103, 193–94; Mariel
    Cuban "disturbance" at, 12, 30–33,
    38–46, 52–59, 67, 78, 153; legacies, 59–63;
    and prison privatization, 193–201,
    206; protests at, 47–52; and punitive
    conditions, 173, 175–76
Fort Indiantown Gap, 32, 38, 44–46
Fort Libertad, 38
Fort McCoy, 32, 35, 38, 42–46, 236–37
Freedom for Immigrants, xiv, xvi, 235, 241,
    244–45
Freedom House, 122, 124
Freeze, Jack, 41, 194

Garcia, Robert, 128, 155
Garcia-Mir v. Meese (1986), 62
gender non-conforming. See
    QTGNC (Queer, Trans, Gender
    Non-Conforming)
General Accounting Office (GAO),
    103
GEO Group, xiv–xvi, 210, 234, 245
Germany, 132, 182; Nazi, 59, 106, 129, 169
Giuffrida, Louis O., 145

Giuliani, Rudy: architect of Reagan's
  policies, 7–8, 54; and Haitians,
  69, 84–88, 159, 175–76; and Mass
  Immigration Emergency Plan, 144–45;
  monitoring of Jesse Jackson, 153–54;
  and prison privatization, 195–96, 199;
  and Salvadorans, 140; and War on
  Crime, 111–17
Golden, Renny, 136, 161, 164–66, 171, 184
Gollobin, Ira, 71, 100
Gonzalez, Sylvia, 47, 152
Gosse, Van, 135–36, 184–85
Grace Commission (President's Private
  Sector Survey on Cost Control), 205–6
Graham, Bob, 57, 66, 70, 78, 89, 173, 181
Grenada, 125, 191
Guantánamo Bay, 58–59, 82, 159, 237–42
Guatemala: rejection of asylum applicants
  from, 10, 106–7, 129–30, 133–36, 143,
  243; and the CBI, 126–28; US-backed
  actions in, 7, 22, 117–20, 184
Guatemalans: and resistance, 13; and the
  Sanctuary movement, 146, 160, 162, 167,
  170–72
Guillermoprieto, Alma, 123

Haig, Alexander, 89–90, 108, 119, 122, 129
Haitians: African American support of,
  66–67, 70–71, 77, 88, 92–93, 97–99, 153,
  240; as asylum-seekers, 26–28, 36, 58,
  66–69, 71–74, 77–80; as boat people,
  63, 68, 76, 93, 98, 101, 129, 239; Creole,
  66, 83, 94, 159, 240; Cuban/Haitian
  entrants, 35–36, 68, 77, 92, 196; and
  foreign policy, 36, 67–71, 74, 77–78, 82,
  86, 93; interdiction of, 9, 79–84, 87, 93,
  102, 104, 159, 233; and Jesse Jackson,
  92, 97–98, 240; Mariel-type migration,
  79–80, 102; national origins, 69–70;
  Navy, 87–88; and Rudy Giuliani, 69,
  84–88, 159, 175–76. See also Cuban-
  Haitian Task force; Duvalier, Francois
  ("Papa Doc"); Duvalier, Jean-Claude
  ("Baby Doc")
Haitian Bridge Alliance, 241
Haitian Program, 67, 73–77, 92

Haitian Refugee Center, 65, 71, 73, 86, 93,
  99–100, 152, 173
Hamm, Mark, 217, 220, 228
Hefner, Tony, 177–78
Helms, Jesse, 8, 130
Helton, Arthur C., 174–75, 200, 216
Heritage Foundation, 122, 205
Hernandez family, 168, 185
Hidalgo, Carlos, 236, 244–45
Hirabayashi v. United States (1943), 19
Hispanic vote, 7, 114–15, 130–33
HIV/AIDS, 226, 239–40
Homeland Security Act, 235
Honduras, xiv, 3, 120, 142, 169–70, 200, 206,
  243
Horowitz, Mike, 99–103
HRC v. Civiletti (1980), 76–77
human rights: Carter's emphasis on, 6; and
  Central American counterinsurgency,
  118–31; and Central American refugees,
  135–39; Cuba, 34; and Haiti, 71–77, 88,
  92–94; liberal, 69; and Mariel reaction,
  28; and private prisons, 211, 234; regime,
  19, 21; and Salvadorans, 106–7; and the
  Sanctuary movement, 161, 170, 174, 176,
  181; Universal Declaration of Human
  Rights, 19–20, 23–24, 26
hunger strikes: at Adelanto, xvi–xvii; at El
  Centro, 106–7, 137, 142; at Fort Allen,
  150–51; at Krome, 12, 94–97, 149–56, 174,
  176, 214; as resistance, 3, 24, 32, 35, 38, 73,
  106–7, 142, 225, 227, 233, 239–40, 244
Hutto, T. Don, 208–9, 243
Hutto v. Finney (1978), 208

ICE (Immigration and Customs
  Enforcement), xi–xvi, 3, 223, 235, 238,
  241, 244–45
Illegal Immigration Reform and Immigrant
  Responsibility Act, 235
immigration: Vietnam War, after, 19, 25–27,
  32, 36; cap on, 20–21, 192; deterrence,
  xiii, 5, 32, 52–55, 67, 81, 103, 151, 198, 207,
  232–33, 239, 242; Extended Voluntary
  Departure (EVD), 134, 137–39; and labor
  (see labor: migrants); mass immigration,

1, 32, 108, 193; pocket freedom, 192; post-
civil rights opposition to, 8, 28, 53, 188.
See also Immigration and Naturalization
Service (INS); Mass Immigration
Emergency Plan; Reagan, Ronald: Cold
War on immigrants
Immigration and Customs Enforcement
(ICE), xi–xvi, 3, 223, 235, 238, 241,
244–45
Immigration and Nationality Act (1965),
20–21, 110, 163
Immigration and Nationality Act (INA)
(1952), 20, 79–82
Immigration and Naturalization Service
(INS): abuse, 178, 198; *Immigration
Detention Officer Handbook*, 177;
Land and Natural Resources
division, 196; Mariel and budgeting,
190–92; Office of Public Affairs, 203;
Operation Sojourner, 181; Operation
Wetback, 19–20, 110, 113; Public
Affairs Conference, 183; Standards for
Detention, 175, 177
Immigration Reform and Control Act
(IRCA), 193, 211–12, 230
Indians. *See* Indigenous people
Indigenous people: anti-Indigenous
sentiment, 2–3, 122–23, 133; Assiniboine,
196; campesino class, 167, 180; in
Central America, 13, 118–24, 134–35,
146; exclusion, 14–17; Ladino, 118; as
martyrs, 171; Maya, 13, 118, 120; Miskito,
121–22, 126, 132; and resistance, 19,
23, 131, 163, 196; Sioux (Lakota), 196;
targeted by United States, 21, 108, 150;
and Thanksgiving, 221
Intelligence Reform and Terrorism
Prevention Act, 235
Interfaith Task Force, 136–37
International Human Rights Law Group,
93
Inter-regional Council for Haitian
Refugees, 156–57
Iran, xii, 6, 22, 60, 118, 125, 145, 200, 212
Isaac, xv–xvi, 245
Islam, 233–34

Jackson, Jesse: and Haitian support,
92, 97–98, 240; at Krome, 153–54;
presidential campaign, 170, 184–85,
191–92; and the Sanctuary Movement,
170–71
Jamaica, 89
Jama v. Esmor Correctional Services, Inc.
(2004), 234
Japanese, 18–19, 28, 98, 170
Jean-Juste, Gérard, 65, 73, 86, 152
Jews, 98, 122, 124, 132, 165, 169; anti-
Semitism, 124, 132
Jim Crow, 15, 17, 22–23
Johnson, Lyndon B., 110, 205
Jozef, Guerline, 241–42

Kahn, Robert, 137, 141, 179
King, James L., 76–77, 86, 92
Kirkpatrick, Jeane, 119, 128
Knauff v. Shaughnessy (1950), 80
Korematsu v. United States (1944), 19
Krome I: conditions, 91–93, 156, 173–75, 195,
212; and Cuban protests, 214, 216, 225;
and Haitian refugees, 66–67, 78; hunger
strikes at, 12, 96–97, 150–55, 174, 176, 214;
and mental health conditions, 157–58;
as processing center, 199
Krome II, 66–67, 78, 90–92, 151, 157, 175
Ku Klux Klan, 18, 30, 41–43
Kurtzban, Ira, 100

labor: anti-union sentiment, 25, 122,
210; convict leasing, 17, 204, 208–9;
incarcerated, 17, 47, 94, 234; migrants,
50, 70, 105, 110, 159, 167–69, 205;
movements, 5, 23–25, 71, 99, 111; and
poverty, 2; and prisons, 42, 199–200,
203; strikes, 24, 94, 156; undocumented,
7, 113; unemployment, 7–8, 42, 65, 128,
212, 229; unions, 71, 111, 118, 126, 159–60,
163, 210; wages, 94–95, 205, 234
La Resistencia, 211, 213, 214
Latinx: Afro-Latinx, 2–3, 108, 133–34;
Latino threat, 110; migrants, 25, 41;
reproductive violence against, 241;
rightwing views of, 169

Lawyers Committee for International Human Rights, 174, 200
left-wing politics, 23, 108, 118, 124
Lenin, 236–39
Leshaw, Gary, 216, 220–21
Levin, Mark, 217–19
Lewis, David, 48–51
Lewis, John, 217, 226
liberation theology, 23, 124, 135, 161, 165, 169, 182
Logan Act, 191–92
Luttig, J. Michael, 82

Mabry, Russ, 219–20
Mahoney, Larry, 151–52
Malone, Harry, 105–7
Mara Salvatrucha gang, 144
Mariel Cubans: boatlift, 8, 28–38, 43–44, 53–54, 60–67, 71, 74–77, 84, 102, 116, 155, 172, 189–91, 228, 236–38; Carter and, 31, 34–36, 39, 45–46, 49, 116, 134, 155, 191; Castro and, 29–37, 54, 60–61, 68, 102; causing "disturbances," 12, 30–33, 38–46, 52–59, 67, 78, 153 *Garcia-Mir v. Meese*, 62; prevention of another crisis, 8, 55, 79, 237; Radio Mariel, 218; and xenophobia, 32, 37, 43–45, 101
Martinez, Pilar, and sister, Elba, 147–49, 167, 181–82, 185
Marxism, 118, 122, 125, 129, 181
masculinity, 35, 49, 223–24
Mass Immigration Emergency Plan, 5, 13, 101–3, 150, 144–45, 188–89, 194, 199, 233
May Day, 34, 97
McCone Commission, 24
McDuffie, Arthur, 36, 40
medical care, xv–xvi, 46, 104, 152, 175
Meese, Edwin, 62, 190, 212, 215–17, 220–24
mental health: crisis, 95, 151, 207; depression, 95, 157–58, 167, 199–200; emergencies, 157–58; facilities, 205; FBI's population profile, 223–24; individuals, 46, 51, 84–85, 157–58, 172–75, 203, 220, 223–24; institutions, 51. *See also* suicide
Merkt, Stacy, 181

Mexican American Legal Defense and Educational Fund, 113
Mexicans: abuse of, 56; in asylum movement, 162, 165, 167, 169, 181–82; and crime, 110–11; at El Centro, 106–7; and federal immigration legislation, 17–20; labor in the US, 25; Mexicanization of enforcement, 19; OTMs (Other than Mexicans), 134; and private prisons, 201–2, 215; undocumented, 105, 117, 197–98
Mexico: asylum in, 139–41; and US border, xiv, 6–9, 16–17, 109, 115, 117, 143, 147, 233; and the CBI, 90; and the Siglo XXI detention center, 244
Miami Action Plan (1982), 116–17
Mica Amendment, 88
migrants: counterinsurgency and detention, 1–2, 5, 7, 11, 15–16, 149, 232–33; economic, 74, 98; illegalized, xii, xviii, 2, 141; labor, 50, 70, 105, 110, 159, 167–69, 205; processing, 99, 189; "undesirable" Mariel migrants, 29–37, 54, 60–61, 68, 102
Milagro, 147–48
missionaries, 119, 123, 135, 147, 161, 169
Morrison, Bruce, 139
Morrow, Douglas, 127
Mowad, George, 199–200, 215, 221, 230
Muñoz, Inés, 159

National Association for the Advancement of Colored People (NAACP), 66, 92–93, 97
National Association of Manufacturers, 115, 125
National Council of Churches, 43, 71, 93, 214
National Gay Newspaper Guild, 44
National Origins Act, 18
National Security Council, 90, 123–24, 145, 180
Native Americans. *See* Indigenous people
nativism, 5, 7, 17, 25, 40
Naturalization Act of 1790, 14
Navidad Roja, 121–23
Nelson, Alan: correspondence with Rudy Giuliani, 144–45, 153–54; and detention,

93, 98–99, 190; and exclusion, 100, 242; on racial profiling, 114; on Salvadoran incarceration, 108; on Sanctuary movement, 172, 180–81

neoliberalism: apologists for, 151–52; carceral systems, 13, 23, 45, 188, 232; and the Caribbean, 85, 108, 128, 144; economics, 1, 9–10, 22–23; governance, 138; and personal responsibility, 22, 25, 69, 197; Reaganism, 52, 206, 231; trade-and-aid, 9–10, 69, 90, 125, 244

New Underground Railroad, 147–48, 161–65

Nicaragua: Contras, 117–20, 134, 136, 182; and the EVD, 138; exiles, 118, 122–23; fleeing violence, 133–36, 206; and Jesse Jackson, 170; Miskito, 132; refugees, 98; revolution, 6, 117–18; in Sanctuary movement, 166; Sandinistas, 118, 121–26, 133; and the USSR, 115, 118, 126, 129

Nicgorski, Darlene, 181

Nissen, Ted, 202, 204, 206

Nixon, Richard, 25, 71, 110–11

No More Cages, 96, 241

North, Oliver, 129, 145, 180

North American Free Trade Agreement (NAFTA), 10, 144, 233

nuclear weapons, 23, 67, 145, 170, 213

Oakdale detention facility: honoring of prison staff, 224–25; and local economy, 199–201; and prison privatization, 205, 207, 211, 229–31; uprising, 12, 186–90, 194, 212–23

Oakdale II, 230

Obama, Barack, xiii–xiv, 238, 243–44

Off Our Backs (organization), 94, 96, 156, 158

Off Our Backs (periodical), 94, 241

Office of Immigration Litigation, 141–42, 230

Office of Legal Counsel, 79–82

Office of Management and Budget (OMB), 58, 99–103, 190

O'Neill, Paul, 203, 210, 213

Operation Distant Shore, 233

Operation Gatekeeper, 233

Operation Hold the Line, 242

Operation Pipil, 180

Operation PUSH (People United to Save Humanity), 170

Operation Sojourner, 181

Operation Terror, 19

Operation Urgent Fury, 125

Operation Wetback, 19–20, 110, 113

Orantes-Hernandez v. Smith (1982), 141–43

Organization of American States, 90, 93, 125–26

Owino, Sylvester, 234–36, 245

Owino v. CoreCivic, Inc., 245

Padilla, Hernán, 155, 158–59

Palestinian Liberation Organization, 124

Panama, 22, 91, 170

Partnoy, Alicia, 235, 245

Peñalver, Rafael, 226–27, 229

Philippines: Filipino laborers, 18; Philippine-American War, 21; Philippine Independence Act, 18

Pindling, Lynden O., 65

Poland, 85, 98, 138, 166

police: Air Police, 38–39; Bahamian police officers, 65; broken windows policing, 113; counterinsurgency training, 22, 109–10, 113, 134, 145; false arrest, 190–91; misinformation among, 61; SWAT, 219, 222; violence, 36–37, 146–47, 152–53, 167, 216

Presbyterians, 147, 163, 168–69, 214, 219

President's Private Sector Survey on Cost Control (Grace Commission), 205–6

prisons: as cages, xiii, 215, 220; for-profit, xii–xv, 10, 188–89, 202–11, 229, 231–35, 243; hostages, 157, 187, 212, 217–21, 224, 226, 228, 231; mass incarceration, xiii–xiv, 1, 3, 11, 21, 231; maximum security, 105, 201; mixed-use, 3, 10, 188, 195, 210–12, 229–30; overcrowding, 10, 63, 78, 92, 104, 111–16, 155, 174, 188–89, 193–94, 204–8, 216, 224, 230–31, 243; solitary confinement, xv, 12, 51, 94, 142, 157, 174–77, 213, 217, 225, 244–45. *See also* abolition; Bureau of Prisons (BOP)

Project Jobs, 113–14

Proyecto Libertad, 137, 179, 242–43
Pueblos sin Fronteras, xvi
Puerto Rico Bar Association, 156, 210

QTGNC (Queer, Trans, Gender Non-
    Conforming), 2–3, 33, 38, 42–45, 47,
    63, 167
Quakers, 147, 162–62, 171
queer folx, 23, 44, 47, 63, 167, 221, 224,
    237–40; homosexuals, 29, 31, 35,
    38–39, 44–47, 61–63, 178, 218. *See also*
    QTGNC (Queer, Trans, Gender
    Non-Conforming)
Quinlan, Michael, 217, 219, 221, 224

Radio Mariel, 218
Radio Martí, 214
Ramos, Nicole, xv, 241
Ratner, Michael, 240
Reagan, Ronald: bridge from Carter, 52,
    54, 214; Central American Marshal
    Plan (*see* Caribbean Basin Initiative
    [CBI]); Cold War on immigrants, 4–11,
    13, 15, 52, 149, 188, 232–33, as governor
    of California, 5, 24–25, 53, 99–100,
    145; and Hispanic vote, 7, 115, 130–33;
    and neoliberalism, 52, 206, 231; 1980
    election, 49, 54; overturning of Carter's
    policies, 119–23, 134, 137–41; and welfare,
    24, 53, 100
Reagan imaginary: definition, 1; and
    migration, 52, 60, 68, 101, 103, 112, 118,
    129, 144, 230; and private prisons, 208,
    229; and white nationalism, 6–9, 25
rebellions, 13, 16, 21, 24, 36–37, 186–87,
    213–17, 228–29, 233. *See also* Atlanta
    uprising; Oakdale detention facility
Red Christmas, 121–23
Red Cross, 59, 88, 219, 242–43
refugees: and counter publics, 135; crisis,
    19, 27, 118, 129–30, 188; Haitian asylum
    cases, 70–71, 77, 85, 107; politics, 20, 26,
    33–35, 74, 85–87, 129–32, 138; "refugee-
    as-victim," 10–11; from Southeast Asia,
    6, 26, 36, 129
Refugee Act (1980), 20, 28, 35, 62, 66, 108,
    134, 137–39, 142

Religion, in prisons, xvi, 198–99, 219.
    See also Islam; Religious Freedom
    Restoration Act; Roman Catholicism
religious organizations: and African
    Americans, 97–98; in El Salvador, 118,
    123–24; and resistance, 71, 107; and the
    Sanctuary movement, 135–37, 159, 162,
    167–71, 180–81; support of Cubans, 43,
    192, 212, 216; support of Haitians, 77, 93,
    159, 240
Religious Freedom Restoration Act, 234
Reno, Donald, 149, 181–84
Reno, Janet, 63
Republican Party, 21, 24, 42, 53, 58, 130, 208
Rescue Committee for Haitian Refugees,
    71, 73
resistance: asylum and, 134–37, 147, 233–34;
    and the Bureau of Prisons, 199, 201,
    226, 228; and civil rights, 149–50, 163;
    and foreign policy, 150, 161, 172, 176;
    Indigenous people and, 19, 23, 131, 163,
    196. *See also* civil rights; hunger strikes;
    Sanctuary movement
retaliation: in detention cases, xii–xiv; in
    detention's structures, 2–6, 11–15, 21–25,
    244; against Central Americans, 108,
    113; against Cubans, 38, 52, 54, 60, 63,
    212–14, 220, 224–25, 228–29; against
    Haitians, 72, 94–97, 241; and resistance,
    xvii; and the INS, 142, 149–50, 242;
    and the Sanctuary movement, 164–67,
    172–79, 185, 188
Revolutionary Communist Youth Brigade,
    178
Rex84, 145, 212
riot. *See* rebellions
Rodriguez, Alejandro, 167–68
Román, Agustín, 217, 221–22, 227–28
Roman Catholicism: and Cubans, 47, 219,
    222, 228; and Haitians, 98; Human
    Rights Commission, 138; missionaries,
    119, 147, 161; nuns, 137, 161, 179, 181;
    priest, 73; and private prisons, 210;
    Protestant/Catholic divide, 165; and the
    Sanctuary movement, 165; US Catholic
    Conference, 48, 50, 98
Romero, Óscar, 118, 135, 147, 155, 163

Roosevelt, Franklin, 18
Ruiz, Jr., Cecilio L., 172, 177–78
Russia. *See* Soviet Union

Sacred Heart Church, 165, 200
Sanctuary movement: caravan, 146–47;
    harassment of, 9, 12, 117, 145, 147–48,
    176–85; New Underground Railroad,
    147–48, 161–65; and religion, 107,
    135–37, 163–167; and resistance, 3, 13, 143,
    149–50, 189, 233, 244; speech acts, 150,
    166; and storytelling, 160–62, 165–67
Sandidge, Sally, 213
Sandinistas, 118, 121–26, 133
Santería, 219, 222
School of the Americas, 22
sex: deviance, 32, 42, 63; heteronormativity,
    43, 167; masturbation, 56
sex workers, 29, 31, 39, 181
Sheehy, Thomas, 210
Shoob, Marvin, 62, 192, 216, 225–26
Simpson-Mazzoli immigration bill, 83
Singleton, John V., 202–3
slavery: and citizenship, 14–15; and
    insurrection, 14, 69, 94; and law, 17; and
    the Underground Railroad, 161–62, 170;
    and US history, 11, 23, 204, 208–9, 242
Smith, William French: and DeConcini's
    report, 104–5; DOJ budget increase,
    112–13; and executive authority, 99–101;
    and Haitian asylum-seekers, 80, 83–86;
    Orantes-Hernandez v. Smith (1982),
    141–43; and private prisons, 195–99;
    and Reagan's task force, 54–57; and the
    asylum movement, 163
solidarity: with Central Americans, 107,
    124, 135–36, 149, 161–62, 168, 170–71,
    177, 179; with Cubans, 40, 44–45,
    211; in detention centers, 12; with
    Haitians, 67, 72, 93–94, 149, 153, 156, 159,
    161–62, 241; with migrants, xvi, 40, 185;
    transnational, 3–4, 15, 23–25, 118, 142,
    169. *See also* Committee in Solidarity
    with the People of El Salvador;
    Sanctuary movement
Somoza, Anastasio, 118, 122–23
South Africa, 151, 163, 169–70

Southside Presbyterian Church, 147, 163
Soviet Union, 18, 26, 36, 98, 119, 124–25, 132,
    180; relationship with Cuba, 52, 91, 115,
    118, 120, 129
Spanish, language, 40, 121–22, 159, 163, 192,
    201, 222, 235
Spanish-American War, 21
suicide, xii, xvi, 12, 45, 72, 95, 151, 156–57, 187,
    219, 228
Sunbelt, 23–25, 144, 188, 194, 203–4, 208–12,
    243
surveillance: border, 108; of Cubans, 52, 60,
    102; in detention facilities, 97, 190; state,
    9, 12–13, 21, 142, 150, 212, 235

Talerant, Prophete, 157
Tanton, John, 8
Task Force on Immigration and Refugee
    Policy, 8, 54–55, 79, 92, 112
Task Force on Violent Crime, 9, 112
Taylor, Berniece, 236–37
terrorism, 6, 54, 109, 179–81, 212, 214, 235;
    counterterrorism, 81, 142, 145, 150,
    235
Third World Liberation Front, 24
Toboso-Alfonso, Fidel Armando, 62–63
Tomsho, Robert, 134
torture, xv, 118, 123, 134–35, 139, 146–47, 157,
    160, 166–67, 176, 180, 208
Trafficking Victims Protection Act, 234
trauma, xiv–xviii, 4, 12, 15, 26, 143, 149, 155,
    157, 161, 167, 169, 175, 193, 238
Trump, Donald, xiv, 3, 5, 238, 241, 243
Turnage, James B., 176, 183

Unitarians, 147
United Farm Workers, 25
United Nations, 19–20, 28, 35, 65, 74, 119,
    122, 138, 141, 152, 159; Human Rights
    Commission, 176
United States: empire, xii, xviii, xix, 1–3,
    10, 13–16, 21–22, 32, 52, 58, 126, 168, 233;
    militarism, xiii, xix, 21, 26–27, 127, 170,
    242; settler colonialism, xix, 1, 5, 15, 56;
    state violence, 2–5, 12–15, 20–21, 26, 76,
    108–9, 135, 149, 160, 165, 229. *See also*
    foreign policy

Universal Declaration of Human Rights, 19–20
University Baptist Church, 147–48, 160, 166, 183
uprisings: at Atlanta penitentiary, 12, 187, 190–92, 212–24, at Attica state prison, 217; and Black Nationalists, 145; Cuban-led, 63; at Elizabeth Detention Center, 233–34; and Esmor Correctional Services, 235; at Fort Smith, 42; leftist, 117; in Miami, 36, 40–41; at Oakdale detention facility, 12, 186–90, 194, 212–23; at Otisville correctional facility, 152; at Talladega prison, 228; in Watts, Los Angeles, 24
US Agency for International Development, 87–88, 109
US Air Force, 31, 38, 41, 46, 219
USA PATRIOT Act, 235
US Border Patrol: academies, 109; creation of, 18; facilities, 132, 156, 243; fear of disease, 76; and Haitian whippings, 241; and Mexicans, 134; and rebellions, 219, 222, 227, 233; replacement of, 235; and resources, 9, 110, 193; and Salvadorans, 140; Tactical Unit (BORTAC), 142, 176–77, 186–87; and the Sanctuary movement, 178–82; in Tucson, Arizona, 172
US Citizenship and Immigration Services, xiii
US Coast Guard, 61, 64–68, 81–82, 87, 104, 219
US Committee for Justice to Latin American Political Prisoners, 72
US Constitution, 14, 17, 79, 82, 99, 140, 145, 177, 179, 181, 204
US Department of Health and Human Services, 30, 42, 45, 58, 157
US Department of Homeland Security, xv, 235, 241–42
US Department of Justice (DOJ): and budgets, 188, 190, 194–96; and Central American migration, 130; and crime, 111–13, 117; and Cubans, 85–86, 173, 187; and Haitians, 154–55, 173; Law Enforcement Assistance

Administration, 205; and Oakdale, 199, 201, 215, 221–25; and War on Drugs, 142–43
US Marshals, 154, 219
US-Mexico border, xiv, 6–9, 16–17, 109, 115, 117, 143, 147, 233
US National Guard, 30, 218–19
US Navy, 109
US Public Health Service, 66, 219
US State Department: and Cuba, 34, 58, 192; and El Salvador, 106; and Haiti, 73–76, 83–88; journalist hire, 151; and Poland, 85; Reagan's overturning of Carter's policies, 119–13, 134, 137–41; and private prisons, 197
USSR. See Soviet Union
US Supreme Court, 18–20, 79–80, 192, 208, 233, 238

Valladaras, Armando, 126, 220
Valley Industrial Park facility (VIP), 195–96
Varelli, Frank, 180–81
Vega, Ana Lydia, 159–60
Venezuela, 89–90
Veterans for Peace, 241
Vietnam, El Salvador as, 121, 160
Vietnamese: at Fort Chaffee, 42; resettlement, 59
Vietnam War, 6, 23, 169–70, 180; draft avoidance, 161; and foreign policy, 119; immigration after, 19, 25–27, 32, 36; and public sentiment, 60; veterans, 109–11, 117, 208
violence. See rebellions; uprisings
Violent Crime Control and Law Enforcement Act, 233
Vodou, 70, 76
Voting Rights Act, 23

Wackenhut Corporation. See GEO Group
war: civil wars, 7, 17, 21–23, 107–9, 118–23, 133, 136, 160, 170, 184, 244; warfare, 1, 2, 6, 9, 13, 21–22, 33, 108, 110, 117, 128–29, 133, 144
War on Crime, 10, 25, 110–11
War on Drugs, 103, 109–17, 142–44, 190, 230, 232

War Powers Act, 125

whites: anti-Cuban sentiment, 60; anti-Haitian sentiment, 65, 71–73, 98, 101, 158, 175; US citizens, xii, 13–14, 17, 169, 171; Cubans, 33, 40; white flight, 23; and nationalism, xiv, 1–3, 7–10, 25, 32, 41, 48, 56, 63, 101, 109, 111, 113, 117, 143, 183; and Reagan, 5, 53; as rebellion victims, 36; and saviorism, 12, 161, 164, 185; settler colonialism, 15, 17, 56

White, Frank, 42, 53–55, 58, 63

Women's Task Force for Haitian Political Prisoners, 94

World Refugee Day, xvi, 243

World War I, 18

World War II, xvi, 1, 18–19, 22–23, 28, 45, 87, 98, 105, 111, 129, 198

xenophobia: anti-Blackness, 8; anti-Haitian sentiment, 65, 71–73, 101, 158, 175; and the CBI, 91, 144; and Clinton, 238; during Cold War, 31, 80; and empire, xviii; and HIV/AIDS, 239; and Latin America, 129–31, 143; and Mariel Cubans, 32, 37, 43–45, 101; and private prisons, 189, 193–200; public, 2, 73, 200; and Trump, 5; and World War I, 18

Yasui v. United States (1943), 19

Young, Andrew, 74

Youth International Party, 153, 179